AA

Explorer
Scotland

Gilbert Summers

AA Publishing

Page 3: Brodick Castle, Arran, Islands of the Clyde
Page 4: Fraserburgh buoys
Page 5 (top): looking towards Hoy, Orkney
Page 5 (left): on the fringe, Edinburgh Festival
Page 5 (right): Plockton
Pages 6 and 7 (top): Tobermory, Mull
Page 7: the Folk Museum, Fochabers
Page 8: walking by Rest and Be Thankful, Arrochar
Page 9: Threave Castle, southeast of Castle Douglas
Page 25: the Clyde in 1878
Page 255: the Eriskay ferry at South Uist
Page 273: Balmoral Hotel, Edinburgh

Written by Gilbert Summers
Revision verified by Gilbert Summers
Original photography by Steve Day, Eric Ellington, Marius Alexander and Ken Patterson

Revised third edition 1999. Reprinted 1999
First published 1995
Edited, designed and produced by AA Publishing 1995, 1997, 1999.
© The Automobile Association 1995, reprinted 1995, 1997.
Maps © The Automobile Association 1995, 1997, 1999

Distributed in the United Kingdom by AA Publishing, Norfolk House, Priestley Road, Basingstoke, Hampshire, RG24 9NY.

The contents of this publication are believed correct at the time of printing. Nevertheless, the publishers cannot be held responsible for any errors or omissions or for changes in the details given in this guide or for the consequences of any reliance on the information provided by the same. Assessments of attractions, hotels, restaurants and so forth are based upon the author's own personal experience and, therefore, descriptions given in this guide necessarily contain an element of subjective opinion which may not reflect the publishers' opinion or dictate a reader's own experiences on another occasion.
We have tried to ensure accuracy in this guide, but things do change and we would be grateful if readers would advise us of any inaccuracies they may encounter.

A CIP catalogue record for this book is available from the British Library.

ISBN 0 7495 1891 X

Published by AA Publishing (a trading name of Automobile Association Developments Limited, whose registered office is Norfolk House, Priestley Road, Basingstoke, Hampshire RG24 9NY. Registered number 1878835).

Colour separation by Fotographics Ltd
Printed and bound in Italy by Printer Trento srl

Titles in the Explorer series:
Australia • Boston & New England • Britain • Britanny • California • Caribbean • China • Costa Rica • Crete • Cuba • Cyprus • Egypt • Florence & Tuscany • Florida • France • Germany • Greek Islands • Hawaii • India •Indonesia • Ireland • Israel • Italy • Japan • London • Mallorca • Mexico • Moscow & St Petersburg • New York • New Zealand • Paris • Portugal • Prague • Provence • Rome • San Francisco • Singapore & Malaysia • South Africa • Spain • Tenerife • Thailand • Turkey • Turkish Coast • Venice • Vietnam

AA World Travel Guides publish nearly 300 guidebooks to a full range of cities, countries and regions across the world. Find out more about AA Publishing and the wide range of services the AA provides by visiting our web site at www.theaa.co.uk.

How to use this book

ORGANISATION

Scotland Is, Scotland Was

Discusses aspects of life and culture in contemporary Scotland and explores significant periods in its history.

A–Z

An alphabetical listing of places to visit. The book begins with sections on Edinburgh and Glasgow, and is subsequently divided into regions. Places of interest are listed alphabetically within each section. Suggested walks, drives and Focus On articles, which provide an insight into aspects of life in Scotland, are included in each section.

Travel Facts

Contains the strictly practical information that is vital for a successful trip.

Hotels and Restaurants

Lists places to stay and places to eat alphabetically by region. Entries are graded budget, moderate or expensive.

ABOUT THE RATINGS

Most places described in this book have been given a separate rating. These are as follows:

▶▶▶   Do not miss

▶▶   Highly recommended

▶   Worth seeing

MAP REFERENCES

To make the location of a particular place easier to find, every main entry in this book is given a map reference, such as 176B3. The first number (176) indicates the page on which the map can be found, the letter (B) and the second number (3) pinpoint the square in which the main entry is located. The maps on the inside front cover and inside back cover are referred to as IFC and IBC respectively.

Contents

My Scotland by Gilbert Summers

Gilbert Summers is a Scot who has spent many years living in Scotland and earning his living writing about his native land, working closely with the tourism industry. He has produced a variety of material for many international publishers. Much to the surprise of his friends, in 1996 he became the manager of a marine aquarium in Macduff, but continues a freelance writing career in his spare time.

Growing up in the northern part of a pre-motorway Scotland brought its own pleasingly skewed perceptions of the shape and form of the nation. Aberdeen was a dramatic granite city in the south, Edinburgh was an age away and only really existed as an illustration on a tin of shortbread. Skye and the west coast were fantastically exotic. Orkney and Shetland were definitely abroad. Yet all were encompassed by 'Scottishness'.

Since then, distances have 'shrunk', both in my perception and because of improved road and rail networks. Now, travel in Scotland is measured out in more manageable statistics: over five hours to the Moray Firth coast from the border near Carlisle; just an hour from Inverness to Ullapool and the ferry to the Western Isles and less than one hour by train from Edinburgh to Glasgow. But the vague feeling of many Scotlands still clings on.

It is remarkable how little time it takes to reach widely contrasting places, and for me this is one of the best things about Scotland. If the Edinburgh Festival crowds begin to wear you down, there are high brackeny green hills close at hand in the Pentlands. Or you can lose yourself in native Scots pinewoods that lie within easy distance of, say, Inverness airport.

As a native, I have always wondered why Scotland, with all its diversity in ancestry, landscape and culture, drapes itself in tartan finery as an instantly recognisable symbol of Scottishness. The humble cloth of the Celt – once despised, even outlawed – has become a powerful marketing tool. Yet, this convenient stereotype hides a complex character. I have always exhorted any traveller to pull aside the tartan curtain and discover other threads of the nation's complex story, such as Picts and Vikings, or the close links with France and the Low Countries or even why more Scots took the government side at the Battle of Culloden than joined to fight with Bonnie Prince Charlie.

Scotland is certainly fertile ground for romantics. Hills that make the heart ache, city skylines with castles and spires, tales of heroism in the glen – you can find them all. Maybe delving too deep isn't necessary. Just sit back and enjoy the sheer variety of it all!

Scotland Is

The Scottish image

Misty glens, lochs, mountains, tartan, bagpipes and kilts: these are the most familiar images of Scotland. How these essentially Highland aspects came to represent the whole of Scotland – Highland, Lowland, urban and rural – is one of the oddities of the nation's history.

TARTAN Today, you can cross the Border and hear bagpipes in a Southern Uplands town, eat shortbread from a tartan wrapper in the middle of Glasgow and take in a Highland Games within easy reach of Edinburgh. All this is well before you reach the real Highlands. Scotland, at least those aspects of it dealing with tourism, embraces its kilted image wholeheartedly: tartan sells.

The glorious paradox is that if a tartan-clad Highlander had appeared in a Lowland town a few centuries ago, he would have been locked up, if not shot on sight. The Highlanders were regarded as barbarous thieves by Lowland Scots. After the crushing of the final rebellion against the Hanoverian dynasty on Culloden Moor near Inverness, the tartan was even banned by Act of Parliament. Tartan was associated with revolt

The new face of Scottish tradition?

and lawlessness. Now, thoroughly rehabilitated, the kilt and its associated paraphernalia represent the whole of Scotland, Highland or Lowland, Gaelic-speaking or otherwise, to many of today's visitors.

BAGPIPES The unmistakable tones of the bagpipe or Highland war pipe form the soundtrack to the romantic image of Scotland. Perhaps originally a device for signalling across long Highland distances, the bagpipe survived partly through its use in Highland regiments, and now plays its role in many pipe bands. Most Scottish towns have at least one band, and the pipes create instant Highland atmosphere at all kinds of gatherings from protest marches to weddings.

SCENERY As for the misty glens and bens, a love for this kind of landscape grew out of the cult of the picturesque embraced by the Romantic poets (William Wordsworth, strongly associated with the English Lake District, made several tours of the Scottish Highlands). Today, a taste for wild scenery is for many people the main reason for visiting Scotland.

The scenery is certainly splendid, and it is perfectly possible to see some of Scotland's most rugged places without leaving a main road. This is why Glencoe appears on the headboard of many a coach. It provides a matchless combination of awesome scenery and chilling tale of the Highlands of old: a massacre of the local clan by a perfidious clan militia took place there in 1692. Further west, the island of Skye makes a startling impact when the Cuillin Hills etch themselves against a blue sky.

Morning mist over Flanders Moss, from the edge of the Trossachs

With scenic grandeur like this, and the romance of kilts and other Highland paraphernalia, it is all too easy to forget the other aspects of Scotland. The country has some of the finest stretches of unspoilt coast-line in Europe: on the east coast, both sheer cliffs and sandy beaches provide superb scenery. The Border towns, with their textile traditions and strong sense of community, are full of character and do not need any dressing up in Highland guise. The Northern Isles, notably Shetland, are a world away from 'Highlandry' and have a vivid Scandinavian heritage. Then there is the modern Scotland, as expressed in style-conscious Glasgow or cosmopolitan Edinburgh. Scotland can offer you ceilidhs (Highland-style evenings of song and dance) if you want them, but make the most of its wealth of other attributes as well.

❏ After the Battle of Culloden in 1746, many rebels were condemned to death by the authorities. One of these unfortunates was a Highland piper. He pleaded for mercy on the grounds that he was a musician, but the judge defined his pipes as a weapon of war and the sentence was duly carried out. ❏

Many Scottish postcards tend to perpetuate the tartan cliché

Perhaps the best-known Scottish festivity is Hogmanay – the last night of the year and its hung-over aftermath. Until recent years it was far more important than Christmas north of the Border.

HOGMANAY Though none can agree on the word's origins (possibly dialect French 'au geux menez' 'bring [gifts] to the beggars'), Hogmanay is still strong in Scotland. Until recent times the night of 31 December, Hogmanay Night, was the most important in the Scots calendar. Other deep-winter festivals, derived from early pagan fire rituals, survive in places, for example the swinging of fire-balls, with the combustible material held in place by wire, in Stonehaven, or the 'burning of the clavie', a kind of portable bonfire in a basket, at Burghead in Moray. Most famous of all is Up-Helly-Aa, a Viking celebration in Shetland, when people go guising (dressing up in costume) and enjoy various shows, including the spectacular burning of a Viking longship. Hallowe'en and Beltane or May Day festivities can also be found in a few places in modern Scotland.

Other types of event are those comparatively modern ones such as Highland Games and agricultural shows. Highland Games are popular in many towns and have spread beyond the Highlands. A combination of musical, dancing and athletic skills all happening in the same arena, often simultaneously, they are held in towns and villages throughout the Highlands and beyond.

HIGHLAND GAMES Clan societies and other promoters of Scotland's romantic martial image give the Games an ancient history, arguing that they were originally held so that clan chiefs could select the most talented people for their retinues. However, most seem to have originated in early Victorian times, when a resurgence of interest in things Scottish resulted in the formation of various Caledonian Clubs. Games gave the members an excuse to cavort in tartan finery. Yet another explanation is that the Games were trials of strength devised by bored lumberjacks cutting down the Highland forests. No matter what their origins, be prepared to enjoy parachute jumps and guest appearances by TV characters as part of the Games 'tradition' as well.

RURAL EVENTS Agricultural shows are as entertaining as Highland

Fringe Sunday in Edinburgh's Holyrood Park – truly cosmopolitan

On the festival cavalcade

Games and serve as a showcase for Scottish agriculture. They take place throughout the Lowlands. Great meeting places for the rural communities, they embrace not just the serious business of selling agricultural machinery and livestock, but also displays of just about anything else from trick cycling to terrier racing.

> ❏ Unlike Highland Games, the Borders Common Ridings are definitely not held for the benefit of visitors. These ancient celebrations of horsemanship in the Border towns owe their origins at least in part to a need to reaffirm town boundaries in the face of frequent cross-border raiding parties over the centuries. ❏

CULTURAL FESTIVALS The Edinburgh International Festival is the spectacular flagship of the mainstream cultural events in Scotland. In fact, the capital suffers from Festival 'overkill' in late August, partly due to the size of the Fringe, the less formal and more unruly younger brother of the 'official' Festival. This huge lucky dip spreads out of the halls and theatres on to the streets of the capital. Nobody could visit Edinburgh during the Fringe and possibly miss it! Also adding to the throng is the Edinburgh Military Tattoo and a range of smaller events

Highland events – the hammer thrower at the Pitlochry Games

> ❏ The Gaels, that is the Gaelic speakers of Celtic origin whose linguistic stronghold is in the far northwest of Scotland, have their own big cultural event for Gaeldom, the autumn National Mod, which is sometimes rather unkindly and unjustifiably described in the press as the 'Whisky Olympics'. ❏

13

such as the Book Festival and the Jazz Festival. In January, rival Glasgow holds the Celtic Connections festival, a homage to Celtic music, with performers from all over the world playing and tutoring hands-on workshops for prospective players or instrument makers. Folk festivals are also held in many places at various times of the year, two of the most notable being in Shetland: the Folk Festival in April and the Accordion and Fiddle Festival in October.

Three languages are spoken in Scotland: Gaelic, (Lowland) Scots, and English. All Gaels are bilingual. Some Lowlanders still tend to undervalue their native tongue, while the use of a broad Scots vowel by a child of English parents living in Scotland can sometimes be greeted with near horror.

14

THE FIRST LANGUAGE Gaelic was once the principal language over much of Scotland, but has been in slow retreat, originally in the face of Anglo-Norman settlers, for seven centuries. Today, Gaelic's stronghold is the far north and west, notably the Outer Hebrides, where there are 66,000 or so Gaelic speakers. However, increased funding for Gaelic broadcasting, especially television, in the early 1990s has resulted, ironically, in Gaelic being heard in parts of Scotland – for example, the extreme northeast – that have had virtually no Gaelic speakers for centuries. Gaelic enters the

LOWLAND SCOTS In its late medieval heyday, the Scots tongue, which evolved from a Northumbrian form of Anglo-Saxon, had roughly the same relationship to 'English' that Dutch has to German. Today it is diluted and impoverished by its kinship with 'Standard English', and has the further disadvantage of non-standardised spelling. However, its rich borrowings from Norse, French, German and Dutch can still be heard, especially in the northeast, which most linguists consider to be its heartland. Even in its densest forms it roughly follows Standard English in most grammatical forms, but

This Gaelic sign in Fort William literally means 'a hundred thousand welcomes'

vocabulary of Scots and English speakers most often in anglicised or part-anglicised placenames or topographical features such as ben, loch, strath, glen or cairn. Sassenach, slogan and ceilidh are other Gaelic words commonly encountered. As the panel at the top shows, many places on the west coast possess only a Gaelic name.

differs considerably in vocabulary and pronunciation.

TRAPS FOR THE LISTENER The linguistic nuances of Scotland are worth listening out for. For example, there are Scots constructions using an everyday English vocabulary. 'I'll see you the length of the bus-stop' is all but opaque to many non-Scots, yet does not use any exclusively 'Scots' words. It means 'I will escort you as far as the bus-stop'. There are single words which mean something different to Scots and English. 'Messages' means shopping to most Scots (and French, for that matter), with the mysterious 'going the messages', that is, doing the shopping, a further complication.

❏ If you are a non-Scot and your car breaks down – beware. A mechanic telling you 'I doubt you'll need a new starter motor' is giving you bad news, not good. In Scotland 'I doubt' often means 'I regret that…' or 'I am afraid that…'. ❏

15

Dingwall in Highland Region also uses the traditional Gaelic welcome

SCOTS: A SEPARATE LANGUAGE?

Perhaps the listener will skite (slip) on a creishy (greasy) chip paper on a dreich (dull) day, accidentally breenging into (colliding with) the farm's dour (unfriendly) orraman (spare hand) daundering (walking slowly) down to the roup (auction)!

Language experts talk of 'the great vowel shift', that is, the change in vowel qualities which took place in medieval times (and makes the works of English medieval writer Geoffrey Chaucer difficult for English speakers today). This shift did not occur in northern word forms. Thus 'take' is 'tak', 'bowl' is 'bool', 'cow' is 'coo', and 'most' is 'maist' (and so on) in Northeast Scotland today. Then listen for a

scattering of surviving weak Anglo-Saxon plural forms: 'shoes' are 'sheen', 'eyes' are 'een'. Add Scottish constructions to the northern vocabulary and characteristic pronunciation, and it takes a brave linguist to say that Scots is just a dialect of English.

But do not worry – you will be understood everywhere and might hear no Scots tongue at all. Bilingual Scots, in the sense of those who can still speak 'dense' Lowland forms as well as English, modify their language into a near Standard English (with a Scots accent, naturally) for the benefit of everyday intercourse with the rest of the English-speaking world.

ENGLISH IN SCOTLAND

The overheating of England's property market in the mid-1980s saw many English people take advantage of the high selling prices in the south to move into rural Scotland where property was much cheaper. It is possible to travel in many parts of the Highlands and hear no local native voices at all.

❏ The linguistic historian Billy Kay has memorably described Lowland Scots as 'a language spoken by consenting adults in private'. ❏

In the Scotland of old, diet and wealth were interrelated; the same is true today. But instead of trips to the supermarket to load up the estate car, the wealthy merchants and lairds and the powerful clan chiefs took advantage of direct trading links across the North Sea to acquire the dainty spices and French wines that went with their status.

16

A MEAGRE DIET It is significant that Scotland's most famous dish, haggis, is an ancient folk recipe for using up the cheapest cuts of meat. In a nation with a somewhat unpredictable climate and a history of economic uncertainties, everyday Scots cooking in the past had much to do with eking out ingredients.

Today, poverty in the bleak housing schemes of deindustrialised Scotland is a factor in health statistics which no amount of tartan packaging can totally conceal. In low-income households a dependence on cheap and convenient high cholesterol and otherwise unbalanced foods ensure Scotland is a poor performer in the healthy-eating league table: deaths through heart disease are the worst in Europe.

Paradoxically, Scotland today has numerous advantages when it comes

The Waterfront Wine Bar in Leith, near Edinburgh

to 'local produce'. Peterhead is Europe's largest white fish landing port. Scottish seafood is sought out by top chefs south of the border and in Europe. (In fact, locals grumble that the best is exported.) Aberdeen Angus beef, though eclipsed by overseas breeds in recent years, is making a comeback and still has considerable cachet. Scots farmers remind anyone who will listen that their beef is 'grass-fed' on natural pastures. Meanwhile, Scottish farmed venison, with all its low-fat virtues, is widely available on restaurant menus.

THE SCOTS AS HOME BAKERS The largest soft-fruit growing area in the EU lies within Tayside in the hinterland of Dundee. With the prevailing climate just right for raspberries and their cousins, as well as strawberries, it is no coincidence that Dundee is famous for its jams. The Scots sweet tooth not only sends

Shortbread – distinctive product and unmistakable packaging

masquerade as tradition and even the humble cup of coffee is translated into creaking mock Scots as a 'tassie o bean bree' ('tassie' is 'cup', 'bree' is 'soup', or 'brine'). There is much more to good Scottish food than 'flambéeing' the steak in whisky or coating the ice cream in oatmeal, and the discriminating diner will find plenty to please, not just an updated local tradition. Other styles, from Italian to Punjabi, are also well represented, notably, but not only, in larger towns.

some of its population to an early grave but also shows itself in a still sturdy tradition of home baking, including shortbread and other traditionally fattening goodies. Finally, the humble oat, until well into the present century still a staple of Lowland farmhands, has recently won new converts with the discovery of its role as a good source of soluble fibre.

EATING OUT TODAY Foodies will be able to find a high standard of cuisine north of the border. Some restaurants advertise 'Taste of Scotland' menus, which means they belong to an organisation dedicated to high standards and the fresh and creative use of Scottish local produce. However, an establishment offering 'Scottish' cuisine will not automati-cally be of the highest order. In a few places there still exists the ersatz Scots menu, where catering packs

❏ 'The little Highland Mutton, when fat, is delicious, and certainly the greatest of luxuries. And the small Beef, when fresh, is very sweet and succulent... Amongst the poorer classes in Scotland, beef is eaten only at Martinmas, when a Mart or Ox is killed; and the only other butcher meat they eat throughout the year is an occasional Braxy.'

Edward Burt's Letters from the North of Scotland, 1730

A 'mart' is an animal, such as an ox or sheep, killed for salting for winter.
A 'braxy' is a sheep that has died of braxy, an intestinal illness. ❏

To many people, especially from the more urban south, the appeal of Scotland lies in its 'unspoilt' qualities: the silent hills and open skies of the northlands represent a near-mystical, changeless purity. But is the north really the untouched wilderness, a description so beloved by the writers of tourist brochures?

18

THE FATE OF SCOTLAND'S WOODLANDS

In environmental terms, the upland landscapes that cover 75 per cent of Scotland tell a sad story of destruction and forest clearance, started originally in the Southern Uplands and the Lowlands by Bronze Age man about 3,000 years ago. The needs of agriculture meant that by the Middle Ages much of the forest south of the Highlands had gone.

Harbouring wolves and brigands, the Highland forests too were destroyed. Charcoal made from Highland oaks was used in early iron smelting. Queen Elizabeth I of England (1558–1603) decreed that English trees should be reserved for shipbuilding, so her smelters turned to the Highlands, aided and abetted by Scottish Lowland businessmen. Until coke replaced charcoal around 1813, Highland forests were destroyed wholesale for smelting purposes.

By 1743 the last wolf had gone, following the brown bear, reindeer, elk, boar and beaver into oblivion. Then the great flocks of sheep – still a feature of the Highlands today – arrived with flockmasters firing whole hillsides, eager to extend the grazings. The modern type of sporting estate seen today, encouraging red deer on an open hillside, also evolved. High populations of nibbling sheep and deer still prevent forest regeneration. In the eastern Highlands, grouse moor management involves annual burning of open hillsides, to encourage young heather growth.

When reafforestation was at last tackled, much of it was in blocks of sitka spruce or other alien species, now seen throughout the Highlands,

The Black Wood of Rannoch – a rare surviving example of Scotland's natural pine forest

even in traditional beauty spots such as the Trossachs. Elsewhere, it is the open 'hillscape', burned and over-grazed, degraded for quick profit and described by some ecologists as a wet desert, that is the wilderness enjoyed by millions each year.

FINDING THE REAL WILDERNESS Yet the picture is not all gloomy. Real wilderness, in the sense of an unchanged landscape, give or take a few ski developments, lies above 900m or so. Meanwhile, on lower ground, there is a more sensitive attitude to forestry planting, at least in some places, and a wide range of habitats, many in the care of conservation bodies. Little chunks of high-grade landscape survive even in the Lowlands in the form of river gorge woodlands, Lowland raised bog and also wetlands, notably at the Loch of Strathbeg in the northeast.

The oakwoods on the east side of Loch Lomond still ring with spring birdsong. An echo of the great wood of Caledon can be found in the Black Wood of Rannoch on the south shore of Loch Rannoch. Here the characteristic habitat survives: an open woodland with an understorey of juniper and heather. Crossbills call in the treetops and it is still possible to see capercaillie, the big grouse of the woods. Around Rothiemurchus on Speyside, near Aviemore, and by Loch Maree in Wester Ross, on the Beinn Eighe side, wild country can be enjoyed in a comparatively 'undegraded' state.

Finally, though land misuse is undeniable, the paradox is plain: despite everything, the Highlands, with their vast stretches of open man-made moorland, remain hauntingly beautiful.

A remnant Scots Pine in Glen Falloch. Overgrazing prevents its offspring regenerating

❏ The unique survival of a feudal method of landownership in Scotland – 10 per cent of Scotland is owned by just 13 individuals – has not always worked in favour of conservation and healthy land use. The financial worth of sporting estates is partly measured in deer numbers, so the incentive exists to keep stocks at artificially high levels, to the detriment of the Highland habitat. ❏

19

Why do many Scots still write 'Scottish' and not 'British' in passports and hotel guest-register books? In 1997, the Scottish electorate threw out the only British Parliamentary party still in favour of the Union with England in its present form. For Nationalists, mild or rampant, there are interesting times ahead.

WHO FEELS BRITISH? In 1707, during the rounds of negotiations and bribes in Westminster that ended with the Union of Parliaments and the loss of Scotland's independence, the proposals for each day of negotiation were laid before the Scots who were left to argue amongst themselves. The English Parliament continued its business. When the deal was concluded, nothing had changed for English parliamentary

flourished and withered over the decades. In 1928 the forerunner of the Scottish National Party (SNP) was formed. They gained 11 MPs by 1974 while campaigning under the slogan 'It's Scotland's Oil', though these were reduced to three throughout the 1980s.

By that time, Scotland had become a Labour Party stronghold, with the ruling Conservatives' policies deeply unpopular north of the Border. A wave of well-off southerners who had capitalised on the mid-1980s property boom and were snapping up desirable property all over Scotland further increased

Saltire, symbol of Scotland

representatives. There were new Scots faces at Westminster – but nothing was fundamentally altered to make the English feel British. Neither do many Scots, even to this day.

By the 19th century, the Liberal Party and a succession of pressure groups had pledged themselves to Home Rule for Scotland. They

resentment. Before the key general election of 1992, the media – much of it London-based and supporting the Conservative government – talked up the Nationalists' chances, seeing them as the 'second force' in Scottish politics. However, the SNP's breakthrough did not occur, though its share of the vote increased – as it did again in 1997. From 1992 to 1997, Scotland was governed by a party with barely enough Scottish Conservative MPs to man the

Scottish Office in Edinburgh. They, in turn, were completely wiped out in the 1997 general election, when the Scottish people delivered their verdict on the Conservatives' pro-Unionist agenda.

THE SCANDINAVIAN MODEL

Nationalists argue that Scotland is self-sufficient in food and energy, while proportionately exporting 21 per cent more for every manufacturing worker than the UK as a whole. Of the 11 nations that have overtaken the UK in the world wealth league in the last 30 years, seven are small European nations. And of those, three – Finland, Iceland and Norway – have become independent this century. Nationalists in Scotland look closely at the Scandinavian model of economic success and point to the influence of Denmark, for example, within the EU; with its similar population size, climate, resources and economy. Far older, they point out, than the present Union with England, is the Auld Alliance – the historical tendency for Scotland to unite with France against England. Old trading alliances with the Low Countries, too, are reminders that Scotland formerly looked to Europe and may do so again.

The commitment of the Labour government, elected in 1997, to a Scottish Parliament has sharpened the minds of many Scots, and also the media, to contemplate going beyond this half-way house in a way that has not been discussed in Scotland for

The Vigil for a Scottish Parliament caravan, parked outside government buildings in Edinburgh

21

three centuries. From a position of near hostility, the SNP now seems to view the proposed Scottish Parliament as a springboard to full independence at some point in the 21st century. Whether or not the nation of Scotland is able to grasp this particular nettle, only time will tell.

> ❏ Linda Colley, a professor of history at Yale University, describes Scotland's situation: 'the alienation of the Celtic fringe is not a recipe for a healthy democracy, nor for a happy and long-lasting union'. ❏

Political message on a disused railway viaduct, north of Montrose

One fact is certain: Scotland as the 'Workshop of the Western World' has gone for ever, the nation's smokestack industries, dependent on coal and iron, mostly reduced to dereliction and the memories of old men…

Harvesting in Fife; agriculture now plays a lesser role in the economy

Even as late as the mid-1960s, manufacturing made up 32 per cent of Scotland's GDP and employed 35 per cent of its workforce. By the mid-1990s, manufacturing was down to 22 per cent with only 20 per cent of the workforce in this sector – below the UK average. Today, seven out of ten workers are now in the service sector and not manufacturing anything. However, Scotland is not yet quite a nation of waiters and tartan gift-shop assistants.

ELECTRONICS – THE SUNRISE INDUSTRY Silicon Glen was the apt name coined to describe the sunrise industry of electronics, which currently employs 46,000 people north of the Border. At least 38 per cent of personal computers and 57 per cent of workstations sold in Europe are actually built in Scotland, thanks to financial incentives for inward-bound companies, plus a skilled workforce. The view from IBM's site (where all of its monitor research and development world-wide takes place) is out to the moors of Renfrewshire. Compaq, the world's largest computer manufacturer (and recent buyer of Digital) has a substantial Scottish presence, notably at Erskine, west of Glasgow. There are many more examples from the 550 companies in this sector, many of them household names.

EXPORTS Scotland's most famous export, whisky, continues to be important, though the degree of Scottish control within the industry is limited, as most brands belong to multinationals based outside Scotland. Roughly 70,000 jobs directly or indirectly depend on it UK-wide, while exports per employee are six times the UK average and in total came to £2.39 billion in 1996. Curiously, 55 per cent of production and 70 per cent of the workforce are in the Lowlands, in spite of the product's Highland associations.

Another of Scotland's famous products is textiles. This sector has had a tough time but is still worth £1.76 billion annually. It employs 41,000 people and is centred on the Borders where, for example, one of the nation's few home-grown multi-nationals, Dawson International, employs around 6,000. This concentration in the south of Scotland itself leads to some unusual statistics: the town of Hawick, for instance, exports more than £110 million of knitwear annually, making it one of the largest exporting centres per head of population anywhere in the UK. (All this in a town of around 15,000 people which has the distinction of being the largest in Scotland not to be served by a rail link.)

BLACK GOLD FROM THE NORTH SEA

Oil has made a substantial impact on the Scottish economy since the late 1960s, turning upside-down the local economies of places like Aberdeen, often described as Scotland's oil capital, and Peterhead, a leading fishing port on the north-east coast, whose harbour of refuge found a new role in sheltering and servicing oil supply vessels. In fact, more than 45,000 jobs in Grampian depend on oil. However, some say the boom has passed, not just because the easier finds have been exploited, but also because increasing offshore automation requires fewer workers, while onshore supply bases also require fewer staff. Meanwhile, optimists point to the imminent opening up of a second exploration front in the waters west of Shetland (the so-called 'Atlantic frontier') where surveys have revealed huge accumulations of untapped oil.

OTHER SECTORS The impact of tourism itself should not be overlooked. It contributes £2.4 billion annually to the Scottish economy and supports 177,000 jobs, including 15 per cent of the Highlands and Islands workforce. Meanwhile, fishing, fish farming, agriculture, the financial industry, plus the rump of the surviving engineering sector (which still includes names like Weir Group, British

Textile manufacture – still important in the Borders' economy

Aerospace, Howden Group, John Brown and Motherwell Bridge) should continue to ensure a measure of prosperity north of the Border.

> ❑ Oil experts estimate the recoverable reserves in the fields west of Shetland to be five billion barrels – roughly equivalent to the entire North Sea production for between seven and eight years. However, rigs will have to combat heavy Atlantic swell, strong winds and twice the water depth of the North Sea to gain this new oily bonanza. ❑

Ravenscraig – the heavy industry of yesterday?

Scotland's position on the edge of continental Europe, surrounded by sea on three sides, helps explain her unpredictable weather. The country is a battleground between the continental climate of Europe and the weather systems coming off the Atlantic Ocean.

NOT TRULY TROPICAL The Gulf Stream is often heralded as the saving grace of Scotland's weather. Much emphasised in holiday brochures, this warming oceanic current reaches Scotland as the North Atlantic Drift. It hardly lends a 'sub-tropical air' to the west coast (as is sometimes claimed in print) but it is appreciated by tender tree ferns and cabbage palms at places like Logan Botanic Garden in Galloway and Inverewe Garden in Wester Ross (at the same latitude as Moscow).

Hebridean rain, Berneray, one of the smaller Western Isles

WHERE TO FIND GOOD WEATHER Sunshine in Scotland is most likely to be encountered away from the prevailing southwesterlies: the east coast 'resorts' – Dunbar, St Andrews and Lossiemouth – all have encouraging statistics. The west is far wetter than the east. While Dunbar gets away with 555mm annual rainfall (less than Rome), Inveraray on Loch Fyne enjoys 2,036mm. For many

visitors, wet weather is a risk worth taking. The popular tourist area of Lochaber is one of the wettest parts and July one of the wetter months in the west, but also one of the busiest for tourists.

When it is not raining, the sparkling colours of the hills and sea lochs of the west make some of the finest landscapes anywhere in the world. Besides, the dreaded east coast haar, a summer sea fog, also complicates the picture. Scottish weather is a highly localised gamble, with few rules – except to expect the worst and be pleasantly surprised.

❏ The summit of Ben Nevis has a mean annual rainfall that is rather generous: it is twice that of Fort William – which gets 1,980mm – only 6km away. But if you really want to test your waterproofs, visit the head of Glen Garry which offers a spectacular 5,000mm every year. ❏

Glencoe, one of Scotland's five ski developments

Scotland was

The scanty clues from 'shell-middens', the rubbish tips of early man, suggest that Scotland was first colonised about 8,000 years ago, after the last Ice Age. Over the millennia, different races blended together, leaving only their grave goods, standing stones and cairns as mysterious evidence for today's archaeologists. Then Celtic invaders from Europe arrived about 500 BC with superior metal-working techniques. The Romans came and failed to subdue the northlands, finally withdrawing shortly after AD 212.

26

After the Romans, 'Scotland' roughly comprised a British kingdom in Strathclyde and the southwest, with a capital at Dumbarton. ('Dun-Briton' means the fort of the Britons, who had been the main Celtic tribe until pushed west by European invaders.) A Pictish confederation controlled the north. Within a couple of centuries a new wave of Celtic settlers arrived, this time from Ireland. These were the Scots who established the kingdom of Dalriada with its centre at Dunadd near Crinan in Argyll.

THE SHAPE OF SCOTLAND The Angles arrived in the southeast in the 5th century. This Germanic tribe created a powerful Northumbrian kingdom, which took in the Lothians (around present-day Edinburgh).

Thus, along with the three Celtic ethnic groups (Britons, Picts and Scots), a fourth, non-Celtic power base became important.

The northern expansion of this Anglo-Saxon grouping was checked at the Battle of Nechtansmere in Angus in 685, when the Pictish King Brude defeated the Angles under Egfrith, one of the important events which influenced the final form of Scotland. It also shifted the power base in England south from Northumbria to around the Thames, where it has remained ever since, so the shadowy northern Picts altered the course of English history as well.

Christianity played its part in Scotland's story. A Galloway-born

The Stones of Stenness, Orkney

Dun Troddan Broch, Glenelg

❏ The Roman historian Tacitus records a tantalising snippet on Scotland's first named battle, when red-haired warriors with painted bodies were defeated by a Roman force at Mons Graupius, a site as yet unidentified. There are traces of Roman marching camps as far north as the Moray Firth, though their greatest monument is the remains of the Antonine Wall (AD 142–3), across the narrow waist of Scotland. ❏

Briton, St Ninian, is the first recorded native Christian. However, the later St Columba is better known. He came from Ireland to Iona in Dalriada in AD 563 to convert the northern Picts. As the Britons were already Christian by this time, this forged closer links between the two groupings.

Yet another factor was at work in shaping Scotland. The depredations of the Vikings troubled both the northern Picts and also the Scots on the western seaboard. Some say the repeated pillaging of the Christian settlement and seat of learning at Iona set back the course of civilisation for centuries. The Picts were so weakened by Norse incursions that

Kenneth MacAlpin, King of Scots, was able to extend his kingdom north and east. He was crowned King of Scots and Picts in 844.

Thereafter MacAlpin strengthened an alliance with the Britons, further extending his sway. However, only after the Battle of Carham (on the English side of the Border near Coldstream) in 1025, when the Scottish King Malcolm I defeated the Northumbrians, did they give up the southeast so that the Lothians became part of Scotland.

Finally, the marriage in 1070 of King Malcolm III to Margaret, a daughter of the English King Edward the Confessor, set a pattern of intermarriage between the royal houses of Scotland and England that would also strongly influence the fate of Scotland.

❏ Tacitus uses the word Picti – painted people – as well as Caledonii (hence Caledonian) to describe the northern tribes. Later, Alba (hence Alban and Albion) was the Gaelic word which described the combined Scot-Pictish kingdom north of the rivers Forth and Clyde. ❏

The Wars of Independence refer to a period in Scottish history when Scotland's right to exist as an independent nation was threatened by the expansionist aspirations of the English Plantagenet kings. But it was not quite as simple as that. Nothing between Scotland and England ever was simple.

THE ENGLISH OVERLORDS? In 12th-century Scotland, notably in the time of King David I (c1080), the Norman feudal system had taken root. David had married the daughter of an English earl, gaining lands near Cambridge in England. In feudal terms, land meant an obligation to the overlord, in this case the English king. This bowing of the knee as an English landholder by David (and

Bannockburn prelude – Robert Bruce kills Sir Henry de Bohun in single combat

earlier kings) reinforced a view that the Scots were under English command. This was strengthened by the Treaty of Falaise in 1174, signed by King William the Lion, who, seeking territorial gains, joined a revolt by English barons against King Henry II of England. The barons were defeated; William was captured and forced to sign a treaty of allegiance, confirming the feudal overlordship of England. (Scotland later bought its 'independence' back when King Richard the Lionheart needed money for a crusade.)

A TRAGIC FALL King Alexander III of Scotland ruled a comparatively peaceful kingdom until 1286 when he died after falling from his horse. Through intermarriage, King Edward I of England was the great-uncle of the heir to the Scottish throne, Margaret of Norway. Acting as arbiter, he suggested she marry his son, thus securing close union between the two kingdoms. The Scots agreed but the Maid of Norway unfortunately died, leaving 13 other claimants with varying degrees of legitimacy.

Edward seized his chance in the power vacuum and demanded acknowledgement of his own claim as overlord of Scotland. The claimants complied and Edward chose John Balliol, who became a puppet king, ever after known in Scotland as 'Toom Tabard' – empty coat. However, even he was pushed too far by Edward who demanded his services against the French. Balliol sided with France and saw his army crushed at Dunbar by Edward's forces in 1296. Scotland was occupied by the English thereafter. The Scots aristocracy, spectacularly sycophantic, secured their property by meekly swearing allegiance to Edward. He then destroyed many of Scotland's own records and carried off a variety of relics among them the Stone of Destiny, which was not to be returned to Scotland until November 1996.

This was the background to the campaign called the Scots Wars of Independence. In the midst of Edward's policy of dismantling Scotland's administration and machinery of nationhood, there arose the first of her freedom fighters, William Wallace, who achieved some successes before his betrayal in 1305.

Stirling Castle – the strategic key to the kingdom of Scotland

❏ William Wallace's most famous victory was at the Battle of Stirling Bridge in 1297, where, within sight of the English-held Stirling Castle, Wallace's men fell upon and defeated the opposing forces while they attempted to cross the narrow bridge. ❏

THE BANNOCKBURN CAMPAIGN

Robert Bruce now saw his chance. Bruce came from an old Norman family (de Brus refers to a Normandy place-name and is often anglicised as the Bruce), and, like other Scots nobles, he played his part in the complex politics of English court life. His grandfather had been one of the original 13 claimants to the Scottish throne. He was crowned King of Scotland in 1307 and initiated a seven-year military campaign, which ended at the Battle of Bannockburn in 1314 with a (historically rare) Scots victory. Thereafter, though Scotland and England were not at peace, Scotland won almost 400 years of independence from England.

Scotland's churchmen were unreservedly nationalist throughout the struggle. With the Pope still believing in England's right to rule Scotland they met to prepare Scotland's most famous document, the Declaration of Arbroath, in 1320: 'For so long as a hundred of us remain alive we shall never accept subjection to the domination of the English...'

Robert Bruce, victor at Bannockburn

Mary was queen for only seven years but she played her part in a large-scale drama involving the royal houses of Scotland, France and England. Since her death more than 400 years ago, she has become perhaps the best-known figure in Scotland's history.

Mary, Queen of Scots (1542–87) was at the centre of political upheavals even as a small child. The Stuart monarchs of Scotland had the inconvenient habit of dying when their offspring were too young to rule. Mary's father, King James V, died a week after hearing of his daughter's birth. Within three years this led to English attacks on Scotland – the destructive episodes known as the 'rough wooing'. This was King Henry VIII of England's less than subtle attempt to marry off his own young son Edward to the infant Mary. To get rid of the English invaders, the Scots called on the French for help. The price for this was the removal of Mary to France in 1548 for marriage to the Dauphin, the young French prince, in order to secure a Catholic alliance against England.

SCOTLAND'S TRAGIC QUEEN On her return to Scotland in 1561, Mary was a young and beautiful widow. The Dauphin had died, still in his teens. With Scotland in the throes of the Reformation and a widening Protestant–Catholic split, Mary was, politically speaking, hot property. Politicians (Scottish and English) soon worked out that finding Mary a Protestant husband might

Mary, Queen of Scots

offer the best chance of stability. However, Mary fell for the dubious charms of the lanky young Lord Darnley. (Mary, being very tall, may have enjoyed the novelty of being looked down on.) Though at first she described him as the 'lustiest and best proportioned lang man', the marriage proved a disaster. Darnley took to tavern life in solace, finding that Mary soon excluded him from any real authority. In short, he sulked.

The murder (by Darnley and others) of her secretary and favourite, David Riccio, witnessed by Mary while six months pregnant, indicates the ruthlessness of the conspirators ranged against her in that age of political and religious instability. The birth of a son – the future King James VI of Scotland, James I of England – and his baptism in the Catholic faith

30

at Stirling Castle were a cause for alarm amongst the Protestant factions.

PLOT AND COUNTERPLOT More controversy followed. The house in which Lord Darnley was convalescing after illness blew up one night. Darnley was found strangled in the adjacent garden, his body unmarked by the explosion. Exactly what happened that night in February 1567 remains one of Scotland's great historical mysteries, but suspicion still falls on the third man in Mary's life, the earthy James Hepburn, Earl of Bothwell. Before Darnley's death it was well known both that Mary's reconciliation with him had failed, and that she was pregnant again. Rumours were rife at court about the possible father of her child. In any event, Mary married Bothwell after his acquittal of Darnley's murder.

Renaissance stonework on Falkland Palace, hunting lodge of the Stewarts

The last Scottish scenes in the drama saw the rising of a confederacy of the Protestant Lords of the Congregation against her new liaison, which led to Mary's surrender and imprisonment in Loch Leven Castle. Her pregnancy ended with stillborn twins.

A few months later, in May of 1568, she escaped, gathered an army and suffered defeat at Langside at the hands of the Protestant faction. Subsequently she fled to England, crossing the Border only 11 days after escaping from Loch Leven. There she remained a political pawn in the hands of Queen Elizabeth I, her cousin, who signed her death warrant in 1587.

31

❏ Riccio was ugly, small and hunched (though a fine lutenist) and it is unlikely that his role extended beyond that of musician and chief secretary to the Queen. Court gossip, however, suggested otherwise. ❏

*The Union of Parliaments and Scotland's loss
of independence is a live issue among Scots, in
a way it has never been in England. Now, in
the early days of a new Scottish Parliament,
there is a strong sense north of the border that
history has come full circle.*

SCOTLAND'S FOREIGN VENTURE

After the Union of the Crowns in
1603, when James VI of Scotland
became James I of England, Scotland
shared a monarch with England but
had its own parliament. Poorly
developed Scotland assumed that
this would mean sharing in trade
with England's burgeoning colonies.
When it became clear that England
intended to keep the economic
benefits to herself, the Scots decided
to found their own colonies. The
Darien Scheme, the establishing of a
settlement on the disease-ridden
isthmus of Panama in 1698, proved a

*Christmas in Parliament Square, on
Edinburgh's Royal Mile*

financial catastrophe. Fever struck
the colonists and neighbouring
Spanish possessions rose against
them. The Scots appealed to nearby
English colonies for aid. This was
refused for fear of upsetting Spain.

Everything was abandoned, ruining
both the Scottish aristocracy and the
ordinary folk who had put up funds.
By 1701 anti-English feeling was
running high. There was also a crisis
of succession for Scotland and
England. The Scots Parliament
attempted blackmail. They stated that
unless Scotland gained trading rights
in English markets, they would not
choose the same monarch as England.
Instead of favouring the Protestant
Hanoverian succession, they would

❏ The Earl of Seafield, as Lord Chancellor instrumental in carrying forward the legislation, touched the written Act with the Royal Sceptre (symbolising royal assent) and consigned Scotland to history. As he handed the Sceptre back to a clerk, he was heard to mutter 'Now, there's an end of an auld sang.' Three centuries later, with a new Scottish Parliament, he has been proved wrong. ❏

turn instead to the exiled Catholic Stuart dynasty. Once more for England the threat of a Scottish alliance with Catholic France presented itself.

POLITICAL HORSE-TRADING The foolish blackmail attempt caused England to retaliate with the Alien Act of 1705. This prevented Scots from holding properties in England and banned the purchase of all Scottish goods and services in England. England's parliament thus alarmed the now penniless Scots nobility, many of whom also had English properties, and also closed off Scotland's main market.

The price of peace was accepting the Hanoverian succession and the end of an independent Scottish parliament. As a trade-off, England offered access to her markets in the colonies. In addition, an English army stationed itself at Newcastle, close to the Scottish Border. Discussions began in London, with the Scottish representatives aware that if agreement to England's terms was not secured, Scotland would be invaded.

BOUGHT AND SOLD FOR ENGLISH GOLD? When the final votes were taken, the nobility were heavily in favour and the popular representatives more evenly divided. This is hardly surprising. The Scottish landowners could recoup their losses after the Darien disaster, since bribes were standard parliamentary practices for moving through legislation. The Duke of Atholl was recompensed generously for not making trouble.

The Duke of Argyll became a general, his brother Archie acquired a peerage. Altogether, about £20,000 was spent in buying off the Scottish aristocracy.

Later, the Scots said the deal was crooked, though the machinations were everyday parliamentary routine and only marginally less subtle than modern practices. Robert Burns wrote the song still sung in Scotland today:
'We are bought and sold for English gold,
Such a parcel of rogues in a nation.'

VOTING FOR A NEW PARLIAMENT
Shortly after taking office in May 1997, the Labour government held a referendum, in which almost three-quarters of the Scots who voted were in favour of the principle of a new parliament. The Labour Party were keen to stress the devolution aspect, and emphasised that it would strengthen rather than weaken the UK. Subsequently, the Scotland Bill of 1998 paved the way for the new body, which comes into being in 2000.

James Ogilvy, 1st Earl of Seafield, as portrayed by Sir John Baptiste de Medina

33

In about a century, the Jacobites went from feared political and military force to a suitable sentiment for Victorian drawing room song. Most celebrated of all is Prince Charles Edward Stuart, the Bonnie Prince Charlie of Jacobite hagiography.

WHO WERE THE JACOBITES?

Decades of conflict between the monarch, the church and the state (both in Scotland and England) came to a head with the exile of the Catholic King James VII (II of England) in 1689.

Though opinion on the matter was divided, a Convention of Estates (political representatives who formed a decision-making committee) in Scotland eventually went along with England and accepted William of Orange, husband of Mary, the daughter of the exiled King James VII. The Scottish supporters of the exiled James were furious. Thus originated the Jacobites (from the Latin Jacobus, for James). They rallied round John Graham of Claverhouse, the 'Bonnie Dundee' of later Jacobite image-building.

He led them against a government army in the Battle of Killiecrankie in 1689. Fortunately for later tourism, he chose a most scenic location in Perthshire for his side's victory and his own demise, killed by a stray bullet.

The Jacobites had created their first saint, but, deprived of a figurehead, they were soon stopped in their tracks at nearby Dunkeld. There the grimly fanatical Cameronians, earlier persecuted by the Catholic faction, took their revenge.

'IT WAS A' FOR OOR RIGHTFU' KING...'

(It was all for our rightful king.) It is sometimes forgotten that the exiled Stuarts were actually the rightful blood line. This belief in the justice of their cause was instilled into James Francis, the Old Pretender, King James VII's son, as he grew up on the Continent. In turn, it was also fostered in the last Stuart king's grandson, Italian-born Charles, the Young Pretender, who as Bonnie Prince Charlie became the most famous Jacobite of all.

UPRISINGS Encouraged by Catholic France and Spain, this court in exile waited for the

Highlander statue on top of the Glenfinnan Monument

"THAD'S A DH'FHASAS
FLÙR AIR MACHAIR
MAIRIDH CLIÙ NA
H-AINNIR CHAOIMH
"THE PRESERVER OF PRINCE CHARLES
EDWARD STUART WILL BE MENTIONED
IN HISTORY AND IF COURAGE AND
FIDELITY BE VIRTUES, MENTIONED
WITH HONOUR"
JOHNSON

call, which came with an uprising in 1715. Its leader, John, Earl of Mar, was known even in his own lifetime as Bobbin John, from his habit of changing sides – an indication of the political complexities of the times. Mar led an army out of the hills to an inconclusive battle above Stirling on the hillslopes of Sheriffmuir. The affair had fizzled out by the time the Old Pretender 'James VIII' actually landed on Scottish soil at Peterhead, so he wisely did not stay long.

The 1719 rebellion was even more farcical. Spanish mercenaries were landed on the northwest coast near Dornie. They linked up with local Jacobites in Glen Shiel. Mortar fire from a detachment of government troops soon dealt with the matter. 'Sgurr na Spainteach', Spaniards' Peak, in Glen Shiel, commemorates the incident. In between times, there were other plans and other invasion fleets which failed to materialise or were blown off course by storms.

THE LAST REBELLION Later, France and Britain went to war. Eager to encourage any destabilisation of her island neighbour, France fitted out the hot-headed, handsome Bonnie Prince Charlie and sent him off to Scotland in 1745 to raise support. After some successes, the mad escapade ended with Charles's army cut to pieces on the battlefield of Culloden. Charles was in Scotland

for less than a year. The Jacobites were never a threat again. Soon the bloodshed had been sanitised and transformed into romantic notions of exiled kings across the water and a great many maudlin songs.

When Charles first landed on Scottish soil on Eriskay in the Outer Hebrides, he was told by the local chief to go home. He said he had come home. Only about 6,000 of the 30,000 fighting men in the Highlands of the time rallied to his cause.

35

> ❏ King James VII was the last of the Catholic Stuart dynasty, a line which had originated with the grandson of Robert the Bruce. ❏

Glenfinnan, where Bonnie Prince Charlie landed on the Scottish mainland some 250 years ago on 19 August 1745

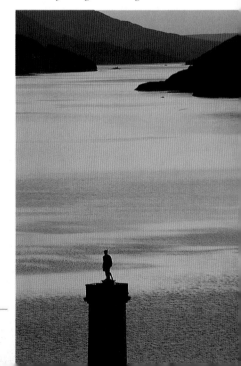

Far from being absorbed by the expanding greater Britain, Scotland retained its identity in the 18th century with an intellectual renaissance which tended towards a liberal-minded patriotism. It played an important role in the international movement known as the Age of Reason.

Some people label the entire period between the Union of the Crowns in 1707 and the death of the influential writer Sir Walter Scott in 1832 as the Scottish Enlightenment. However, if Scotland did have a true post-Union Golden Age, then most commentators place it within the second half of the 18th century.

EDINBURGH'S GREATNESS In its heyday, the movement was centred upon Edinburgh. The New Town was its architectural expression, but the Enlightenment embraced many other fields from medicine to philosophy, agriculture to economics. This was the time of Edinburgh-born David Hume, one of the more influential philosophers of the Western world; of Kirkcaldy-born Adam Smith, who wrote *Wealth of Nations* as the cornerstone of the new

Adam Smith, whose Wealth of Nations *was a masterpiece of political economy*

science of political economy; of Edinburgh's pioneering geologist James Hutton; of chemists such as Joseph Black, discoverer of carbon dioxide, and of many more who laid the foundations of a range of modern disciplines, many of them flowering out of the seedbed of Edinburgh University.

INTELLECTUAL LIFE Edinburgh was the first university in the world to introduce a chair of English Literature, and it also led the way in important pioneering medical work. No less than three generations of Monros held the Professorship in Anatomy. Glasgow-born William Cullen not only established a tradition of chemical research work, but also became Professor of Chemistry at Edinburgh in 1756 and lectured in clinical medicine at the Royal Infirmary, exploring the links between the two disciplines.

Between 1750 and 1790 Edinburgh was certainly a stimulating place to live. It was also a place where those creating the intellectual wealth were well aware of their role. They recognised the paradox that a lead in so many fields had been taken, paradoxically, in a poor nation that had so recently lost status.

Even with New Town construction under way, the sheer proximity of many families of both high and

❑ George III's chemist, Amyat, commenting on the intellectual life of Edinburgh society in the 1750s, remarked: 'Here I stand at what is called the Cross of Edinburgh, and can, in a few minutes, take 50 men of genius and learning by the hand.' ❑

36

A map of Scotland dating from 1797

humble birth in the tall cramped tenements of Edinburgh's Old Town seemed to generate a special atmosphere, a cross-fertilising of ideas which was widely commented upon by outsiders. They noted the debating and literary societies, the interest in written essays and stimulating conversation, as well as in the concrete forms of communication, such as building roads, bridges and canals. Referring to this ready access to scientists, engineers and all kinds of thinkers and writers, the English visitor Amyat (chemist to King George III) wrote that the philosophers in Scotland 'tell us what they know, and deliver their sentiments without disguise or reserve'.

By 1789 Thomas Jefferson, travelling in Europe on political business, wrote that 'no place in the world can pretend to be competition with Edinburgh'. Yet half a century later, the light had dimmed. An urge for rapid political change, embodied in the French Revolution and the Romantic movement, had overwhelmed the moderation and harmony which were the goals of the greatest Enlightenment thinkers.

Royal Society of Edinburgh, founded in 1783

❏ David Hume to Elliott of Minto in 1757: 'is it not strange…that, at a time when we have lost our Princes, our Parliaments, our independent Government, even the presence of our chief Nobility, are unhappy in our accent and Pronunciation … speak a very corrupt Dialect of the Tongue…is it not strange… we shou'd really be the People most distinguish'd for literature in Europe?' ❏

The great mercantile cities of the Lowlands went about their business of making money. The powerful Highland landowners were similarly motivated. To improve their estates, they cleared their tenants from ground they had worked for centuries. Today this process might be called ethnic cleansing.

The series of evictions and forced emigration known as the Highland Clearances did not happen immediately after the defeat of the Jacobite rebel forces at Culloden in 1746. Nevertheless, after Culloden, the old-style clan chiefs were stripped of their powers. The reality of hard economics asserted itself in the poor lands of the north.

fish and meal. Also, kelp was gathered, dried, and burned and the ash used in the manufacture of soap and glass. This made money for landowners with coastal properties.

The landowners raised rents to increase profits and altered leases to reduce individual landholdings, in order to compel tenants to spend more time fishing or kelp-gathering.

An abandoned croft at Arnol, on the Isle of Lewis in the Western Isles

THE IMPROVING LANDLORDS A programme of improvements was implemented by new landowners, only some of whom were still of Highland stock, as they tried to make money from their property. The second half of the 18th century saw the founding of state-sponsored fishing stations such as Tobermory and Ullapool. The potato was first grown and soon became a staple. Better nourishment allowed the Highland population to expand.

A SHORT-LIVED PROSPERITY
Britain's wars employed Highland manpower and were also a market for Highland produce such as cattle,

Far from evicting tenants, landowners in the first decades of the 1800s – the majority of whom were absentees – actually required manpower to make money.

The slump came at the end of the Napoleonic Wars in the early 19th century, when the market for cattle collapsed. Agricultural improvements, successful in the Lowlands, simply did not work on the thin, acid Highland soils. New chemical processes made kelp-gathering unnecessary, and even the fishing became unprofitable. The landowners turned to sheep to make money. Unfortunately, the tenants' farming activities – the growing of potatoes and the pasturing of cattle – conflicted with the needs of the new-style Cheviot or black-face breeds.

> ❏ 'Much the same thing is done today by town councils who uproot people from their old shabby but neighbourly streets and place them in ultra-modern, clinically clean but often inhuman high-rise flats, usually against their will.'
> *Dunrobin Castle Guidebook*, printed 1991. Dunrobin was the home of the initiators of the Sutherland Clearances. ❏

VIOLENCE IN THE GLENS The people of the glens were evicted. The violence that accompanied the policy flared up in a now infamous list of Highland place-names, of which Strathnaver on the Sutherland Estates is perhaps the best known.

In 1785, the last Earl of Sutherland's daughter, Elizabeth Gordon, married one of the richest men in England, George Granville Leveson-Gower, second Marquess of Stafford. He had made a fortune in coal and wood and owned a vast estate in England. With his marriage came most of the northern Scottish county of Sutherland, including Dunrobin Castle.

In the programme of estate improvements, around 5,000 Highlanders were cleared up to 1821. They were either settled on narrow coastal strips or forced to emigrate, mostly across the Atlantic. In Strathnaver, many of the tenants were unable to salvage their belongings as their houses were burned before their eyes. The estate factor, Patrick Sellar, was even charged with arson and homicide, as some homes were fired with old people still inside them. He was acquitted.

The same pattern of evictions by landowners – titled aristocrats, entrepreneurs and industrialists – stretched from Shetland to Perthshire. Many sincerely believed it was for the best. Today, in the Highlands, with their silent glens admired by city-dwellers, visitors creep reverently round the treasures in the castles of the descendants of these 'improvers'.

Dunrobin Castle, Golspie, Sutherland

The Scots have always been adventurers. Soldiers and merchants travelled in Europe from the very early days of the Scots nation. Then, when ships became large enough to undertake longer voyages, Scots left their homeland and became entrepreneurs and explorers, as well as simply colonists, all over the globe.

In 1297, Sir William Wallace, the Scottish freedom fighter, wrote to the Senators of Lübeck and Hamburg thanking them for helping Scottish merchants and offering safe conduct for any of their representatives at Scotland's ports. This is an early reference to Scots entrepreneurs abroad. It is estimated that Poland had 30,000 Scots living and operating in business there in the 17th century.

Dunbar acknowledges its famous son, John Muir

TO THE FOUR CORNERS OF THE GLOBE Scots were prominent in the Far East. William Jardine, born in Lochmaben (Dumfriesshire), was an independent China trader, who joined forces with James Matheson to form the Hong Kong-based Jardine Matheson of today. Its early profits were amassed in the unsavoury

opium trade. Hugh Falconer from Forres and William Jamieson of Leith were early pioneers of tea plantations in India. Fraserburgh-born Thomas Glover introduced modern technology to Japan, particularly in shipbuilding. He ordered Japan's first slip dock, which in turn led to the expansion of the now multinational company Mitsubishi.

Not only was Thomas Glover a trusted adviser and personal friend of Mitsubishi's founder, Yataro Iwasaki, he also imported the first steam locomotive and the first telegraph line. Incidents in his extraordinary life are said to have inspired Puccini's opera *Madame Butterfly*.

The Scots turned westward as well, building Glasgow's early wealth on plantations of Virginia tobacco and Jamaican sugar. Later developments such as the Prairie Cattle Company Limited, Texas's first major joint stock venture in cattle ranching, were actually Edinburgh based. More than half the Hudson Bay Company's senior staff were Scots. Even more significantly, at least 13 US presidents claimed Scots ancestry.

These emigrant Scots or their descendants became involved in every sphere. The son of a poor country tailor in an upcountry parish in Aberdeenshire went on to found *Forbes Magazine*, the still-successful US financial journal. Bertie Charles Forbes (1880–1954) became a millionaire in the process. James Gordon Bennet (1795–1872) left his native Keith in Moray in the northeast, and went on to found the *New York Herald*. In industry, the best-known Scot is the steel magnate Andrew Carnegie from Dunfermline; his name has become a byword for

Dunfermline-born industrialist Andrew Carnegie

philanthropy. The squalor of the Glasgow slums of the early 19th century produced Allan Pinkerton, the founder of the oldest and largest private investigation agency in the world. In 1867 a young Scottish emigrant, John Muir from Dunbar, began to develop the idea of environmental conservation while walking in the Sierra Nevada. It was to lead to the founding of the conservation movement in the USA.

There were, naturally, the oddities: the Scots who suddenly popped up in unexpected places, like the businessmen who formed the African Lakes Corporation in 1878 or the Scottish lace workers in Spain who founded the first Spanish football club. Less surprising, perhaps, is a certain James Chisholm, who founded the first pub in Sydney, called the Thistle Tavern – presumably around the same time as another Scot, Lachlan Macquarie, brought order as the first governor of the former penal colony of New South Wales.

THE HOMELAND Whatever the reason, religious persecution, lack of opportunity, forced clearance, voluntary emigration or just a sense of adventure, Scots men and women have been the country's leading export over the centuries. Small wonder the Clan Donald has over 100,000 members worldwide. For many the call of the homeland is still strong. Libraries throughout Scotland, carrying records on microfiche formerly only available at New Register House in Edinburgh, do brisk business with genealogical inquiries.

❏ The word Scot in Polish also means a commercial traveller, and the Poles have a simile 'as poor as a Scots pedlar's pack'. Evidently not all Scots were successful in business. ❏

The image of Scotland as a resourceful, industrial place sits uncomfortably with the more romantic notion of misty bens and glens. Yet, in times gone by, the output of heavy industry and, in particular, shipbuilding, ensured that Scottish products went around the world and that 'Clyde built' (that is, a product of the many shipbuilding yards along the River Clyde) meant the very finest of its kind.

The Scottish industrial belt was formerly a diagonal corridor across the waist of Scotland, less than 48km wide from coast to coast. It took in the coalfields of Ayrshire and the south of Edinburgh, the Vale of Leven dyeing industries south of Loch Lomond and Angus textile manufacturing (all now mere vestiges of their former size, if there at all). Paradoxically, it also included some of Scotland's best farmland.

THE KEY TO PROSPERITY: COAL AND IRON Amongst these activities, those based on locally available coal and iron had the highest profile – if only because of the effect they had on

The Clydeside birth of a Cunarder, the Queen Mary

the environment and landscape. It is arguable that the real cradle of the Industrial Revolution in Scotland lay east of Glasgow, in the Falkirk area, where the Carron Company was founded in 1760, close to iron mines.

However, by the early years of the 19th century, the easily workable blackband iron ore of Lanarkshire had been discovered. What had been the fruit garden of the west of Scotland was demolished in a search for this important mineral. The air of Lanarkshire filled with grime and smoke as ironworks sprang up, using local coal to fuel the furnaces. The stage was set for Clydeside to become one of the world's greatest shipbuilding centres. Though England's River Tyne was also important, most of the developments in ship design and, in particular, marine engines and boilers, were made on Clydeside.

> ❏ The Carron Company's most famous product was the carronade, a short-barrelled, large-bore cannon used in Britain's imperialist wars. ❏

THE SONG OF THE CLYDE Formerly, the shipyards stretched practically unbroken all the way downstream to Greenock, but these days most are long gone. Even as recently as 1929, the Clyde built 20 per cent of the world's shipping. Then the so-called Clyde symphony or the 'song of the Clyde' was at its height: the noise of thousands of riveters banging home the red hot rivets which held together the locally made steel plates.

42

Sunset over the Clyde shipyards

THE ROMANCE OF SHIPS Glasgow, of course, had all kinds of other manufacturing operations, including the production of railway locomotives. Dundee and the Angus hinterland thrived on textiles, Edinburgh had her printing and publishing industries, as well as shale oil extraction to the west. Even modest Aberdeen could claim a surprisingly large engineering sector, while the Borders were well known for textiles.

Yet only shipbuilding and the proud and graceful products which sailed the waters of the globe acquired the romance and mystique that come with the associations of distant places. Though the local coal and iron that helped build the ships have long been worked out, the

❏ During World War II, the Clyde shipyards still had the capacity to build 2,000 ships, repair more than 23,000 and convert hundreds more. To put it another way, the workforce built or repaired 13 ships every day for five years. ❏

hammers are not yet silent. The Clyde still sees the launch of large vessels – as ever, diagonally into the narrow river. But on the banks of today's Clyde there are also long stretches of filled-in docks and redeveloped sites. Only at places such as the Denny Ship Model Experiment Tank at Dumbarton (see page 140) are there echoes of the great, grimy days of the Clyde, the river that made Glasgow.

Edinburgh

Royal Botanic Garden

Scottish National Portrait Gallery

YORK PLACE

New St Andrew's House

3 Moray Place Bank Gardens

MORAY PLACE

Queen Street Gardens

Royal College of Physicians

St Andrew Square

Bus Station

St Jam Centre

Register House

AINSLIE PLACE

ST COLME ST

St Georgian House

CHARLOTTE

ROSE STREET

GEORGE STREET

Assembly Rooms & Music Hall

ROSE STREET

Scott Monument

PRINCES STREET

Waverley Shopping Centre

2 West Register House

QUEENSFERRY ST

HOPE SQUARE

ROSE STREET

Freemasons' Hall

PRINCES STREET

Floral Clock

Royal Scottish Academy

THE MOUND

WAVERLEY BRIDGE

Fruitmarket Gallery

City Art Centre

Lauriston Castle

SHANDWICK PLACE

WEST END

West Princes Street Gardens

Ross Open-air Theatre

National Gallery of Scotland

BANK

Lady Stair's House

St Giles Cathedral

COCKBURN

City Chambers

HIGH TH

Parliame House

Gladstone's Land

LAWN MKT

Zoo Scottish Agricultural Museum

CANNING STREET

LOTHIAN ROAD

CASTLE TERRACE

Edinburgh Castle

★

Camera Obscura

VICTORIA ST

Scotch Whisky Heritage Centre

JOHNSTON TERRACE

GEORGE IV BRIDGE

National Library of Scotland

COWGAT

CHAMBERS ST

Royal Museum Scotlan

Traverse Theatre

Century 2000

SPITTAL ST

GRASS MARKET

CANDLE MAKER ROW

Museum of Scotland

Festival Square

Usher Hall

Royal Lyceum Theatre

George Heriot's School

Greyfriars Kirk & Greyfriars Bobby Statue

University of Edinburgh Medical Scho

MORRISON STREET

WEST APPROACH ROAD

BREAD ST

WEST PORT

College of Art

FOUNTAIN BRIDGE

LAURISTON PLACE

A   B   C

STIRRING FIRST IMPRESSION By road, only a couple of hours or less from the Border with England, the A68 plunges over the edge of the Southern Uplands to reveal the Lothians, Edinburgh's countryside, spread out below: the sweep of the Pentland Hills stopping short at the edge of the city; further round, the dark profile of Arthur's Seat dominating the other more gentle rises on which Scotland's capital is built; then the long reach of the Firth of Forth with just a hint of the Highlands beyond. This is the setting for one of the world's most distinguished cities, now once again to be the seat of the Scottish Parliament.

From the air, on the final approaches, the city map is plain: the castle on its high rock and the Palace of Holyroodhouse in its Royal Park act as head and tail for the backbone of the Royal Mile, which runs through the Old Town. Across the green space of Princes Street Gardens, symmetrical patterns reveal the plan of the neo-classical New Town. Moments after this port-wing view, and over the high spans of the Forth rail and road bridges, the traveller touches down.

By rail, you reach the centre at Waverley Station. On emerging, the skyline seems familiar: the profiles of castle and battlement, the gothic-spired Scott Monument and Greek-porticoed art galleries, popular postcard images, are known worldwide.

From every angle, Edinburgh strikes theatrical poses. The neo-classical collection of monuments on top of Calton Hill seems about to frame some Greek tragedy. Above the rooftops of the Royal Mile, the long red ridge of

Edinburgh Castle dominates the city skyline

▶▶▶ CITY HIGHLIGHTS

Salisbury Crags skirts the rocks of Arthur's Seat – it could well be a painted backdrop for one of Sir Walter Scott's melodramas. At one o'clock each day a cannon cracks out, puffing blue smoke over the castle battlements. This is not another uprising, only Edinburgh squeezing extra drama out of a time check. Edinburgh generates excitement and a sense of expectation. This is where things happen...

OLD EDINBURGH Edinburgh's **Castle Rock** dates from the last Ice Age. An eastward grinding glacier nibbled away at its hard volcanic plug, leaving three steep sides and a ramp running down eastwards. An archaeological dig in the 1990s to establish the age of settlement on the Rock found some chewed herring bones, now carbon-dated to around 800 BC.

The Castle Rock was a Dark Age stronghold, fortified by the Saxon King Edwin in the 7th century. The oldest building in Edinburgh today is the 11th-century **St Margaret's Chapel** within the castle, named after Queen Margaret. She married King Malcolm, whose Celtic court was at Dunfermline, then the capital. As a Saxon southerner she persuaded the court to move to the Saxon-influenced Lothians. Edinburgh became the capital thereafter.

By the 12th century, the huddle of little houses protected by the castle had spilled down the ramp – the embryonic **Royal Mile** – perhaps as far as today's Tron Kirk in the High Street. Margaret's son, King David, founded **Holyrood Abbey**, another landmark in the shaping of the old city.

The castle was sacked by King Edward I of England in 1296 and many of the nation's records were destroyed. After the English withdrew, Edinburgh became a royal burgh in 1329, and thereafter faced the wars and vicissitudes of Scotland's long struggle under a weak monarchy with a powerful and ambitious neighbour on her southern border. The High Kirk of St Giles was burned in 1385 by King Richard II of England, the Royal Mile torched in 1542 during the 'rough wooing' (see page 30).

As a means of defence, Edinburgh was a walled town. Bits of wall survive today, near St Mary's Street and above the Grassmarket. In the main, the community remained within its high walls until the mid-18th century. Then it crossed the marshy defensive gap, now the site of Princes Street Gardens, to found the New Town.

NEW EDINBURGH In the creative heat and spirit of optimism of the Age of Enlightenment, the city laid the foundations of the townscape of today. The first **New Town** comprises the rectangle bounded by **Charlotte** and **St Andrew squares** to west and east and **Princes** and **Queen streets** to the south and north. Other development schemes followed on around Moray Place and, less successfully, along Royal Terrace.

The great public buildings and monuments which enhance the city environment so much today were built at the same time: the **Royal Scottish Academy** and the **National Gallery**, honey-coloured columned temples floating in garden greenery when viewed from the east; the fluted shapes of more columns of Calton Hill's unfinished National Monument, which block and change the views east along Princes Street from every angle.

Amid all this neo-classicism, the monument to Sir Walter Scott shoots out of the trees like a Gothic sky-rocket. Architecturally isolated, Scott's immortalisation in sandstone plays its part in the theatrical quality of Edinburgh and has become an essential symbol of the city. Towering above Holyroodhouse, the impossible profile of **Arthur's Seat** looks like a backdrop for one of Scott's own theatrical melodramas – or an entirely appropriate setting for the cultural overkill generated annually through the Edinburgh International Festival, the Fringe and other attendant festivals.

For all its swingeing parking fines and crowds, as well as the proportion of well-meant but uninspiring productions that turn the Fringe into something of a lucky dip, Edinburgh undoubtedly remains an exciting place. Away from the city centre's cosmopolitan throng, life in the New Town goes on as it has done for more than two centuries, below the plasterwork in elegant drawing-rooms or amid the shade of the private gardens overlooked by palace-fronted façades: altogether a curious meeting of past and present.

SCOTLAND'S BURGHS
A Scottish burgh, a term first used in the 12th century, was a town with certain rights; when these rights were granted by the monarch, a town became a royal burgh. The rights were mainly to do with mercantile matters, such as the granting of the right to hold fairs or markets, in order to raise money for the Crown, as well as for the community itself. Characteristics of a burgh usually included a mercat (market) cross, to indicate the place of the market and the town centre, as well as a tolbooth, a civic building that served as an administrative centre and, very often, a courtroom and prison too. Burghs disappeared with a local government reorganisation in 1975.

47

Calton Hill commands some fine views over Edinburgh – see page 49 for an example

Visitors view the former Royal High School near Calton Hill

▶▶ Calton Hill 45D3

Robert Louis Stevenson's favourite view of Edinburgh was from this hill to the east of Princes Street. Even in Stevenson's day it carried its extraordinary neo-classical collection of buildings: the **Old Observatory** (the only surviving building by New Town planner James Craig), the **City** or **New Observatory**, the **Dugald Stewart Memorial** (loosely based on the temple of Lysicrates in ancient Athens), the unfinished **National Monument** and the **Nelson Monument** which ignores its neo-classical neighbours and is shaped instead like an upturned telescope. If the walk up the steps to the hilltop is too much, take the car. Look for the turning by the former Royal High School. The hill is open at all times.

▶ Camera Obscura 44C1
594 Castlehill
Open: Apr–Oct, Mon–Fri 9.30–6; weekends 10–6. Nov–Mar, daily 10–5. Admission charge
This building has a varied history: the lower storeys were built in the 17th century, and the upper castellated storeys added in 1853, when the building first became a camera obscura. As well as panoramic projections of Edinburgh, thanks to its revolutionary design and mirrors, the centre offers Edinburgh-related exhibitions.

▶ Canongate Kirk 45D2
Canongate
This church was built in 1688 for the congregation when King James VII converted the abbey kirk at Holyrood into a chapel for the Knights of the Thistle. Of greater interest, though, than this fairly plain cruciform church, is the adjoining **graveyard**. Graves include that of Mrs McLehose, an attractive young woman who was abandoned by her husband. Robert Burns conducted a passionate correspondence with her (just that and no more, since Burns was confined to his Edinburgh lodgings with a twisted knee). She outlived him by 45 years. Also here is the grave of Robert Fergusson, the brilliant Edinburgh poet who inspired Burns, though they never met. When Burns visited, he was shocked to find Fergusson's grave unmarked, and paid for his headstone.

Itinerary

Three days in Edinburgh

DAY 1 Rampart views from **Edinburgh Castle** aid orientation in this fairly simply laid out city, and a self-guided castle tour, taking most of a morning, is worthwhile. Then go downhill, diverting for **Victoria Street** shopping. (Use the steps at West Bow.) Try, say, Jacksons on the **Royal Mile** for lunch, or head to the Kalpna by Nicholson Street, or take a chance with a pub lunch anywhere on the Mile.

Be selective if time is short. The **Museum of Childhood** is fun, or continue to **Huntly House**. The **Palace of Holyroodhouse** is also popular, though this option may give too much history. Alternatively, go to **Calton Hill** for city views, en route for the **National Gallery** at the foot of the Mound. You should just catch it before closing.

DAY 2 Yesterday the Old Town, today the New. Start at the **National Portrait Gallery**, then go on to the **Georgian House**. In between, try Jenners in Princes Street for shopping. For lunch, choose from the many options nearby: La Lanterna on Hanover Street if on a budget, or Martin's on Rose Street. In the afternoon, explore northwards through the New Town to reach the Royal Botanic Garden, then return via Stockbridge and shops. In the evening, check out Leith's eating places, or, if the weather is fine, walk in the Royal Park to enjoy great views from Arthur's Seat, followed by a beer in the Sheep's Heid at Duddingston.

DAY 3 The **Waverley Market** is useful for last-minute souvenir shopping. If you have time, revisit the Royal Mile. The **Scotch Whisky Heritage Centre**, the **Writers' Museum**, and **Gladstone's Land** are all within easy reach of the centre.

TIME-KEEPING
The firing of the one o'clock gun from the ramparts of Edinburgh Castle originated from a request by the Leith Dock Commission in 1861 to locate a time ball on top of the Nelson Monument (which was visible from the docks). Punctually every day since then (except in wartime and on Sundays) an audible signal has boomed out across the city and simultaneously the time ball has dropped down its pole on the monument, enabling mariners of old to check their chronometers and nowadays making tourists jump visibly as they stroll along Princes Street at lunch-time.

49

Edinburgh Castle from Calton Hill

A ROYAL MYSTERY

In 1830, workmen discovered a tiny coffin hidden in the royal apartments in Edinburgh Castle. Within was a baby with an embroidered 'J' legible on the golden shroud. This added to rumours that Mary, Queen of Scots' own infant had died and been substituted. The prime suspect is the Countess of Mar, since the future King James VI was brought up with the Earl and Countess's own son, whom he resembled closely, as contemporary portraits show.

▶▶▶ Edinburgh Castle 44B1

Open: Apr–Sep, daily 9.30–5.15. Oct–Mar, daily 9.30–4.15. Admission charge

Possibly Scotland's most famous landmark, Edinburgh Castle dominates the city centre with its silhouette of ramparts and rooftops. Almost a million visitors every year swarm over its buildings, from the 11th-century chapel to its latest addition, a restaurant with one of the finest views anywhere in the city.

Edinburgh Castle was an important royal court from at least the 11th century. Through the Middle Ages, its buildings were mainly around the highest point of the Castle Rock. King David II built the first strong defensive line across the eastern neck after 1356.

Little of the very early works survives. Today's **Great Hall** of King James IV dates from the early 16th century, but has been much altered. The massive **Half Moon Battery** dates in part from the latter half of the 16th century. As the castle's royal role became less important than its military one, successive waves of buildings and defences were dictated by military needs and warfare, which severely damaged the castle on many occasions.

The castle fired its last shot in anger in 1745 at Bonnie Prince Charlie's men, who failed to take the high rock. Thereafter, as well as a barracks and administrative centre, the castle also became a military prison. It still serves as a military headquarters.

Start your tour by the **Esplanade**, the mid 18th-century parade ground. Beyond the Victorian gatehouse, you find yourself below the vast walls of the **Half Moon Battery** and **Forewall Battery**. Beyond the **Portcullis Gate** the upper levels are reached.

Reminders of a constant military presence include the handsome **Governor's House**, dating from 1742, now the Officers' Mess, and the **New Barracks**, whose bold blocking has dominated the skyline since the 1790s. The former hospital, to the right (beyond tiny **St Margaret's Chapel**), is now part of the Scottish United Services Museum, a place of monosyllabic attendants and immaculate uniforms. (The main historic collection is in the Queen Anne Barracks.)

The Vaults, beside the Victorian prison, have more atmosphere. These dripping, dank corridors of naked rock have been barracks, stores, bakehouse and, as memorably described in Robert Louis Stevenson's *St Ives*, a prison for French soldiers (look for their graffiti). However, the most famous denizen today is **Mons Meg**: she squats evilly on a spotlit plinth next door to her audio-visual introduction.

Back above ground, on Crown Square, is the **Scottish National War Memorial**, an emotional ambush of grey light, tattered flags and endless names. Opposite is the anticlimax of the **Great Hall**. Like the small room in the Palace in which Mary, Queen of Scots gave birth to the James who was to rule both Scotland and England, this just fails to grab the imagination. However, also here is a very illuminating display on the story of the castle, plus the **Honours of Scotland Exhibition**. This is a highlight,

The Scottish United Services Museum, Edinburgh Castle

where you can view the oldest regalia in Europe: the Scottish crown, sceptre and sword of state. In close-up, the royal crown seems a bit like the castle itself: a little battered and frequently repaired over the centuries, yet the pride of a poor nation.

▶ City Art Centre 44C2

Market Street
Open: Mon–Sat 10–5; during Festival Sun 2–5.
Admission free
The city's own art gallery is housed in a six-floored former warehouse. It stages a changing programme of exhibitions and displays the city's collection of Scottish paintings. It brings world-class exhibitions to the city, from the Chinese Warriors to the Pharaohs.

▶ Craigmillar Castle 45D1

Off the A68
Open: Apr–Sep, daily 9.30–6.30; Oct–Mar, Mon–Wed and Sat 9–4.30, Sun 2–4.30, Thu 9.30–12. Admission charge
If Edinburgh Castle were less of a magnet, and if Craigmillar Castle were not situated quite so near one of Edinburgh's less salubrious housing developments, then the impressive Craigmillar would have many more visitors. In Mary, Queen of Scots' time, the imposing fortress was held by Sir Simon Preston, one of her staunchest allies. Behind the massive curtain wall, somewhere in the 16th-century range of buildings, the murder of her husband Darnley was planned (see pages 30–1).

City Art Centre

THE SCOTTISH REGALIA
On 24 June 1953 the Regalia of Scotland were taken from the castle to St Giles Cathedral, where they were presented to Her Majesty the Queen. The galaxy of lords and earls who guarded the Honours of the Nation were dressed in ermine and grand costumes. The Queen, however, wore a simple coat and hat. Still clutching her handbag, she touched the oldest crown in Europe. The incongruity is still remembered in Scotland to this day, though in the official portrait of the event, by Stanley Cursiter, the handbag has been carefully painted out.

MONS MEG
This siege gun or bombard was made in Mons in the 1440s and sent by its owner, the Duke of Burgundy, to his nephew by marriage, King James II, in 1457. The gun had a firing rate of, at the most, one cannonball every 30 minutes. Though cumbersome to move over the rough roads of its day, it did take part in sieges before finally bursting while firing a salute in 1680. It was later displayed in the Tower of London, before its return to Edinburgh Castle.

Edinburgh Castle from Princes Street Gardens

Walk

A flavour of old Edinburgh

A pleasant stroll to attractions on both sides of the Royal Mile, before dropping down to the Grassmarket and a fine view of the castle. Allow 2 hours; *see map on page 44.*

Amid the general visitor melee on

Looking east down the Royal Mile in the direction of the Palace of Holyroodhouse

Castlehill at the very top of the **Royal Mile**, look out for the **Witch's Well** (on the wall) which recalls the last witch burned here in 1722. Nearby is **Cannonball House**, which has a cannonball embedded in the gable with a variety of explanations as to how it got there. Further down the hill are the *Camera Obscura* (see page 48) and the *Scotch Whisky Heritage Centre* (see page 63). Keep on down the hill to the roundabout.

In the Lawnmarket, there are numerous souvenir shops to distract you, but for a hint of old Edinburgh, turn right just after the roundabout into the short Upper Bow. Go to the end of this truncated street and look over the railings to see Victoria Street curving down below. Now imagine the shape of the town before Victoria Street was built: Upper Bow plunged steeply down to join the lowest point of Victoria Street, called West Bow, which leads into the Grassmarket. The insignificant lane you have just come down used to be the main road into old Edinburgh from the west. Return to the Lawnmarket on the Royal Mile. Opposite is **Gladstone's Land** (see page 54), one of a number of restored 17th-century properties in this area.

Lady Stair's House (the Writers' Museum, see page 57) is also on the north side of the street – cut through an alleyway to reach it – with **Deacon Brodie's** Tavern occupying the corner site. Deacon Brodie, a respectable locksmith by day and a villain by night, inspired Robert Louis Stevenson's *The Strange Case of Dr Jekyll and Mr Hyde.*

Turn right into George IV Bridge and right again to reach Victoria Street, which has a good range of shops and cafés. West Bow leads into the **Grassmarket**. The right to hold regular markets here was granted by King James III in 1477. The area gained notoriety as the hanging place of common criminals, as well as Covenanter martyrs (see page 55). Look for the **St Andrew's Cross**, railed and set into the cobbles, which marks the gallows site.

For an impressive view of the castle, cross over the Grassmarket, go halfway along and follow The Vennel up in a series of steps to a well-preserved portion of the city wall. This is **Telfer's Wall,** 1628–36, which now defines the boundaries of George Heriot's School beyond. From here, there is an excellent view north to the castle. Return to the Grassmarket, then bear right, passing **Mr Wood's Fossil Shop** which offers souvenirs with a difference (very small trilobites are a snip). Then go up **Candlemaker Row**, where tourists risk life and limb standing in the middle of the road to photograph the statue of **Greyfriars Bobby** (see page 55) at the far end. Make your way back to the Royal Mile along George IV Bridge.

❑ Beneath Edinburgh City Chambers in the High Street, site of the former Royal Exchange, lies Mary King's Close. This narrow street was abandoned after the plague of 1645, and sealed off to prevent the disease from spreading. It was subsequently covered by the foundations of the later buildings on the High Street. The 17th-century time capsule survives today and is used for storing council documents. It can be visited on conducted tours. ❑

❑ The Old Town right up to the 18th century, and even later, was a rather smelly place. This fact was recorded by numerous visitors. Household wastes of every description were emptied from the tall tenements into the narrow High Street with a warning cry of 'gardyloo' from on high (the phrase comes from the French *gardez l'eau* – 'beware, water'). This was the cause of great embarrassment to James Boswell as he escorted the distinguished man of letters, Dr Samuel Johnson, up the Royal Mile before they set off for their Hebridean Tour in 1773. The odour is also remembered by a famous fiddle tune, somewhat ironically entitled 'The Floo'ers (flowers) o' Edinburgh'. ❑

The City Chambers, built as the Royal Exchange

Edinburgh

'THE CADIES'

In the Old Town there used to be an entirely unofficial part-courier, part-guide, part-security service known as 'the cadies'. They knew every nook and cranny in the warrens around the Royal Mile and no visitor could arrive in town without their knowledge. For generations, Edinburgh had fewer robberies and less house-breaking than other Scottish cities simply because of the all-seeing eyes of the cadies. The word, from the French *cadet,* survives today as caddy, the term now used for someone who helps with golf clubs.

54

The Georgian House, Charlotte Square

Greyfriars Bobby, Edinburgh's best-known dog

▶ Fruitmarket Gallery   44C2
Market Street
Open: Tue–Sat 10–6, Sun 12–5. Admission free
Another of Edinburgh's high-profile arts venues, the Fruitmarket emphasises contemporary art and design with a strong international flavour. Combine it with a visit to the City Art Centre opposite (see page 51).

▶▶ Georgian House   44A2
Charlotte Square
Open: Apr–Oct, Mon–Sat 10–5, Sun 2–5, last entry 4.30. Admission charge
Right in the middle of Robert Adam's magnificent palace-fronted block at No. 7 Charlotte Square, the National Trust for Scotland has re-created the look of 1796, when the elegant building was new. From the magnificent drawing-room with its candlesticks aglitter, to the well-scrubbed areas below stairs, it demonstrates the impact that the New Town made on Edinburgh life for its wealthier residents.

▶ Gladstone's Land   44C2
477 Lawnmarket
Open: Mon–Sat 10–5, Sun 2–5, last entry 4.30. Admission charge
When the local merchant, Thomas Gledstanes acquired the property that now bears his name in 1617, it was a typical 16th-century building that would have resembled John Knox House further down the street (see page 57). Gledstanes modernised it by adding a stone front and stone arcading. Like so much of the Royal Mile, this

ancient tenement was scheduled to be swept aside, but instead a purchaser presented it to the fledgling National Trust for Scotland in 1935. The Trust restored it and uncovered its by then hidden arcades, now unique in Edinburgh. Some fine painted ceilings also survive from Gledstanes' time and are set off by period room settings.

▶ **Greyfriars Kirk**   44C1

Greyfriars Place
Open: Kirk Easter–Oct, Mon–Fri 10.30–4.30, Sat 10.30–2.30;
Nov–Easter, Thu 1.30–3.30: churchyard daily. Admission free
King Charles I's attempt to introduce the English Episcopal Service Book to Scotland in 1637 was widely opposed. The following year a large crowd gathered in the churchyard of the Greyfriars to sign the National Covenant. This important manifesto professed loyalty to the king but warned him not to interfere in the affairs of the Kirk. It can be seen to this day within the church. Thus were born the Covenanters, participants in the religious wars of the 17th century. The kirkyard itself, where 1,400 Covenanters were imprisoned in 1679, is on the site of a 15th-century Franciscan friary and has many 17th-century grave monuments.

The Covenanters Prison
in Greyfriars Kirkyard

It was also the burial place of John Gray, the owner of Greyfriars Bobby, a dog who refused to leave his master's grave. The kind-hearted graveyard attendant fed him at first. Soon the faithful terrier was a well-known phenomenon, cared for by the locals. He soon adopted a local restaurant, delighting its owner who did extra business because of the publicity. People came from long distances to see the dog arrive each lunchtime.

When a law was passed forbidding ownerless dogs, Bobby's supporters appealed to the Lord Provost who gave the dog immunity by way of an inscribed collar. Bobby died in 1872 but the tale did not end there. A baroness erected a fountain at one end of nearby Candlemaker Row. Later still, in 1961, the story of Greyfriars Bobby was the subject of a Walt Disney film, which explains his appeal to American visitors today. Doggy artefacts are on display in **Huntly House** (see below).

▶▶ **Huntly House**   45D2

Canongate
Open: Mon–Sat, during Festival Sun 2–5. Admission free
This 16th-century building houses the city's museum of life over the centuries. Local silver, glass, pottery, shop signs and a host of other artefacts are all displayed in a warren of interconnecting rooms. It helps to know a little about the history of Edinburgh before you browse around so that, for example, the artefacts connected with King George IV's visit, or the original New Town plan signed by James Craig, are more significant.

55

REGISTER HOUSE
Record keeping in Scotland has had a troubled history. King Edward I of England vindictively destroyed the country's earliest records in the 13th century. Register House was sited in the castle by the mid-16th century, and then in the Tolbooth a century later. Only in 1774 was a foundation stone laid for a custom-built Register House, designed by Robert Adam, and partly financed by funds raised from the sale of estates forfeited by Jacobite lairds (see page 38). The building, at the east end of Princes Street, is still in use today, guarded by a famous statue of Wellington.

From its earliest days as Scotland's capital, Edinburgh has had strong literary connections. Thomas Nelson, J Bartholomew, Oliver & Boyd and W & R Chambers are some of the famous publishing houses with origins in Edinburgh.

SCOTLAND'S POETIC GOLDEN AGE
Medieval Edinburgh was a literary place. Gavin Douglas, c1474–1522, Dean of St Giles, translated the *Aeneid*, the first translation of a Latin poet ever printed in English.

William Dunbar, c1460–c1520, was a court poet whose work was in print by 1508, the earliest example of Scottish typography. Sir David Lyndsay of The Mount scandalised the courtiers with his *Satyre of the Thrie Estatis* in 1540. The piece returns regularly to the Edinburgh Festival.

56

Originally a wig-maker in the Grassmarket, the poet Allan Ramsay later set up Britain's first circulating library, and his is the first of the 'modern' names associated with literary Edinburgh. Then came Robert Fergusson, who captured the spirit of the Enlightenment in Edinburgh and inspired a later generation, among them Robert Burns.

A vibrant literary community Conspicuous in the 19th century was Sir Walter Scott, writing of 'mine own romantic town' from his house in Castle Street. As a teenager, he had once met Burns at a local literary gathering. Edinburgh's literary life, with its publishers, tavern life and buzzing creativity, attracted writers from all over the world. It was the first city to recognise the achievements of Charles Dickens by making him a freeman. Charlotte Bronte was also enthralled by the place. Her brother Branwell wrote to the influential Edinburgh-based *Blackwood's Magazine* asking for a job when he was 15. His letter was ignored at the time but is now in the National Library.

Edinburgh in its prime Robert Louis Stevenson was a native of Edinburgh and became one of its most famous Victorian writers. Stevenson wrote of the city not just in romantic terms but in a style which still brings its taverns and low life alive. Scotland's most influential 20th-century poet, Hugh MacDiarmid, also had strong Edinburgh connections through a variety of publishing enterprises. The novelist Muriel Spark was educated at James Gillespie's High School for Girls, model for the Marcia Blane School in her novel *The Prime of Miss Jean Brodie*.

Today it is still possible to rub shoulders with poets and writers, even moderately famous ones, in one of the city's 'literary' pubs such as Milne's Bar on Hanover Street. The Bohemian life survives in Edinburgh, perhaps as a reaction to the city's Calvinistic and prim outlook.

Burns' memorabilia, The Writers' Museum

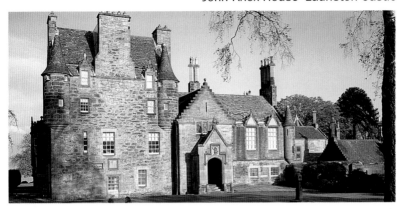

▶ John Knox House   45D2

45 High Street
Open: Mon–Sat 10–5, last entry 4.30. Admission charge
Nobody seems to know if John Knox (see panel) really did live in this house in the High Street. However, a folk tradition was enough to save it when threatened with demolition as long ago as 1849. The late 15th-century building, with its projecting first floor gallery, is a reminder of what the Royal Mile would once have looked like: narrow and lined by tenements with their projecting floors virtually shutting out the light. The house was damaged by the English Earl of Hertford's men in 1544, when it was owned by Mariota Arres and James Mossman. Their initials are on the wall above the shop door. Mossman was the keeper of the Royal Mint to Mary, Queen of Scots, and was eventually hanged for his allegiance. Today there is an exhibition on the lives of both Mossman and Knox within the property.

▶ Lady Stair's House
(The Writers' Museum)   44C2

Off Lawnmarket
Open: Mon–Sat 10–5, during Festival Sun 2–5.
Admission free
This building, bearing the date of 1622, was only later associated with the first Earl of Stair's widow, who died in 1759. The close on which it was built was at one time the main communication between the Old Town at the Lawnmarket and the New Town. The house was given to the city in 1907, and it is now a museum of Burns, Scott and Stevenson memorabilia.

▶ Lauriston Castle   44A2

Off Cramond Road South
Open: Apr–Oct, Sat–Thu 11–5; Nov–Mar, Sat–Sun 2–4.
Admission charge
A little away from the main tourist thoroughfares, Lauriston Castle makes a worthwhile excursion, perhaps combined with a quiet walk along the River Cramond. Built in 1593 on the site of a tower destroyed in 1544, the castle's original owner was John Napier (1550–1617). This Scottish mathematician was the inventor of logarithms. The castle was presented to the city in 1926 and its Edwardian interiors are carefully preserved.

Lauriston Castle near Cramond

57

JOHN KNOX
Born at Haddington (see page 115), John Knox (1513–72), architect of the Reformation in Scotland, became filled with Lutheran reforming zeal in 1544 and was called to the ministry in 1547. He led an adventurous life, including a spell as a French galley slave, following capture at St Andrew's Castle. He preached in England and on the Continent, as well as making his mark in Scotland, where his views were uncompromisingly antagonistic to those of Mary, Queen of Scots.

EDINBURGH'S OLDEST HOUSE
Moubrey House, next door to John Knox House, is probably even older than its more famous neighbour and can therefore claim the distinction of being Edinburgh's oldest dwelling, built by Andrew Moubrey c1472.

The National
Gallery of Scotland

▶▶▶ Museum of Childhood 45D2

High Street
Open: Mon–Sat 10–5, during Festival Sun 2–5.
Admission free

If you have never quite forgotten your last trainset or your doll's house, then the Museum of Childhood should awaken echoes of those lost days. There is a collection of older material such as Victorian dolls and German automata, but the eerie part is the objects half recognised from one's own childhood. There, behind glass, is that even larger set of Meccano to which you always aspired. If you have children, then you should consider visiting, though the younger members may be overcome by the massed ranks of historic teddies. Even without children, this museum should still be on the 'must visit' list.

▶▶ (Scottish) National Portrait Gallery 44C3

Queen Street
Open: Mon–Sat 10–5, Sun 2–5. Admission free

The Scottish National Portrait Gallery was built with much Caledonian zeal following the impetus given by the funding provided by John Ritchie Findlay, who owned *The Scotsman* newspaper. At its opening in 1889 it was stated that 'a gallery such as this is … the highest incentive to true patriotism we can possibly have'. Since then, the images of the famous Scots who stare down from the walls have become part of Scotland's fabric, reproduced both in scholarly books and on shortbread tins, so that the viewer coming upon Nasmyth's Robert Burns may find it quite familiar – a veritable icon of Scotland.

Take time, however, to look at the setting of these famous Scots. The architect Robert Rowand Anderson was an Edinburgh native but amid the orderly neo-classicism on the very edge of the first phase of the New Town, he created a Gothic palace, now one of Edinburgh's few - monuments to Gothic revivalism. Inside, the late Victorian fashion for mural painting found expression in a processional frieze of famous Scottish figures – a miniature portrait gallery in itself – with other wall-sized scenes from Scotland's story, set between the sandstone columns.

A MUSEUM FOR ADULTS?
The founder of the Museum of Childhood, Patrick Murray, an Edinburgh town councillor, insisted it was a museum portraying a specialised field of social history. A bachelor, he did not actually like children – or at least he pretended not to. He formerly displayed in the museum entrance hall a design for a memorial window to 'good' King Herod!

The Stuart monarchs are here, naturally, including the only portrait of Mary, Queen of Scots in the collection which was made in her lifetime – a small bronze bust of Mary, aged around 17 years. Flora Macdonald, who played her role in later Jacobite schemes, is also on view, as is King George IV entering Holyroodhouse in 1822. This visit of the monarch marked the rehabilitation of tartan, which is much in evidence in many other works.

Poets, painters, novelists, engineers, philosophers and famous fiddlers are all here – and not only from distant times. Though the heyday for the medium of portraiture has gone, there are many powerful pictures from nearer our own time, with figures such as Hugh MacDiarmid, Norman MacCaig and Muriel Spark among the subjects. Some of the more recent pictures in the collection are the result of the gallery acting upon the results of a survey amongst gallery users. They were asked which natives they would most like to see on the walls and Edinburgh-born Sean Connery has entered this hall of fame as a result.

A GREAT ARCHITECT
William Henry Playfair (1789–1857) not only designed the National Gallery (which was finally completed in the same year that he died), but is also associated with many other buildings in and around the New Town, which still lend distinction to the city's profile. These include Donaldson's Hospital, St Stephen's Church and, on Calton Hill, the National Monument, the New Observatory and the monument to Dugald Stewart.

59

Roman treasure in the Royal Museum of Scotland collections

The Museum of Childhood, a top attraction on the Royal Mile

▶▶▶ National Gallery of Scotland　　44B2
The Mound
Open: Mon–Sat 10–5, Sun 2–5. Admission free
William Playfair's National Gallery was completed in 1857 and rates among the top two or three classical designs in Edinburgh. Its sparingly ornamented length, honey-coloured in the thin Edinburgh sunlight, has a simple dignity entirely in keeping with its role as a repository for Scotland's finest art.

Inside, its human scale makes it easily accessible. There are no vast and intimidating halls, but controversy raged in the conservative Edinburgh art world when the present display was first opened in the late 1980s. Against a rich red background, many paintings are hung very high and close together. Visit it for some of the best Old Masters in the United Kingdom outside London, for its Impressionists and, naturally, for its Scottish paintings. There are also important collections of prints, drawings and watercolours.

Looking over Hillend Ski Centre towards Edinburgh

Walk

From Swanston to Colinton Dell

A rural walk south of Edinburgh in the footsteps of Robert Louis Stevenson, with spectacular views back towards the city. Allow about 3 hours for the walk (one way).

Take a bus or car to the southern edge of the city. Bus travellers can alight at the Hillend Ski Centre on the

A703 and cross Lothianburn Golf Course by a path to reach the attractive little hamlet of Swanston to the west. Those with a car can take it all the way to the hamlet, where there is a car park.

Swanston is associated with Robert Louis Stevenson – his family had a summer cottage there – and is part of the setting for his unfinished novel *St Ives*. The former Stevenson family home (private) is still there as described in the work: 'It had something of the air of a rambling

The Hermitage of Braid, on the way from Edinburgh to Swanston

infinitesimal cathedral ... grotesquely decorated with crockets and gargoyles, ravished from some medieval church.' (In real life, these were salvaged from the restoration of St Giles.)

For a longer expedition (than just to Swanston itself) which needs good footwear and the best part of a morning or afternoon, follow the track into the Pentland Hills south of Swanston. The objective is the broad ridge, seen to the south, of Caerketton and Allermuir Hills, two of the Pentland 'tops'. Alternatively, Caerketton (the one with screes) can be reached by missing Swanston entirely and going up towards the ski centre at Hillend, striking upwards on a path to the left of it. Either way, you join a skyline path westward along the heathery hilltops, enjoying superb city views. Take in Capelaw Hill before descending an easy path and track to Bonaly Country Park. (There is a car park for those making a separate excursion.) Follow Bonaly Road down into the suburb of Colinton to reach Spylaw Park. Turning right (towards town) soon brings the walker to Colinton Parish Church above a bend in the Water of Leith, another place which Stevenson knew well; his maternal grandfather, the Reverend Dr Lewis Balfour, was minister here. It is childhood memories of this leafy dell with its mossy banks and river that Stevenson recalls in his lines: 'Here is the mill with the humming of thunder./Here is the weir with the wonder of foam.' Buses run from Colinton back into the city centre.

▶ Palace of Holyroodhouse   45E2

Open: Apr–Oct, daily 9.30–5.15; Nov–Mar, daily 9.30–3.45.
Admission charge

As late as the 1890s, Robert Louis Stevenson in his
Picturesque Notes on Edinburgh observed that 'The Palace
of Holyroodhouse has been left aside in the growth of
Edinburgh, and stands grey and silent in a workman's
quarter among breweries and gasworks'. This was the
low point in the story of what is still the official residence
of the royal family in Scotland. The palace evolved from
the guest house of the adjacent Holyrood Abbey, now a
ruin.

The first palace, started by King James IV, was damaged
during the English raids of 1544, part of the 'rough
wooing' (see page 30), though the north-west tower (or
the King James V Tower – the left-hand tower on the
frontage) survived the flames to be rebuilt. It contains the
rooms associated with Mary, Queen of Scots.

Holyrood was ablaze again in 1650, the same year as
Cromwell and his troops stayed there while occupying
the north. He ordered some repairs but in the main the
work seen today is the result of a major remodelling in
1671–80, during the reign of King Charles II. His brother,
King James VII (James II of England), was sometimes in
residence there.

However, it is most strongly associated with Mary,
Queen of Scots (see page 30) though the site of the murder
of Riccio is no longer marked with red paint but instead
by a discreet plaque. After such highlights as grand levees
held by the transient Bonnie Prince Charlie and later by
King George IV in his 1822 visit, it fell into decline, though
Victoria and Albert used it in 1850. Much restoration
work this century has restored its dignity. As well as portraits of monarchs (some of them mythical) there are
tapestries and fine furniture from the royal collections. It
closes to visitors and transforms itself from a tourist centre to a high-security establishment whenever a member
of the royal family comes to visit.

Palace of Holyroodhouse
– detail of entrance gates

61

THE LAW COURTS
Behind St Giles,
Parliament House, the
seat of Scottish govern-
ment until 1707, now
houses the Supreme Law
Courts of Scotland. There
are portraits by Raeburn
among other artists, as
well as a hammerbeam
roof to admire.

ROYAL PORTRAITS
Jacob de Witt, a
Dutchman living in
Edinburgh, signed a con-
tract with His Majesty's
Cash Keeper in 1684 to
deliver 110 portraits of
Scottish kings within two
years at £120 per year.
These ran from the possi-
bly mythical King Fergus I
to the then contemporary
King Charles II – so at
least in one case de Witt
had a likeness from which
to work. The painter ful-
filled his contract at more
than one a week and at
least 80 of the portraits
can be seen today.

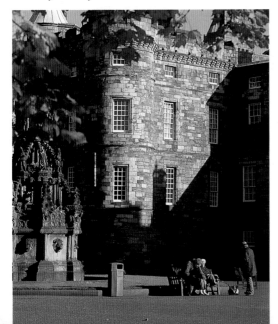

Palace of Holyroodhouse,
officially the Scottish
residence of the royal
family

Edinburgh

THE OLD PHYSIC GARDEN

Few of the passengers arriving at Waverley Station notice the plaque which records the site of the first public botanic garden in Edinburgh. The Old Physic Garden was in the hollow now occupied by the station and adjacent post office. The area saw many changes, not the least of which was the draining of the Nor' Loch which once provided Edinburgh Castle's defences to the north (in part of today's Princes Street Gardens). The partial draining of the ancient loch flooded the Old Physic Garden in 1689 and many of its precious plants were lost.

Royal Botanic Garden – an all-weather, all-year attraction

A PRESBYTERIAN PROTEST

A humble cabbage-stall owner called Jenny Geddes earned her place in history on 23 July 1637. King Charles I had declared St Giles a cathedral and had ordered the use of the Anglican service-book. No sooner had the Dean of Edinburgh started this unfamiliar service to the staunchly Presbyterian congregation than Jenny Geddes threw her prayer stool at him, screaming 'Daur ye say mass in my lug! (Dare you say Mass in my ear?)'. More missiles followed and a full-scale riot ensued. Her great gesture over, Jenny quietly returned to cabbage selling.

▶▶ The People's Story   45D2

Canongate
Open: Mon–Sat 10–5, during Festival Sun 2–5. Admission free

The People's Story is just that – a museum recording the experiences of the ordinary folk of Edinburgh from the 18th century to the present day. As such it does not portray a sanitised view of a city in which bad housing and poor working conditions co-existed with a genteel preoccupation with middle-class respectability. It is overtly political in its cameos of the local trades and the workers who put in long hours for small rewards. The overwhelming impression is of generations of drudgery for all kinds of people, from skilled craftsmen making barrels for the local brewing industry down to humble domestics whose first job was to polish the steel in the grate until it shone, then light the mistress's fire to blacken it again. It certainly puts today's Royal Mile in a new light.

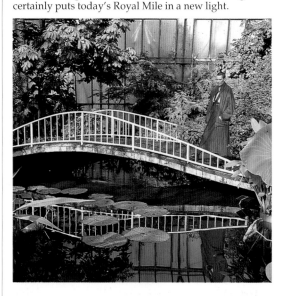

▶▶▶ Royal Botanic Garden   44B3

Inverleith Row
Open: Apr–Aug, daily 9.30–7; Mar, Sep 9.30–6; Feb, Oct 9.30–5; Nov–Jan 9.30–4. Admission free

One of Edinburgh's most precious recreational assets, the garden is 'strollable' from Princes Street via Stockbridge, though you may wish to take the bus back up the hill. It is especially suitable for children as it is dog free – though the squirrels can be a bit persistent. As well as its large rhododendron collection and a magnificent rock garden (best in May), there are substantial areas under glass. The highest point of the garden has a fine view of the city.

▶▶ Royal Museum of Scotland and Museum of Scotland   44C1

Chambers Street
Open: Mon, Wed–Sat 10–5, Tue 10–8, Sun 12–5. Admission charge

This lofty Victorian building, with its soaring columns

and galleries houses the national collection of scientific, natural, historical, geological, archaeological and other objects.

The adjacent new Museum of Scotland building, which was opened in late 1998, houses a collection of artefacts that relate specifically to Scotland. Check out the programme of special talks and lectures that the museum organises.

John Knox in St Giles

63

THE OLD TOLBOOTH
It was formerly considered good luck to spit on the heart shape which marks the Old Tolbooth site beside St Giles. This was perhaps a contemptuous gesture towards the town authorities who used the Tolbooth as a prison.

JOHN KNOX
John Knox's statue can be seen inside St Giles, but the fiery reformer's grave is no longer marked. He was buried in the old St Giles churchyard, which is now covered by flagstones.

ST GILES
St Giles, the kirk, was probably founded by Benedictine followers of Giles, the saint, who brought the name from the south of France. In 1466, the Preston Aisle of the kirk was completed, in memory of William Preston who had acquired the armbone of the saint in France. This relic disappeared about 1577, but St Giles' other armbone is still in St Giles Church, Bruges.

The story of Scottish whisky is told on the Royal Mile

▶ St Giles: the High Kirk of Edinburgh   44C1
High Street
Open: Mon–Sat 9–5, Sun 1–5; and for services.
Admission free

Often called St Giles' Cathedral, though purists argue it only achieved this status briefly, St Giles was at one time the only kirk within the walls of old Edinburgh. The tower of St Giles, whose crown was completed in 1500, is one of the few remaining examples of 15th-century work to be seen in the High Street today. Much of the kirk has been altered and reworked over the centuries. Today's dull cladding is the result of 19th-century 'restoration'. Only the tower and crown escaped this grey stone.

Once the venerable church even had a long arcade of booths, the 'krames', leaning against the north side. These were removed in 1817 along with the 'luckenbooths', other small shops which contributed to the crowded narrowness of this part of the High Street. Just to the west of the kirk is the site of the Old Tolbooth, also removed in 1817. Now causeway stones mark the spot in the shape of a heart.

▶ Scotch Whisky Heritage Centre   44C1
354 Castlehill
Open: daily 10–5.30, last tour 5; extended hours in summer.
Admission charge

The problem with whisky-making is that it is not in itself a visually dramatic process, much of it consisting of waiting around until the enzymes do their job. The Scotch Whisky Heritage Centre injects a measure of fun into the subject by taking the hi-tech approach, with talking tableaux and commentary all viewed while riding along very slowly on a hollowed-out whisky barrel. Whisky's story is told from its ancient origins via tales of smuggling and prohibition to modern marketing methods.

The Scottish patriot Fletcher of Saltoun wrote in 1698: 'As the happy situation of London has been the principal cause of the glory and riches of England; so the bad situation of Edinburgh has been one great occasion of the poverty and uncleanliness in which the greater part of the people of Scotland live.'

Top: an ornate ceiling inside the head office of the Royal Bank of Scotland at 36 St Andrew Square

64

THE MOUND
In the great building spree that went on in 18th-century Edinburgh, somewhere had to be found for the material dug out for foundations. In the case of the Royal Exchange (today's City Chambers) the rubble became the Castle Esplanade. Meanwhile, Geordie Boyd, a local tailor, started dumping earth into the quagmire of the old Nor Loch. So did everyone else, and 'Geordie Boyd's mud brig' grew and grew. Two million cartloads later, in 1830, it became The Mound, the elegant roadway linking the Old and New Towns.

An 18th-century vision Many stories of the squalor of the Old Town of Edinburgh are documented. As the more peaceful 18th century began in Scotland, improvements began within the Old Town itself. But the long-term solution was for the city's inhabitants to escape entirely from the rocky ramp running down from the castle.

George Drummond, Lord Provost of Edinburgh, had a clear vision of a new Edinburgh rising on what was then only a low ridge between the castle and the sea. A competition to design a new town was organised, which was won by a young and unknown architect, James Craig. His 1767 design shows a simple grid of streets balanced by a square at either end. This is the Princes Street to Queen Street area, with Charlotte Square and St Andrew Square at either end.

Princes Street If you stroll along Queen Street today, you can see how it echoes Princes Street: it is built up on one side only and has gardens (still private) opposite. Down amid the hubbub and 'High Street' shopfronts on Princes Street, it is hard to believe that in Craig's original scheme the area was meant to be entirely residential. He designated today's Thistle and Rose streets, lesser byways between the grand thoroughfares, as the abode and business place of tradesmen and shopkeepers. The use of the lanes behind Thistle and Rose streets to service the back doors of the wealthier residents was a clever element in his deceptively simple scheme.

Princes Street did not remain residential for long. The main tide of commercial developments began to flow from east to west by the mid-19th century. Before that, the residents, whose grand drawing-rooms looked out to the castle over the trees in the gardens, had fought another battle. A speculator wanted to build along the south side of Princes Street and the indignant citizens,

Period atmosphere in elegant Charlotte Square

determined to preserve their views, had to take their case to the House of Lords before the project was stopped. (The city fathers of the day were quite happy to allow the speculator to build.) Today's low-profiled Waverley Market is a reminder of those far-off legal battles.

String-pulling Stand on what used to be the bare ridge, and is now George Street, about halfway along, and look up and down the street. In Craig's plan the two squares, Charlotte and St Andrew, at either end of the view, also had churches. While the green copper dome of the former St George's (now West Register House) is plain on the western skyline, to the east in St Andrew Square there is a fine town house instead of a church.

A place of worship was never built there because of civic string-pulling by Sir Laurence Dundas. Rich, powerful and

PRINCES STREET
Princes Street was to be called St Giles Street, but King George III objected as it reminded him of the St Giles district of London, which was notorious for its lowlife at the time. So the most famous street in Scotland became Prince's Street after the Prince Regent, before assuming its plural form in 1848.

65

one-time Commissary General of the army in Flanders, Dundas acquired the site and altered the plan to suit himself. He employed Sir William Chambers to design the magnificent façade which is seen today, and this fine town house is now the headquarters of the Royal Bank of Scotland. It has ornate ceilings in its main hall, well worth looking at even if you do not have an account there. The city fathers got their kirk eventually, built on a less satisfactory site, round the corner in George Street. This is St Andrew's, still in use today and open to visitors.

By the end of the 19th century, the first New Town was complete, paving the way for further phases to the north, east and west, and creating Edinburgh's unique neo-classical ambience.

The grand façades of Edinburgh's New Town

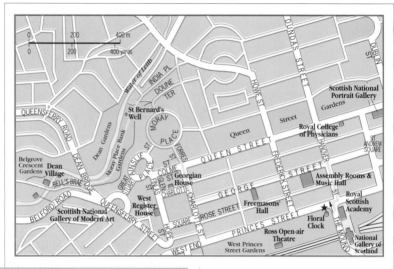

Walk

The New Town

Discover the surprisingly intact second phase of the New Town in the streets that lie north of Charlotte Square. Allow 3 hours.

Starting from the **Floral Clock** on Princes Street, opposite the Royal Scottish Academy, walk north to George Street, turning left at the **statue of King George IV**. Go past the **Assembly Rooms**, now a major Festival Fringe venue, where Sir Walter Scott publicly admitted to writing the Waverley Novels during a grand dinner in 1827.

Continue down George Street to **Charlotte Square** at the west end, which balances **St Andrew Square** at the east. The Robert Adam-designed north façade of Charlotte Square is impressively harmonious, while intrusive dormers and other additions detract from the other three sides.

Continue downhill to **Moray Place**, typical of the New Town with its private gardens, cobbled roads and grand façades. Leave by **Doune Terrace**. Cross the **Water of Leith** to shop in Stockbridge, otherwise turn

left along undistinguished India Place. Keep going to enter the wooded valley of the Water of Leith and go down steps by the bridge. **St Bernard's Well**, half-hidden in the greenery, is a former mineral spring in the shape of a Grecian temple with a statue of Hygeia, designed by Alexander Nasmyth in 1789.

The footpath continues to **Dean Village**. Overhead is Thomas Telford's road bridge, built in 1832. A 1643 Baxters (Bakers) 'coat-of-arms' survives on the abutment of the original bridge below. Climb back to the busy streets by cobbled Bell's Brae, the former main road.

St Bernard's Well

▶ **Scottish Agricultural Museum** *44A1*

Ingliston, 11km west of Edinburgh
Open: Apr–Sep, daily 10–5; Oct–Mar, Mon–Fri 10–5.
Admission free except during Royal Highland Show
This is Scotland's national farming museum,
adjacent to Scotland's premier agricultural show-
ground site. It covers all aspects of bygone rural life,
including trades associated with farming, and social
and home life in the countryside. There are good
displays of equipment and artefacts and evocative
photographs.

▶ **Scottish National Gallery**
   of Modern Art *44A6*

Belford Road
Open: Mon–Sat 10–5, Sun 2–5. Admission free
Housed in former school premises, an excursion here
could be made via a stretch of the Water of Leith footpath,
joining it perhaps at Dean Village. Scotland's own collection of moderns includes works by Derain, Matisse,
Picasso, Giacometti, Hockney and Hepworth among
many others. Scotland's own artists are not neglected,
with the Scottish colourists – Peploe, Cadell, Fergusson
and Hunter – well represented. The gallery also has a
popular café.

An adaptation of The Rev
Robert Walker Skating
by Raeburn – symbol of
Edinburgh art

67

▶ **(Edinburgh) Zoo** *44A1*

Corstorphine Road
Open: Apr–Sep, Mon–Sat 9–6, Sun 9.30–6; Mar and Oct,
Mon–Sat 9–5, Sun 9.30–5; Nov–Feb, Mon–Sat 9–4.30, Sun
9.30–4.30. Admission charge
The zoo once suffered all the problems of financing a
traditional, wide-ranging animal collection in a time
when other leisure attractions were siphoning off visitors.
Now its collection is smaller. The sad solitary elephant
has gone and, along with some new and spacious enclosures, there is a very substantial animal-themed gift shop
(a good money-earner for the zoo). A few of the fairly
primitive enclosures still remain – for the tigers and some
of the other big cats, for instance – but the penguins and
gorillas (awesome in close-up through the glass) look
happy enough. Young children will undoubtedly appre-
ciate it, though parents may get backache from lifting
them up to see. Also, pushing a buggy on the sloping
grounds is something of an endurance test. There is a
breeding programme for endangered species.

PENGUINS ON PARADE
Edinburgh Zoo's 'Penguin
Parade' is an old-
established institution.
The penguins are
shepherded out of their
modern, spacious enclo-
sure daily in the summer
months and trundle round
a grassy area nearby.
Formerly, they were
walked right out of the
zoo, but their appearance
on the pavements by
Corstorphine Road caused
traffic accidents as drivers
were distracted. Their per-
ambulations these days
are less extensive.

Edinburgh

RESERVING ACCOMMODATION

The Edinburgh and Scotland Information Centre (see page 272) helps visitors find accommodation, though the queues can be quite long. Try the advance central reservation service (tel: 0131 473 3855) but note that it cannot be used to book accommodation at Festival time.

Accommodation

Sit on the top deck of a bus coming in on the main road from Cameron Toll through the district of Newington and you can get some idea of the range of accommodation. The hotels and guest-houses are lined up as far as the eye can see – and that is just one street, though it changes its name as it heads towards The Bridges and central Edinburgh.

However, do not be misled into thinking that finding the right place to stay will be easy, since Edinburgh is a hugely popular destination. If you are visiting specifically to 'do' Edinburgh at Festival time, then book well ahead. Otherwise, late August and early September are best avoided altogether. Finding somewhere at a reasonable rate will be much easier outside that period, and easier still out of season (November to Easter). If you do find yourself in the city during the Festival and need somewhere to stay, it's worth persevering with the Edinburgh and Scotland Information Centre, 3 Princes Street (tel: 0131 557 1700), who will certainly assist. It would be misleading to suggest that accommodation is impossible, more that things are *very* busy.

HOTELS Many international chains are represented in Edinburgh, for example the Edinburgh Sheraton, with its views of the castle, or the Hilton, down in a dip by the Water of Leith. Then there are the city's former railway hotels: the grand-style Caledonian with its sumptuous Pompadour Restaurant and, dominating the skyline at the other end of Princes Street, the equally luxurious Balmoral. (This used to be called the North British, taking its name from the other pre-1923 railway company which ran services into Edinburgh.)

Also in the expensive bracket are the Howard Hotel in elegant Great King Street, the popular George on George Street, the Roxburghe in Charlotte Square, the Carlton Highland on North Bridge and the King James Thistle off Princes Street at the east end.

Quality can be enjoyed without paying the earth. Notable for its personal service

Echoes of the great railway age – the Caledonian Hotel

A Princes Street landmark – the clocktower of the Balmoral Hotel, formerly the North British, at Princes Street, east end

and country club atmosphere in the city is Channings on South Learmonth Gardens. The Malmaison, with a strong French influence, is in a quiet location close to the waterfront in Leith, yet only 10 minutes from the city centre.

GUEST-HOUSES There is a wide choice of guest-houses. Many can be found south of the city centre: try the Thrums Private Hotel in Minto Street, Newington, for example. As a general rule, the smaller establishments tend to be some distance from the city centre – though this should not be a problem as Edinburgh bus services are adequate. Remember if coming by car to enquire about parking at the establishment of your choice, since Edinburgh traffic wardens strike without mercy after 8am.

In all cases, rates during the off-season period between November and Easter are cheaper and there are often special break prices or other kinds of deals from the larger hotels.

HOSTELS There are two permanent Edinburgh youth hostels at: 7 Bruntsfield Crescent EH10 4EZ, tel: 0131 447 2994; 18 Eglinton Crescent EH12 5DD, tel: 0131 337 1120. These are supplemented in summer by additional hostel accommodation using university student residences. For advance bookings, contact the District Office, 161 Warrender Park Road EH9 1EQ, tel: 0131 229 8660. All are within easy reach of the main visitor attractions.

OUT OF TOWN Another option is to choose accommodation outside the city. The Norton House Hotel and the Royal Scot are on the west side of the city within easy reach of Edinburgh Airport. South of the city, the Roslin Glen Hotel in the conservation village of Roslin is close to Rosslyn Chapel, with its magnificent medieval stonecarving.

PARKING
If you are bringing a car to Edinburgh, it is best to check exactly what the parking arrangements are, especially if you wish to lie in in the morning. Parking laws are rigorously applied after 8am.

HISTORIC FEATURES
You might notice the extra-wide front doors in some of the city's New Town properties that are now hotels. Together with generous hallways between inner and outer doors, these were originally built to park sedan chairs when not in use! Similarly, the New Town's George Street was not built so broadly with central parking in mind but to let a coach-and-six do an easy U-turn!

Edinburgh

Food and drink

Edinburgh's colourful pub signs

Edinburgh sees itself as a cosmopolitan city so you will find cuisines from around the world on offer in its restaurants. However, many establishments come and go, and chefs move around, so it is always best to take up-to-the-minute local advice if you want a meal to remember.

RESTAURANTS In addition to a wide choice of independent restaurants, the main hotels all have good restaurants, with the Grill Rooms at the Balmoral and the Sheraton, and the Pompadour at the

70

IN THE HAGGIS SEASON...
Haggis may be Scotland's national dish, but it can be dull, or dry, or greasy or gritty – though it can also be spicy and delicious. If you want to try it, you will sometimes find it on Scottish-themed restaurant menus as a starter.

Caledonian being particularly notable. On the other hand, the area surrounding the university, especially around Nicolson Street, has a number of eating places offering particularly good value. Leith, Edinburgh's seaport, is the venue for a number of enterprising restaurant developments and should not be overlooked. This is a place to head for in the evening to eat, drink and to see and be seen in one of the trendy wine bars.

For consistent quality, Martins in Rose Street North Lane and The Vintner's Room down in Leith are examples of top-flight imaginative cuisine, but it is almost unfair to single them out as the city has so many good restaurants to choose from: Atrium, Jacksons, the Malmaison, Brasserie, L'Auberge, Duck's at Le Marché Noir, The Witchery by the Castle. For top quality at top prices, try Jeff Bland's cooking at No.1 The Restaurant (in the Balmoral Hotel). If you want quality on a budget, try The Kalpna in Nicolson Street, with

Bags of atmosphere at the Café Royal Oyster Bar

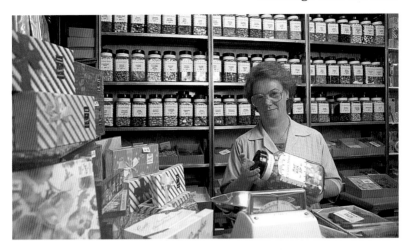

its reasonably priced, inspiring Gujarati vegetarian cooking; to join a cross-section of the natives enjoying an evening out, try the Waterfront Wine Bar in Leith.

The only thing which is really hard to track down in Edinburgh is an easily identifiable local cuisine, though the East Lothian countryside is market-garden country, supplying plenty of local produce. The other name for Edinburgh's eastern hinterland is 'Scotland's Granary', which has in turn helped to develop a tradition of fine baking, though probably no more so here than in other parts of Scotland. Local food-lovers are more likely to whisper reverently about the near-legendary Valvolla and Crolla delicatessen in Haddington Place, with its authentic Italian ambience.

WHOLEFOODS Edinburgh's fairly enlightened attitude (for Scotland) to food can be deduced from the success of Henderson's in Hanover Street. This vegetarian wholefood self-service restaurant is not a new place capitalising on the current trend for healthy eating. Instead it has survived and prospered on the same site for decades – since long before the notion of healthy food reached the rest of high-cholesterol Scotland.

The heavyweight traditional Scottish breakfast is still available in most guest-houses and 'B & B's, but you can skip it and linger instead over a croissant and coffee in one of the city's numerous café bars. Home-baked cakes for afternoon tea are easily found – try Clarinda's in the Canongate – and the Sheraton offers delicious traditional Scottish shortbread, though you need not go so far upmarket.

EDINBURGH ROCK The quintessential Edinburgh souvenir is sold at any number of tourist shops, and could be just the gift for someone with a (very) sweet tooth. If you prefer a different kind of food souvenir, look for authentic Scottish cheese in a delicatessen.

Scotland's sweet tooth – Casey's sweet shop

ROLL PLAY

An Edinburgh baker's is a good place to note the regional differences in the names for various bread goods and fancies. Muffins describe at least two types of bun. Pancakes are even more of a problem. Are they the same as crumpets, or even pikelets? Aberdeen rolls in most Edinburgh bakers are butteries, sometimes rowies. And what exactly are Jap cakes and German biscuits? If you think this is complicated, try ordering a pound of potted hough from the butcher next door.

Tartan brollies – practical souvenirs of Edinburgh

OPEN FOR BUSINESS
Especially in the height of the season, many shops catering for visitors are open every day. Off-peak, the city has late night opening on Thursdays (7.30–8pm), and super-stores stay open late right through the week, all year round.

The elegant interior of Jenners

Shopping

MAIN SHOPPING AREAS Do not make the mistake of assuming that Edinburgh's shopping ends with Princes Street. Far from it. With the exception of Jenners, which is the city's last independently owned major store, and a very few other places, Princes Street has little more to offer than can be found on a dozen other British high streets. This is not to say that the shops are necessarily bad – just that there is not a huge choice of unique or characterful Scottish wares along its length.

Within a few moments' walk of Princes Street are two covered malls. The St James Centre was built on the site of part of the New Town and is no better or worse than other modern malls elsewhere in Britain. The Waverley Market beside the Scott Monument is much more interesting.

SCOTTISH GOODS Shopping in Edinburgh is worthwhile, but the best shops are not all in one place. The city offers a good range of Scottish products. Stores selling imported souvenirs abound along the Royal Mile, but there are several high-quality outlets as well. The Edinburgh Old Town Weaving Co, at 555 Castlehill, offers a good cross-section of Scottish wares made on the premises, including bagpipes and kilts. Scottish Gems, at 24 High Street, has a fine selection of silver and gold jewellery. Judith Glue, just below St Giles, has an excellent range of Orkney knitwear and Scottish gifts.

SPECIALIST SHOPS Small individual businesses still survive in Victoria Street, along with Byzantium, an interesting antiques and crafts market. A little further on in the Grassmarket, among the odd mixture of down-and-outs and exclusive designer shops, is Mr Wood's Fossils, which sells all kinds of fossils. Also within easy reach of Princes

Street is the William Street/Stafford Street area, where there are a number of smaller specialist fashion and gift shops, of which Studio One in Stafford Street is a long-established example.

SHOPPING OUT OF THE CENTRE Further afield, the districts of Bruntsfield and Morningside are worth a stroll along the main streets, down the high canyons of the Edinburgh tenement blocks. Stockbridge, towards the Water of Leith, is also worth a look, and only minutes from

A Royal Mile souvenir shop – tartan all the way

73

the city centre. Edinburgh Crystal at Penicuik, about half an hour from the city centre by car, runs factory tours showing the glass-blowing process and has hand-cut products. (You can also buy this range in the city.)

BOOKSHOPS Edinburgh's literary leanings are confirmed by the large number of bookshops scattered around, many of which are second-hand stores. Among new book retailers are James Thin, The Edinburgh Bookshop and Waterstones. These, and many more, some with late opening hours, make the city a browser's paradise.

ART AND ANTIQUES Antiques shops seem to come and go, but try Bruntsfield Place or Causewayside where they gather in clusters. It is best to ask around for up-to-the-minute information. Some antique shops have a good selection of Scottish paintings, but Edinburgh is exceptionally well-endowed with specialised galleries, with excellent selections of both contemporary and antique material.

The Firth Gallery in William Street specialises in living Scottish artists, the Dundas Street Gallery in Dundas Street tends towards contemporary figurative and landscape work, while Stills on Cockburn Street exhibits work by both Scottish and international photographers. For those who hunt around, bargains and high-quality work can be found in the city. If tracking them down takes you off Princes Street then that is all the better – the real Edinburgh can be found en route.

JENNERS
The last independent store on Princes Street, Jenners has been an Edinburgh institution since 1838. It offers a good range of wares, from Edinburgh Crystal to exclusive fashions and a large toy department. This traditional department store is housed in a handsome building of 1895, with lots of baroque detail outside and a mock Jacobean galleried interior.

Nightlife

It may not be Paris or Las Vegas, but Edinburgh belies its sober and respectable image with a vibrant nightlife.

The annual rash of Fringe posters

THEATRE AND CONCERT HALLS The Traverse Theatre on Cambridge Street (tel: 0131 228 1404) puts on the most stimulatingly experimental material, while the Royal Lyceum Theatre on Grindley Street (tel: 0131 229 9697) stages more 'middle-of-the-road' plays. The Kings Theatre on Leven Street (tel: 0131 229 1201) has a varied lightweight programme including variety and pantomime. The Usher Hall on Lothian Road (tel: 0131 228 1155) is the city's old-established concert venue, now sharing the prestige with the Festival Theatre on Nicolson Street (tel: 0131 529 6000). The Queen's Hall on Clerk Street (tel: 0131 668 2019) is a more intimate concert setting, while The Playhouse, Greenside Place (tel: 0131 557 2692) sees a lot of big showbiz names.

FILM The independent Dominion on Newbattle Terrace in Morningside (tel: 0131 447 2660) is particularly good, while the Filmhouse on Lothian Road (tel: 0131 228 2688) is the place to see off-beat, less commercial or foreign-language films.

OTHER KINDS OF NIGHTLIFE The city's casinos include the Stanley Berkeley in Rutland Place (tel: 0131 228 4446) and Stanley Martell on Newington Road (tel: 0131 667 7763). Both offer free membership with 24 hours' notice.

Alternatively treat yourself to a Scottish evening, with lots of songs and dancing. Several of the downtown hotels hold these on a regular basis. Try the Carlton Highland Hotel on North Bridge (tel: 0131 556 7277) or the King James Hotel, Leith Street (tel: 0131 556 0111).

There are at least half a dozen club venues offering something for fans of Techno, rave, chart sound, mainstream and/or the gay scene. Try Café Graffiti, in the former Mansfield Place Church (tel: 0131 557 8003), and Club Mercado in Market Street (tel: 0131 226 4224).

74

FESTIVAL NIGHTS
Remember that Edinburgh's nightlife, like the city itself, moves up a gear during the Festival. Everywhere is crowded and full of visitors. This is the season when Edinburgh appears truly cosmopolitan.

LISTINGS
For up-to-the-minute events information in Edinburgh, try *The List* available from all city-centre newsagents, or *The Scotsman* on Saturdays, whose weekend section is very strong on entertainment events throughout Scotland, but emphasising Edinburgh. The latter is a useful place to find information on folk music in the capital.

Fringe actors – an encounter at every street corner

Practicalities

AIRPORT TRANSFERS Edinburgh Airport, Edinburgh EH12 9DN (tel: 0131 333 1000) is 11km from the city centre. Airport buses run at peak times every 15 minutes (every hour off-peak) between the terminal building and Waverley Bridge. They take 30 minutes (45 minutes in the rush hour) and cost roughly a quarter of the taxi fare.

ARRIVING BY TRAIN OR BUS Waverley Station could hardly be closer to the city centre and there is a taxi rank right within the station. The main bus station is at St Andrew Square, moments away from Princes Street along which run the principal city bus services (see below).

TOURIST INFORMATION For the main Edinburgh Tourist Information Centre see page 272. For information about Edinburgh at the airport, check with the Tourist Information Desk (tel: 0131 333 2167).

GETTING AROUND BY BUS Edinburgh has an extensive bus network, with two main bus companies covering most of the routes. On Lothian Region Transport (LRT) maroon and white buses, you pay the driver on entry with the exact fare. LRT offers a variety of unlimited travel tickets to visitors. Further information from the LRT information office at 27 Hanover Street (tel: 0131 555 6363).

On SMT Eastern Scottish green and cream buses, you pay the driver on entry, and change is given. Some of these services are small coaches known as Citysprinters. Further information from The Bus Shop, St Andrew Square Bus Station (tel: 0131 663 9233).

TAXIS Black taxis are widely available within the city. There are a number of taxi ranks, and taxis showing an illuminated 'For Hire' sign can be hailed in the street. Black taxis cannot be picked up at Edinburgh Airport, but a fleet of other licensed cabs (usually saloon car types) is available there.

TRAVEL TO THE AIRPORT 75
Both main rail lines converging on Edinburgh, from Glasgow and from the north, pass the airport practically adjacent to its perimeter. So far, nobody has thought to build a station. Airport to city-centre connections are by road, through the suburb of Corstorphine, which can get very busy at peak times, to Princes Street. Allow a good hour before check-in time if you are catching a plane.

If time is short – take a bus tour

Glasgow

CHANGING IMAGE Not so long ago, the idea of down-to-earth Glasgow becoming a serious challenger to Edinburgh's supremacy in the cultural and entertainment stakes would have been dismissed as impossible (especially by the complacent capital). But throughout the 1980s Glasgow ran a broadly based campaign to change its image. The native Glaswegians' friendliness, adaptability and innate loyalty to their native city was harnessed to turn Glasgow into one of the most exciting places in Britain. Today, a thousand cameos of downtown Glasgow with its fine civic buildings rival the grand panorama of Edinburgh. The buoyant enthusiasm of the folk of the west make Edinburgh's stand-offishness seem

Glasgow

Look up for the best details on Glasgow's buildings

78

all the more absurd. Glasgow's choice of cultural, entertainment, eating and shopping attractions matches anything the capital can offer, except perhaps at Edinburgh Festival time. In short, Glasgow has arrived.

The story of the city is essentially one of trade, though long ago it was a religious centre of some importance. St Kentigern, or Mungo (c518–603), is said to have built its first church on the site of the present cathedral, thereby founding the settlement which later became a royal burgh, though not until 1611. This status gave certain trading rights, though the prosperity of the city's traders and burgesses grew slowly at first, their activities hindered by the shallow silty river. Only after the Reformation, which ended Glasgow's role as a religious seat, did commerce really get under way. By 1688, the first pier had been built on the Broomielaw, on the riverside.

After the Union of 1707, the pace accelerated as it became easier to trade with the English colonies in America. Set on the western seaboard, Glasgow was well placed for this trade, and it soon began to rival Bristol in importance. In came rum, cotton and tobacco; out went manufactured goods such as hats, shoes and linen. One group of merchants in particular, came to rival the aristocracy because of their wealth and power: Glasgow's Tobacco Lords.

'WORKSHOP OF THE WESTERN WORLD' The Glasgow talent for adaptability and resourcefulness showed itself in the way that new markets were founded after the collapse of the tobacco trade after America became independent in 1775. Using the nearby resources of coal and ironstone, Glasgow was soon a city with a heavy

Typical Glasgow street scene. St George's Tron Church closes off the view west down George Street

manufacturing base in the throes of the Industrial Revolution. At its height it became the 'Second City of the British Empire' and was the 'Workshop of the Western World' throughout the 19th century. This confidence expressed itself in fine civic buildings, both in the Merchant City – that part of Glasgow lying west of the old High Street – and further west in the streets, which were built on a relentless grid, disregarding local topography. It is in this inner city that the finest architecture can be seen today.

However, the ores and the coal which formed the backbone of the heavy industry, in particular around Lanarkshire immediately to the south, gradually became worked out. Even by the early years of the 20th century, Glasgow was losing touch with the shifting patterns of the world economy. By mid-century, many of the shipyards were uncompetitive and its locomotive works were finding it difficult to compete for orders.

Glasgow today is a postindustrial city, now emerging from a phase of urban renewal, with something of the spirit of the enterprising Victorians playing a part in the city's rebirth. Indeed, Glasgow is the 1999 UK City of Architecture and Design.

The city still has some problem peripheral housing schemes (but then so indeed has Edinburgh). There are still holes in the Merchant City, a few sites with grand plans still unfulfilled. But anyone strolling through the fashionable Italian Centre (an 18th-century warehouse conversion) or the sophisticated Princes Square (everything that a modern shopping mall ought to be but more often than not isn't) can see that the new Glasgow has something rather special.

THE RIVER CLYDE
Mention the River Clyde to the locals and soon the phrase 'doon the watter' (down the water/river) will be heard. This refers to the now all-but-vanished summer holiday tradition of the toiling masses in the Clydeside conurbation who escaped from the shipyards, foundries, engineering works, mills and offices, on a trip by steamer down the Clyde to the playground of the lower estuary – to Rothesay, Dunoon, Helensburgh or any one of the other Clyde resorts (see Bute, page 231).

A CLEAN RIVER
Salmon returned to the River Clyde in 1983. Because of pollution, they had not been found there for the previous 120 years.

Medieval stained glass at the Burrell Collection; see page 81

Glasgow

AN EXPLODING MYTH
One enduring Glasgow myth is that the Kelvingrove Art Gallery and Museum was built back to front, and that the architect committed suicide by jumping from the tower. It isn't and he didn't!

▶▶ Art Gallery and Museum   76A4
Kelvingrove Park
Open: Mon–Sat 10–5, Sun 11–5. Admission free
This arresting turn-of-the-century-building in red sandstone sits in Kelvingrove Park. Often known as the Kelvingrove Art Gallery, it houses one of Britain's finest civic art collections. Within, individual galleries or wings lead off from its high, cold and echoing central hall. French paintings of the Barbizon, Impressionist and Post-Impressionist periods are here in plenty as well as the Old Masters, with 17th-century Dutch work particularly prominent. 'Home-grown' work is likewise strong, with The Glasgow Boys, a late 19th-century artistic flowering, represented by Hornel, Henry, Guthrie, Walton and others. Also featured are works by the Scottish colourists – Peploe, Cadell, Hunter and Fergusson.

The museum is strong on European arms and armour, with good displays of silver, pottery, glass, porcelain, and archaeological and ethnographic materials. The Natural History section has an important taxidermy department.

▶ Botanic Gardens   76A4
Great Western Road
Open: daily 7–dusk. Admission free
The original botanic collection was in a physic garden of the university, which moved to its present site on Great Western Road in 1842. The centrepiece of the garden today is the magnificent Kibble Palace of 1863, a sort of glass 'big top' originally built for a well-to-do Glasgow merchant called John Kibble at his Clyde coast home. He decided to give it to the city, provided he could use it for 20 years, and it was reassembled in the garden in 1871. It has been a warm and ferny refuge ever since, its bleached statues reflected in the ponds of colourful waterlilies. Exterior features include a herb garden, a sequential border and an arboretum. Specialities are a renowned orchid collection, and the national collection of begonias.

80

The 18th-century elegance of Pollok House, in whose grounds the Burrell Collection now stands

▶▶▶ Burrell Collection 76A1

Pollok Country Park, 7km southwest of Glasgow
Open: Mon, Wed–Sat 10–5, Sun 11–5. Admission free

Sir William Burrell was a wealthy Glasgow shipowner with a wide-ranging taste for *objets d'art*. This magpie started collecting as a boy and was still acquiring pieces at the time of his death in 1958, aged 96. Even by 1901, when the city staged the Glasgow International Exhibition, Burrell was the largest single lender for the displays, which included medieval tapestries, ivories, wood and alabaster sculpture, stained glass and bronzes, Roman glass, 16th- and 18th-century Dutch, German and Venetian table glass, plus silver, furniture, Persian rugs and many paintings including works by Manet, Whistler and Monticelli. He acquired his first Degas just a little later, an indication that his eclectic tastes were already fully formed when he still had more than half a century of collecting ahead of him. In 1944 he gave the whole collection of 8,000-odd items to the city, along with almost half a million pounds to build a suitable home for them. As one of the conditions attached was a rural and pollution-free setting, matters languished for some years but a site was found by 1967 and, after a competition and a 12-year building phase, the magnificent Burrell Collection opened in Glasgow's Pollok Park in 1983.

At the Art Gallery and Museum, Kelvingrove

▶▶▶ Gallery of Modern Art 77D2

Royal Exchange Square
Open: Mon, Wed–Sat 10–5, Sun 11–5. Admission free

The Gallery of Modern Art (opened 1996) started life as a tobacco baron's mansion in 1780, then became a bank, an exchange or meeting and entertainment place for businessmen, then a library.

The Gallery of Modern Art is one of Scotland's major contemporary art venues, on four floors, each identified by one of the elements: fire, earth, water or air, with appropriate signage. It displays Glasgow Museums' collection of art, craft and design from 1950 to the present. Artists who have become internationally known since the 1980s are emphasised, and the gallery actively acquired works from beyond Scotland, for example, Papua New Guinea and Ethiopia. The gallery runs a wide-ranging programme of temporary exhibitions and events and makes a substantial impact on the contemporary arts in Scotland.

BUYING WORKS OF ART
Sir William Burrell used 28 school exercise books between 1911 and 1957 to record the purchase of each item. He bought cautiously, and though he used trusted dealers in London and Paris, he often sought a second opinion and liked to haggle over prices. Though wealthy, he was up against the even greater wealth of a number of American art magnates such as John Paul Getty.

The Kibble Palace, Glasgow Botanic Gardens

POLLOK HOUSE
Pollok Park, the setting of the Burrell, comprised the former policies (grounds) of Pollok House, donated to the city in 1967. Five minutes from the Burrell Collection, Pollok House, built c1750 with later additions, now houses a further European painting collection as well as furniture, ceramics, glass and silver.

Glasgow

EARLY 18TH-CENTURY GLASGOW

The writer Daniel Defoe was most impressed by Glasgow and wrote in his *Tour Through the Whole Island of Great Britain*: 'It is a large, stately and well-built city, standing on a plain…and the five principal streets are the fairest for breadth, and the finest built that I have ever seen in one city together.' This was before rapid industrialisation brought its special problems of poor housing and degradation.

▶▶ Glasgow Cathedral   77E3

Cathedral Street
Open: Apr–Sep, Mon–Sat 9.30–6, Sun 2–6; Oct–Mar, Mon–Sat 9.30–4, Sun 2–4; also for services. Admission free

Now a little isolated from the main thrust and vigour of the modern city centre, Glasgow Cathedral is one of the most ancient and historic sites in the city. The short trip eastwards is well worth making and is an easy walk from the Merchant City. The site has been occupied since the early days of Christianity here and is associated with Glasgow's patron saint, St Kentigern or Mungo. He founded a church here, possibly in the early 7th century. The earliest identifiable work is 13th century.

There are five elements to the cathedral, which has an unusual shape: the nave, the choir, the upper and lower chapter houses, the lower church and the Blacader Aisle. The late-medieval roof, 32m above the nave, incorporates 14th-century timber. The choir and nave are separated by a 15th-century screen or pulpitum, a rare survivor from pre-Reformation times. The unique lower church, below

Glasgow Cathedral

the choir, was a 13th-century extension on the sloping site, and contains St Mungo's tomb. The Blacader Aisle, where spotlights pick out the fascinating ceiling bosses, is the 'youngest' part of the fabric, built by Archbishop Blacader (1483–1508). The Necropolis behind the cathedral is likewise worth a stroll.

▶ City Chambers   77D2

George Square
Open: Mon–Fri, tours at 10.30, 2.30. Admission free

The exterior of the City Chambers is exotic enough, with its turreted, colonnaded façade in Venetian style, topped by a tower and festooned with carving. Inside it verges on the outrageous, with a mosaic basilica of an entrance hall, marbled staircases and galleries, epitomising the 'over the top' exuberance of high Victoriana. The building was intended to restore confidence after the City of Glasgow Bank collapse, and was opened by Queen Victoria in 1888.

Glasgow's transformation from religious seat to commercial centre resulted in the original community expanding westwards from its High Street, cathedral, mercat cross and other trappings of a market town. It was this 'new town', at the heart of Glasgow today, which became the Merchant City.

The growth of trade Glasgow's expansion could only be funded by trade, but the shallow, silty nature of the river at first hindered the aspirations of the traders and burgesses. The first pier was built on the nearby Broomielaw by 1688 and over the years the river was deepened. Gradual commercial expansion meant that the rural grazings west of the High Street were required for commerce. Various manufacturing concerns, as well as vast warehouses and the grand mansions of the successful traders sprang up in successive waves. Expansion gathered pace in the 18th century as a planned development of gridded streets.

Glasgow became one of Europe's most important tobacco ports, with its nerve centre within the Merchant City. The ships which came in with the golden leaf from Virginia sailed again with cargoes ordered by the planters on the far side of the Atlantic. Thus the Merchant City prospered, even surviving the economic hiccup of the American colonies gaining independence.

Architectural style The city developed urban characteristics unique in Scotland. Most notable of these is the compact Glasgow square, usually enclosing a church: one example is at Nelson Mandela Place, west of Queen Street Station. Another feature is the deliberate placing of prominent buildings to close off vistas.

The Victorians, with their emphasis on civic pride, brought other styles to the Merchant City. However, decline set in during the 20th century, when the 18th-century warehousing became redundant, and the old tobacco exchanges outmoded. The area became a little run down until the design-led late 20th-century renaissance. Now the Merchant City is again the focus of innovation, though this time it is the small, specialist (and exclusive) retailers of fine clothes, furniture and other up-market supplies who have brought new life to this fascinating and historic area.

Top: chimney pots are numbered for each tenement flat

COTTON
After American Independence the business community of the Merchant City diversified by investing in cotton spinning. Glasgow became second in importance only to Manchester, England, in this industry.

The Duke of Wellington *by Marochetti*

83

Walk

Glasgow city centre

A walk that takes in the architectural riches, past glory and modern regeneration of the Merchant City area. Allow 2½ hours.

See map on pages 76–7.

Near Queen Street Station, admire the early French Gothic style of the **Glasgow Stock Exchange** (1875). Go down Queen Street, with its views across statue-spiked George Square, to the **Gallery of Modern Art** in the former Royal Exchange. Originally a mansion, it had a colonnaded classical façade stuck on later to enhance the view from Ingram Street.

Go through **Royal Exchange Square** (there is a good tearoom) for the shopping delights of pedestrians-only **Buchanan Street**. The modern charms of the discreet **Princes Square** development, airy yet compact, contrast with the **Argyll Arcade** beyond, built in 1827 as Scotland's first shopping

Glasgow offers the best shopping choice in Scotland

arcade. The arcade opens into Argyle Street. The shops move generally downmarket the further east you go, so, unless you intend a weekend visit to the flea market at the **Barras** further yet to the east (see panel, page 86), turn up Candleriggs to reach the heart of the old **Merchant City**. Some 18th-century warehouses survive. The Italianate style City Hall (1817) is still a concert hall, though only the façades of the markets remain. The Merchant City is still in the throes of regeneration: note the **Café Gandolfi** in Albion Street round the corner, an example of the new Merchant City enterprise.

Thread through Wilson Street, past more interesting new shops on **Ingram Square** and the massive, classical old **Sheriff Court**. Continue west to Virginia Street, named after the New World trade. **Virginia Court**, half-way along, has ancient cart ruts in its cobbles. Nearby is the former **Tobacco Exchange**, now bookshops and antique stalls. Then make your way through to **George Square**, with Robert Adam's **Trades House** (his only surviving work in Glasgow) in the near vicinity, and, to the north, **Hutchesons' Hall** on Ingram Street.

▶ Greenbank Garden 76A1

Flenders Road
Open: daily 9.30–sunset. House Apr–Oct, Sun 2–4. Admission charge

Greenbank is 10km south of town in fairly plush Clarkston. Set around a fine Georgian house, originally built for a Glasgow merchant, the five-hectare policies (grounds) include a big walled garden. Greenbank is run as a demonstration garden, with a variety of small-scale features. It is owned by the National Trust for Scotland.

▶▶ Hunterian Museum and Art Gallery 76A4

University Avenue and Hillhead Street
Open: Mon–Sat 9.30–5 (Mackintosh House closed 12.30–1.30). Admission free

William Hunter (1718–83) trained at Glasgow University and became a famous physician in London. He bequeathed substantial scientific collections to his parent university and the Hunterian opened in 1807 as Scotland's first public museum. The emphasis is now on geology, archaeology, coins and art. Exhibits include the fossil of the Bearsden shark (named after a suburb of Glasgow) as well as the city's own meteorite!

The Hunterian Art Gallery has existed as a separate (but practically adjacent) entity since 1980. It includes European works from Rembrandt to Reynolds as well as Scottish 19th- and 20th-century work. The Print Gallery exhibits works from the largest print collection in Scotland, from Dürer to Hockney. Also prominent is the American-born painter James McNeill Whistler, whose estate was gifted in 1935. Charles Rennie Mackintosh is well represented too. Furniture and fittings from the architect's home are displayed in the Mackintosh House – a reconstruction of the principal rooms of his own home.

▶ Hutchesons' Hall 77D2

158 Ingram Street
Open: Mon–Sat 10–5. Admission free

Hutchesons' Hall was built in 1802 to a design by David Hamilton, one of the city's most talented local architects. It has a National Trust for Scotland visitor centre and shop.

CHARLES RENNIE MACKINTOSH (1868–1928)
Mackintosh gutted the end-of-terrace house at 78 Southpark Avenue, Hillhead, Glasgow and refitted it in his own unique style. It came into the hands of the university in 1945 and was demolished in 1963. Prior to demolition a detailed survey was carried out and much was salvaged, ultimately to be lovingly rebuilt almost 20 years later in the Mackintosh section of the Hunterian Art Gallery.

85

Mackintosh's distinctive style in the Hunterian

St Mungo, who now has a museum named after him

BARRAS FLEA MARKET
At the weekend a visit to the People's Palace can be combined with a browse around the Barras, Glasgow's flea market. It lies within easy walking distance north of Glasgow Green.

86

GLASGOW GREEN
In the days when Glasgow was a hotbed of communism and the struggle for workers' power, Glasgow Green was used as the Clydeside orators speaking platform. The authorities retaliated in the 1930s by planting flower-beds in strategic positions to discourage crowds from gathering.

At the Museum of Transport

▶ **St Mungo Museum**   77E3
Cathedral Square
Open: Mon, Wed–Sat 10–5, Sun 11–5. Admission free
With picture windows that reveal the skyline of the soaring cathedral and the knobbly monuments of the Necropolis, this museum of religious life and art also takes a broad overview of human ways of dealing with big issues – life, death, the hereafter – and how they are treated across the world. Salvador Dali's *Christ of St John* of the Cross is here, just round the corner from a many-limbed Shiva as Nataraja, the Lord of the Dance. Dali's masterpiece is hung so high that it is best viewed from the gallery on the other side of the room. From Japanese shrines to Aboriginal paintings, the religious art and artefacts of all kinds of cultures are brought together here. A separate gallery shows material from human rites of passage – birth, marriage and so on – more anthropological, perhaps, than religious in the usual sense. Take time to read the comments boards, where visitors are asked to write a few notes on what they think of the museum experience. Quite a few note the close relationship between religion and conflict.

▶ **Museum of Education**   76B1
Scotland Street
Open: Mon–Wed 10–5, Sun 2–5. Admission free
Housed in a Mackintosh building of 1904, the former Scotland Street School now pays homage to education in Scotland and gives a sense of how it felt for pupils, right down to the squeak of pencils on slate. Inside are period classrooms from various eras, and changing exhibitions.

▶▶▶ **Museum of Transport**   76A4
Kelvin Hall, 1 Bunhouse Road
Open: Mon, Wed–Sat 10–5, Sun 11–5. Admission free
This spacious site round the back of the Kelvin Hall holds all kinds of historic transport exhibits. It is great fun, and not just for children, with huge steam locomotives, brooding and awesome, tramcars and buses, Hillman Imps (Scotland's fairly awful last home-produced motor car) and other gleaming vehicles from past eras. The fire engines and ship models are hugely popular and there is

also an evocative 1938 Glasgow street scene. The museum is just across the road from the Art Gallery and Museum at Kelvingrove with the Hunterian within easy reach.

▶▶▶ People's Palace   77E1

Glasgow Green
Open: Mon, Wed–Sat 10–5, Sun 11–5. Admission free

In the heart of the ancient park known as Glasgow Green the People's Palace, as the name implies, is for and about the 'ordinary people' of Glasgow. This late Victorian sandstone edifice has a museum at the front and a huge glass conservatory, known as the Winter Gardens, at the back. The latter is heated so that palms and other tender plants can flourish, and there is also a café, which makes it a popular place for idling and for posing for wedding and other photographs. To go from the clear light and bustle of the Winter Gardens through the swing-doors to the museum is an odd experience, a little like discovering someone's attic.

The story of the Tobacco Lords is told in the museum, together with those of the radical weavers, the temperance and Co-operative movements, and women's suffrage, alongside the ephemera of countless everyday lives, from tram tickets to ration books, as well as reconstructions of typical Glasgow working-class tenement accommodation.

Just down the road, off the Green, is the former **Templeton's Carpet Factory**, yet another of Glasgow's exuberant pieces of Victoriana, sometimes called the Doge's Palace. Multi-coloured brick and tile have been used to create an extraordinary Venetian-style façade (the building can only be viewed from the outside). Also on Glasgow Green, which, in spite of renewals, still has a faintly neglected air, is the Doulton Fountain, a 14m high terracotta creation, formerly an important exhibit at the 1888 International Exhibition at Kelvingrove.

A shop front from the Glasgow street in the excellent Museum of Transport, where it always remains 1938

Provand's Lordship, one of only two remaining medieval buildings in Glasgow

Charles Rennie Mackintosh, architect, designer, water-colourist and leading exponent of art nouveau in Scotland

▶ Provand's Lordship

77E3

High Street
Open: Mon, Wed–Sat 10–5, Sun 11–5. Admission free
Close to the cathedral is Glasgow's only other city-centre medieval building, Provand's Lordship. The word 'Provand' is the same as 'prebend', a clergyman who is paid from cathedral revenue and officiates there. The Provand or Prebend of Balornock once inhabited the house.

It was built in 1471 as a manse (minister's house) for the long-vanished hospital adjacent. With its characteristic steeply pitched roof with crow-stepped gables and armorial panels, it was, in its day, a suitably dignified residence for churchmen. Later in its long history it had less distinguished occupants. Glasgow's hangman occupied a one-storey lean-to cottage next door. Now a lone survivor, Provand's Lordship has become a city museum housing period furniture. The dark rooms, with their low doorframes, small windows and worn steps have a curious musty atmosphere about them (yes, the house is said to be haunted). As well as the interesting furniture, there are displays on the many changes of use the building has undergone in its 500-year history.

▶ Queen's Cross Church

76C4

Garscube Road
Open: Mon–Fri 10.30–5, Sun 2.30–5. Admission free
This is the only church designed by Charles Rennie Mackintosh. Built in 1897–9 it is now the headquarters of the Charles Rennie Mackintosh Society, with a small exhibition area, library and shop.

▶ (Glasgow) School of Art

76C3

Renfrew Street
Open: tours Mon–Fri 11, 2, Sat 10.30. Closed last 2 weeks in Jun. Admission charge
This is Mackintosh's masterpiece, a work of world stature, though crowded by later developments, and is still a breathtaking design. The School of Art is sometimes described as the first and finest architectural work of the modern European movement. Here all of the Mackintosh characteristics are seen to good effect: the sinuous swirls of the forms of nature, the bold and uncluttered lines, the detailing and supreme awareness of the effect of light and shadow.

▶▶ Springburn Museum

77E4

Atlas Square
Open: Mon–Fri 10.30–5, Sat 10–4.30. Admission free
Springburn was a hamlet with a few weavers and quarrymen on the north side of Glasgow until the railways came in 1842. Thirty years later it was the centre of a railway empire. Most of the 27,000 Springburn folk were at one time connected with the railway in some way. The workshops of the Caledonian and the North British Railways were here, as well as two more builders, one of them, Hyde Park, the largest in Europe. Their products were exported all over the globe. Now almost everything has gone, and the shriek of the steam dinosaurs has long been silenced. The Springburn Museum records a vanished way of life and the industrial heritage of the community.

▶▶ The Tenement House 76B4

145 Buccleuch Street
Open: Mar–Oct, daily 2–5, last admission 4.30
Admission charge

A young girl moved into the tenement building with her mother in 1911. They were pleased to have such well-appointed accommodation. The young girl was a certain Miss Toward. She never married and after her mother's death lived there alone until 1965. A relative who bought the flat realised that it was a 'time capsule' of Glasgow life, because Miss Toward had never thrown anything away and had never changed the layout of her home. Here, preserved in its entirety, was a slice of tenement life from the early years of the 20th-century.

The flat consists of a hall and four rooms: the bedroom (reserved usually for the lodger in Miss Toward's case); the parlour or best room, used for special occasions, for example when the kirk elder or a minister called; the bathroom – a sure sign that this was a very well-appointed tenement for its date (it was built in 1892); and the kitchen, complete with a large black cooking range with coal bunker.

Glasgow School of Art, a remarkable example of Mackintosh design

FOSSIL GROVE
Among Glasgow's many green spaces, Victoria Park is notable for its Fossil Grove. This is a roofed area in which excavations have exposed the fossilised stumps and roots of trees which grew here 330 million years ago.

THE COAL BUNKER
Miss Toward of the Tenement House had a kitchen coal bunker which held 540kg at a time and would have been typical of that era. Pity the poor coalmen on the Glasgow tenement stairs!

89

Accommodation

As befits Scotland's largest city and one where tourism is rapidly increasing, Glasgow has a very reasonable choice of accommodation at all price levels. An increasing number of quality hotels have opened up quite close to the city centre, mainly to serve the business and conference market, partly because of the Scottish Exhibition Centre down by the Clyde. Another trend has been the welcome arrival of a few smaller, intimate, town-house style establishments amid the city's Georgian terraces. Accommodation in the university halls of residence should not be overlooked at the budget end of the market. The city's Tourist Information Centre (see page 272 for its address) can also organise special short breaks in the city.

OUT OF TOWN It is easy to get into the countryside from Glasgow – Loch Lomond is only half an hour away – so it is also worth considering out of town accommodation if exploring the city. Organisations such as the Farm Holiday Bureau, National Agricultural Centre, Stoneleigh, Warwickshire, England CV8 2LZ, tel: 01203 696909, offer farmhouse accommodation in the silence of the moors and upland grazings of the Campsie Hills, for example, both of which are well within an hour's journey of the city centre.

Though Glasgow does not have quite the same accommodation bottlenecks as Edinburgh, it nevertheless gets quite busy. Don't forget that there are Tourist Information Centres which can find accommodation both in Paisley and also at Glasgow Airport, as well as the main city-centre office.

TOP HOTELS Starting at the top end, the Glasgow Hilton has all the style and high levels of service (and, of course, prices) you would expect from this international chain.

Glasgow accommodation caters well for all price brackets, from the budget to the luxurious, as here at the Devonshire Hotel

Many original features survive in the elegant Victorian townhouses of Devonshire Place, including stained glass at the Devonshire Hotel

91

(Driving there is tricky, though the tall building is visible enough. The hotel even goes to the length of providing a little map to help you find your way to the car park.)

The Moat House International, the Glasgow Marriott (right in the centre) and the Holiday Inn Garden Court (likewise in the thick of things) are all worth considering if you are looking for the no-nonsense professionalism of the larger establishment. The Kelvin Park Lorne is fairly moderately priced – ideal for the Art Gallery at Kelvingrove and large enough to have a good range of facilities, yet still small enough to be friendly. (The locals' 'genius for instant friendship' is most noticeable in the service industries – receptionists sometimes genuinely remember guests.)

The Devonshire Hotel at 5 Devonshire Gardens is a town house of deluxe standard just by Great Western Road. (Do not confuse this with One Devonshire Gardens, a couple of doors down, which is equally luxurious and slightly more expensive.)

Also at the top end and out of town is Cameron House Hotel and Country Club, on the banks of Loch Lomond, with a superb range of leisure facilities. Other possibilities, if you want a country base with easy access to the city centre, are the areas around Balloch (at the south end of Loch Lomond), Helensburgh (a Clyde resort) and Drymen, east of the loch.

HALLS OF RESIDENCE For travellers on a budget, there is a good selection of all kinds of bed and breakfasts and guest-houses available, as well as university halls of residence (see panel). Locations include Sauchiehall Street, ideal for the shops, Clyde Street, a good base for the Merchant City, and Cathedral Street, and all offer reasonable value for money. Glasgow also has a large youth hostel in a good location at 7/8 Park Terrace G3 6BY, tel: 0141 332 3004.

CAMPUS ACCOMMODATION
For details of Glasgow's on-campus accommodation – there are at least six halls of residence for Glasgow University alone – then contact Glasgow University's Conference and Vacation office at 81 Great George Street, Glasgow G12 8RR (tel: 0141 330 5385), or Strathclyde University Residence and Catering Services at 50 Richmond Street, Glasgow G1 1XP (tel: 0141 553 4148).

PACKAGE DEALS
Glasgow is now a popular destination for English-based coach firms and other operators who offer a complete package of travel and accommodation. For more details, contact the Greater Glasgow and Clyde Valley Tourist Board – address in Travel Facts, page 272 – and ask for the latest list of package holidays.

Food and drink

As in other cities, fashionable places to eat and drink in Glasgow come and go, as do chefs. You need to strike up a conversation with a local or follow the recommendations of local restaurant critics (see panel page 96) for up-to-date news. Glasgow has ambience in plenty when it comes to eating and drinking: it's all part of its downtown vibrancy and new-found confidence – it is probably the most exciting place to be in Scotland for an evening out. There is also a core of well-loved favourites which are easy to track down.

Glasgow specialises in the kind of place which offers competent cuisine along with bags of atmosphere, so that any minor shortcomings are easily forgiven. Another characteristic is the many pubs and restaurants which now occupy buildings originally designed for other commercial uses – you can catch yourself staring upwards from your glass of beer at the fine old woodwork of a former bank, or the decorated tiles of a Victorian insurance office. There are themed places as well, which are very popular with locals. Yet another category is the restaurant with a pub or café attached.

Scotland's patriot, William Wallace, has given his name to several pubs

ASK A CABBIE
One way of getting a really up-to-date tip on the best places to eat is to ask a taxi driver. Certainly, Glasgow is noted for its friendliness (though the same can be said about plenty of other places in Scotland). However, Glasgow's talkative cabbies definitely made an impression on the American Society of Travel Agents when it held its annual conference there in 1997. Their helpfulness was officially recognised by the Scottish Tourist Board, which awarded a commemorative plaque to the local taxi drivers' association in acknowledgement of their role as 'outstanding ambassadors of tourism!'

RECOMMENDED RESTAURANTS The well-loved Ubiquitous Chip off Byres Road offers a menu which is probably as near as one can get to a local cuisine, with a pronounced Scottish flavour. Much the same can be said about the Buttery in Argyle Street, with its Victorian décor. Another favourite with a loyal clientele is the long-established Rogano in Exchange Place, which first opened its art-deco doors in 1935. Seafood is a speciality here.

A Glasgow institution for Italian cuisine is La Parmigiana on Great Western Road, which has a loyal local following for its tuna with borlotti beans, *rabbit alla cacciatore* and other slightly out-of-the-ordinary dishes. Also hugely popular, especially with the business crowd, is Yes, on West Nile Street, where the purple and red decor provides a striking setting for an eclectic cuisine making strong use of Scottish ingredients: try the gateau of haggis, neeps and tatties! Stravaigin, on Gibson Street, looks world-wide for its inspiration; it has a refreshingly laid-back attitude, but the quality of its cooking, in the Hanoi duck soup, Chilean *curanto* or Mexican *estofado de lengua*, is top-notch. The café-bar restaurant Papingo on Bath Street is a good-value venue for modern Scottish cooking: roasted vegetables with honey, garlic and balsamic vinegar, or mussel, leek and crab soup, for example. If you want to splash out, try the restaurant at One Devonshire Gardens for painstakingly prepared modern cuisine.

PUBS Glasgow's pubs are very varied, but city-centre ones can be very spruce. Typical of this kind is the Drum and Monkey, formerly banking premises in St Vincent Street. It is popular with business people who have lunch in its small and intimate back room with its dark wooden pews, and has a more boisterous main hall. Not far off in West Regent Street, a similarly successful transformation can be seen at De Quinceys. At one time the Moorish tiles that brighten the walls of the premises looked down on the main business hall of another banking company; now they provide an impressively stylish background to a scene of cheerful drinking.

TEAROOMS Glasgow's tea-rooms have always been something of an institution. The Willow Tea Room is a surviving, though restored, typical Mackintosh design in Sauchiehall Street. These days, tea and coffee are also served throughout the day in any of a number of bistro-style establishments. The Victoria and Albert in Buchanan Street serves tea or coffee with home-made shortbread in the morning in its bar, and the Jenny Tearoom beside the Gallery of Modern Art in Exchange Square has a reputation with the serious tea drinker.

The Rogano, an old-established part of Glasgow's restaurant scene

93

A STREET NAME
Sauchiehall Street is really sauchie-haugh street: 'sauchies' are willows and a 'haugh' is a watery field. The willow reference is echoed in the Willow Tea Room on the street.

FOR SHOPPERS
Princes Square has a reasonable standard of refreshments. Try the October Café right on the top floor, with its notice-ably bright atmosphere – perhaps an effect of being so near to the glass roof.

Glasgow

94

ST ENOCH SQUARE
Built on the site of the old St Enoch Station, St Enoch Square is now a massive under-cover shopping mall, a touch better than most 1990s malls thanks to its interesting architecture, with exposed girders and pipes. However, it is not as upmarket and intimate as Princes Square.

Shopping

There are more shops in Glasgow than anywhere else in Scotland. All the usual High Street names can be found but, thanks partly to Merchant City enterprise, there is also a very good selection of smaller specialist outlets. Glasgow is style- and fashion-conscious, so clothes shops proliferate, though not all of them survive.

MAIN AREAS The main shopping streets are found from Argyle Street northwards as far as Sauchiehall Street, taking in streets on both sides of pleasingly pedestrianised Buchanan Street, northwest of which is a grid of streets well worth exploring. The Merchant City lies to the east of it and should be explored. There are further shopping possibilities around Byres Road to the west which should not be overlooked. Except for Byres Road, most of Glasgow's shops are in easy walking distance of Buchanan Street. The best of the new-style malls are likewise found around Buchanan Street: Princes Square and the Buchanan Galleries which open directly off it, and the St Enoch Centre just across Argyle Street and less upmarket, but worth exploring if only for its design.

OUTLETS FOR SCOTTISH GOODS If you are looking for high-quality Scottish wares, then Geoffrey (Tailor) Highland Crafts – quite far along Sauchiehall Street (but worth the walk) – is just the place for Scottish knitwear or tweed souvenirs, or for an entire Highland outfit. Hector Russell, Kiltmaker, in Renfield Street will also oblige in much the same market niche.

The Barras (or Barrowland) is an essential part of the Glasgow shopping experience – but don't make it the only one!

Old-established John Smith's, Glasgow's own bookshop, has a huge selection of material on Scotland and Glasgow. Postcards home could be written with something exclusive picked up at the Pen Shop in Princes Square, which is a useful shopping mall for gifts as well as fashions, including reasonably priced knitwear at a branch of the Jumpers chain.

DESIGNER SHOPS If you ask about designer shops in the Merchant City, locals may well point you towards Mademoiselle Anne in Stockwell Street, which has women's collections. Another Merchant City treat for (male) shoppers is Slater Menswear, famous throughout Scotland for its huge array of suits and casual clothing at discounted prices. For antiques the Virginia Galleries are well worth a browse. The galleries comprise a number of small antique businesses with surprisingly reasonable prices considering their location. The atmospheric Argyll Arcade (dating from 1827) offers a choice of 32 jewellers' shops. Catherine Shaw, in Gordon Street and the Argyll Arcade, has giftware in Charles Rennie Mackintosh's style.

Glasgow shopping

Jewellers in plenty in the Argyll Arcade

Typifying the new Glasgow style is the Italian Centre, just off Ingram Street, of which the city is inordinately proud, particularly because this gathering of shops includes labels seen nowhere else in the United Kingdom outside London.

FLEA MARKET If you tire of the chic shops of the Merchant City, then a trip to the Barras flea market will prove a refreshing antidote – though remember that the market is open at weekends only. The Barras is a reminder that Glasgow has not yet become too precious in its new image. The name may have been translated into 'Barrowland' in an attempt to prettify it, but it still remains a boisterous flea market in a hotch-potch of sheds and warehouses. There at least, the prospect of a real bargain flits just ahead at the next stall, and even if it remains out of reach, the market nevertheless provides great entertainment.

PADDY'S MARKET
Do not confuse the Barras with Paddy's Market, near the river. Paddy's Market gets its name from the penniless Irish immigrants of a century ago who would literally sell the shirts off their backs, so desperate was their poverty. Something of the same air of desperation still hangs around today. This little lane of stalls belies Glasgow's upbeat new image.

95

Princes Square – modern shopping at its most sophisticated

Nightlife

Glasgow has a huge selection of pubs and bistros plus a range of venues offering musical entertainment from proper ceilidhs (not fake affairs for tourists) to new wave.

LISTINGS
The List, available from all city-centre newsagents, gives information on events in Glasgow and Edinburgh. *The Herald* newspaper on Saturdays lists entertainment activities with a Glasgow emphasis.

THEATRE AND CONCERT HALLS The city's cultural flagship is the Royal Concert Hall, Sauchiehall Street (tel: 0141 287 4000), a first home for the Royal Scottish Orchestra, which, along with Scottish Ballet and Scottish Opera, has its headquarters in the city. The Royal Scottish Academy of Music and Drama, Stevenson Hall, Renfrew Street (tel: 0141 332 5057) offers a varied programme of international performances. The Tramway, Albert Drive (tel: 0141 287 4000) is an exciting venue for opera, drama and dance. The Tron Theatre, Trongate (tel: 0141 552 4267) offers the best of contemporary Scottish and international theatre. The Pavilion Theatre, Renfield Street (tel: 0141 332 1846) puts on variety shows, rock and pop concerts, while the Kings Theatre, Bath Street (tel: 0141 287 4000) has drama and popular productions. With the Citizens' Theatre, Gorbals Street (tel: 0141 429 5561), the City Hall and the Henry Wood Hall, these are just some of the performing spaces on offer.

FILM An alternative to the regular cinema chains, the Glasgow Film Theatre, Rose Street (tel: 0141 332 6535) is an independent concern, offering new releases, classic revivals and popular re-runs.

OTHER NIGHTLIFE These are some examples from the broad spectrum: Glasgow's 'Grand Ole Opry', 2 Govan Road (tel: 0141 429 5396) is where the local cowboys hang out for the country and western music. Archaos, Queen Street (tel: 0141 204 3189) is the biggest club in Glasgow and offers an eclectic musical mix on its three dance floors. The Arches, Midland Street (tel: 0141 221 4001) offers house, Techno and big music names at one of the city's largest venues. Victoria's, Sauchiehall Street (tel: 0141 332 1444) is a popular upmarket nightclub with supper bar: the hunting ground of professional footballers and models, with several floors to suit all musical tastes. The Riverside Club, Fox Street (tel: 0141 248 3144) is *the* ceilidh place in town, like an upstairs barn with a tiny stage. The Renfrew Ferry, Clyde Place (tel: 0141 429 8676) looks like a floating conservatory but is actually the former Renfrew ferry: another great ceilidh place with other kinds of music as well (best to check the local press for details). The Scotia Bar, Stockwell Street (tel: 0141 552 8681) is an old-fashioned little pub with lots of impromptu performances, mostly of folk music.

The ground-breaking Citizens' Theatre, at the heart of Glasgow's art scene

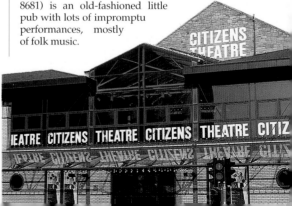

Practicalities

AIRPORT TRANSFERS Glasgow Airport (tel: 0141 887 1111) is 13km from the city centre with an express bus service that takes 30 minutes at a very reasonable fare. These buses connect with the hourly service to Edinburgh city centre. There is also a railway station at Paisley Gilmour Street, about 3km away. Metered taxis are available, with fares upwards of £12 to the centre. The Airport Tourist Information Centre (tel: 0141 848 4440) can reserve accommodation, though the main information centre is in the city centre – see page 272.

ARRIVING BY TRAIN OR BUS Glasgow Central is the city-centre train terminus for services from the south (London Euston is about five hours away). Glasgow Queen Street is the terminus for services from Edinburgh (around 45 minutes by rail) and the north and west (Aberdeen and Fort William for instance). Glasgow's main bus station is Buchanan Bus Station, Killermont Street.

*The Drum and Monkey,
St Vincent Street*

PUBLIC TRANSPORT WITHIN GLASGOW Glasgow is the only Scottish city with an underground network, a modernised and useful service open 6.30–10.30 daily with trains every six to eight minutes all day. Flat rate tickets are on sale at all stations on the underground, which takes the form of a large circle. For information call at St Enoch Square Travel Centre (tel: 0141 226 4826). This important source of travel information for Glasgow's excellent fully integrated transport network is located beside the St Enoch Centre, right in the city centre, and also has details of Glasgow's extensive suburban rail network.

There are many bus companies operating within the city. Several different types of multi-journey or flexible tickets are available, some combining rail, bus and underground. The Family Day Tripper Ticket, allowing travel as far afield as Loch Lomond, is good value.

TAXIS Black cabs are widely available throughout the city, and main taxi ranks are located at the stations. A fleet of airport taxis operates the service from the airport.

ACROSS THE BORDER Unless indulging in the tartan frolics of Gretna or Gretna Green – 'Joke Anvil Weddings Performed Here' says one advertisement – crossing the border is a low-key affair. (It was different when eloping couples from England came to Gretna Green, where Scots law allowed them to marry simply by declaration before witnesses – this became illegal in 1940.) Sometimes a piper plays at Carter Bar where the A68 enters Scotland, but otherwise at first sight things look much the same.

However, Scotland is distinct from England, even in its southern sector – from banknotes to buying beer in pubs, a subtly altered culture is all around. Geographers call the area the Southern Uplands – blue waves of hills, resonant with tales of ancient skirmishes in these fought-over lands – a dramatic sight from Carter Bar. Further west, in the Galloway Forest Park north of Newton Stewart, the end of the park road is within walking distance of The Merrick, the highest mountain (843m) in southern Scotland, with a vista of dark lochs, birchwoods and purple slopes which resemble the Trossachs further north (see pages 160–1).

AYRSHIRE Continuing north from Galloway, the sheep-cropped moors and conifer blocks blend into Ayrshire, another area with a highly characteristic landscape. There is a lushness in the river valleys, woods and hedgerows reminiscent of South Wales – a parallel sustained by the signs, in places, of now-vanished heavy industry, coal and ironworks, backed by green hills. Further north, the typical Ayrshire view is across hawthorn hedge and pasture to a long horizon dominated by the smudgy profile of Arran and Kintyre, a setting more Highland than Lowland.

Beyond the geological edge of the Southern Uplands, and into the southern part of the central corridor across Scotland, the scenery changes again. The summery yellow grainfields of East Lothian have red-pantile roofed villages with hills as a backdrop, or even the sheer unexpectedness of the vista from the prehistoric site on the top of Cairnpapple Hill behind Linlithgow, with the Forth Valley spread out like a geography lesson.

Marking the Border at Coldstream

Borders landscape near Galashiels

As well as its fine landscapes, southern Scotland has highly individual townscapes and communities of character. The characteristic pastel-washed frontages and wide streets of the Galloway towns are surprising for anyone with preconceptions of dour grey Scottish communities. No one who accidentally stumbles upon a Common

100

Typical river valley scenery near Walkerburn, west of Galashiels

THE RIVAL COUNTY TOWNS
After Berwick became English, Greenlaw saw its chance to become the county town of the Scottish county of Berwickshire. However, nearby Duns also wanted this status and managed to achieve it several times. Each time it did so, little Greenlaw built another fine civic building. A 17th-century courtroom and prison, an 18th-century hotel to accommodate visiting lawyers and court officials, and a 19th-century town hall all add to the fine townscape of today's Greenlaw. It was superseded by Duns for the last time in 1903.

Riding in one of the Border towns can fail to notice the groundswell of loyalty to place and culture. These are mainly modern revivals of the ancient customs of marking out the bounds of the community, as well as great celebrations of horsemanship – another Border speciality. (A Scottish Border MP once requested that the date of a general election be changed so that it did not clash with the Selkirk Common Riding, which he enjoyed attending.)

LAND OF BURNS Similarly in Ayrshire, where you cannot turn a corner without finding a signpost pointing to some aspect of the life of Robert Burns, there is a genuine and unique regard for Scotland's poet. This is not something that tourism promoters have foisted upon reluctant communities, but instead an affection for the ploughman poet and pride in his achievements.

From bards to model villages by the tumbling cataracts of New Lanark, from stern Border towers to the softness of East Lothian, from the faded Victorian resorts of the golf-mad Clyde coast to the breathtaking bird cliffs of St Abbs, the south of Scotland offers a slice of real Scotland without too much tartan ribbon (even if you can find a pipe band in a Border town just as easily as further north). In fact, the area's variety and complex character may ultimately satisfy much more than that of the weather-dominated north. It is not an area to hurry through.

AYRSHIRE ELECTRIC ILLUSIONS
The A719 at a point within sight of Culzean Castle, 14km south of Ayr, is called Croy Brae, or more familiarly, Electric Brae. Because of a particularly effective optical illusion, the road gives the impression of going downhill when it is actually going up. The site got its name as it was formerly thought that electricity had some part to play in the phenomenon, though this is now known not to be the case. Take care when travelling on this road as you are likely to encounter puzzled motorists freewheeling 'uphill' to satisfy their curiosity.

THE EDINBURGH LIGHT HORSE

Sir Walter Scott was a countryman at heart, with the landowner's ideal of an ordered society where everyone knew their place. He and some friends founded the Edinburgh Light Horse, a kind of 'Home Guard', in response to a threatened Napoleonic invasion in 1797. They galloped around enthusiastically but saw little real action. However, in the troubled times when workers began to protest about working conditions, Scotland's champion did manage to threaten to sabre some mill workers at Moredun Mill and took a few pot shots at dissenting miners at Cross Causeway, both in Edinburgh.

▶▶▶ Abbotsford House   99D3

Off B6360, tel: 01896 752043.
Open: mid-Mar–May and Oct, Mon–Sat 10–5, Sun 2–5; Jun–Sep, daily 10–5. Admission charge
Sir Walter Scott's creation of his own version of Scotland and its heroic past is embodied in the house that was his life. Here is the door from the Old Tolbooth in Edinburgh, there is the desk made with wood from a Spanish Armada ship. Look at Rob Roy's gun, Bonnie Prince Charlie's quaich (cup), James IV's hunting bottle (did he club game with it?), the keys of Lochleven Castle and other treasures.

▶ Ayr   98B3

A preference for a fortnight in the Mediterranean sun instead of a traditional seaside holiday, plus the demise of traditional industries such as coal mining, have left Ayr and its hinterland facing a challenging future. Nevertheless, Ayr is a bustling place (but take care with the parking system which needs vouchers from local shops and garages). It makes a good base for keen golfers.

Non-golfers can pursue the life of Burns. There seem to be so many places in the vicinity in which Burnsiana is displayed that after a day or two you will recognise his handwriting from several paces off. Take your pick from the **Auld Kirk**, where many of Burns's contemporaries are buried, the **Twa Brigs o Ayr**, the older of which is

Scottish memorabilia from Abbotsford

15th-century or earlier, plus the odd statue or two…then follow signs to Alloway.

Alloway▶▶, a pleasantly leafy suburb of Ayr, is disturbed only by incessant coach loads from all nations on their way to the shrine of Scotland's national bard. **Burns Cottage,** with a museum adjacent (*Open* Apr–Oct, daily 9–6; Nov–Mar, Mon–Sat 10–4, Sun noon–4. *Admission charge*), is an excellent starting point. Down the road the **Tam o'Shanter Experience** has a 10-minute presentation on Burns, then the poem Tam o'Shanter springs to life in a three-screen theatrical event (*Open* Apr–Sep, daily 9–6; Oct–Mar, daily 9–5. *Admission charge*). Nearby, the Burns Monument's neo-classical columns rise from a clipped garden, one of many contrasts with the poet's life of poverty and struggle. Also moments away are the **Auld Brig o Doon** and **Alloway Kirk**, both immortalised in the poem Tam o'Shanter, a tale of drunkenness and orgy in a setting now taken over by suburban respectability.

Dalgarven Mill

On the Burns trail Incurable romantics will pursue the poet east to **Mauchline,** a village sitting dourly on a grassy ridge in the hinterland of hawthorn-hedged fields. There they will find the **Burns House Museum** (*Open Easter–Sep, Tue–Sat 10–4, Sun 2–4. Admission charge*) and – even better – a breathtaking view from the **Burns Memorial Tower** just up the road. Burns signposts are everywhere. You can even follow them to the grimly workaday town of **Kilmarnock,** where in a country park stands **Dean Castle.** A rare volume, the first or Kilmarnock Edition of Burns poetry is on display, but just as interesting are the early musical instruments and European armour collections (*Open* castle daily 12–4, restricted winter opening; grounds daily dawn–dusk. *Admission charge*).

Elsewhere in Ayr's hinterland, **Dalgarven Mill** – the Ayrshire Museum of Countrylife and Costume, north of Kilwinning, is in a restored water-powered flour mill (*Open* Easter–Sep, Mon–Sat 10–5, Sun 11–5; Oct–Easter, Tue–Sun 10–4. *Admission charge*). Also within easy reach of Ayr are the **Magnum Leisure Centre,** much trumpeted for its modern approach to leisure now that the traditional Clyde Coast seaside holiday is out of favour, the **Scottish Maritime Museum** (see page 117) and **Culzean Castle** (see page 110).

THE SOUTHERN UPLANDS FAULT
The Southern Uplands Fault, where the midland plain gives way to the high ground of southern Scotland, is most conspicuous in the east. Running into East Lothian and prominent from the main A68 south of Dalkeith (Midlothian), the ancient tough rocks of the Lammermuir Hills form an escarpment above the soft sandstones to the north. A convenient layby on the A68 at Soutra Hill offers superb views back to the Pentlands, Edinburgh, the Firth of Forth and beyond.

TOURIST INFORMATION
Ayr: Burns House, Burns Statue Square (tel: 01292 262555).

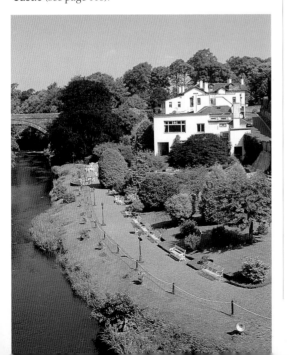

The gardens beside the Brig o Doon in Ayr

Robert Burns (1759–96) is the best-known figure in Scottish literature, though whether for his poems or for his pursuit of the lasses is perhaps another matter. Large tracts of Ayrshire and the area around Dumfries have plenty of signposted places of interest associated with his life.

SATIRICAL OBSERVATIONS

As an observer of others' follies, Burns wrote plenty of scathing and satirical observations of both people and state. A poem to the 'Scotch Representatives in the House of Commons' contains the line, often quoted by the distilling industry: 'Freedom and Whisky gang thegither' (go together). It also contains this observation on the Scots army regiments:
'But bring a Scotchman frae his hill
Clap in his cheek a Highland gill
Say, such is royal George's will And there's the foe,
He has nae thought but how to kill Twa at a blow.'

[A gill is a measure of whisky; royal George means King George.]

Robert Burns

Ayrshire beginnings With his farming background and his daily toil, Burns might have lived and died anonymously as just another Ayrshire farmer, struggling with poor soil and the primitive agricultural practices of the day. Instead, his immortality was assured through poetry filled with shrewd observations on human nature, with lyricism and optimism, and above all, belief in the brotherhood of man.

His father was a farmer who moved to Ayrshire from Kincardineshire, on the east coast, and built a cottage on some land he had acquired. This 'auld clay biggin' still stands, a shrine to the thousands who have flocked there since the beginning of the 19th century. Burns's father was a hard worker determined to educate his family. Robert and his brother Gilbert acquired a reasonable, if sporadic, education. Robert read avidly when he was not helping on the farm. He had committed 'the sin of rhyme' by the time he was 15 years old, while on the farm of Mount Oliphant.

Poems and passion After his father's death in 1784, he and his brother rented the farm of Mossgiel near Mauchline. Robert soon gained a local reputation as a maker of rhymes (among his other vices). In a period when passion and poverty went together with fierce creativity, Burns wrote some of his best-known works. This culminated in the publication of the famed Kilmarnock Edition of *Poems, Chiefly in the Scottish Dialect* in 1786. Around the same time there were writs from Jean Armour's father, livid at his daughter's association (pregnancy, to be precise) with Burns, the poor farmer; penance in the local kirk (for fornication); thoughts of emigration – only 'the feelings of a father' kept him in Scotland; and also an affair with Highland Mary which ended in mysterious circumstances.

Highland Mary (Mary Campbell) is a figure about whom very little is known. She died in October 1786, possibly after bearing him a child. Certainly, Burns felt terribly guilty about her in later years. It is said she consented to be his wife, but he was already committed to Jean Armour, whom he later married.

Through the success of the Kilmarnock Edition, Burns gained sudden fame. He was soon lionised by the literary classes of Edinburgh and welcomed as a ploughman poet into genteel drawing-rooms. He went along happily with the image.

The songwriter Burns was also a maker of songs. In 1787 he started his completely unpaid contribution to James Johnson's *Scots Musical Museum*, reworking and improving many songs and fragments, a huge body of work still popular to this day. By 1788 he was back once again with Jean Armour. He married her and gave up the hopeless struggle of farming at Mossgiel, deciding instead to move to Ellisland Farm not far from Dumfries. He took up employment with the Excise, although he was still determined to succeed as a farmer. The farm at Ellisland failed in 1791.

In between his commitments to the Excise and the needs of the farm, he worked on with further volumes of *The Scots Musical Museum* as well as his own poetic

outpourings. Illness and low spirits dogged him as the 1790s progressed. Rheumatic fever took its toll in 1795 as he struggled to maintain the output for *A Select Collection of Original Scottish Airs for the Voice*. By July 1796, at the age of 37, he was dead.

Memories of Burns The Burns 'industry' followed on thereafter. The first of many biographies was published by 1797, the year after his death, and the Irvine Burns Club, started in 1826, claims to be the oldest continuously operating club of its kind. Today, his birthday (25 January) is celebrated throughout Scotland – and far beyond, wherever Scots gather – with Burns Suppers, a unique format of haggis, whisky, poetry and song. No other British poet has achieved anywhere near the same kind of popular appeal. On Burns Night even buttoned-up Scots have a good time, with their stern Calvinistic streak temporarily obscured by the outlook that, at least for one evening

'...man to man, the warld o'er
Shall brithers be for a' that.'
Burns would certainly have approved.

THE BROW WELL
Though places associated with Burns are scattered throughout Ayrshire and Galloway, perhaps the saddest lies adjacent to the B725 southeast of Dumfries. The Brow Well is a rock-cut well close to the sea. It was once famed for its mineral properties, and the poet, desperately ill with rheumatic fever and possibly bacterial endocarditis, visited it while sea-bathing nearby, in a last attempt to recover his health. He died three days after he returned from Brow.

Burns Cottage in Alloway, near Ayr

AE FOND KISS
The curious affair by post (see page 48) which Burns had with Mrs Agnes McLehose in Edinburgh resulted in a great deal of correspondence, some frigid literary exercises in neo-classical idiom and one great, truly great, love poem and song of parting, 'Ae fond kiss and then we sever', with its haunting fourth verse:
    Had we never lov'd sae kindly,
    Had we never lov'd sae blindly!
    Never met – or never parted,
    We had ne'er been broken hearted.
This was written in 1791, as 'Clarinda', as Burns addressed her, was preparing to rejoin her husband in the West Indies. Burns never saw her again.

98C3

TOURIST INFORMATION
Biggar: (Easter–Oct) 155 High Street (tel: 01899 221066).

▶ **Biggar**

The town of Biggar, equidistant from Glasgow and Edinburgh, has retained its own character and a sense of heritage. The original settlement is associated with 12th-century Flemish immigrants who arrived under the patronage of the Scottish kings. The incomers built 'mottes', earthen mounds once topped with wooden castles. A motte survives behind today's High Street.

Biggar is essentially a centre for a rural hinterland, and the **Corn Exchange**, with its clock tower, still dominates the wide main street, scene of former markets. **St Mary's Kirk** dates from 1545 – the last kirk to be built before the Reformation – and is open to view. It is a collegiate church, founded by Lord Fleming, Mary, Queen of Scots's uncle, to support teaching priests. All this can be taken in on a few minutes' walk from the main street. The town also has a puppet theatre – not a common feature of Scottish towns – as well as several museums.

Gladstone Court Museum, a tribute to the energy of the local museum trust, is an indoor 'street' of shops with a good range of nostalgia-inducing artefacts (*Open* Apr–Oct, Mon–Sat 10–12.30, 2–5, Sun 2–5. *Admission charge*). **The Greenhill Covenanter's House,** downhill towards the Biggar Burn behind St Mary's, is a 17th-century farm relocated stone by stone. It sheds some light on the Covenanting movement (see page 55) and the complexities of the Scottish religious wars by way of artefacts and displays (*Open* Easter–early Oct, daily 2–5. *Admission charge*). For a total contrast, visit **Biggar Gasworks Museum▶** (*Open* Jun–Sep, daily 2–5. *Admission charge*). Thanks to North Sea Gas, traditional gasworks have vanished from most places, but not from

Biggar Gasworks (no longer operating) is Scotland's oldest surviving rural gasworks (1839)

An old-fashioned chemist's shop at Gladstone Court Museum, Biggar

Biggar. Sometimes they fire it up, creating an olfactory trip down memory lane for some. **Moat Park Heritage Centre** tells of Biggar's early history, and also focuses on embroidery, with samplers and patchwork coverlets, and on geology (*Open* Easter–mid-Oct, Mon–Sat 10–5, Sun 2–5. *Admission charge*).

▶▶▶ Caerlaverock Castle and National Nature Reserve
98C1

Open: Apr–Sep, daily 9.30–6; Oct–Mar, Mon–Sat 9.30–4, Sun 2–4. Admission charge

Caerlaverock Castle is unique in Britain. No other castle builder employed this odd triangular moated design. The castle sits in its moat, massive and menacing in red sandstone, and offers another puzzle. Nobody knows who built Caerlaverock, which is of late 13th-century origin. It was taken by King Edward I of England around 1300 and regained by the Scots by 1312, only to suffer further in later Anglo-Scots conflicts. Unexpectedly, for this frontier fortress, there is an ornate 17th-century range within: Nithsdale's Building, built by the Lords Maxwell. But all is scarred and ruinous – a troubled history in stone.

Caerlaverock National Nature Reserve▶▶▶ Combine a castle visit with de-luxe birdwatching on the marshes: particularly good away from high summer, best of all on a calm winter's day. Among the birds here are 13,000 barnacle geese from Spitzbergen, with superb views possible of the flocks from the visitor centre or from the conveniently placed hides. This is one of Scotland's major wildlife spectacles if you time it right. The reserve is open all year.

▶▶ Castle Kennedy Gardens
98A1

Open: Apr–Sep, daily 10–5. Admission charge

The Earl of Stair built these pleasure grounds. As a Field Marshal, instead of toiling with a wheelbarrow and shovel, he used his troops to build the main landscape features. (They were supposed to be chasing Covenanters.) The result is gardening on a grand scale, with superb vistas down the monkey puzzle avenue, woodland walks and lakes, and swathes of rhododendrons in spring. May is probably the best month to visit. The gardens are undoubtedly worth the excursion to the west of Galloway, and could easily be combined with a visit to Logan Botanic Garden (see page 120).

CASTLE REMAINS
Within Castle Kennedy Gardens is the shell of Castle Kennedy, burned down in 1716, but now lending an antique air to the parklands. The Victorian Lochinch Castle in the grounds is strictly private.

THE DEBATABLE LAND
The Debatable Land was the name given to disputed territory between England and Scotland, between the Rivers Sark and Esk, not far from Carlisle, England. Grazing was its only use as buildings were forbidden. In 1552 it was split in two and a settlement agreed.

107

Two sides of Caerlaverock Castle's triangular moat

The magnificent Adam interior of Chatelherault Lodge, near Hamilton

TOURIST INFORMATION
Castle Douglas: (Apr–Oct)
Markethill (tel: 01556 502611).
Coldstream: (Apr–Oct)
Town Hall, High Street
(tel: 01890 882607)

The past uniform of the famous Coldstream Guards

▶ **Castle Douglas**   98C1

This is a cheerful sort of place, with its busy main street at the centre of a simple grid. The town's designer, Sir William Douglas, was a rich local merchant who rebuilt the old village in 1792. Now bypassed by the A75, Castle Douglas has plenty of shops to make strolling worthwhile.

Adjacent Carlingwark Loch was once a source of marl, the limey clay used as fertiliser which originally made the town prosperous. To the northeast is the Motte of Urr, the largest man-made castle mound in Scotland. The former 12th-century administrative headquarters of the de Berkeleys is now an impressive green hump by the river, visible from the B794.

A few minutes from Castle Douglas, **Threave Garden**▶▶ is the training ground for the National Trust for Scotland's gardeners. There are always fresh plantings and new ideas to see within its 26 hectares. Early spring (April) has spectacular drifts of daffodils with over 200 cultivars. Later, the peat garden – that speciality of the cool, moist Scottish climate – is a high point. Most aspects of Scottish gardening can be seen on trial here, from the traditional flower border to the Victorian hothouse (*Open* daily 9.30–sunset; walled garden and greenhouses daily 9:30–5; visitor centre Apr–Oct, daily 9.30–5.30. *Admission charge*).

Threave Castle▶▶ This gaunt 14th-century tower rising out of the watery scenery on an island in the River Dee was once owned by Archibald the Grim. It is an appropriate setting for the name. The Lord of Galloway built his fortress with the intention of intimidating. Formerly the main power-base of the Black Douglases, the strongest of the Scottish nobles until they overreached themselves in a conflict with King James II, Threave was successfully besieged in 1455 by the king's forces. Excavations have revealed a lot about medieval defensive buildings as well as the most complete medieval riverside harbour in

Scotland. There is a pleasant walk, though wet in places, from the farmyard car park to the riverside. Ring a bell for the boatman. Even when the castle is closed, the walk is still worthwhile, with close-up views from the bank. Threave Wildfowl Refuge is nearby (*Open* Apr–Sep, daily 9.30–6. *Admission charge*).

▶▶ Chatelherault
98B3

The wealthy Duke of Hamilton asked William Adam to design a hunting lodge and kennels within the grounds surrounding Hamilton Palace. Chatelherault was part of one of the most ambitious landscaping works in 18th-century Britain. Nothing remains now of the 3-mile avenue, the lake or the canalised River Clyde. Even Hamilton Palace was demolished in 1927 after most of the land was sold for mining. Today there is only a country park – plus a £7 million restoration of Adam's one-room deep façade, part of which is a visitor centre telling the extraordinary story. It is well worth the diversion from the M74. (*Open* Apr–Sep, Mon–Sat 10–5, Sun 12–5.30 (Oct–Mar 5pm). *Closed* occasional Fridays. *Admission free*)

COLDSTREAM
Birthplace of the Regiment

▶ Coldstream
99E3

A pleasant village just north of the border, Coldstream, like Gretna Green, once did a brisk trade in marrying elopers. This is recalled on a plaque by the little tollhouse on the Scottish side of John Smeaton's elegant 1760s bridge. Coldstream is also associated with the Guards regiment of the same name. Items from their past can be seen in the Coldstream Museum (*Open* Apr–Sep, Mon–Sat 10–4, Sun 2–4; Oct, Mon–Sat 1–4. *Admission charge*).

North of the village is **The Hirsel**▶, once the home of Sir Alec Douglas-Home, Lord Home of The Hirsel, who was Prime Minister from 1963–64. Walks through varied habitats of woodland (with rhododendrons in spring), farm and loch,

which are enjoyed by birdwatchers in particular. A craft complex and visitor centre in a converted farm building sheds light on the life of a Borders country estate (*Open* grounds daily, sunrise–sunset; museum and crafts centre Mon–Fri 10–5; Sat–Sun 12–5. *Admission free; parking charge*).

109

THE COLDSTREAM GUARDS
The primacy of the Grenadier Guards as the senior regiment in the Guards Division of the British Army is disputed by the Coldstream Guards. Both regiments share 1660 as their official founding date. When on parade the Coldstreamers will not stand next to the Grenadiers, instead taking the left of the line. Their motto is *Nulli secundus* – second to none.

FOUND IN THE LOCH
Not only valuable marl came out of Carlingwark Loch by Castle Douglas. Among other historical artefacts, a forge was once recovered from the waters. It is thought to have been used by King Edward I's forces as they passed this way during one of their forays in around 1300.

Threave Castle, near Castle Douglas

NATIONAL GUEST FLAT

In 1946, the top floor of the main part of Culzean Castle was put at the disposal of General Dwight D Eisenhower as a token of the Scottish people's gratitude for his role as Supreme Commander of the Allied Forces in Europe in World War II. It has become known as the National Guest Flat and its story is told in the Eisenhower Room in the castle today.

AN ITALIAN INFLUENCE?

The unique studded façade of Crichton Castle dates from the 1580s. The Palazzo Steripinto in Sciacca, Sicily (1501) is a possible source of inspiration, as the 5th Earl of Bothwell was in exile in southern Italy.

Culzean Castle has fine Adam architecture, extensive gardens and superb views to Arran and Ailsa Craig (a steep, rocky island once the plug of a volcano)

►► Crichton Castle   99D3

Open: Apr–Sep, daily 9.30–6. Admission charge

This forbidding, brooding castle is easily missed if you hurry along the A68, intent on Edinburgh. It is worth stopping, not least because of the fine Lothians countryside in which the castle is set. Built between the late 14th and late 16th centuries, it is associated with the Earls of Bothwell. Mary, Queen of Scots was here in January 1562, attending the wedding of her half brother to Lady Janet Hepburn. The son of that marriage, the 5th Earl of Bothwell, frequently in exile, commissioned the castle's unique feature: the diamond-faceted façade of the north range. Beyond the castle a pathway leads through some fine rural scenery to Borthwick Castle (a private hotel).

►►► Culzean Castle and Country Park   98A2

Open: house Apr–Oct, daily 10.30–5.30 (last entry 5); country park daily 9.30–sunset. Admission charge

Culzean, pronounced 'Kul-*ain*', is the National Trust for Scotland's most popular attraction. Set on its clifftop perch, it has been associated with the Kennedy family since the 14th century. The present building was commissioned by the 10th Earl of Cassillis, and is one of Robert Adam's most famous designs, taking 20 years to reach completion in 1792. The structure itself, with its ornate plasterwork, oval staircase and round drawing-room, plus 230 hectares of 'policies' (grounds), came into the hands of the National Trust in 1945, to be held for all time. Now the once-private grounds swallow up more than half a million visitors every year, though fewer visit the castle itself. Stabilising the wind- and salt-eroded sandstone of the structure and the outbuildings was only one problem for the Trust to solve. Simply running the estate is a huge operation. This is conservation and countryside education on a large scale. Within the extensive policies are woodland walks, a walled garden, a swan pond, deer park and aviary, as well as a helpful Ranger Service, based in a reception and interpretation centre.

▶ **Dalbeattie**   98C1

Dalbeattie presents an uncharacteristic Galloway town-scape of silver granite, like a little detached chunk of Aberdeen, but its granite has brought prosperity – even the Grand Harbour of Valletta in Malta used it. The town is a good base for exploring the coastline, especially around

The beach at Yellowcraigs, Dirleton, with Fidra offshore

111

Rockcliffe and Kippford, two little communities dozing quietly by the firth. Kippford is favoured by sailing enthu-siasts, while Rockcliffe has more the air of a retirement haven. Further up the Water of Urr is Palnackie, where a flounder tramping festival is held annually in the muddy creek. Also nearby is Orchardton Tower, a 15th-century tower house unique in Scotland because it is circular.

▶▶ **Dawyck Botanic Gardens**   98C3

Open: Mar–Oct, daily 9.30–6. Admission charge

On the B712 southwest of Peebles, this specialist garden of the Royal Botanic Garden in Edinburgh lies a little off the main tourist routes and as such is often overlooked. It is worth seeking out, especially in late spring and early summer when the garden is ablaze with rhododendrons. The plantings here are on a large scale, with grand conifers and shrubs and woodland walks.

▶▶ **Dirleton Castle**   99D4

Open: Apr–Sep, daily 9.30–6; Oct–Mar, Mon–Sat 9.30–4, Sun 2–4. Admission charge

Overlooking the village green of Dirleton, this ancient fortress dates back in part to the early 13th century, when its great circular towers, now overlaid with later work, were built by the Anglo-Norman de Vaux family. The strategically important castle, commanding east–west routes round the Lammermuirs, was captured by King Edward I of England in 1298. It also has a pit-prison, cut from the solid rock. Left in ruins by Cromwell's troops in 1650, the castle became part of the Archerfield estate. The site lies within a much later wall enclosing a 17th-century bowling green, ancient yews and a fine garden. This last feature, an attraction in its own right, is at its best in high season. Historic Scotland, the organisation that cares for the castle, has recreated a Victorian garden here. Combine a visit with a walk at Yellowcraigs, for fine coastal scenery. An access road is signed just east of the castle.

The South

Eyemouth, an active fishing port

A STABBING AT THE ALTAR

In assessing his chances of securing the throne of Scotland, Robert the Bruce (see page 29) had to deal with other powerful families with Scottish interests at the English court. For this purpose the encounter was typical of the murky politics of the day. He met with John Comyn (the Red Comyn) at Greyfriars Kirk in Dumfries. Most historians believe that they had been jointly plotting against King Edward of England and that Comyn had let the English know about this. Bruce had been warned and left England in great haste. At his meeting with Comyn he accused him of treachery, and the fatal stabbing followed. The game was up. To return to King Edward was impossible. Bruce had to declare his intention: to win Scotland's Crown.

Decorative tiles in a Dunbar shop

▶ **Dumfries** 98C2

With its old bridges, museum and Camera Obscura, a reasonable range of shops and plenty of Burns strands to follow, Dumfries is a pleasant rather than a breathtaking town. Known as the Queen of the South, it is the largest centre for some distance around, with a good mix of light industry and commerce, tourism and historic sites. Now that it is bypassed by the terrifyingly busy A75, the town

environment has greatly improved. The prevailing street colour is the distinctive pink of the local sandstone. Dumfries grew up around the ford on the River Nith, becoming a royal burgh in the 12th century. The now-vanished Greyfriars was the scene of the stabbing of the Red Comyn by Robert the Bruce, an incident that led to the Scottish Wars of Independence (see panel). Much later, and flying in the face of Jacobite romantic myth, Dumfries wanted no truck with Bonnie Prince Charlie, who helped himself to town funds as well as the lead off the roof of St Michael's Church.

Like Ayr, Dumfries has capitalised on its Robert Burns connections (see pages 104–5). He moved here in 1791 to take up his post as an excise officer and now lies buried in a grand mausoleum in St Michael's churchyard. The house in which he died is also a museum (*Open* Apr–Sep, Mon–Sat 10–5, Sun 2–5; Oct–Mar, Tue–Sat 10–1, 2–5. *Admission free*). The Globe Inn, known to Burns, is still a pub, complete with the chair he used and the window on which he scratched some radical verses.

Robert Burns Centre▶ Modern input to the Burns cult takes the form of this handsome former mill building by the River Nith. The centre offers an exhibition on the Dumfries Burns connection (*Open* Apr–Sep, Mon–Sat 10–8, Sun 2–5; Oct–Mar, Tue–Sat 10–1, 2–5. *Admission free*).

▶▶ **Dunbar** 99D4

Boasting high sunshine records – when the coastal 'haar' (sea fog) stays away – and low rainfall, Dunbar is a curious mix of traditional resort, decayed port and elegant Georgian sea town. By the harbour are the shattered fragments of one of medieval Scotland's most important fortresses, controlling an important coastal route used by the English invaders. The Scots were defeated here in

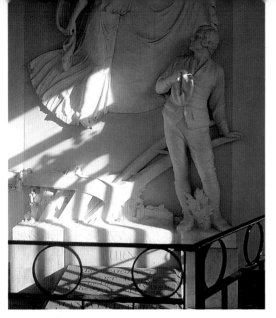

FIRST STEAMBOAT
Dalswinton Loch lies 10km
north of Dumfries. The first
steam-powered boat ever
built was tested on its
waters in 1788. The
designer was William
Symington, an engineer
who was born not far off at
Leadhills. His engine developed 0.45 horsepower
(0.34KW), barely enough to
turn the cranks.

*Burns's Mausoleum, one
of many stops in and
around Dumfries on the
Burns trail*

1296. In 1650, the Covenanting army met the same fate at
the hands of Oliver Cromwell.

Today, the townscape owes its origins partly to funds
generated by intense trading activities in the 18th century,
which included, briefly, whaling. The handsome 17th-
century town house pre-dates these times, though
Dunbar or Lauderdale House, blocking the eastward
High Street view, was built by one of the powerful trading
families in the town. There are other fine buildings to be
admired, but a stroll will inevitably lead seawards, past
the Cromwellian Old Harbour to the New or Victoria
harbour, dating from 1842. In spring, kittiwakes nest on
the old castle and other harbourfront buildings.

Dunbar lies next to the **John Muir Country Park**▶▶, 70
hectares of excellent coastal habitat, varying from
salt marsh to sea buckthorn, around the Tyne estuary. It
offers plenty of walks at all seasons and has the further
attraction of completely altering its character at high tide.

▶ Eyemouth Museum   *99E3*

*Open: Apr–Jun and Sep, Mon–Sat 10–5, Sun 1–3; Jul–Aug,
Mon–Sat 10–6, Sun 11.30–4.30; Oct, Mon–Sat 10–4.
Admission charge*

A converted Georgian church in the fishing port of
Eyemouth is the setting for this successful
community venture. Eyemouth Museum
was set up in 1981 to record the cente-
nary of the Great East Coast Fishing
Disaster of October 1881, when 189
fishermen lost their lives in a sudden
hurricane. The tale of the disaster is
commemorated in a magnificent
tapestry, and the museum also
touches on other aspects of folk life
in the area, including agricultural
developments. A visit here could be
combined with birdwatching around
St Abbs' Head.

AN UNFORTUNATE NAME
The former county town of
Duns is recalled in the
uncomplimentary 'dunce'.
This is ironic, as it refers
to John Duns Scotus
(1266–1308), a philoso-
pher and leading divine
said to have been born in
the town. The modern
usage came about
through later criticism of
his teachings.

TOURIST INFORMATION
Dumfries: 64 Whitesands
(tel: 01387 253862)
Eyemouth: Auld Kirk,
Market Place (tel: 01890
750678).

Lochcarron Woollen Mill, Galashiels

THE QUEEN'S WAY
The A712 between Newton Stewart and New Galloway as it passes through the Galloway Forest Park is known as the Queen's Way. The original Queen's Way was the old pilgrim road used by Mary, Queen of Scots, among many other monarchs, which led down to Whithorn (see page 120).

Outdoor refreshments by the Tyne, Haddington

▶ **Galashiels**   99D3

A sturdy, workaday mill town, rather than a picturesque place, 'Gala' has lots of shops to browse in for knitwear bargains. In fact, the textile theme is inescapable, notably at **Lochcarron Cashmere Woollen Mill**▶▶ (*Open* Mon–Sat 9–5, also Sun 12–5 Jun–Sep. *Tours Mon–Fri only. Admission charge*) The museum there, with its traditional spinning and weaving artefacts, tells the story of the town's development as an important textile manufacturing centre. There is also a factory tour and a mill shop.

▶▶ **Galloway Forest Park**   98B2

Between the rivers Cree and Ken, the open moors below the grey hills of Galloway lost their original tree cover long ago. From 1922 onwards the Forestry Commission reclothed many of the slopes using alien species, designating the 620sq km area a Forest Park in 1943 and leaving a third of it as open land. Like all Forestry Commission properties, it offers unlimited public access unless areas are closed for tree felling. There are many marked forest trails and opportunities to fish or camp, and the park is also bisected by the Southern Upland Way (a long-distance footpath). Among the points of interest are the 16km forest drive near Clatteringshaws Loch, the Raider's Road, linking the A712 and the A762, and the peerless views from the road end at Glen Trool. The Bruce's Stone, commemorating the first victory in the Independence Wars, can also be found here.

▶▶ **Gatehouse of Fleet**   98B1

Peaceful in pastel colours, Gatehouse of Fleet on the edge of the hills was founded in the 1760s as a mill community. Looming over the A75 access road just southwest is the 15th-century **Cardoness Castle**, a typically austere tower house (*Open* Apr–Sep, daily 9.30–6; Oct–Mar, Sat 9.30–4, Sun 2–4. *Admission charge*). In the other direction, the B796 north out of Gatehouse offers a flavour of the empty hinterland and high hills of Galloway, as well as a long view to the viaduct over the Big Water of Fleet. Use this road if you are visiting the Gem Rock Museum at Creetown (*Open* Easter–Sep, daily 9.30–6; Oct–Nov, Mar–Easter, daily 10–4; Dec–Feb, Sat–Sun 10–4. *Admission charge*), as it is much more attractive than the A75.

Mill on the Fleet▶▶▶ (*Open* Easter–Oct, daily 10–5.30. *Admission charge*). A visitor centre in a former bobbin mill tells the tale of Gatehouse's cotton spinning, offering a high-tech interpretation. Visitors are provided with hard hats, inside which are tiny loudspeakers that are activated at various points in the displays to provide commentary – an approach that some people can find a little disconcerting.

A gentle corner of the Galloway landscape in Scotland's southwestern corner

TOURIST INFORMATION
Galashiels: (Apr–Oct)
3 St John's Street
(tel: 01896 755551).
Gatehouse of Fleet:
(Apr–Oct) Car park
(tel: 01557 814212).

115

▶▶▶ Haddington 99D4

One of the most pleasing towns of the Lothians, the counties surrounding Edinburgh, Haddington was the former administrative headquarters of the old county and for centuries played an important part in Lothian affairs. A 12th-century royal burgh, it also lay at the centre of one of the most favoured agricultural regions of Scotland, and had continental trade through the now silted up port of Aberlady to the north.

Today it retains its triangular medieval street plan, and the fine, mainly Georgian, buildings of the town centre have been preserved and carefully painted to create a co-ordinated and harmonious façade along the High Street rivalled by few other Scottish towns. The air of a prosperous old community is enhanced by other trappings of a Scottish burgh: the impressive town house originally built by William Adam, the market cross, courthouse and 14th- to 15th-century St Mary's Church, with its warm, red stones reflected in the river. This is a town to study at a slow pace, admiring the detailing of wrought-iron balconies, ornamental urns, cornice-decoration and so on. Note also the closes running off the main thoroughfares. Tucked round a corner in Sidegate, a plaque records the exact heights of the River Tyne floods: the last big one was in 1948.

SCOTTISH TWEED
The traditional explanation for the name 'tweed' is that a merchant in London received a consignment of Scottish cloth and misread the word 'tweel' (twill). Because of the River Tweed the name stuck. This is probably a myth, though at least two Scottish tweed mills claim they sent the consignment. There is a written reference from Aberdeen in 1541 to 'small twedlyne' – tweedling. According to philologists, the words tweel and tweeling, tweed and tweedling have been around a long time and have nothing to do with rivers. Besides, the traditional version does not explain Harris tweed, given that Harris in the Outer Hebrides is so far away.

The South

A LONG RIDE

Mary, Queen of Scots rode from Jedburgh to Hermitage Castle and back in a day, just over 80km, to visit the wounded Earl of Bothwell, trusted lieutenant on Border matters. Though this is sometimes romantically described as a foolhardy venture undertaken on her own, it was not in fact unusual to cover such a distance in a day and, besides, the queen was in company with many members of her court and a squad of soldiers.

TOURIST INFORMATION

Hawick: (Apr–Oct) Drumlanrig's Tower, Tower Knowe (tel: 01450 372547).

▶ Hawick   99D2

Hawick is the largest of the Border towns. Its long and bustling main street is worth a browse for woollen shops with keenly priced cashmeres. At one end is **Drumlanrig's Tower**. This visitor centre portrays the local history of the area. A few minutes' walk away **Wilton Lodge Park** is also attractive, with Victorian walled gardens and its own museum and art gallery.

▶ Hermitage Castle   99D2

Open: Apr–Sep, daily 9.30–6. Admission charge

Off the B6399 in bleak Border country, the grimness of Hermitage Castle echoes the emptiness around. High in atmosphere, reeking of the violence of the medieval borderlands, Hermitage is particularly impressive if the clouds are low on the hills. One of the tales about this 14th-century keep concerns the wicked Lord Soulis, who was so cruel that the locals eventually revolted, wrapped him in lead and boiled him to death in a cauldron.

▶ Innerleithen   99D3

A compact mill town by the confluence of the Leithen Water and the mighty Tweed, Innerleithen is home to some famous knitwear names, notably Ballantynes. Sir Walter Scott used it as the setting for his novel *St Ronan's Well*, published in 1821.

A Borders' time capsule

Robert Smail's Printing Works▶▶▶, run by the National Trust for Scotland, is perhaps the main attraction within the town (*Open* Easter, May–Sep, Mon–Sat 10–1, 2–5, Sun 2–5; Oct, Sat 10–1, 2–5, Sun 2–5. *Admission charge*). The local printers, which served the community for well over a hundred years, remained in the original family's hands until purchased by the Trust in 1986. The Victorian office, paper store, composing room, and machine room all survived as a unique time capsule. Most importantly, so did 50 'guard books' – a record of every item ever printed at the works, as well as endless ephemera from the past. There are now print demonstrations.

Just minutes away to the south is one of the most interesting grand homes in the Borders. **Traquair House▶▶▶** (*Open* Apr–May and Sep, daily 12.30–5.30; Jun–Aug, daily 10.30–5.30, last entry 5. *Admission charge*) boasts that it is the oldest continuously inhabited house in Scotland and that it has been associated with the Stuarts or Maxwell-Stuarts, the Lairds of Traquair, since 1491. Before that it was a hunting lodge used by the Scottish monarchs. Over the centuries it has been transformed from a grim Borders keep to a stately mansion, and has remained practically unchanged since the end of the 17th century. Curiously, for a house occupied by frequent holders of high office during Scotland's troubled past, the mansion only once saw violence – in 1688,

ST RONAN'S WELL

The sulphurous waters of St Ronan's Well were said to be particularly effective for 'ladies desirous of becoming in an interesting condition'. According to local legend, the sulphur content is the result of the local holy man, St Ronan, catching the Deil (Devil) with his shepherd's crook and immersing him in the waters.

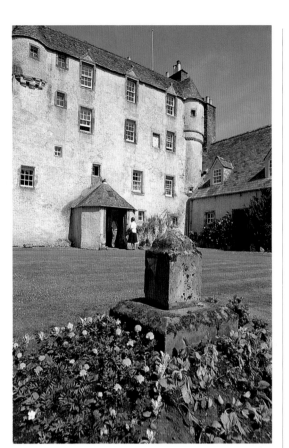

Traquair Castle, left, a fine fortified Borders castle, and below, the Traquair coat of arms

when a mob from Peebles stormed the building and destroyed religious artefacts.

The lairds were staunch Catholics, which is why the house has a secret staircase intended as a quick escape route for priests. As Catholics, they were also Jacobites. A total of 27 Scottish and English monarchs have been guests at Traquair, and Bonnie Prince Charlie is said to have visited. Family lore and the paraphernalia and treasures of generations, including notable Mary, Queen of Scots' relics, are further attractions of the house, which is also pleasantly unintimidating in scale. If there is only time for one Borders house, then make it Traquair

▶ Irvine   98B3

Scattered around the riverside area of the New Town of Irvine, the **Scottish Maritime Museum**▶ has a variety of craft, including a lifeboat, a tug and a puffer (an inshore supply boat) moored in the harbour by floating pontoons, an undercover exhibition, a typical shipyard worker's cottage and a Victorian boatshed, the largest of its kind ever built. The latter used to be on the Clyde, and was reconstructed here, brick by brick (*Open* Apr–Oct, daily 10–5. *Admission charge*). A ferry runs from nearby Ardrossan to Brodick on the Isle of Arran (see page 230).

117

Above: Jedburgh's mercat cross, symbol that the town enjoyed certain trading rights. Right: Kelso Abbey, at the heart of the town Sir Walter Scott described as the most beautiful in Scotland

118

TOURIST INFORMATION
Jedburgh: Murray's Green (tel: 01835 863435).
Kelso: (Apr–Oct) Town House, The Square (tel: 01573 223464).
Kirkcudbright: (Apr–Oct) Harbour Square (tel: 01557 330494).

A FLATTERING DESCRIPTION
With its long waterfront, Lord Cockburn described Kirkcudbright as 'the Venice of Scotland.' Clearly, he never saw it with the tide out.

THE UNION CANAL
Linlithgow is a good place to discover the Union Canal, ideal for strolls along the tow-path. There is an impressive aqueduct about 3km to the west. Linlithgow has a canal museum and cruising opportunities. Enquire at weekends in summer.

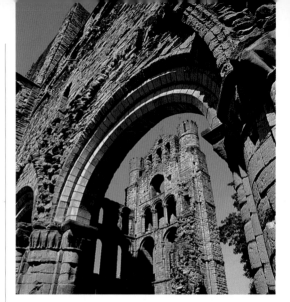

▶▶ Jedburgh 99D3

Jedburgh, on the A68, is a typical Borders town, with a history of tweed making. The local weavers were the first to combine two colours in their weave, thus inventing tweed. Even the Tourist Information Centre and car park are on the site of a former mill. The original woollen developments were centred round the activities of the monks in the Border abbeys, of which Jedburgh's is the best preserved.

The shell of the once great building of **Jedburgh Abbey**▶▶▶ still dominates the town skyline though it was destroyed by English forces during the 'rough wooing' (see page 30). The Abbey Visitor Centre makes an excellent introduction to the vanished monastic life of the Borders (*Open* Apr–Sep, daily 9.30–6; Oct–Mar, Mon–Sat 9.30–4, Sun 2–4. *Admission charge*). Also of note is Mary, Queen of Scots' House, a near-contemporary fortified or 'bastel' (like the French bastille) house, now a museum (*Open* Mar–Nov, Mon–Sat 10–5, Sun 12–4.30; Jun–Sep 10–4.30. *Admission charge*). The former prison on the site of the vanished castle (Castle Jail) was once a Georgian model prison but is now another museum. The town has further associations with Sir Walter Scott and Bonnie Prince Charlie.

▶▶ Kelso 99E3

When the writer H V Morton passed this way in the 1920s, he was struck by the appearance of the main square in Kelso. 'Surely I was in France! An enormous *grande place* paved with whinstone forms the heart of the town. Round it rise those tall, demure, many-storied houses…which seem to know almost as many stories as a concierge.' Little has changed except the traffic. Stroll from the square past the poignant fragment of **Kelso Abbey**, which was severely damaged by the Earl of Hertford's forces in 1545. All 112 inhabitants were slaughtered. The Tourist Information Centre is almost opposite. Rennie's handsome bridge of 1803 spans the Tweed moments further on. From the parapet there is a fine view to **Floors Castle▶** (*Open* Easter–Sep, daily 10–4. *Admission charge*), the largest inhabited house in Scotland. It offers glittering excesses of fine French furniture, porcelain, paintings and tapestries, as well as extensive parkland and walks.

Mellerstain House▶▶, a highly attractive Adam mansion with fine views, to the northwest of Kelso, has typically ornate Adam plasterwork and decoration and also beautiful terraced gardens (*Open* Easter, May–Sep, Sun–Fri 12.30–5. *Admission charge*).

▶▶▶ Kirkcudbright 98B1

Pronounced 'kir-*coo*-bree', Kirkcudbright has a typically spacious Galloway layout and its genteel, brightly painted Georgian streetscapes give it a dignified and harmonious air. The 16th-century **Maclellan's Castle** is a ruined turreted mansion conspicuous on the skyline and an exception to the prevailing 18th-century work (*Open* Apr–Sep, daily 9.30–6. *Admission charge*). There are a few antique shops to browse around, as well as the Harbour Gallery, though the main artistic connection is **Broughton House**, with its collection of the works of Edward Hornel (1864–1933) of the famed 'Glasgow Boys' (*Open* Apr–Oct, daily 1–5.30. *Admission charge*). The picturesque Tolbooth and mercat cross complete the harmonious groupings within this Solway town, which has one other pleasing feature: **The Stewartry Museum▶▶** is a traditional museum with no hi-tech fripperies (*Open* May, Mon–Sat 11–5; Jun and Sep, Mon–Sat 11–5, Sun 2–5; Jul and Aug, Mon–Sat 10–6, Sun 2–5; Oct–Apr, Mon–Sat 11–4. *Admission charge*). Visitors can discover the Dorothy L Sayers connection and find out why the founder of the American navy was once locked in the local tolbooth.

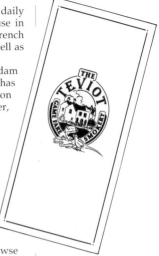

FIVE RED HERRINGS
The renowned detective novelist Dorothy L Sayers had two aunts and an uncle in Kirkcudbright. She used the local area as a setting for one of her Lord Peter Wimsey novels, *Five Red Herrings*, published in 1931. Another and more famous work set in Galloway – at least in part – is John Buchan's *The Thirty-Nine Steps* (published in 1915).

The Scottish Parliament met in 15th-century Linlithgow Palace on several occasions, most 'recently' in 1646

▶ Linlithgow Palace 98C4

Open: Apr–Sep, daily 9.30–6; Oct–Mar, Mon–Sat 9.30–4, Sun 2–4. Admission charge

Birthplace of Mary, Queen of Scots, this once magnificent royal palace is now a cold shell. It was burned, probably accidentally, during the last Jacobite rebellion in 1745. It is worth a diversion from the M90, and a visit can be combined with a look at nearby St Michael's Church.

98A1

A SEA-FISH POND

On the way to Logan Botanic Garden, it is possible to see the unusual feature of a sea-fish pond. Built originally in 1800 as a source of fresh fish for nearby Logan House, it contains tame cod which can be fed by hand. Curiously, the pond was damaged by a wartime mine.

A RECORD CLAIM

The Whithorn excavation team reconstructed a Viking Age house on the site of their dig for the benefit of visitors. It was built of poles and brush-wood and sadly it burned down. Seeking compensation through their insurers, the team made the first ever Viking Age insurance claim.

Logan Botanic Garden, where many species from the southern hemisphere enjoy some of Scotland's mildest air

►► Logan Botanic Garden

Open: Mar–Oct, daily 9.30–6. Admission charge

Galloway trumpets its prevailing mildness to persuade visitors to stay. Nowhere is the benign influence of the North Atlantic Drift more apparent than in Logan Botanic Garden. This specialist garden of the Royal Botanic Garden in Edinburgh specialises in tender plants which would not survive in other parts of Scotland. It has much success with the arrestingly exotic Australasian tree ferns, as well as cabbage palms and a whole range of temperamental southern hemisphere species.

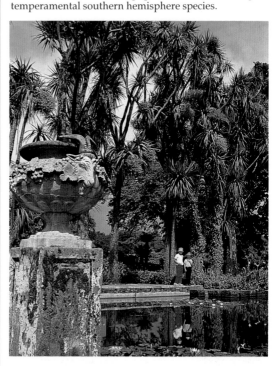

►► The Machars

98B1

Lush green is the key colour of the Machars, to which are added the black and white of cattle in the pasture and the yellow splash of gorse on the little rough hillocks. This is gentle, rolling countryside, with the big hills of Galloway receding to the north. A triangle lying between Wigtown Bay and Luce Bay, the Machars are sometimes overlooked by visitors but have a curious serenity. Perhaps this echoes their early religious links. Here, at Whithorn, not on the island of Iona, is the cradle of Christianity in Britain.

Whithorn Dig and Visitor Centre►► This archaeological attraction (*Open* Apr–Oct, daily 10.30–5, last tour 4.30. *Admission charge*) is on the site of the first Christian community in Scotland and displays material from AD 400 dug up on the site. The ruined Whithorn Priory and a museum are adjacent. Whithorn became a place of pilgrimage for the Scottish kings.

Whithorn is associated with St Ninian. His chapel on a grassy headland at Isle of Whithorn (not actually an island) is an anticlimax, though his cave makes a worthwhile walk down a lane and along the pebbly shore.

The town of Wigtown is also attractive, with a wide main true. It is associated with the drowning of two Covenanter martyrs, tied to a stake before the incoming tide in 1685. You can visit the site, down by the endless mud flats of the shore.

▶▶▶ Melrose   99D3

Melrose is a cosy, tweedy town that is almost too neat to be true. It has an abbey, romantically ruined in red sandstone, visible from the road. Next door, the National Trust for Scotland sells various gifts and dried flowers grown in Priorwood Garden (*Open* Apr–Sep, daily 9.30–6.30; Oct–Mar, Mon–Sat 9.30–4.30, Sun 2–4.30). There are plenty of gift and clothes shops. Melrose is overshadowed by the beautiful Eildon Hills where a stiff walk (starting across the golf course) offers outstanding views.

Trimontium Exhibition▶▶ This is a fascinating account of one of the Romans' main forts in Scotland, just a few fields away at Newstead (*Open* Apr–Oct, daily 10.30–4.30. Closed 12.30–1.30 on Sat, Sun. *Admission charge*). Alternatively there are a number of excursions from Melrose, including Dryburgh Abbey and Scott's View (see page 126).

A grim reminder of the Covenanters at Wigtown

The River Bladnoch as it reaches the sea near Wigtown; it rises high on the Galloway moors

▶ Moffat   98C2

The ram statue on the Colvin Fountain in the middle of the town square is a reminder of Moffat's origins in the wool trade, though it also had a reputation in the 18th century as a spa town. The woollen bargains at Moffat Weavers at the southern end of town are popular with tourists. Moffat is on the A701, a scenic route to Edinburgh known as 'the Beeftub road'. As well as the **Devil's Beeftub**, a hollow carved out by a glacier at the head of the valley, there are more glacial features to be seen up the Moffat Water by the A708. This passes the Grey Mare's Tail, a geologically classic waterfall pouring over the lip of a hanging valley. Hardy walkers can penetrate beyond the waterfall, either to circle round Loch Skeen or to reach the broad rounded summit of **White Coomb**, which at 822m is one of the highest hills in the Southern Uplands.

A CANNY LOCATION
Why did the Romans build their main fort at Trimontium? According to the Trimontium Exhibition in Melrose, when the legions came over the Cheviot, they made for the most conspicuous landmark, the triple-peaked Eildon Hills, instantly recognisable from any angle, and right in the centre of southern Scotland.

The South

AN AMERICAN CONNECTION
Arbigland Garden can be combined with a visit to Sweetheart Abbey. The garden is attractively sheltered by mature trees, and has a pleasantly tinkling burn, a Japanese Garden, poolside primulas and sea views. However, its claim to fame is its connection with John Paul Jones, the founder of the American navy. He was born in a cottage on the estate and worked in the gardens as a boy. A museum tells the story (*Open* May–Sep, Tue–Sun 2–6).

122

TOURIST INFORMATION
Lanark: Horsemarket, Ladyacre Road
(tel: 01555 661661).

Shambellie House Museum of Costume

The corn mill at New Abbey, which, along with a picturesque abbey and a museum of costume, make the village worth seeing

▶▶ **New Abbey**   *98C1*

New Abbey is a little village on the A710, dominated by the red ruins of **Sweetheart Abbey**. This religious seat was founded in 1273 by Devorgilla, wife of John Balliol. On his death she had his heart embalmed in an ivory and silver casket, an act recalled in the abbey's name. The abbey suffered from its proximity to the Border in the Wars of Independence. At the Reformation its riches were disposed of, and the building gradually deteriorated. Today, visitors can enjoy a peaceful stroll through the pointed Gothic ruins. The 18th-century **New Abbey Corn Mill**▶ is moments away from the abbey (*Open* abbey and mill Apr–Sep, daily 9.30–6; Oct–Mar, Mon–Wed and Sat 9.30–4, Thu 9.30–12, Sun 2–4. *Admission charge*). The great grinding stones, powered by water via an impressive set of gearing, produce oatmeal of various grades. Walk a bit further to reach the **Shambellie House Museum of Costume**, an outstation of the Royal Museum of Scotland. It shows material from the National Costume Collection (*Open* Apr–Oct, daily 11–5. *Admission charge*).

▶▶▶ **New Lanark and the Falls of Clyde**   *98C3*

The River Clyde seems a world away from its downstream industry here amid the farms and orchards of Lanarkshire, on the edge of the hills. It roars through a wooded gorge over spectacular waterfalls ('linns') in a setting unique in Scotland. This alone would be well worth the detour, but it is only one part of the experience. The river was harnessed to power cotton mills in an unusual experiment in workers' welfare. The model village of New Lanark has survived intact and there is a visitor centre within the mill complex (*Open* daily 11–5. *Admission charge*).

A remarkable industrial and social experiment, embodying the principles of welfare and worker care, took place in the upper reaches of the River Clyde in the late 18th and early 19th centuries. Two hundred years later, there is still a great deal to see.

In 1783 a successful Glasgow businessman, David Dale, bought this wooded bowl with its roaring river as a potential site for a spinning mill. Before the end of the century New Lanark had become the single largest industrial enterprise in Scotland. Some of the river's force was diverted, a little way downstream, to turn giant water-wheels which, with belts and drives, powered noisy cotton looms housed in vast mill buildings. In 1793, over 1,100 employees tended these machines, of whom 800 were young boys and girls.

Social benefits Dale the master was no despotic employer. Hours were long, but substantial housing was provided as well as educational facilities. Many of his child-workers were orphans who were, by the standards of the day, well fed and cared for. Another source of workers was Highland emigration: New Lanark employed people who would otherwise have headed for the New World because of repression and depressed economic conditions in their native lands to the north.

Robert Owen This Welshman was born in 1771 (32 years after Dale) and also made his way in the spinning industry. He had strong ideas about equality and social welfare. In 1799 he married David Dale's daughter. Along with two partners he then bought New Lanark and assumed management in 1800. Already embodying principles of welfare and worker care, the model village became the setting for Owen's own social experiments and even more benevolent management style.

After some business vicissitudes in the early years of the 19th century, Owen was able to put his principles into practice with new Quaker backers. To the four great mills and blocks of workers' houses were added the New Institute for the Formation of Character (1816) and Robert Owen's School (1817), as the first steps in the creation of his vision of a society without crime, poverty or misery – the fundamentals of 'Owenism'.

THE FALLS OF CLYDE
The linns which comprise the Falls of Clyde are in a delightful wooded river gorge and are well worth the walk upstream. (Go through the gap in the wall at the far end of the village.) Some of the water is diverted through tunnels to run a hydroelectric power station. When this is not operating, for example during station maintenance work, the falls are at their best.

Bell tower on New Buildings, New Lanark

Robert Owen, an entrepreneur of vision who transformed the banks of the Clyde at New Lanark with his model working village

TOURIST INFORMATION
Newton Stewart (Apr–Oct):
Dashwood Square (tel:
01671 402431).
Peebles: High Street
(tel: 01721 720138).

NO CARE FOR TREES
Neidpath Castle eventually came into the hands of the Douglas Earls of March. The 3rd Earl inherited it but cared little for this country property, instead leading a spendthrift life in London. He even sold for timber a fine stand of ornamental trees planted by his father and grandfather. This vandalism was subsequently condemned by William Wordsworth's *Sonnet Composed at Neidpath Castle*: 'Degenerate Douglas! oh the unworthy Lord!'

Traditional ironmongers, Peebles

▶ Newton Stewart   98B1

A kind of gateway between the Machars and the Galloway Forest Park, Newton Stewart has a good range of shops (including antiques). Near by, the Wood of Cree is a Royal Society for the Protection of Birds nature reserve, the largest oak wood in the southwest. Species include several summer warblers, plus dippers and grey wagtails. The scenically outstanding Glen Trool road (see page 114) is easily reached from the town.

▶▶ North Berwick   99D4

Within easy commuting range of Edinburgh, North Berwick has developed from a small fishing port into a holiday resort. Its little harbour is jammed with pleasure craft, its harbourfront granary is converted to flats, and its fine quality Victorian and Edwardian architecture likewise suggest prosperity. The golf course reaches almost to the town centre. Behind the town is the conspicuous cone of the North **Berwick Law**, a 187m high volcanic plug. Views from the top are excellent and take in the Bell Rock Lighthouse, off Arbroath in Angus. North Berwick gives easy access to some fine coastline, notably westwards along the sands towards Yellowcraigs (see page 111). East of the town, on the way to Tantallon, is another fine beach at Seacliff. Other nearby attractions include the historic aircraft collection at the **Museum of Flight** at East Fortune (*Open* Jul–Aug, daily 10.15–6.15; mid-Mar–Jun and Sep–mid-Nov, daily 10.30–5; mid-Nov–mid-Mar, Mon–Fri 11–3. *Admission charge*. Free in winter).

Tantallon Castle▶▶▶ This 14th-century former Douglas stronghold straddles a headland, a grim fortified wall of eroded red sandstone, with the Bass Rock as a backdrop (*Open* Apr–Sep, daily 9.30–6; Oct–Mar, Mon–Wed and Sat 9.30–4, Thu 9.30–12, Sun 2–4. *Admission charge*).

▶▶ Peebles   99D3

Respectable, well-scrubbed Peebles is well within day-trip range of Edinburgh and is accordingly busy throughout

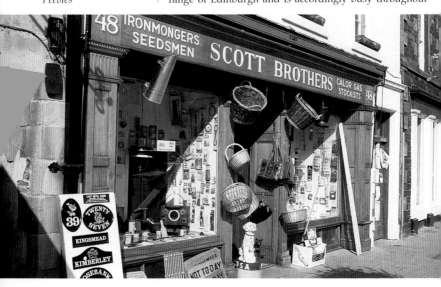

the year. There is a good choice of shops for antiques and fashions, and probably the best old-fashioned ironmonger in Scotland. The town was the birthplace of William and Robert Chambers, of *Chambers Dictionaries* fame. After making their fortune in Edinburgh, they endowed their home town with the impressive municipal buildings on the main street, now housing a library and museum.

Neidpath Castle▶▶ (*Open* Easter–Sep, Mon–Sat 11–5, Sun 1–5. *Admission charge*). A few minutes west of the town, this stronghold can be reached on foot along the River Tweed as a pleasant alternative to going by car. An L-plan tower house, originally built by the Hayes family, Neidpath has survived remarkably intact. It was 'modernised' for comfort in the 17th century, though retaining its medieval outward appearance, but fell into decay by the early 19th century. It was restored by the present owners, the Earls of Wemyss.

▶▶ Rosslyn Chapel   99D3

Open: Mon–Sat 10–5, Sun 12–4.45. Admission charge

The finest example of medieval stone carving in Scotland (if not Britain) can be found a few minutes' stroll beyond the former mining village of Roslin. Perched above the wooded Roslin Glen, Rosslyn Chapel was founded in 1446 by William Sinclair, 3rd Earl of Orkney. The church, still used as a place of worship, is really only the choir of a much larger design which was never completed. It is associated with Scott's romantic poem The Lay of the Last Minstrel. There are fine wooded walks from the site, with both Rosslyn Castle and Hawthornden (both private) hidden in the glen below.

'Maude' (former Class J36) at Bo'ness

LITERARY VISITORS
Rosslyn Inn (now a private house), adjacent to the Chapel, was the main lodging for many famous folk who came to see the wonders of the place. The Wordsworths stayed there, leaving very early to visit Sir Walter Scott at his first marital home at nearby Lasswade (the Scotts were still in bed when they arrived). Before that, Robert Burns stayed, and Dr Samuel Johnson and James Boswell took lunch and tea there, on their way back from their Hebridean tour.

A branch line – re-created

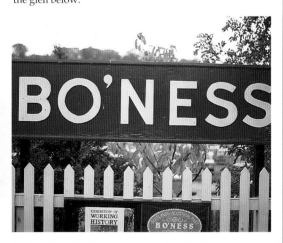

▶ Scottish Railway Preservation Society (Bo'ness and Kinneil Railway)   98C4

Open: Jul–Aug, Tue–Sun 10.30–4.30 (6 trains). Apr–Jun and Sep–mid-Oct, Sat–Sun 11.20–4.30 (5 trains). Admission charge

At Bo'ness on the Forth, a typical Scottish branch line has been re-created, offering a 6km trip uphill to Birkhill (with extensions likely) where a former clay mine can be visited. It captures the feel of a vanished age and could be tied in with a trip to Linlithgow.

BASS ROCK BIRDS
The gannet's Latin name, *Sula bassana*, recalls its long association with the Bass Rock. Gannets occupy about 14,000 nest sites on the Bass. There are smaller numbers of kittiwakes, guillemots, razorbills and puffins. Boat trips go from North Berwick.

Drive

Border views and abbeys

Smailholm Tower for Border views

The river valleys and rounded hills of the Borders make rewarding country for touring. This route is 64km, easily driven in a day if no diversions are taken.

Take the A68 north from Jedburgh, then the B6400 east. The unmistakable high tower of the **Waterloo Monument** on an ancient earthwork was raised in 1815 on the instructions of William Kerr, 6th Marquis of Lothian.

Continue past the modern village of Roxburgh, to reach **Kelso** with its ruined abbey.

Take the B6364 northward and soon you will see a dark square of battlements rising ahead. Take a minor road to Hume. Built by Lord Hume in the 1790s on the site of the original **Hume Castle**, the site offers one of Scotland's best views.

Travel west to cross the A6089 at a staggered crossroads for the view from **Smailholm Tower**, a 16th-century fortified border keep associated with Sir Walter Scott. Then drop gently down westwards to find signs for the peaceful riverside **Dryburgh Abbey**.

Scott's View, Scott's favourite viewpoint for the Eildon Hills, is signposted. The minor road leads to the A68 and Melrose, with its abbey. Detour to Selkirk, or return to Jedburgh on the A68.

▶ Scottish Mining Museum   99D3

Open: Mar–Oct, daily 10–4. Admission charge

The former Lady Victoria Colliery is in the former mining village of Newtongrange, at one time the largest of its kind in Scotland. Pit and village were under the sway of domineering pit managers, a story told by tableaux which follow the career of a typical miner. There is also an impressive steam winding engine. Industrial heritage enthusiasts can also take a coal trail down to Prestongrange on the coast near Musselburgh where there are other mining artefacts.

▶▶ Selkirk   99D3

Sir Walter Scott presided as sheriff in Selkirk, and his **Courtroom** (*Open* Apr–Sep, Mon–Sat 10–4, also Sun 2–4 from Jun–Aug; Oct, Mon–Sat 10–5, Sun 2–4; Jul–Aug, daily 10–6. *Admission charge*) tells of his life, writings and time spent as a judge. **Halliwell's House▶▶** is now an interesting museum. Ask to see the excellent videos about the Common Ridings (*Open* Apr–Jun and Sep–Oct, Mon–Sat 10–5, Sun 2–4; Jul–Aug, daily 10–6. *Admission free*). **Abbotsford House** is nearby (see page 102).

▶ South Queensferry   98C4

South Queensferry makes a pleasant evening excursion from Edinburgh to view the great bridges both upriver and down. Alternatively, tie it in with a day visit to **Hopetoun House▶** to the west, where architects William and John Adam created a spectacular mansion that is now filled with valuables (*Open* Apr–Sep, daily 10–5.30, last entry 4.30. *Admission charge*). Also near by is **Dalmeny House**, where porcelain from the Rothschild Mentmore collection is among the impressive range of items on display (*Open* Jul–early Sep, Sun 1–5.30, last entry 4.45. *Admission charge*).

QUEEN MARGARET
The queen in the name South (or North) Queensferry refers to Queen (and Saint) Margaret, the Saxon wife of the uncouth King Malcolm. She is associated with the ancient ferry-crossing here, which connected the old capital at Dunfermline with the Lothians.

TOURIST INFORMATION
Selkirk (Apr–Oct): Halliwell's House (tel: 01750 20054).

127

A vanished way of life at Newtongrange

AN EARLY FORTH BRIDGE DESIGN
Commenting on the flimsiness of an 1818 design for a chain bridge across the mighty Forth near South Queensferry, a later Victorian engineer noted 'it would hardly have been visible on a dull day and after a heavy gale it would no longer be seen on a clear day either'.

'King Coal', now a museum within easy reach of Edinburgh

The estuary of the Forth was the last great challenge of the Victorian railway age. In 1873 the railway companies of the east coast trunk route oversaw the laying of a foundation stone for a Forth Bridge designed by Sir Thomas Bouch. But then the Tay Bridge – which he had designed – fell, and his plans for the Forth were abandoned.

MAINTENANCE COSTS
The phrase 'painting the Forth bridge' has passed into common usage to describe a never-ending job. The painting area has been estimated as 59 hectares and 31,800 litres of Forth Bridge oxide of iron brushing paint are needed to coat it from end to end. Originally, many of the bridge painters were ex-sailing ship crew, accustomed to shinning up and down holding only a rope. Today, hydraulic lifts and cradles are used.

A new Forth design was supplied by Benjamin Baker of the engineering company Fowler and Baker. This was based on the cantilever principle, invented in the Far East, and used steel instead of the treacherous cast iron of the first Tay Bridge. The contract for the work was signed in 1882, with William Arrol as the main contractor.

Building progress The next four years were taken up with building the coffer dams, sinking the caissons (watertight chambers used for laying foundations underwater) and building the piers on which the immense weight of steel would rest. The superstructure was built in the following four years. While the first Tay Bridge has sometimes been described as an optimist's bridge, the Forth is a pessimist's bridge. The engineers were all too aware of the effects of lateral wind pressure, which had been the downfall of the Tay design. Exhaustive scale-model tests were carried out and all the various calculations were based on a 'worst-case scenario' – the freakish situation in which a hurricane blew its way up one side of the Forth and down the other.

Facts and figures The bridge cost 57 lives during construction before it was opened in March 1890 – and still proves an endless source of astonishing statistics, not the least curious of which is the fact that the bridge is almost a metre longer on a hot summer day than in midwinter. It consumed 54,860 tonnes of steel, 148,300 cubic metres of granite (on the approach viaducts), 21,330 tonnes of cement and almost seven million rivets. The last one was banged into place by the Prince of Wales at a spot marked by a plaque. It was the monument of the age.

The Forth Bridge, impressive from every angle

▶▶▶ St Abbs   99E4

The great seabird colonies of northern Scotland, particularly Shetland, are justly famous. But there is one place in southern Scotland where, for very little effort, in May and June in particular, a spectacular 'bird city' can be seen which rivals anything the north can offer. The cliffs and stacks of St Abbs Head are favoured by 10,000 guillemots alone. This portly, penguin-like auk is just one of the many species that make the experience a cacophony of noise, and, not least, smell (a distinctly fishy one). Razorbills, fulmars and kittiwakes add to the din. The cliffs can be viewed with relative ease, as some of them are offshore stacks. If time permits, walk the whole length of the path from the Northfield Farm car park to the lighthouse, starting at the eastern end to walk anticlockwise round the reserve. There are magnificent sea views all the way, with the biggest seabird colonies bursting into view by the lighthouse itself. Birdwatchers haunt the spot at autumn migration time as well. There are lots of rare birds – ask the warden for details.

BIRD SPECIES
St Abbs Head specialities in autumn migration include sooty and manx shearwaters and arctic and great skuas. Summertime sees plenty of gannets going to and from the Bass Rock breeding grounds near North Berwick.

EARLY CHARITY
In the early 19th century, the Wanlockhead proprietor, the Duke of Buccleuch and Queensberry (owner of Drumlanrig Castle), passed through and gave £5 to the miners to drink his health. Instead they 'considered they should testify their respect and gratitude by making the £5 the commencement of a charitable fund for the relief of miners when sick, or rendered unfit for work by age, as also for the benefit of their widows'. Whether or not this gave the duke food for thought is not recorded.

129

St Abbs, where clear waters and a diverse underwater flora create a Mecca for divers

▶ Wanlockhead   98C2

Wanlockhead is Scotland's highest village, though it is a considerable distance from the Highlands. It stands amongst the bald, bleak domes of the Lowther Hills, a strange, almost claustrophobic, gathering of steep-sided glaciated bumps buffering Strathclyde and Galloway. The Lowthers are cut by impressive road passes, notably the Dalveen and the Mennock, the latter leading to Wanlockhead and its neighbour, Leadhills.

Britain's most important non-ferrous metal mining area used to be there, in the endless winds and open moors. Gold was found in the reign of King James IV, but lead made fortunes for local landowners. The mine closed in the 1930s, a story told in the **Museum of the Scottish Lead Mining Industry** (*Open* Apr–Oct, daily 11–4.30, last tour 4; Nov–Mar, by appointment. *Admission charge*). There are several other historical threads to follow, ranging from the vanished branch line, once Britain's highest railway, to the Covenanters, whose strongholds were here.

Gulls on offshore rocks, St Abbs

Central Scotland

130

Nicoll Moncrief's gratitude seems to be as much to King James (VI of Scotland, I of England) as to God. This carving is in the village of Falkland

A MEETING OF TWO CULTURES This region has two distinct characters because it bridges the Highland Line, or, more accurately, the Highland Boundary Fault. This is not just a geological distinction but a real divide between two cultures, Highland and Lowland, separated by a mountain barrier and, formerly, also by language and traditions.

It was in the Highland part of Central Scotland that the cult of the picturesque first took root. From the cities of the central belt, the first tourists admired the beauties of the Trossachs and Loch Lomond – not just because they were attractive, but also because they were the first bit of wild Scotland that was accessible from the Lowlands. This led to the growth of resort towns which still cater for visitors today: places such as Callander, Crieff, Dunkeld and Pitlochry, all of which have long-established reputations as holiday spots in or near the Highlands.

The feeling of entering or leaving different cultures is an important element in the Central Scottish 'experience'. Ben Ledi looms at the end of Callander's main street as a reminder that there is real grandeur beyond the cut-price woollen mill sales. At Dunkeld, there is a strong sense of passing between the Highland portals. Alternatively, drive up any of the Angus Glens – or follow back roads beyond Alyth – for a full flavour of the openness in the silent, rounded hills of the Grampian edge. From the unexpected drama of the Reekie Linn waterfall near Kirriemuir, Scotland's mini-Niagara smoking its way

Central Scotland

ROMANTIC PROSPECTS
Though Sir Walter Scott is often said to have put the Trossachs on the tourist map, he was certainly not the first to discover them. As early as 1794 the Statistical Account of Scotland noted under the heading 'Romantic Prospects' that 'The Trossachs are often visited by persons of taste, who are desirous of seeing nature in her rudest and most unpolished state'.

THE HEART OF SCOTLAND
Breadalbane is an ancient name for the heart of Scotland in central Perthshire. Crianlarich, Killin and, further east, Aberfeldy, with all the high hills around, are considered to be within it. The name is derived from two Gaelic words: *braghaid*, the upper part, and *Alban*, Scotland, hence Breadalbane means 'the uplands of Alban', an appropriate enough name for this wild country.

VIEWING THE FAULT LINE
Perhaps the best vantage point for viewing the Highland Boundary Fault is from the top of Conic Hill behind Balmaha on the shores of Loch Lomond. The climb can be made along part of the West Highland Way. From the hilltop, the fault line runs out and through the main Loch Lomond islands to the west, while it disappears eastwards towards Callander. The pink and pebbly conglomerate rock is characteristic of the geology of the edge of the Highlands.

over a high ledge, to the heights of Ben Lawers, Central Scotland's much trampled-upon highest mountain, scenic drama can be found in plenty.

Yet Central Scotland is not without a very attractive Lowland character. Northeast Fife, with its long beaches backed by finely trimmed golf courses, seems a long way both from the Highlands and the legacy of the Industrial Revolution. This portion of Fife missed out on the effects of industry, so plain in other parts of the Lowlands. Instead, it kept its essentially rural character. Its European heritage from its early trading links with the Low Countries is seen today in architecture, especially on the coast. Thus St Andrews and the East Neuk of Fife have very distinct personalities, being Scottish without being either tartan or grimy. Angus is almost wholly rural, though here the Grampian hills are always a backdrop, forming one side of Strathmore, the long rural corridor which leads northeastwards from Perth up to the Mearns on the edge of the old county of Kincardineshire.

Central Scotland's industrial background includes linoleum at Kirkcaldy, Dunfermline's specialised damask ware and also industries based on the city of Dundee, still noted for its jam and journalism. Brewing is still associated with Alloa in the old county of Clackmannan below the Ochil Hills. Perhaps the most interesting chunk of industrial heritage can be found at Culross overlooking the Forth, where a small Scottish burgh seemed to be passed over by progress for more than two centuries until restoration.

Just as the shipyard workers of the industrial Glasgow of old would escape at weekends to the mountainous beauty of the Trossachs and the millworkers of Dundee would go northwest to the long Angus glens, so it is still the hills and mountains which inevitably call to visitors today. To take in the essence of Central Scotland, find a high point near the Highland edge: Callander Crags behind Callander, the highest section of the Duke's Road in the Trossachs, Dumyat (pronounced 'De-*my*-att') behind Stirling, the delectable Duncryne Hill on the southern edge of Loch Lomond, or the Caterthun hillforts on a Grampian shoulder in Angus. Northwards, waves of hills roll on to the end of Scotland. Southwards is all the grit and liveliness of the Lowland towns. That is the essence of Central Scotland.

The Tay Valley in Perthshire. The river begins life in Loch Tay and reaches the sea at Dundee

THE SIGNAL TOWER
The Bell Rock lighthouse by Robert Stevenson was built on the Inchcape Rock, a reef submerged at high tide, about 18km southeast of Arbroath. It was first lit in 1811 and was a magnificent achievement for its day. To facilitate rock to shore communication when the lighthouse was under construction, a signal tower was built, which was also the shore base for the light. This is today's Signal Tower Museum where the story is told in full.

▶▶ Aberfeldy
130B2

The largest settlement in the area known as Breadalbane, Aberfeldy is a pleasantly peaceful place. It makes a good centre for exploring the local walks and trails, notably along the Moness Burn to view the '**Birks of Aberfeldy**' in the wooded den. These birchwoods were made famous by Robert Burns who penned the lyrics of the Scottish song of the same name. Aberfeldy itself has a watermill and a distillery to visit. **Castle Menzies** is near by to the northwest on the B846 (*Open* Apr–mid-Oct, Mon–Sat 10.30–5, Sun 2–5, last entry 4.30. *Admission charge*). This 16th-century, fortified Z-plan tower is in the care of the Clan Menzies. To reach it by road means crossing the River Tay by the finest of General Wade's bridges (see panel). This handsome, five-arched, hump-backed structure was designed by the architect William Adam and built in 1733.

▶ Arbroath
131D2

A salty, seagull-strafed, seacoast town, Arbroath in Angus gave its name to the Arbroath smokie, a smoked, split haddock. Smokies can be bought from several

Blair Castle

WADE'S BRIDGES
General Wade, the military road builder, built many fine bridges in Scotland, but none were so grand as his work at Aberfeldy. It was not to everyone's taste. Dorothy Wordsworth toured with her brother William in 1803 and, among many carping comments on things Scottish in her journal, she described how the party 'crossed the Tay by a bridge of ambitious and ugly architecture. Many of the bridges in Scotland are so...'

merchants in the narrow streets of the 'fishing quarter'. Arbroath mixes its fishing activities with the slightly time-warped air of a 1950s traditional Scottish holiday resort. There is very fine coastline to explore north of the town, as well as the hinterland of Angus within easy reach. In the centre of the town stand the red sandstone walls of the 12th-century **Arbroath Abbey**▶ (*Open* Apr–Sep, daily 9.30–6; Oct–Mar, Mon–Sat 9.30–4, Sun 2–4. *Admission charge*), scene of important events in Scotland's history (see panel). Other aspects of the town's history are portrayed in the curious **Signal Tower Museum**▶, close to the harbour. By way of a change from maritime themes, the museum has a display on one of Arbroath's specialist industries: the manufacture of lawnmowers (*Open* May–Sep, Mon–Sat 10–5; also Sun 2–5 Jul and Aug. *Admission free*). Contributing to the town's holiday air is **Kerr's Miniature Railway**▶▶. This ride-on track, running parallel to the high embankment of the adjacent main Edinburgh-Aberdeen railway, has delighted generations, as photographs on the entrance kiosk reveal (*Open* Easter–Sep, Sat–Sun 2–5; also Mon–Fri 2–5 in Jul–mid-Aug. *Admission charge*).

▶ **Balquhidder** *130B2*

The Braes (slopes) of Balquhidder and Balquhidder Glen, in which lie the long reaches of Loch Voil, are often missed by those rushing north on the A84 from Callander. Once a place in which desperate men from broken clans chose to settle – though it was also the stronghold of the MacLarens and the Macgregors – the area around Balquhidder has glorious scenery which is worth exploring. Many people visit the **grave of Rob Roy** (see pages 137 and 161) in Balquhidder kirkyard, something of an anticlimax, while others make their way to the end of the public road, in order to climb the choice of **Munros** (see panel, page 149 for definition) within easy reach. Another worthwhile walk is to hike up through the trees to the windy heights of Kirkton Glen (start by the church) where the little jewel of **Lochan nan Eireannaich** (Loch of the Irish) sits below the crags of an old hill pass to Glen Dochart. Listen for the ring ouzel (the mountain blackbird) which sings here in summer.

▶ **Blair Atholl and Blair Castle** *130B3*

Blair Atholl is famed chiefly for **Blair Castle**▶ ▶ whose white-painted turrets are conspicuous from the A9. The old established settlement that grew up near the castle also has a mill and a folk museum to visit. Blair Castle itself (*Open* Apr–late Oct, daily 10–6, last entry 5. *Admission charge*), the ancestral seat of the earls then the dukes of Atholl, dates from at least 1269. There are many stories associated with it, in particular its role in the Jacobite rebellion of 1745, and many rooms filled with furniture and artefacts accumulated over the centuries. It is the archetypal Scottish castle, though you may tire of hearing that the Duke of Atholl was the only person in Britain allowed to keep a private army.

135

THE DECLARATION OF ARBROATH
In the Scots Wars of Independence, the country's leading churchmen were firmly nationalist. In 1320 they met in Arbroath Abbey to write a famous document in Scotland's story, the Declaration of Arbroath. Its most widely quoted passage is: 'For so long as a hundred of us shall remain alive we shall never accept subjection to the domination of the English. For we fight not for glory, or riches or honour, but for freedom alone which no good man will consent to lose but with his life.'

TOURIST INFORMATION
Aberfeldy: The Square (tel: 01887 820276).
Arbroath: Market Place (tel: 01241 872609).

THE FALLS OF BRUAR
North of Blair Castle, accessible from the old A9, these falls are within the extensive landholding of the Blair Charitable Trust. Robert Burns visited on his Highland tour and suggested to the Duke of Atholl that he might plant more trees to create even more beauty around the falls. The suggestion was taken up and the falls today are noted for their mature larch trees.

Near Aberfeldy: fishing the River Tay, and Castle Menzies (detail)

THE BRACKLINN FALLS

For a wager, Sir Walter Scott once rode a pony across the rickety old bridge that spanned the gorge below the Bracklinn Falls. Today's bridge is more substantial, but take care with children on the slippery rocks and tree roots near the edge of the gorge, beyond the bridge.

TOURIST INFORMATION

Blairgowrie: 26 Wellmeadow (tel: 01250 872960).
Callander (Mar–Dec): Rob Roy & Trossachs Visitor Centre, Ancaster Square (tel: 01877 330342).

SOFT FRUITS

Around Blairgowrie and up into Strathmore is the largest soft fruit growing area in the EU. Raspberries, tayberries, loganberries and strawberries thrive in the balance of sunshine and moisture.

▶ Blairgowrie   131C2

A busy centre with a good range of shops, Blairgowrie first prospered from the River Ericht as it powered its way out of the Highlands. Flax mills were built on its bank and by the early 19th century the town was booming. A second wave of prosperity followed after raspberry growing on a commercial scale was introduced. Today, the crop is still important, with the long rows of raspberry canes in the surrounding fields looking a little like vineyards.

The old **Keathbank Mill▶ ▶** (on the north side of town off the A93) has been converted into a visitor centre. The water wheel and machinery still turn to impress visitors with their awesome scale. Also on display is the largest model railway in Britain – a complete 'O-gauge' model of Norton Fitzwarren junction on the old Great Western Railway. There is a heraldry workshop, too, carving huge coats of arms. (*Open* Easter, May–Oct, daily 10–5. *Admission charge*).

En route to the town, the A93 is bordered for 530m just beyond the River Isla by the 30m high **Meikleour Beech Hedge**.

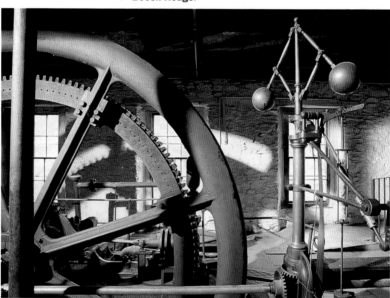

Keathbank Mill

▶ ▶ Callander   130B1

Right on the Highland edge, with Ben Ledi looming at the end of the main street, Callander seems busy throughout the year. The town's bustle is a reminder of its role as a gateway not just to the Highlands but specifically to the Trossachs. The old village of Callander was rebuilt and extended after 1763, when the authorities took over the land of the Drummonds, the previous owners who forfeited them after the 1745 Jacobite rebellion. It is an example of early town planning, and soon Callander took on its role of servicing visitors, which it has had ever since. Escape from the tartan wares of the shopping street to discover picturesque **Bracklinn Falls▶ ▶**, signposted from the

Walk

The Bracklinn Falls

Only minutes from Callander's busy main street lies an escape on the very edge of the Highlands. Allow one hour to the Falls, or three hours for the Callander Crags circuit.

The Bracklinn Falls are signed north (right if coming from Stirling) up a street near the Roman Camp Hotel sign. If travelling by car, drive up this road, soon entering attractive mixed woodland for a short way until the Falls car park is seen on the right.

Take the level path running east from the parking area. Soon the pines flanking the path end to reveal to a pleasing green prospect back across the Lowlands. Continue through a double kissing gate, with the falls sounding close at hand. Descend steps to a bridge over the white water. The path peters out on the far side, amongst the oak trees.

Retrace your steps. The energetic can walk uphill along the road from the car park, into open country with views north of an attractive glen. It is possible to circle back to Callander via the Callander Crags on the skyline, but you will need a stout pair of walking shoes.

east side of the town (see the walk above). Slightly more demanding (for pedestrians) are the **Callander Crags►►**, overlooking a dense bowl of woodland immediately behind the town and threaded by sheltered paths. Waterfall and woodland can be combined in a single excursion by penetrating further up the signposted road into an attractive Highland glen.

Rob Roy and the Trossachs Visitor Centre►► This modern tourist orientation centre interprets the life of Rob Roy Macgregor, Scotland's Robin Hood, by means of audio-visuals and fairly hi-tech displays (including a talking cow). It also sets the folk hero firmly in the Trossachs landscapes (see page 160) (*Open* Jul–Aug, daily 9–7; Jun and Sep, daily 9.30–6; Mar–May and Oct–Dec, daily 10–5; Jan and Feb, weekends 10–4. *Admission charge*).

►► The Caterthuns 131D3
These 2,000-year-old ramparts are Scotland's prehistory at its best. To stand in the centre of a great ring of broken stone with only a curlew call for company is certainly atmospheric. It is well worth the effort of seeking out this breezy high place on the shoulders of the Grampians near Edzell in Angus, with superb views to the Lowlands. The builders of the White and Brown Catherthun hillforts must have been capable of organising manpower in plenty to quarry and build such defences, impressive even in ruin.

Callander's Rob Roy and the Trossachs Visitor Centre makes good use of a redundant church

Crieff Visitors' Centre, paperweights

138

EARLY INDUSTRY
Throughout the 17th century, Culross was the sole maker of baking girdles (griddles). It is said the local smiths invented them after King Robert the Bruce ordered them to provide iron plates so that his soldiers could cook their oatcakes.

The Palace, Culross

▶▶ Crieff   *130B2*

A town at the edge of the Highlands, Crieff seems all hills. Until 1770 it was an important cattle market. It has also been a spa. Down by the River Earn on the A822, is **The Crieff Visitor Centre▶** offering on-site manufacture and sale of pottery and glass paperweights (*Open* daily 9–5.30, restricted winter hours. *Admission free*, factory tour charge). Opposite is **Stuart Crystal▶** with Stuart, Waterford and Wedgwood wares (*Open* Jun–Sep, daily 9–6.30; Oct–May, Mon–Sat 9–5, Sun 11–5. *Admission free*). Just down the road is the sunken Italian garden of **Drummond Castle▶**, with formal terracing ideal for strolls (*Open* Easter, May–Oct, daily 2–6, last entry 5. *Admission charge*). North of the town the **Glenturret Distillery▶▶**, one of Scotland's oldest, offers a tour, audio-visual programme and shop (*Open* Mar–Dec, Mon–Sat 9.30–6, Sun 12–6; Jan–Feb, Mon–Fri 11.30–4, last tour 2.30. *Admission charge*; free in Jan).

▶▶▶ Culross   *130B1*

Because of its very early involvement in coal mining and salt pans, Culross ought to have been just another nondescript industrial community on the banks of the Forth. Instead, after the town's early economic prosperity, the Industrial Revolution bypassed the town for a variety of economic reasons, and it was all but forgotten. Thus Culross entered the 20th century with many 17th- and 18th-century domestic buildings intact. The streetscapes have been preserved and the attractive dwellings, with their red pantiled roofs, restored. Cobbled streets and the old mercat cross give the place the air of a film set (which it is on occasion), but this is a lived-in community. There are some interiors to see, notably the Culross **Palace** (really the town house) of Sir George Bruce, Culross's 16th-century entrepreneur (*Open* palace Apr–Sep, daily 11–5, last entry 4; study and town house Apr–Sep, daily 1.30–5; Oct, weekends 11–5. *Admission charge*).

▶ **Cupar**   *131C2*

Cupar is a handsome enough, typical Lowland Scottish town in the centre of a rural and agricultural area, the Howe (hollow) of Fife. Cupar once made money with its linen manufacture and still maintains its role as the administrative headquarters of the old county of Fife. A network of pleasantly out-of-the-way rural roads includes a fine ridge route to Falkland (see page 145). It is also worth visiting Hill of **Tarvit House**▶▶, an Edwardian mansion (*Open* house Easter, May–Sep, daily 1.30–5.30; Oct, weekends only; gardens Apr–Oct, daily 9.30–9. Nov–Mar, 9.30–4.30. *Admission charge*).

▶▶ **Deep Sea World**   *131C1*

Open: Apr–Jun and Sep–Oct, daily 10–6; Jul–Aug, daily 10–6.30; Nov–Mar, Mon–Fri 11–5, Sat–Sun 10–6. Admission charge

In this visitor centre in North Queensferry, a moving walkway carries you unnervingly along an underwater transparent viewing tunnel where sharks swim by. This is probably as close as you will ever get to knowing how a fish feels in an aquarium. There are also coral reef displays, rock pools to fumble in and a variety of other marine exhibits.

▶▶ **Doune**   *130B1*

Doune was once the Scottish centre for manufacturing pistols. Today this little place with winding streets is chiefly visited by those going to **Doune Castle**▶▶▶, the finest surviving medieval castle in Scotland (*Open* Apr–Sep, daily 9.30–6; Oct–Mar, Mon–Wed and Sat 9.30–4, Thu 9.30–12, Sun 2–4. *Admission charge*). The 14th-century fortress is built to a simple and strong plan: a formidable range of buildings surrounding an inner courtyard. Note the security features, such as a separate stairway for each main hallway and the duke's bedroom's emergency exit. As well as allowing the main quarters to be sealed off if intruders gained the courtyard, the design acknowledges the need for some comfort: the guest bedrooms are built directly above the kitchen, with its 5.5m wide fireplace.

DROVE ROADS
The Crieff tryst or cattle market was an important affair in the days when the Highland black cattle were walked from their pastures in various parts of Scotland to an annual autumn fair. Throughout the north there was a network of 'drove roads' used by the cattle drovers. These old ways through the glens flowed together like tributaries and converged on major markets such as Crieff. The trade ended when railways arrived and could move stock more quickly.

Doune Motor Museum houses the world's second oldest Rolls Royce

THE DOUNE MOTOR MUSEUM
If you thought a MacPherson Strut was a kind of Highland fling, then a visit to one of Doune's attractions will clarify matters. The Doune Motor Museum is essentially the private collection of car enthusiast the Earl of Moray. The 40-odd vehicles in this custom-built museum include the second oldest surviving Rolls Royce (*Open* Apr–Nov, daily 10–5. Admission charge).

TOURIST INFORMATION
Crief: Town Hall, High Street (tel: 01764 650578)
Dunblane (May–Sep): Stirling Road (tel: 01786 824428).
Dundee: 4 City Square (tel: 01382 4346640).

AN ANCIENT WALK
The Darn Road is an ancient route (used by the Romans) which links Dunblane with Bridge of Allan for foot traffic. It makes a pleasant afternoon's walk. On the way, the path passes a cave overlooking the Allan Water, which is associated with Robert Louis Stevenson. He used to holiday nearby as a boy.

Though now surrounded by the urban development of Dundee, Claypotts Castle is one of the most complete examples of a 16th-century Z-plan tower house

▶ Dumbarton   130A1

This town on the Clyde estuary is associated with ship-building, but is worth visiting for two very different features. The first of these, **Dumbarton Castle▶** (*Open* Apr–Sep, daily 9.30–6; Oct–Mar, Mon–Wed and Sat 9.30–4, Thu 9.30–12, Sun 2–4. *Admission charge*), is built on the natural defensive site of Dumbarton Rock, a volcanic plug. Though little remains from its early pre-Viking defensive days, the fortress is associated with Mary, Queen of Scots. She was held there in safety before her departure for France at the age of five. The **Denny Ship Model Experiment Tank▶▶** was the world's first commercial experimental tank for shipbuilders' scale-models, built in 1882 by the local builders William Denny. The hulls of many famous vessels were designed and tested here, including P & O's *Canberra* (*Open* Mon–Sat 10–4. *Admission charge*).

▶ Dunblane   130B1

The little city of Dunblane on the Allan Water has winding streets and little shops and, thanks to a bypass, is a peaceful kind of place, especially around the **Cathedral▶▶**. The seat of the Bishop of the Diocese of Dunblane since the 13th century, this place of worship is the usual Scottish mix of very early architecture and more recent restoration work. (The nave was roofless for 300 years until 1893.) It demands a slow walk round to examine the 15th-century misericords, early effigies and other points of interest (*Open* Apr–Sep, daily 9.30–6; Oct–Mar, Mon–Sat 9.30–4, Sun 2–4 and for services. *Admission free*). **Doune Castle** (see page 139) is a few minutes to the west.

▶ Dundee   131C2

Dundee sits on slopes facing south over the estuary of the River Tay, which is spanned by road and rail bridges. Its centre is an uneasy mix of Victorian edifices, slashed by new roads and partly overshadowed by a covered mall. Scotland's fourth city promotes itself under the banner 'City of Discovery'. The 'Discovery' part of its slogan is a reference to RRS (Royal Research Ship) *Discovery▶▶*, berthed permanently at the Discovery Point floating

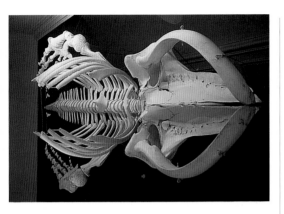

The great Tay whale in Dundee's Barrack Street Museum

THE DOGGEREL POET
William McGonagall, the Scottish doggerel poet (1830–1902), is strongly associated with Dundee. His uniformly bad verse soon met with acclaim, notably from the student and legal fraternity. His eulogies to the Tay Bridge and the stranding of the great Tay whale are just two occasions when his special talents (a complete disregard for metre in particular) were brought to bear.

Dunblane Cathedral, stained glass

exhibition. This was the vessel used by Captain Scott (of Antarctic fame) and built in Dundee in 1901 because of the city's expertise in building whaling vessels (*Open* Apr–Oct, Mon–Sat 10–5, Sun 11–5; Nov–Mar, Mon–Sat 10–4, Sun 11–4. *Admission charge*). The nearby frigate **Unicorn** is the oldest British warship still afloat – she was built in England, in 1824 (*Open* mid-Mar–Oct, daily 10–5; Nov–mid-Mar, Mon–Fri 10–4, last admission 30 mins before closing. *Admission charge*). Then there are the museums to investigate: the **Barrack Street Museum**▶ (*Open* Mon 11–5, Tue–Sat 10–5. *Admission free*) with its natural history collection including the famous Tay Whale eulogised by the notorious William McGonagall, and the **McManus Galleries**▶ the city's municipal museum and art gallery (*Open* Mon 11–5, Tue–Sat 10–5. *Admission free*).

A newer attraction is the **Verdant Works**▶▶ which brings the story of jute to life in a former jute mill (*Open* Apr–Oct, Mon–Sat 10–5, Sun 11–5; Nov–Mar, Mon–Sat 10–4, Sun 11–4. *Admission charge*).

Within the endless coastal suburbia that ends at the golf courses at Carnoustie to the east is **Broughty Castle Museum**▶ (*Open* Mon 11–1, 2–5, Tue–Thu and Sat 10–1, 2–5, also Sun 2–5 from Jul–Sep only. *Admission free*) with tales to tell about whales and other local historical matters. Then there are the **Mills Observatory** (*Open* daily except Sun), opened in 1935, a sweet factory in the style of the 1940s, also open to visitors, and country parks in the Angus hinterlands, while it is not far to the Angus glens.

141

Andrew Carnegie in Pittencrieff Park

142

INDUSTRIAL ESPIONAGE
Dunfermline was already engaged in spinning when, in the early 18th century, Huguenot master weavers set up in Edinburgh using a secret process to make patterns on plain linen cloth. The new damask was a huge success. Dunfermline weaver James Blake got himself a job cleaning the Huguenot looms, memorised the process, then built his own loom. Thus began Dunfermline's damask linen industry.

Dunkeld 'Little Houses' (private)

▶ Dunfermline 131C1

'What Benares is to the Hindu, Mecca to the Mohammedan, Jerusalem to the Christian, all that Dunfermline is to me.' Thus eulogised Dunfermline's most famous son, Andrew Carnegie. The Dunfermline of today is still full of Carnegie associations – it even has a Carnegie Hall – but this 'auld grey toun' above the Forth goes much further back. It was the capital of Scotland in the time of the 11th-century King Malcolm Canmore (the Gaelic *ceann mohr* means great head or chief). This Celtic warlord married Margaret of the English royal house after she was shipwrecked near by while fleeing the Norman Conquest in 1070. Margaret was later canonised and under her good influence, Dunfermline became the religious centre of Scotland.

Dunfermline Abbey▶ with its adjoining monastery and the royal palace still survive, though they have been rebuilt over the centuries. Today there is a strong sense of layers of history around the historic heart of the town, though sorting them out takes time. There are plenty of explanatory panels and models within the palace complex which clarify matters. (*Open* Apr–Sep, daily 9.30–6; Oct–Mar, Mon–Wed and Sat 9.30–4, Thu 9.30–12, Sun 2–4. *Admission charge*.) The 12th-century work in the abbey church may be the finest surviving Scottish-Norman architecture in Scotland. King Robert the Bruce is buried here: his name is written on great stone blocks on the church tower.

Andrew Carnegie Birthplace Museum▶▶ Dunfermline soon turned to commercial matters: brewing and weaving. Andrew Carnegie (1835–1919) was the son of a weaver who emigrated to the USA. In due course Carnegie's business acumen in the steel industry made him rich enough to give away $350 million. Exactly how is told in this museum. The adjacent Memorial Hall is filled with an extraordinary assemblage of Carnegie memorabilia, including numerous 'freedom caskets' – the ornate boxes in which grateful communities gave him the metaphorical keys to their towns and cities. (*Open* Apr–May and Sep–Oct, Mon–Sat 11–5, Sun 2–5. Jun–Aug, Mon–Sat 10–5, Sun 2–5; Nov–Mar, daily 2–4. *Admission charge*.)

Dunfermline's Carnegie Library was the first of nearly 3,000 worldwide. This and other amenities, including the local museum, the Music Institute, the Carnegie Centre (complete with ornate Turkish baths) and the substantial Pittencrieff Park all indicate the generosity of this extraordinary 'local boy made good' who transformed his home town from a grey workaday place into a well-resourced community. Dunfermline may not be the most picturesque of Scotland's towns, but it has an interesting story to tell.

▶ Dunkeld   *131C2*

A classic Highland-edge community, Dunkeld has bene-fited environmentally (if not commercially) from the A9 bypass. As well as some shopping and the picturesque 18th-century 'Little Houses', it also has Thomas Telford's handsome bridge, opened in 1809. This was a toll bridge, and the imposition of the toll caused riots in 1868. Downstream by a footpath is the Birnam oak, last relic of

Carnegie's initials on Pittencrieff Park gates, Dunkeld

LITERARY INSPIRATION
It was while holidaying in the Dunkeld area in 1893 and studying fungi that Beatrix Potter wrote an illustrated letter about a naughty and adventurous bunny to a young friend. The bunny became the famous Peter Rabbit, and an expert local amateur naturalist, Charles Mackintosh, the retired postman, is suspected of being the prototype for Mr McGregor the gardener.

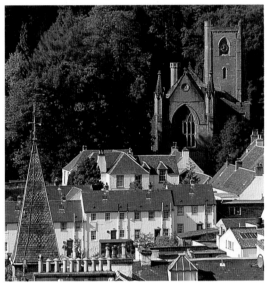

Dunkeld Cathedral and 'Little Houses'

THE HERMITAGE FOLLY
Also known as Ossian's Hall, it was built in 1758 by the 2nd Duke of Atholl's nephew. The curious belvedere overlooks the roaring waters of the River Braan. By 1783 it had acquired a set of mirrors within: a pulley slid back a partition (a painting of Ossian) to reveal them and give the illusion of water pouring in from all directions. This aristocratic toy was not to everyone's taste. It was vandalised in 1821 and again in 1869. The restored shell survives to this day.

Birnam Wood ('Macbeth shall never vanquished be until/Great Birnam wood to high Dunsinane hill/Shall come against him,' prophesy the witches in Shakespeare's *Macbeth*). Dunkeld also has a cathedral, founded in the 12th century and wrecked at the Reformation. Its choir has been restored as the parish church. Walk up the wooded valley of the River Braan (on the opposite side of the A9 to Dunkeld) to **the Hermitage▶▶**, the pleasure grounds of the Dukes of Atholl. On the way, what might be the tallest tree in Scotland can be seen, a 60m-or-so high Douglas Fir. It grows in a hollow by the river at the foot of a slope. The Hermitage is open at all times.

Loch of the Lowes▶▶ Accessible off a minor road on the A923 above Dunkeld, this Scottish Wildlife Trust reserve is a gem of Highland-edge scenery and has ospreys in summer. The visitor centre is open in summer only, but the observation hide is open all year.

Maintaining the fishing fleet, Pittenweem

The East Neuk's heritage is firmly bound up with the sea

►►► East Neuk of Fife 131D1

The chief attraction of the East Neuk of Fife, a land of well-manicured golf courses, lush hedgerows, and rich barley fields and woods all set by a glittering sea, is its little string of coastal communities. The area can easily be reached from Edinburgh, and it makes a very worthwhile day's excursion from St Andrews (see page 154).

The eastern tip of Fife, Fife Ness, is not one of Scotland's most dramatic headlands, though birdwatchers enjoy it at migration time. However, nearby **Crail►►**, easternmost of the villages, is a pretty place with one of the most frequently photographed harbours in Scotland (wait for high tide). Old trading links with the Low Countries are echoed in the architecture, with crow-stepped gables and a Dutch-style town house whose bell, cast in 1520, has a Dutch inscription. There is a good local museum.

Moving west, next comes **Anstruther►**, with its seafront shops selling colourful fishing nets and beach-balls as a reminder of the traditional holiday trade. The **Scottish Fisheries Museum►►►** overlooks the harbour, with a comprehensive presentation on the development of fishing in Scotland, from open boats right through to the most awesome modern catching machines. There are plenty of ship models, as well as the real thing (historic vessels float in the harbour). Children should enjoy the marine aquaria and tableaux full of authentic details, right down to the smell of tarry rope. This museum gives a very strong sense of the endless struggle, frequent tragedy and foundations of prosperity of many east coast communities (*Open* Apr–Oct, Mon–Sat 10–5.30, Sun 11–5; Nov–Mar, Mon–Sat 10–4.30, Sun 2–4.30. *Admission charge*).

Pittenweem►► offers plenty of challenge to the photographer torn between bright-hulled fishing boats and red-pantiled houses. Up a lane near the harbour can be found the cave-shrine of St Fillan, the damp abode of an ancient saint referred to in the name Pittenweem ('place of the cave').

Continuing west, St Monance is another community tied to the sea – its kirk could not stand any closer to the waves. In between these communities is a varied coastline of sand and rock.

Kellie Castle►► (*Open* castle Easter, May–Sep, daily 1.30–5.30; Oct weekends only; last entry 4.45; grounds daily 9.30–sunset. *Admission charge*.) A short way inland, this National Trust for Scotland property dates mainly from the 16th and 17th centuries and was restored in Victorian times. Its walled garden is a peaceful scented haven in high summer and is worked organically.

TOURIST INFORMATION
Anstruther: Scottish Fisheries Museum, Harbourhead (tel: 01333 311073)
Crail: Crail Museum, 62–64 Marketgate (tel: 01333 450869)
Dunfermline: 13/15 Maygate (tel: 01383 720999).
Dunkeld: The Cross (tel: 01350 727688).

▶ Edzell 131D3

Edzell slumbers happily behind its ornate arch commemorating Queen Victoria's visit, and is one of those out-of-the-way places where little ever seems to stir along the wide main street. However, there are a number of points of interest nearby. **Fasque House▶** home of the family of the 19th-century prime minister W E Gladstone, is within easy reach (see page 176), as are the **Caterthuns** (see page 137). **Edzell Castle▶▶** is also worth exploring, and is signed from Edzell along a minor road. The early 16th-century red-stoned tower, a former Lindsay stronghold, features an unusual pleasance or walled garden with unique heraldic and symbolic sculptures (*Open* Apr–Sep, daily 9.30–6; Oct–Mar, Mon–Wed and Sat 9.30–4, Thu 9.30–12, Sun 2–4. *Admission charge*).

SCOTS NAMES
Howe in 'Howe of Fife' means hollow. Neuk, as in East *Neuk*, is the Scots for corner (hence nook).

AN EDUCATIONAL VISIT
Visit the Scottish Fisheries Museum and learn the difference between fifies, zulus and scaffies (they are all different kinds of early fishing craft).

145

▶▶ Falkland Palace 131C1

Open: Apr–Oct, Mon–Sat 11–4.30, Sun 1.30–4.30. Admission charge

The façade of this Renaissance-style former hunting lodge (1501–41) dominates the village of Falkland, tucked below the Lomond Hills. Behind the castle are small but attractive gardens and a Real (royal) Tennis court dating from 1539 (said to be the oldest in Britain).

Pittenweem, one of the most picturesque of Fife's many coastal villages

▶▶ Fife Folk Museum 131C2

Open: Easter, mid-May–Oct, Sat–Thu 2–5. Admission charge

Set in Ceres, the very essence of a rural northeast Fife village, this collection of artefacts showing Fife's rural past is housed in a 17th-century weighhouse and adjoining former weavers' cottages. In the village look out for 'The Provost', a curious 'toby-jug' carving, set in a niche in a gable wall by the crossroads.

A simple plaque over a cottage door in Crail, Fife

146

The devil on this Helensburgh dormer stares directly at a church opposite

► Glamis Castle and Angus Folk Museum   *131C2*

Glamis (pronounced 'Glahms') is an ancient castle site. Its present appearance dates from the 17th century, but the main tower is in part much older. It has fine collections of china, tapestry, painting and furniture (*Open* Apr–Oct, daily 10.30–5.30, last tour 4.45; from 10am Jul–Aug. *Admission charge*). The other end of the social scale is represented at the **Angus Folk Museum►**, a National Trust for Scotland property. (*Open* Easter, May–Sep, daily 11–5; Oct, weekends 11–5, last entry 4.30. *Admission charge*). A row of 19th-century cottages have been knocked through to form a continuous passage with rooms, tableaux and display cases covering everyday life in the rural Angus of old.

► Helensburgh   *130A1*

Sir James Colquhoun, 8th Baronet of Colquhoun and Luss, had plans for the little *clachan* (the Gaelic for 'village') near his castle, since it was the fashion of the Georgian age to improve. He bought the land and advertised for weavers but failed to attract any. Then he went upmarket, promoting the new town of Helensburgh (named after his wife) as a residential place. This plan worked, thanks in part to the later improved communications by rail and sea. Ever since, Helensburgh has retained its properous character, its wide streets and grand properties (built by well-to-do Glasgow commuters) earning it a reputation as a 'museum of villas'.

Hill House►► Finest of all the villas is Charles Rennie Mackintosh's masterpiece, now in the care of the National Trust for Scotland. His design was so comprehensive that he even included details for light fittings, carpet patterns and window snibs (Scots for 'catches'). It was built in 1904 as the family home of the wealthy Glasgow publisher Walter Blackie (*Open* Apr–Oct, daily 1.30–5.30, last entry 5. *Admission charge*).

► Hillfoots Towns   *130B1*

The Hillfoots towns of Menstrie, Alva, Tillicoultry and Dollar are strung out below the steep scarp face of the Ochil Hills east of Stirling. They formed the second largest textile manufacturing area in Scotland, using the burns running steeply off the Ochils to power the mills, and the

high green open pastures on the heights to raise the sheep whose wool was processed. Most (but not all) of the manufacturing has gone now, leaving impressive mill architecture at places such as Alva. The hill country above the towns is quite unspoilt and offers a good selection of walks into the Ochils, notably from the **Ochil Hills Woodland Park** between Alva and Tillicoultry.

Dollar►►, to the east, is the most attractive of the towns, while Blairlogie, to the west, is a pleasant village. (The others are rather dour, their attraction lying in the countryside of the Ochils above them.) Behind Dollar, on a high shoulder above a darkly wooded glen, is

Castle Campbell above Dollar

BEN CLEUCH
The highest point in the Ochil Hills is Ben Cleuch (720m). If the clouds are high it offers superb views from the summit of the hills of the Central Highlands. But do not underestimate these exposed broad slopes, especially in winter: use proper footwear and walking equipment. The Ben Cleuch path starts from Tillicoultry or Alva.

TOURIST INFORMATION
Alva: Mill Trail Visitor Centre, West Stirling Street (tel: 01259 769696) Kirkcaldy: 19 Whytescauseway (tel: 01592 267775)

ADAM SMITH
The Adam Smith Centre, Kirkcaldy's civic centre and theatre (built in 1889 and refurbished in 1973), is named after Adam Smith, who was born in the town in 1723. A plaque near Kirk Wynd marks the site of the house where the econo-mist wrote his influential treatise *An Inquiry into the Nature and Causes of the Wealth of Nations.*

Characteristic Wemyss ware cats

Castle Campbell▶▶▶ (*Open* Apr–Sep, daily 9.30–6; Oct–Mar, Mon–Wed and Sat 9.30–4, Thu 9.30–12; Sun 2–4. *Admission charge*). This impressive stronghold is accessible by car or by a very picturesque walk, at one stage through a narrow gorge. The fortress was owned by the 1st Earl of Argyll, Chancellor of Scotland to King James IV, and comprises a basic 15th-century tower house with later additions, including a notable loggia – an arcade with arches. Rearing above the trees at the head of the valley, it is impressively situated and well worth a visit – especially on a clear day, for the views from the ramparts. It could be tied in with a trip to nearby Culross.

▶ Kirkcaldy   *131C1*
Kirkcaldy may not be the most scenic of Scottish towns but it has good amenities, including a fine park and theatre. Visit its Art Gallery and Museum both for a fine collection of Scottish artists (notably Peploe) and its displays of local Wemyss ware pottery (*Open* Mon–Sat 10.30–5, Sun 2–5. *Admission free*).
    Ravenscraig Castle (*Open* Mon–Sat 10.30–5, Sun 2–5. *Admission free*) is an austere, ruined fortress overlooking the Firth, founded by King James II in 1460 and later owned by the Sinclair Earls of Orkney. Also close at hand is the picturesque **Dysart**, with attractively restored properties around a tiny harbour.

One of Scotland's most famous stretches of inland water is the result of a glacier dumping its gouged-out gravels, thus creating a dam at the southern end of the deep trench it had dug. This took place 10,000 years ago, leaving Loch Lomond 8m above sea level, in contrast to the long, narrow sea loch of Loch Long immediately to the west.

THE BANKS OF LOCH LOMOND

By yon bonnie banks and by yon bonnie braes
Where the sun shines bright on Loch Lomond
Where me and my true love were ever wont to gae
On the bonnie bonnie banks o Loch Lomond.

Chorus
Ye'll tak the high road and I'll tak the low road
And I'll be in Scotland afore ye
But me and my true love will never meet again
On the bonnie, bonnie banks o Loch Lomond

MUSICAL CONNECTIONS

The song 'The Banks of Loch Lomond' is thought to have been written by a condemned Jacobite prisoner while in jail in Carlisle, in England, after the 1745 rebellion. His lines about 'yon bonnie banks' have gone round the world, though the unknown lyricist is not the only one to make reference to the loch. Alan Jay Lerner's 1947 hit 'Almost Like Being in Love' has the lines:
'Maybe the sun gave me the pow'r,
But I could swim Loch Lomond and be home in half an hour.
Maybe the air gave me the drive
For I'm all aglow and alive.'

Accessibility Loch Lomond is Scotland's largest loch in surface area. Famed in song, it has exerted its pull on visitors since the late 18th century. The 'bonnie banks' are indisputably bonnie – but probably no more so than those of many a Highland loch lying further north. Loch Lomond's attraction really lies in its accessibility, a characteristic it shares with the Trossachs.

Its Lowland southern end is only half an hour (sometimes less) from Glasgow city centre by road. This makes it commuter and also weekend-cottage country, as a stroll around neat little Drymen, with its exclusive shops, will confirm. The nearest point of the loch to Glasgow is at Balloch, at the head of the surprisingly industrialised Vale of Leven. Though Balloch is hardly

picturesque, **Balloch Castle Country Park** (open all year) has a visitor centre at the castle (which is also the Ranger Service HQ).

To grasp how this loch was made, climb little **Duncryne Hill** south of Gartocharn, for a sublime view of the receding loch, narrowing northwards and squeezed by the hard shoulders of Highland hills. The Highland Boundary Fault with its tough rocks confined the land-shaping glacier. When it reached the soft rocks of the Lowland edge, it widened out, just as Loch Lomond's waters do today.

The eastern side Take the B837 no-through-road up the eastern bank of the loch. **Balmaha**, with humpy Conic Hill behind it marking the geological line where the Highlands begin, is the stepping-off point for boat excursions round

Loch Lomond's islands. These come in various shapes and sizes, though **Inchcailloch** (Scottish Natural Heritage), with its ruined 13th-century chapel and fine woodlands, is particularly outstanding. Cruises land there from Balmaha.

Rowardennan is the end of the road for car explorers, though it is pleasant to continue eastwards on foot up the track which forms part of the **West Highland Way**. This officially signposted 157km long-distance footpath from Milngavie, by Glasgow, to Fort William drops to the lochside at Balmaha for its journey northwards. The car park at Rowardennan is also the favoured starting-off point for the climb up Ben Lomond, Scotland's most southerly (and probably most popular) 'Munro' (see panel).

Car tourers can also sneak up on the loch via Aberfoyle to reach Inversnaid, where the road drops steeply out of the 'hanging valley' of **Glen Arklet** and down to the water. This scantily populated place with its ferny banks and waterfalls is recalled in a poem by Gerard Manley Hopkins. The northern tip of Loch Lomond tails away in the marshy fields at the end of Glen Falloch.

The western side The main A82 road takes the west side of the loch, slicing away at the bonnie banks with road improvements in order to carry the tourists north at ever higher speeds. Thus many visitors miss tiny Inveruglas, from where a private road (walkers only) leads to **Loch Sloy**, the old homelands of the Clan MacFarlane, tucked behind the high hills known as the Arrochar Alps. Further south is **Tarbet**, its name indicating a place of portage: the Vikings once carried their longships from the head of Loch Long and pillaged Loch Lomond's settlements. Also on the A82 is **Luss**, its pretty cottages part of the planned estate village originally built by the Colquhouns.

MUNROS

A Munro is a mountain in Scotland over 914m high. Munro-bagging is a popular sport north of the border. The name recalls the first compiler of Scotland's heights, Sir Hugh Munro, who published a list of 277 peaks in 1891. The actual number of Munros in Scotland changes sometimes as surveys add or eliminate certain peaks. In addition, there can be problems of definition of what qualifies as a discrete mountain. For example, when does a subsidiary top of a Munro become a separate Munro? The current agreed figure is 284.

LUSS

The village name Luss is explained by a charming legend concerning the death of a local girl married to a high-ranking French officer during the 14th-century Anglo-French wars. She died in France but was buried by Loch Lomond. Fleurs-de-Lis (a species of iris and a heraldic device of the Bourbons) were scattered on her grave and, it is said, grew there ever afterwards. Though the story is romantic, it is equally likely that Luss is from the Gaelic word lios, meaning 'garden'.

THE STONE OF SCONE

The Stone of Scone, or Stone of Destiny, was the traditional coronation throne of the Scottish monarchs until it was stolen by King Edward I of England in 1297. Controversy still surrounds this stone. Some Scots believe it is a fake, and that the real Stone of Destiny was hidden before Edward's arrival and briefly found again in the early 19th century though it subsequently vanished. Whatever the truth, the Stone of Scone remains a powerful nationalist symbol in Scotland. It was returned to Scotland in November 1996, and can now be seen in Edinburgh Castle.

TOURIST INFORMATION

Montrose (Apr–Sep): Bridge Street (tel: 01674 672000).
Perth: 45 High Street (tel: 01738 638353).

Scone Palace, one of the very grandest of Scotland's stately piles, is largely an early 19th-century design

▶ Montrose
131D3

A typical east coast Lowland town, Montrose looks both to land and sea, with a maritime past, an involvement in North Sea oil, and one of Angus's main livestock markets. It is also something of a resort, with long beaches and a choice of old-established golf courses. Birdwatchers flock to the basin of the River Esk, which hems in the town to the west, as this Scottish Wildlife Trust reserve is an important and decidedly muddy habitat for waders and wildfowl.

Coastal scenery is impressive, with further natural history interest at **St Cyrus** (Scottish Natural Heritage) to the north. A visitor centre here interprets the formerly important local activity of salmon netting, as well as the nearby bird and plant life. Close by to the south are the long sands of **Lunan Bay**, guarded by the ruined Red Castle above the dunes – an idyllic spot for beach strollers.

The House of Dun ▶ ▶ ▶ (*Open* Easter, May–Sep, daily 1.30–5.30; Oct; weekends only. Grounds daily 9.30–sunset. *Admission charge*). Close to the town, this National Trust for Scotland property was originally built in 1730 to a William Adam design, and has seen extensive restoration work, especially to its spectacular plasterwork. In courtyard buildings Angus Weavers weave real linen napery on traditional handlooms – a rare survivor of an industry once widespread in the area.

▶ ▶ Perth
131C2

Though built on a site still prone to flooding, Perth's strategic position as a major Lowland town with easy access to the Highlands has always given it an important role. It was the cradle of the Reformation in Scotland, after John Knox's preaching sparked off a riot in the town – and it also had bleaching and dyeing industries because of the softness and power of the River Tay's waters.

Rebuilding and renewal mean that very little is left of the ancient town. Instead, there is a grid of handsome streets completed by the early 19th century. They obliterated much of the earlier medieval plan, but include

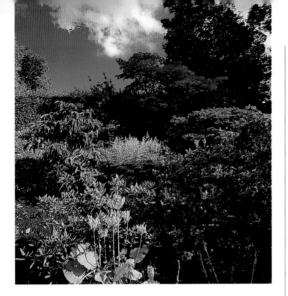

Perth offers the choice of the fast (possibly too fast) A9 heading for Speyside and Inverness, the slow A92 taking the high route over Glenshee for Royal Deeside, and the fast dual carriageway, the A90(M) via Dundee for Aberdeen. Beware if driving on the A92 in the skiing season. It leads to the ski developments at Glenshee, and the bends south of the Spittal of Glenshee are too often treated as a slalom course by car-borne skiing enthusiasts.

Branklyn Garden, Perth

151

Shopping for antiques, Perth

neo-classical buildings such as Perth Academy (1807), the County Buildings (1815–19 – Perth is the county town) and the unique waterworks (1832), now a picture gallery. Meanwhile, amid these stately civic surroundings, Perth gets on with its role as a centre for a mainly rural, well-off hinterland. It has a wide range of specialist shops for antiques, crafts, jewellery, outdoor and sports equipment, a museum, an art gallery on George Street (*Open* Mon–Sat 10–5. *Admission free*) and a thriving repertory theatre. The Regimental Museum of the Black Watch at Balhousie Castle on the North Inch tells the story of the regiment, founded in 1740 (*Open* May–Sep, Mon–Sat 10–4.30; Oct–Apr, Mon–Fri 10–3.30. *Admission free*).

On the edge of town, the small-scale **Branklyn Garden▶▶▶** has outstanding late spring colour from azaleas, blue poppies, and other horticultural treasures (*Open* Easter–Oct, daily 9.30–sunset. *Admission charge*). **Fairways Heavy Horse Centre** is another popular excursion only a few minutes further on the Dundee road. This centre has working Clydesdales, with dray rides, vintage horse implements and video shows (*Open* daily 10–5. *Admission charge*).

Off the Blairgowrie Road, **Scone Palace▶▶** is one of Scotland's grandest stately homes (*Open* Easter–Oct, daily 9.30–5.15, last entry 4.45. *Admission charge*). Scone (pronounced 'skoon') was the traditional crowning place of Scottish monarchs. The site was actually the Moot Hill, within the palace grounds. Scone Palace as seen today dates mainly from the early years of the 19th century. It houses magnificent collections of porcelain, furniture, ivories, 18th-century clocks and 16th-century needlework. In addition to this, there are fine gardens.

Clan skirmish re-enactment by Loch Achray, Trossachs

TOURIST INFORMATION
Pitlochry: 22 Atholl Road
(tel: 01796 472215).

THE SOLDIER'S LEAP
The Battle of Killiecrankie in 1689 was the first attempt by the Jacobites to restore the exiled King James VII. They won after the government forces were unable to resist the wild charge of the Highland clans. However, in his victory, the Jacobite leader, John Graham of Claverhouse, Viscount Dundee, was killed by a stray bullet. Without 'Bonnie Dundee's' charismatic leadership, the rebellion fizzled out. Also in this battle, a certain Donald MacBean, a government soldier, leapt 6m across the River Garry to avoid being impaled on a Highland claymore. The spot is known as the Soldier's Leap.

▶▶ **Pitlochry**   *130B2*

Pitlochry claims to be the geographical centre of Scotland. Its situation amongst the Perthshire hills was noted by Queen Victoria's personal physician when she stayed along the road at Blair Castle. His recommendations on the wholesome air led to many of the well-to-do subsequently building large mansions in this previously quiet weaving village. The Perth to Inverness railway's arrival in 1863 accelerated the growth of the fledgling resort. New hotels were built, including the Pitlochry Hydropathic, and Pitlochry developed a popularity it has retained ever since. Statistics suggest that the population of 2,500 offers 6,700 beds and plays host to nearly a million visitors a year.

Not as dull as it sounds, the **Hydro-Electric Visitor Centre** (*Open* Apr–Oct, daily 10–5.30) overlooking Loch Faskally, only moments from the main street, has a fish ladder – a stepped series of pools enabling fish to get upriver – and an explanation of the complex Tummel Valley hydro-electric scheme. You can see the fish jumping or swimming past the viewing chamber – if you are lucky. Another feature of the town is the Pitlochry Festival Theatre which shows an easily digestible programme right through the main season.

Killiecrankie▶▶▶ is a dramatic battle site set amidst a very scenic river gorge with woodlands and steep rocks. The National Trust for Scotland visitor centre tells the story of both the battle and the gorge itself, where there are superb walks among the tall pines and larches planted by the Dukes of Atholl. Combine a trip here with the Queen's View of Loch Tummel (*Open* site all year; visitor centre Apr–Oct, daily 10–5.30. *Admission charge*).

▶▶ **Queen Elizabeth Forest Park**   *130A1*

The poorly-drained, infertile uplands of Scotland have defeated many a landowner. After World War I, many of these unprofitable areas, for example around the Trossachs and Loch Lomond, were bought by the state for forestry. In 1953, the 170sq km (approximately) owned by the Forestry Commission in some of the most attractive landscapes of the Central Highlands became the Queen Elizabeth Forest Park. At least 100km of forest roads are open to foot traffic. The starting point is the Queen

Elizabeth Forest Park Visitor Centre above Aberfoyle, with its magnificent views back to the Lowlands. As well as waymarked trails in profusion for walkers, right across the area, there is a forest drive by Loch Achray for those who cannot bear to leave their cars, as well as dedicated cycling routes. The amenity value of the forests around Loch Lomond and the Trossachs is heavily emphasised, and even though this is Scotland's best-known tourist area, it is perfectly possible to escape from people.

▶▶▶ Rumbling Bridge   130B2

Rumbling Bridge is a geological curiosity. The phenomenon which brought generations of tourists was the sinister rumbling of boulders grinding in a deep pot called 'the Devil's Mill', in a gorge which the River Devon has cut into the soft rock of the Lowland edge. The place even had its own train station, though the railway has long vanished, and excursionists would picnic by the steep and ferny banks and wander the narrow footpaths and viewing points. They also admired the quaint little bridge of 1713 which spans the gorge and is spanned in turn by a later, higher bridge of 1816, which carries today's A823. Today, there are fewer visitors as the Rumbling Bridge gorge lies in a kind of tourist no-man's land, bypassed by travellers rushing up the M90 for Perth or the M9 for Stirling, but it is a curious spot and makes a pleasant extension to, say, an excursion to Castle Campbell or the Hillfoots towns.

Loch Faskally, near Pitlochry, is part of the complex of lochs used for the generation of hydro-electric power

153

Loch Venachar is the most easterly of the Trossachs lochs, and supplies 'compensation water' to the River Forth, replacing the water taken from Loch Katrine to quench Glasgow's thirst

TREE TYPES
The dominant tree species in the Queen Elizabeth Forest Park, in common with most other commercial forests in Scotland, are the alien sitka and Norway spruce, with some Scots and lodgepole pines in the drier areas. There are also some oak and beech plantings, supplementing the semi-natural oakwoods (whose bark was once harvested for tannin) as well as birch scrub – a reminder of the natural regeneration which would take place if there were fewer sheep and deer.

Central Scotland

Not only is St Andrews famed as the home of golf and of Scotland's oldest university, but it is also a decidedly handsome east coast town. This is the view from the top of St Rule's Tower, near the ruined cathedral

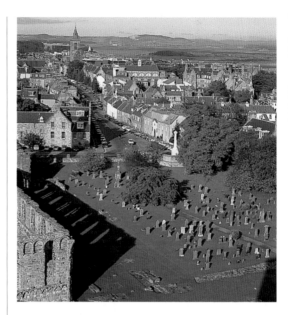

TOURIST INFORMATION
St Andrews: 70 Market Street (tel: 01334 472021).

SCOTLAND'S LARGEST CHURCH
Some say that the design of St Andrews Cathedral was in advance of the building technology of its age. It was by far the largest church in Scotland and one of the longest ever built anywhere in the UK, with a length of about 110m.

A BEACH WALK
For a change from the town, take a stroll along the beach at Tentsmuir, north of Leuchars near St Andrews, where the pinewood-backed sandy beach goes on forever. En route, admire the fine Norman architecture of the parish church at Leuchars. Craigtoun Country Park, also near the town, is great for children.

▶▶▶ St Andrews   *131D2*

St Andrews is unique: an ancient ecclesiastical capital, the oldest Scottish university town, and a world golfing Mecca. According to legend, a Greek monk, Regulus (or Rule), carrying relics of St Andrew, one of Christ's disciples, was shipwrecked here and founded a church. Thereafter the cult of St Andrew was focused on this part of Fife. The monk's name survives as St Rule's Church (or tower) still standing near the ruined cathedral and probably from the early 12th century. Its topmost point makes a good place to view the town's medieval street plan.

Founded in 1160, **St Andrews Cathedral▶** is today a mere ruined fragment of what must once have been awesome architecture. It was damaged by natural disasters and then laid low by the Reformers. The cathedral's stonework was ultimately pillaged for use elsewhere in the town. Its on-site museum is well worth a visit for the glimpses of vanished magnificence. The ruins are open any time, the museum daily.

Teetering on the sea's brink, **St Andrews Castle▶▶** tells a tale of drama and religious conflict, and boasts an impressive bottle dungeon. A claustrophobic underground experience can be had following the route of sappers as they counter-mined during an attempt to tunnel under the castle during a 16th-century siege. The tunnel is electrically lit now (*Open* Apr–Sep, daily 9.30–6; Oct–Mar, Mon–Sat 9.30–4, Sun 2–4. *Admission charge*).

There are other local museums and the **Sea Life Centre** (*Open* daily 10–5; Jul–Aug 10–7. *Admission charge*) to visit, plus a golfing museum and excellent long beaches on either side of the town. Visitors can stroll round the many college precincts of Scotland's oldest university (founded in 1411), before sampling some of the finest shopping of any provincial town in Scotland. (The combination of university, visitors, and a prosperous farming hinterland ensures that high-quality wares are on offer.)

Scotland is often called 'the home of golf' and, brushing aside any suggestion that the game probably originated in the Low Countries, claims it for her own. Certainly, Scotland has a number of very old-established courses, often lying close to town centres, where, had it not been for the early rights of golfers, the land would have been swallowed up by developments long ago. Nowhere is this better seen than in St Andrews.

Seaside pastime It is quite possible that golf came over when the medieval trading links with the Low Countries were strong. By the time of the early Stuart monarchs, a game with sticks and balls was taking up the time of both king and commoner alike. In 1457, King James II decreed that soldiers should not play golf. In 1503, King James IV treated himself to a new set of clubs.

Some say the sport originated with a piece of driftwood, a sea-washed pebble and a rabbit-burrow – all three are found on the Fife coast amongst the turf, links and dunes. In the days before mowing machines were invented, golf had to be played where grass was naturally short. Usually only on seaside links did the exposure, poor soil and nibbling rabbits all combine to keep the turf close-cropped. Bunkers developed from natural hollows into which a golf ball would frequently roll. Wind erosion on the thin grassy skin already damaged by players' efforts to hit out would soon create a sandy hazard.

The Old Course All this substantiates St Andrews Old Course's claims to 15th-century origins. The Old Course is still the ultimate dream of many, which may explain why, for instance, Japanese visitors have acquired a reputation for slow play over it – they want to savour every moment. It represents traditional design at its very best. However, remember that there are other courses, both adjacent to the Old Course and right along the Fife coast.

A GOLFING HAZARD
One of the former hazards of the Old Course was the goods shed of the nearby railway yard on the Fife coastline from Leuchars. This demanded a high approach shot on the 17th to clear the roof. Though the railway has gone in one of the more short-sighted closures of the 1960s, the outline of the old shed has been preserved as the golf school of the nearby luxury hotel which now occupies the site of the former sidings. Meanwhile, a campaign continues to re-open the line.

St Andrews, the Old Course

155

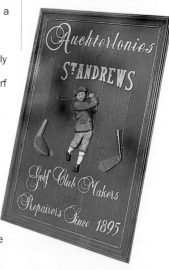

A JACOBITE BATTLE

The Battle of Sheriffmuir, on the open slopes of the Ochil Hills above Stirling, was fought in 1715 between the rebellious Jacobite forces under the Earl of Mar and the government army under the Duke of Argyll. Unusually, it ended in a draw, with each of the opposing wings pushing back the other, but neither side gaining overwhelming advantage. Argyll took his forces off to Dunblane, while Mar's men withdrew to Perth. As it was November, many of the Highland rebels wanted to go back home for the winter, and the rebellion fizzled out.

▶▶▶ Stirling   130B1

Whoever controlled Stirling controlled the Scotland of old. It was the lowest bridging point of the River Forth running east, with marshes to the west, the Campsie Hills to the south, and the Ochil Hills (and the Highlands) northwards. Stirling Castle preserves its impregnable air, rising out of the former marshlands. Downhill from the castle, the Old Town has the air of an old-established Scottish burgh, with its mercat cross, tolbooth and Church of the Holy Rude (c1456) as the ancient symbols of commerce, the law and the church. Further down, Victorian developments begin with handsome shopping streets and a railway station, and spread into the suburbs.

Stirling Castle▶▶▶ (*Open* Apr–Sep, daily 9.30–5.15; Oct–Mar, daily 9.30–4.15. *Admission charge*). Most visitors to Stirling get at least as far as the Esplanade with its breathtaking panorama, but it is well worth penetrating the castle complex itself. This former royal court with its fine Renaissance work was sadly misused after Scotland's James VI deserted it to become King of England as well. Much has been restored, including the Renaissance palace of James V and the Chapel Royal of 1594.

The National Trust for Scotland tells the story of one of Scotland's very few victories against the English at the **Bannockburn Visitor Centre▶**, 4km southeast of Stirling (*Open* Apr–Oct, daily 10–5.30; Mar, Nov–Dec, daily 11–3.

Walk

Old Stirling

See map opposite.

Fragments of an old Scottish townscape survive in this walk through the historic heart of Stirling below the castle. Allow two hours.

Follow the impressively rough-hewn old town wall opposite the tourist information centre uphill past the old school, now an attractive hotel, to the historic buildings of St John Street. These include the Erskine Marykirk, a grand classical church (1842–6), now fronting a modern youth hostel; and the old **Detention Barracks** (1847), now the Old Town Jail museum.

The **Church of the Holy Rude** lies beyond, with Cowane's Hospital (the Guildhall, a summer ceilidh venue) near by. A gate between them leads to the cemetery, with a fine view of the castle from the Ladies Rock. Steps and a gate lead to the Esplanade, next to the castle. The distant views here include the Arrochar Alps to the west, Ben Chonzie northwards, and the Pentland Hills behind Edinburgh.

After visiting the **castle**, go downhill past **Argyll's Ludging**, Scotland's finest surviving Renaissance mansion (open to visitors), and pass the façade of **Mar's Wark**, all that remains of a Renaissance palace damaged during the '45 rebellion. Broad Street, complete with cannon and tall 18th- and 19th-century tenements, gives way to Victorian developments and the main shopping streets.

King Robert I on Stirling Castle Esplanade

Admission charge). The informative displays are housed in a modern building.

The National Wallace Monument▶▶ recalls Scotland's first freedom fighter (William Wallace), and has an audio-visual presentation as well as views from the top of the tower after 246 steps up a spiral staircase (*Open* Mar–May and Oct, daily 10–5; Jun, Sep, daily 10–6; Jul–Aug, daily 9.30–6.30; Feb and Nov, weekends 10–4. *Admission charge*).

The summer programme of costume drama set in the castle and in the atmospheric streets, changing exhibitions at the Smith Art Gallery and performance at the MacRobert Arts Centre are further choices for visitors.

The view from the ramparts of Stirling Castle towards the Church of the Holy Rude

TOURIST INFORMATION
Stirling: 41 Dumbarton Road (tel: 01786 475019).

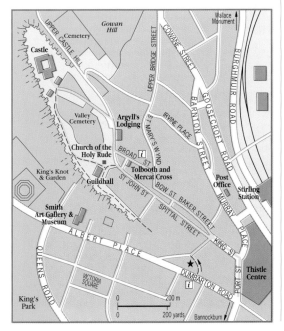

THE REASONS FOR BANNOCKBURN
The Battle of Bannockburn was not what King Robert I (the Bruce) wanted. He was forced into this pitched battle with the might of the English knights after his brother, Edward, besieging Stirling Castle, accepted an offer from its English governor that 'if by midsummer a year thence he was not rescued by battle, he would yield the castle freely'. This committed King Edward II of England to rescue his governor and fight the Scottish forces in a pitched battle.

Drive

Perthshire's glens

A drive round some typical Highland glens with ribbon-lochs and characteristic glaciated U-shaped profiles. This

The Queen's View, Loch Tummel

is a good autumn drive, when the roads are quiet and the colours spectacular. The trip totals 184km via Glen Lyon but not including the Loch Tummel extension. Allow one long day, or alternatively stop overnight in the Kenmore area.

Take the A85 west from Perth, noting 15th-century Huntingtower on the outskirts of the town. On this section, south of the Highland Boundary Fault, the green landscape of well-worked farmland and woods rolls out across the shallow bowl of Strathearn, the

Falls of Dochart, Killin

valley of the River Earn, reaching as far south as the Ochil Hills.

Continue through **Crieff**, keeping on the A85. The town has plenty of shops and a cluster of visitor attractions on the edge of town (see page 138).

Because of its position on the Highland Boundary Fault, the village of **Comrie**, further along the A85, is known as the earthquake centre of Scotland. **Earthquake House**, built as a recording station in 1874, lies just west of the town. The hills close in towards St Fillans, on the eastern end of **Loch Earn**, a popular loch for watersports. There is a major water sports centre at Lochearnhead. Note, en route, the fine views south to the bulk of Ben Vorlich.

At Lochearnhead, turn north up **Glen Ogle**. This grand glen, according to Queen Victoria's diaries, reminded her of a print of the Khyber Pass. The old railway (closed 1965) with its decaying viaduct is now a walkway, though not totally peaceful because of the roar of peak-season traffic in the confines of the hills. Try the layby at the head of the pass for views of the **Meall nan Tarmachan** and **Ben Lawers** ranges.

After turning right at Lix Toll, on reaching Killin, watch out for pedestrians peering into cameras on the narrow bridge over the **Falls of Dochart**. There are friendly little shops in this attractive community, which has an alpine flavour when there is snow on the slopes above.

Continue eastwards, then take the unclassified road north towards Glen Lyon, unless it has recently snowed on the tops – this road traverses high ground. The National Trust for Scotland's visitor centre blights the bright green flanks of **Ben Lawers**. The Trust is a conservation body, but ironically Ben Lawers' mountain flora is threatened by too many visitors, so pass on into Glen Lyon.

Turn east down this typical Highland glen, with a 'big hoose' behind its wall, warning notices to keep off the hills during stalking, forestry on the slopes, farming on the river flats and a hydro-electric scheme at the head of the glen. Note the Fortingall Yew where Glen Lyon opens out. This is reputed to be more than 3,000 years old, possibly the oldest tree in Europe. The Fortingall Yew is said to be the birthplace of Pontius Pilate, whose father is supposed to have been a legionnaire stationed in Scotland. Victorian guide book writers were notoriously imaginative.

Low-lying cloud shrouding Schiehallion and Loch Rannoch

Continue by going north to **Loch Tummel** and then circling back by way of Pitlochry, or for a more direct route rejoin the A9 east of Aberfeldy to return to Perth.

H V Morton in In Search of Scotland *sums up the Trossachs. He complains how a traveller can wander around for months looking for essential Scotland 'enduring heat, cold, fatigue, high teas, Sabbaths, kirks, and at the end comes suddenly on the whole thing in concentrated form, boiled down to the very essence...' Even more exasperating, as he points out, the place is conveniently near Edinburgh and Glasgow.*

WORDSWORTH IN THE TROSSACHS
Among the many poems inspired by his Trossachs visits, Wordsworth composed *Stepping Westward* after exploring Loch Katrine. *The Solitary Reaper* with its lines 'Breaking the silence of the seas/Among the farthest Hebrides' owes its origins not to some west coast lass, but to a fieldworker the poet heard singing as she worked near Balquhidder.

160

SS Sir Walter Scott, steam power on popular and beautiful Loch Katrine (pronounced 'Kattren')

Definitions The Trossachs phenomenon is a curious one. For a start, nobody can quite agree on where it is. It certainly centres on the narrow pass that leads from Loch Achray through to the huge car park at the east end of **Loch Katrine**. Usually it goes over the hills and knolls southward to take in **Aberfoyle** and **Loch Ard**. **Ben Ledi** is a part of it to the east. Sometimes it is taken to mean all of this area as far as the **Braes of Balquhidder** and the banks of **Loch Lomond** at Inversnaid.

Then nobody can agree on what the word Trossachs means. Generations of writers have accepted an early explanation that it means 'the bristly country' in Gaelic – yet no Gaelic word in current use supports this. The standard work for Victorian travellers, *Murray's Handbook* of 1894, dismisses it as the rugged country. Possibly it derives from an obsolete Gaelic word *trasdaichean* meaning a transverse glen joining two others.

Popularity in the Romantic age Wherever it is and whatever it means, it was firmly on the tourist trail before the end of the 18th century, thanks to the Romantic movement with its cult of the picturesque. A Callander minister, writing in the *Old Statistical Account* for 1794, states that 'The Trossachs are often visited by persons of taste, who are desirous of seeing nature in her rudest and unpolished state'. Before then, shaggy landscapes were considered uncouth and vulgar, without order or harmony – as well as being downright dangerous and probably filled with savages as well.

The Romantic poets came to admire the wooded peaks mirrored in shimmering lochs. William and Dorothy Wordsworth, accompanied by Samuel Taylor Coleridge, passed through in 1803. Though the scenery hardly needed the extra attention, Sir Walter Scott took the landscapes around Ben Ledi and Loch Katrine (as well as Stirling Castle) in *The Lady of the Lake* (1810) and peopled them with heroes, knights, hermits and fair ladies. This dramatic verse narrative was an overnight sensation and helped propel the Trossachs towards becoming the very byword for Scottish scenery. New inns were built and roads opened up. At the eastern gateway, Callander's shopkeepers prospered.

Modern visitors The Trossachs are just as popular today, and a few new visitor attractions have opened. The **Rob Roy and the Trossachs Visitor Centre** in Callander (*Open* Jan–Feb, weekends 10–4; Mar–May, Oct–Dec, daily 10–5; Jun, Sep, daily 9.30–6; Jul–Aug, daily 9–7. *Admission charge*) tells the Trossachs story through the eyes of the local hero and popular rogue Rob Roy Macgregor, who knew these Highland-edge landscapes well. (His clan found them convenient for hiding cattle stolen from Lowland farms.) At Aberfoyle, the **Scottish Wool Centre** offers a worthwhile variation on the Scottish combination of large giftware shop with attractions attached. The Story of Scottish Wool from prehistoric times to the present is told by way of a presentation in a 150-seat arena and in summer there are live demonstrations of shearing and working sheepdogs, as well as a chance to try carding and spinning (*Open* Apr–Sep, daily 9.30–6; Oct–Mar, daily 10–5. *Admission charge*). These modern developments add a wet-weather dimension to the attractions of the Trossachs.

However, the best way to understand the place is to walk – up **Ben Aon** overlooking Loch Achray; round the head of Loch Katrine in Glen Gyle to discover the old Macgregor graveyard; up Ben Ledi in the heart of the Trossachs. After all, visitors have had so much enjoyment doing just that for two centuries.

HILLTOP RITUALS
Ben Ledi, tallest of the Trossachs hills, is associated with Beltane rites, ancient fire ceremonies on hilltops formerly practised by the Celts. The coming of their summer was 1 May. A folk memory of this lingers on but has attached itself to Midsummer Eve instead, when the uphill path to this 879m high hill can be quite busy as people gather to watch the sunset at its most northerly point.

161

The ferryman who takes visitors to the atmospheric Inchmahome Priory, on an island in the Lake of Menteith, near Callander

Far right: Macduff harbour
Right: whisky is exported from Scotland across the world – this bottle ended up in Australia

BEYOND THE GRAMPIAN HILLS The northeast region, strictly speaking, lies north of the Highland Line, the geological fault which runs from Helensburgh in the west to Stonehaven in the east. Yet the northeast has good Lowland farmlands and the densest forms of the Lowland Scots tongue. It used to be described as 'the Grampian cocoon' – the land beyond the Grampian hills, isolated from developments in Central Scotland. This may explain the survival in some vigour of its old tongue, as well as a kind of independent spirit and attitude among many of the locals. But modern communications, as well as new settlers and the impact of North Sea oil, have made their mark in this essentially rural area.

The northeast is different: not like the empty, wet and rugged deserts of the Highlands with their original inhabitants in exile; nor even like the brisk and busy central corridor of Scotland which spawned the industrial revolution. It is a community tied together by the twin bonds of its sea-going and its farming heritage. Its main centre, Aberdeen, the third largest city in Scotland, sometimes seems to operate like a very large market town, in spite of all the peripheral industrial estates which grew up in the wake of the oil finds in the shallow seas to the east and north.

Geographically, the northeast can be interpreted as a series of shelves, running down from the frost-shattered granite heights of the Cairngorms to the gently rolling, well-farmed Lowlands. These descending steps end

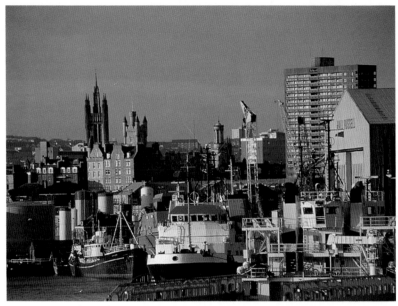

Oil supply vessels in Aberdeen harbour

spectacularly in a coastline whose beauty is hardly matched in the United Kingdom – preserved partly by remoteness, partly by the unglamorous workaday fields behind it, and also because it is usually very chilly.

CASTLES The 'cocoon' effect means that many great castles have survived, away from the destructive mainstream of Scotland warfare and safely tucked out of sight behind their stone walls and woodland 'policies' (grounds). Some still control farms and grand estates, others are now in the care of bodies such as the National Trust for Scotland and are open to the public. If you travel in the northeast, there seem to be signposts with castle logos at every turning.

DISTINCT AREAS The northeast splits into a number of areas. There is the city of Aberdeen itself, with its wide commuter belt, taking in places from Ellon in the north, Inverurie, Alford, Banchory and other little country towns which expanded in the oil boom. North from this area to Kinnaird Head, the northeast tip, is Buchan, built on fishing and farming, with granite towns and villages tucked into the folds of open farmland. The old county of Banff, at least in its lowland stretches, is transitional, softening the bleak edges of Buchan and merging in turn with the softer airs of Moray, in the rain shadow of the high hills in the inner Moray Firth.

Running west of Aberdeen is the valley of the River Dee, given royal approval by Queen Victoria and still, at least in part, a playground for the wealthy, not just aristocrats on hillground and forested estates, but also the occasional foreign millionaire. Deeside eventually runs into the great whalebacks of the Cairngorms, whose northwestern slopes face Speyside and the upper reaches of Moray. North and northeast of the Cairngorm plateau are the

THE TURRA COO
One tale of northeast thrawnness (stubbornness) is that of the (locally) famous Turra Coo. Turra is Turriff, a small market town, and a coo is a cow. In 1912 a local farmer refused to cooperate with the new National Insurance Act. He was fined but refused to pay. The Sheriff Officer poinded (seized) a cow. After a failed attempt to auction it in Turriff – before a crowd of 1,500 intent on merriment – it was sold in Aberdeen, but bought by sympathisers. The coo was taken back home to its first owner, watched by another large crowd and the local brass band. This spawned a minor industry in Turra Coo commemorative post-cards, pottery, glassware, etc. A memorial was erected in 1971.

lonely glens of former upper Banffshire, once hazy with the smoke from illicit stills.

WHISKY Today the whisky industry, centred on the River Spey, is big business. Grand malt whisky names – Macallan, the Glenlivet, Glenfiddich, Glenfarclas, and so on – stretch all the way to the sea, sounding every bit as distinguished as the famous wines noted as place names in France's Rhône valley.

Provost Skene's House, Aberdeen

King's College, Old Aberdeen

166

Granite detail from the entrance to St Nicholas's churchyard

▶▶▶ Aberdeen   *162C2*

With a population of well over 200,000, the glittering granite and spacious streets of the United Kingdom's most northerly city make an impact on first-time visitors. Built between the river mouths of the Dee and the Don, this old-established place – a royal burgh since 1124 – once had strong trading links with Europe, while servicing its agricultural hinterland and developing other industries such as textiles.

Before the end of the 18th century, it was exporting its characteristic silver-grey granite to London and other places and also building the distinctive townscape seen today around Union Street (the main shopping thoroughfare). Unlike the soft sandstones of Edinburgh and Glasgow, tough granite did not suit ornate carving. Instead it was

used boldly in blocks, parapets and spires. In sunshine, the mica chips become a million mirrors, in rain, the stones reflect only the grey sky.

Many of Aberdeen's places of interest are within walking distance of each other. The east end of Union Street is the former centre of the early settlement, indicated by the mercat cross. Aberdeen's is one of the most splendid in Scotland, dating from 1686, and arcaded with

167

'EDUCATION, SALVATION AND DAMNATION'
One of the finest groupings of granite architecture in Aberdeen overlooks Union Terrace Gardens. St Mark's Church of 1892, with its handsome dome and colonnaded portico, is flanked by the central library, inspired by Renaissance styles, and on the other side by the exuberant Edwardian flourishes of His Majesty's Theatre. Together they form a trio which was dubbed 'Education, Salvation and Damnation'.

heraldic panels and portraits. Opposite is the 17th-century **Tolbooth** or **Old Town House**. (It once held prisoners before trial, and tours of the old cells are available.) Note the Flemish medieval-style turrets on the adjacent **New Town House**, a reminder of old trading links. The Shiprow opposite, one of the oldest streets in the city, leads down to the harbour.

Aberdeen Maritime Museum▶ The 16th-century **Provost Ross's House** is a unique survivor on the old Shiprow, between the market place and quayside. The museum portrays the city's sea-going past, from early times via fishing boats and tea clippers right up to the oil boom (*Open* Mon–Sat 10–5, Sun 11–5. *Admission free*).

Marischal College▶▶ was founded in 1593 by the Earl Marischal as a Protestant alternative to the Catholic King's College in Old Aberdeen (see page 168). The two combined to form Aberdeen University in 1860. Marischal's arresting façade (with the Marischal Museum within) was built from 1891 onwards, breaking all rules about granite and its severity. The spectacularly ornate work is set off by the gilded flags, and this giant granite wedding cake is still the second largest granite building in the world. (Only El Escorial, near Madrid, Spain, is larger.) (*Open* Mon–Fri 10–5, Sun 2–5. *Admission free*).

Provost Skene's House▶ Past the eye-catching façade of Marischal College and almost underneath the ugly modern block of St Nicholas House, this steeply gabled, rubble-built structure is the remnant of a once closely packed area of town houses. It dates in part from 1545. It is now a museum of civic life with restored furnished period rooms and a painted chapel, as well as a café (good for afternoon tea) (*Open* Mon–Sat 10–5. *Admission free*).

AN ABERDEEN SAYING
There is an old saying still current among Aberdonians: 'Tak awa Aiberdeen and twal mile roon aboot – an far are ye?' ('Take away Aberdeen and 12 miles (19km) round about and where are you?'), meaning that without Aberdeen the area would be lost and worthless.

ROYAL CASTLE INSPIRATION
By late Victorian times the east end of Union Street, called the Castlegate, was downright seedy. Even today, respectable, upright native Aberdonians are a bit uncomfortable about it. The 19th-century city planners had the answer. Right in the middle they built a Salvation Army Citadel (1893–6). It survives as such today, with a handsome baronial tower. This castle-like design was inspired by another symbol of strength and righteousness: Balmoral Castle. The resemblance is purely external.

The Northeast

Right: one of the colourful exhibits from the Aberdeen Maritime Museum

Old Aberdeen

Aberdeen Art Gallery►► has excellent collections of 18th- to 20th-century work (*Open* Mon–Sat 10–5, Sun 2–5. *Admission free*). Close by is **St Nicholas Kirk►**, the first place of worship in Aberdeen, founded in the 12th century.

Old Aberdeen►►, once a separate community near the River Don, lies north of the main city near the precincts of **King's College►**. The university was founded in 1494 and its cobbled streets and artisans' cottages make it an atmospheric campus. **King's College Chapel►►** with its crown spire is a fine example of an early collegiate chapel (*c*1500). The tall oak screen and the ribbed wooden ceiling and stalls have ornate medieval woodcarving. The King's College Visitor Centre (*Open* Mon–Sat 10–5, Sun 12–5. *Admission free*) is a good starting point for a tour.

Beyond the handsome Georgian **Old Aberdeen Town House►►** is the Chanonry, leading to St Machar's Cathedral and Seaton Park. The River Don curves round this park, then flows under the picturesque 14th-century Brig o'Balgownie.

St Machar's Cathedral► St Columba sent St Machar to build this church near the sea, where a river flowed in the shape of a shepherd's crook. The nave was possibly rebuilt in red sandstone by around 1370, then finished in granite by the mid-15th century. The building was damaged during the Reformation and in the 17th century, but extensively restored in the 19th century (*Open* daily 9–5. *Admission free*).

Aberdeen has sandy beaches, a funfair, leisure centres, swimming pools and spacious parks – in short, many of the trappings of a holiday town. It also has a large number of indoor venues specifically geared for children. If all else fails, you can always lose them for a while in the large maze in the city's Hazlehead Park.

The Satrosphere, signposted from the west end of Union Street, is undoubtedly Aberdeen's top children's attraction (*Open* Apr–early Oct, Mon–Sat 10–5, Sun 1.30–5; mid-Oct, Mon, Wed–Fri 10–4, Sat 10–5, Sun 1.30–5. *Admission charge*). Do not be put off by the 'interactive science and technology exhibition centre' description: it is a hands-on, absorbing experience for any child with imagination. There are endless experiments and demonstrations for children. They can play with mirrors and light, create a giant bubble a metre wide, play tunes on 2m pan pipes, whisper into a parabolic reflector and be heard across the hall, become a TV newsreader, balance balls in streams of hot air, build a waterwheel and become involved in dozens of other activities. Allow plenty of time to make the most of it.

Other Aberdeen attractions Jonah's Journey in Rosemount Place takes its theme from life in Bible times – here children can visit a nomad's tent, dress up and grind corn (*Open* Mon–Sat 10–12, Sun 2.30–4.30). **James Dun's House**, just by the Art Gallery in Schoolhill, sometimes has special exhibitions with children's themes, so is worth checking out. Older children will enjoy the interactive computers at the Maritime Museum (*Open* Mon–Sat 10–5, Sun 11–5. *Admission free*) and some of the exhibits (probably the shrunken heads!) at the Marischal College Museum (*Open* Mon–Fri 10–5, Sun 2–5. *Admission free*).

The Winter Gardens at the **Duthie Park** are popular with families. **Hazlehead Park** (pictured at the top of this page) also has a domestic animal zoo, as has **Doonies Farm**. Most of Aberdeen's parks have good playgrounds – try the one on the Beach Esplanade, where there is also a traditional fairground (in summer). Out of town, **Storybook Glen** near Maryculter is a sheltered valley where fibreglass models of cartoon and fairytale characters loom disconcertingly out of the undergrowth (*Open* Mar–Oct, daily 10–6; Nov–Feb, Sat–Sun 11–4. *Admission charge*).

FLORAL FACTS
Seaton Park is only one of the city's open spaces. Aberdeen lays special emphasis on flowers and is a frequent winner of the 'Britain in Bloom' award. Aberdeen's flower displays were initiated using 60 tonnes of daffodil bulbs and 600,000 crocuses in one phase alone. Rose bushes outnumber the locals by nine to one.

A ghoulish exhibit from the Marischal College Museum

TOURIST INFORMATION
Banff: Collie Lodge
(tel: 01261 812419).
Braemar: The Mews, Mar
Road (tel: 13397 41600).
Ballater: Albert Hall,
Station Square (tel:
013397 55306).

Braemar has recorded Britain's lowest temperature: –27.2°C

BALMORAL
Balmoral Castle is the private holiday home of the royal family and only opens its grounds and ballroom to the public for a short time each year (*Open* Easter–May, Mon–Sat 10–5; Jun–Jul, daily 10–5; last entry 4). Usually the ballroom houses a painting exhibition from the Royal Family's private collection. In August, when the royals are in residence, the castle serves as a high-security royal playground.

Lonely Corgarff Castle

▶▶ Ballater   162A1

Well-scrubbed and handsome Ballater has profited greatly from the needs of the royals at Balmoral for everything from bread to gumboots. With Balmoral just westward, there are more 'By Royal Appointment' signs here than anywhere else in Scotland.

Local excursions include the not-to-be-missed **Glen Muick** (pronounced Mick) with red deer sightings all but guaranteed. Also worth exploring are the birchwoods around Dinnet, notably **Loch Kinord** and the **Burn o Vat**, and a good network of trails around **Glen Tanar**, near Aboyne. Hardy walkers can explore the **Mounth passes** – a series of high-level ancient trails leading across the massif of The Mounth. Northwards is 16th-century **Corgarff Castle**, with its star-shaped defences added in 1748.

▶ Banff   162B3

Pressure from a local conservation group saved some of Banff's attractive Georgian domestic architecture from redevelopment into the retail anonymity that blighted so many other Scottish towns, and this old seacoast town is worth a stroll in its own right. However, its main attraction is **Duff House▶**, a restored Adam mansion, now the principal outstation of the National Galleries of Scotland, with displays of Scottish portraiture of the 18th and 19th centuries and fine period furniture (*Open* Apr–Sep, daily 11–4; Oct–Mar, Thu–Sun 11–4. *Admission charge*).

▶▶ Braemar   162A1

The A93, coming west up Deeside, climbs out of the Dee valley and turns southwards, seeking a pass over the Grampians. Braemar sits on the turn. It can feel a little transitory, yet it is an old-established resort, benefiting like Ballater from the royal presence at Balmoral. The **Highland Heritage Centre** (*Open* daily 9–5. *Admission free*), takes up the theme of the royal connection and the Braemar Highland Gathering. There is an excellent selection of local excursions, including the **Linn of Dee**, a picturesque rocky cleft, west of Inverey. Also near by is the **Devil's Punchbowl**, a water-worn rock feature among the pines at the Linn of Quoich. The **Colonel's Bed** is yet more rock and water: a narrow gorge with slippery shelves in Glen Ey. For the ambitious walker, **Glen Derry** gives access to the eastern end of the Cairngorms, as well as the pass of the Lairig Ghru leading through to the Spey.

The northern Picts lived in and around the Grampians between the 4th and 9th centuries AD. The Mounth, the hill ground between Deeside and Angus, was an important barrier. Moray was their final stronghold before defeat and gradual absorption by the ascendant Scots whose union with them formed the first kingdom of Scotland known as Alba (see page 27).

Burghead The most important Pictish centre was Burghead, on the coast near Elgin. A great promontory fort survived until a 'new' town of Burghead was built on a grid plan in 1805–9, destroying much of the Pictish ramparts and timber-laced walling that had stood there for more than a millennium. Six Pictish bull carvings survive from that time, outlined boldly in stone.

The bull is just one of the symbols which tantalise modern archaeologists and historians. The Picts left earthworks such as coastal headland forts in the northeast and inland sites like Bennachie, a hill near Inverurie, but it is their symbol stones which are the most vivid evidence of this long-gone culture. A few stones are still in their original locations, some have been re-erected or placed in museums, others have been built into walls or lost entirely.

Standing stones The **Picardy Stone** near Insch is typical, a whinstone pillar with, among other subjects, a clearly executed double-disc and Z-rod (a recurring symbol in Pictish

art), serpent and mirror. The **Maiden Stone** near Pitcaple is an impressive, red granite monolith of considerable presence, especially when slanting light highlights the curious so-called 'Pictish elephant', one of the most mysterious of the designs. This is a late (9th-century) work.

Most magnificent of all is **Sueno's Stone** on the outskirts of Forres, with its many figures galloping on the face of a 2½m monolith. Theories abound on the meaning of this stone and all the others. Some suggest that Sueno's Stone is war reporting on a grand scale – recording, ironically, the Scots victory over the Picts. Some see the other stones as monuments, others as proclamations. Nobody knows, but the designs have both power and inspiration. Tracking them down can make for interesting excursions in this northern corner.

THE MEANING OF THE STONES
The Picts were divided into two realms, the northern and southern. Many of the finest symbol stones belong to the northern grouping. Their language was ousted by the arrival of the Scots from Ireland and they left no written records. It is known that inheritance was through the female line – though Pictish kings reigned, their sons did not succeed them. Do the symbols carved on the stones indicate lineages, alliances and power within the leading Pictish families?

Left and below: the Maiden Stone, near Pitcaple

Whisky is one of Scotland's top exports, worth £2.1 billion in 1993, and is important in the economy of many communities. There are more than 40 distilleries in Moray alone, the greatest concentration anywhere in Scotland. More than just a distinctive plume of steam in the attractive wooded river valley, these distilleries sustain engineers, coppersmiths, painters, plumbers, maltsters and many more trades.

DALLAS DHU
Amidst all the live distilleries, busy bubbling, frothing and producing odd aromas, you can also visit a distillery of the past. In the care of Historic Scotland, Dallas Dhu near Forres is a time capsule and allows a more intimate inspection than working distilleries (*Open* Apr–Sep 9.30–6; Oct–Mar, Mon–Wed and Sat 9.30–4, Thu 9.30–12, Sun 2–4. *Admission charge*).

172

Copper stills at the Glen Garioch Distillery, Oldmeldrum

For centuries *uisge beatha* (the Gaelic for 'water of life') has been produced in Scotland from the simple ingredients of barley, water, yeast and, usually, peat smoke. There are two main distinctions: malt whisky and grain whisky. Most drinkers would say that malt has a more complex flavour and bouquet. Certainly, modern marketing techniques have given it more cachet and a higher price! Malt whisky uses only malted barley. Grain whisky may use malted barley but also other cereals, notably maize. A single malt is the product of a single distillery, while a blend, as its name suggests, is a blend of malt and grain whiskies – the higher the proportion of malt whisky, the better (or more expensive) the blend.

Experts broadly classify malt whiskies into Highland, Lowland, Islay and Campbeltown types. This can be generalised into eastern, notably from Speyside, and western, from the islands, mainly Islay. Of the two, the western malts are noticeably 'peaty'. The malt which is the basis of malt whisky has usually (but not necessarily) been bought from local maltings. Malt is germinated barley that has been killed off and then dried (sometimes with peat smoke).

The whisky-making process To make whisky, grind a large quantity of malted barley and add hot water to it in a large circular vat of several thousand litre capacity called a mash tun. Eventually, the result will be wort, a sweet-smelling liquid. Hold this in a worts receiver or underback below the mash tun. Use the solids in the mash tun, called draff, for winter cattle food.

Take the wort and add it with yeast to another enormous vessel, known as a wash-back, where it will ferment. Then pump this liquid, called the wash, via a wash charger into a wash still, which is a large copper container. Heat it, using gas if available. Condense the vapours in a worm – a coiled copper water-cooled tube. Repeat this process at least twice. Then run the distillate into a spirit safe. This is the part that needs most expertise. Both the beginning and end of the distilling process produce impurities. The whisky is, so to speak, in the middle.

Next, procure casks. Old sherry casks are particularly recommended. Add water to the whisky and place in the casks. Leave for several years before bottling as a single malt. Then sell worldwide as a prestige product!

THE ANGELS' SHARE
This is the name given to the whisky that was definitely there when the distillery staff put it into the cask but has gone, five or more years later, when the casks are broached for bottling or blending. Nothing untoward has taken place. There is a natural evaporation through the wood of the casks.

173

Casks – and their contents – maturing at the Glenfiddich Distillery, Dufftown

Distillery tours If you attempt any form of distilling in your kitchen, Customs and Excise will be very interested. The process is strictly commercially licensed and takes place only in Scotland's distilleries (and the product is most definitely spelt 'whisky', without an 'e'). Many distilleries place strong emphasis on visitor facilities and attempt to inject some drama and excitement into a process which is visually undramatic but nevertheless requires skill, method and large-scale investment.

A typical visit includes some kind of audio-visual presentation, with the malt whisky company describing their brand as the 'true taste of Scotland' and laying great store on historical roots. (Awkward facts detracting from 'Scottishness', such as the owning company being an overseas-based multinational, are skipped over.) Then there is a tour, of varying degrees of liveliness, depending on the guide; and afterwards a return to the hospitality area where a dram is usually offered. There will often be some kind of historic exhibition and nearly always a shop. No tour of Speyside is complete without taking in at least one distillery.

DOLPHINS

The Moray Firth contains the largest inshore colony of bottle-nosed dolphins in Britain. (The species otherwise tends to favour offshore waters.) Leaping dolphins can be seen anywhere at any time in the Firth. The entrances to the inner firths can be rewarding for dolphin watchers, as can the mouths of the rivers Findhorn and Spey (Spey Bay is particularly good for seals as well). The bottle-nosed dolphin can be recognised by its uniform grey with a paler underbelly and a tall dorsal fin.

Painted ceiling in Crathes Castle; the original castle was built in 1323 on land granted to the Burnett family by Robert the Bruce

▶ Craigellachie   162A2

A typical Speyside community dependent on the whisky industry and visiting anglers, Craigellachie is noted for its cooperage, now the **Speyside Cooperage Visitor Centre▶▶**, where the skills of barrel making are demonstrated (*Open* Easter–Sep, Mon–Sat 9.30–4.30; Oct–Easter, weekdays only. *Admission charge*). Also near by is **Craigellachie Bridge▶**, designed by Thomas Telford which crosses the Spey with an iron span cast in Wales.

▶▶ Crathes Castle   162B1

Open: castle Apr–Oct, daily 11–5.30, last entry 4.45. Grounds daily 9–dusk. Admission charge

This 16th-century L-plan tower house has many rare original features, notably four rooms with painted ceilings, as well as a ghost of a green lady and fine old furniture, locally made. Crathes is also noted for its gardens, made into compartments by close-clipped yew hedges and containing many unusual species

▶ Dufftown   162A2

A planned town founded in 1817, Dufftown has wide streets which centre on a square and landmark **clock tower** (which houses the local museum). The little town is bound up with distilleries, including famous malt whisky names such as Glenfiddich, which is overlooked by the ruins of the 13th-century Balvenie Castle (itself a malt whisky name). The **Glenfiddich Distillery Visitor Centre▶▶▶** offers one of the very best audio-visuals and tours, showing all the stages from malting through to bottling (*Open* all year, Mon–Fri, 9.30–4.30, also Sat 9.30–4.30, Sun 12–4.30 Easter–mid-Oct. *Admission free*).

Though a planned town, Dufftown's story as a settlement goes as far back as AD 566, when Mortlach Church was founded, one of the earliest religious sites in Scotland. There are Pictish stones and a 'leper's squint', a hole through which lepers could observe proceedings inside the church.

▶ Elgin   162A3

Elgin has rebuilt its townscape over the centuries, yet retained fragments of early times. A medieval street plan can still be made out, with narrow alleyways leading off the main street. Some arcaded façades from 18th-century shops also survive. Take in the view from the top of the Lady Hill at its west end. This was the site of the castle – a little of the wall remains – occupied by King Edward I of England in the Wars of Independence.

Elgin Cathedral▶ ('The Lantern of the North') was founded in 1224 and burned in 1390 by the notorious Wolf of Badenoch, the black sheep of the royal Stuart family (following excommunication by the local bishop). The cathedral was rebuilt and in use until the Reformation, when it suffered the usual fate of great religious seats in Scotland. Much of its stonework was pillaged and used elsewhere, though the historic structure was taken into the care of the nation in 1825 (*Open* Apr–Sep, daily 9.30–6; Oct–Mar, Mon–Wed and Sat 9.30–4, Thu 9.30–12; Sun 2–4. *Admission charge*).

'Acorn to Cask', the story of whisky barrels at Craigellachie

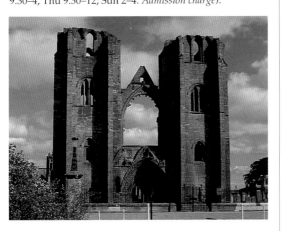

Elgin Cathedral adds distinction to the skyline of the 'capital' of Moray. Much of the surviving work dates from the 13th century

175

Elgin Museum▶ is reckoned to be one of the finest museums in the north. Among other exhibits it features the oldest dinosaurs found in Britain – though, like the museum itself, they are quite small (*Open* Apr–Oct, daily 10–5. *Admission charge*).

Other attractions in town include **Johnstons of Elgin▶**, a woollen mill specialising in cashmere, with a visitor centre and mill tours. The town also has a motor museum and a preserved meal mill. Near by, out on the levels of the Laich of Moray, is **Duffus Castle▶**, the impressive remains of a motte and bailey castle with a 14th-century tower. Unusually for Scotland the moat is still water-filled.

Spynie Palace▶, the ruin of a former bishop's mansion with good views from the tower, is to the east. Elgin's former port, **Lossiemouth▶**, is now a resort and fishing town, with a busy airbase near by. A beautiful coastline stretches out to east and west. Also near by is **Pluscarden Abbey▶ ▶**, originally a 13th-century foundation, suppressed during the Reformation. In 1948, monks from Prinknash Abbey, in Gloucester, started restoration (*Open* daily 5am–8.30pm. *Admission free*).

THE BATTLE OF MONS GRAUPIUS
The Roman historian Tacitus tells how Agricola's forces, ranging north in the summer of AD 83, finally brought to battle and defeated the Caledonian warriors by a hill within sight of the sea in the north of Scotland. This was the Battle of Mons Graupius, which also gave the name Grampian, possibly due to a 1470s printing error when 'm' was substituted for 'u'. Many historians favour a Grampian location for the battle, possibly Bennachie near Inverurie. The real battle site has never been found.

THE MOUNTH
The Mounth, from the Gaelic *monadh* – ('moorland' or 'mountain'), is the name given to the hillmass south of Deeside. The Mounth passes were once important throughroutes to the north. Today, they survive as hill tracks marked on maps: the Capel Mounth, the Firmouth, the Fungle and many more, now mainly the haunt of leisure-time walkers and mountain bikers. Motorable passes include the A93 over Glen Shee and the B974 Cairn o Mount.

TOURIST INFORMATION
Forres: 116 High Street (tel: 01309 672938). Fraserburgh: 3 Saltoun Square (tel: 01346 518315).

One of Fyvie Castle's main attractions is its outstanding art collection: portraits by Batoni, Raeburn, Ramsay, Gainsborough and others

► **Fettercairn**   *162B1*
Car travellers who tire of the fast dual carriageway A90 should try an interesting route to the northeast via Fettercairn, a little place on the southern edge of the Grampian Hills. Fettercairn has an 1861 Gothic arch recalling the visit of Queen Victoria, and a malt whisky visitor centre open May to September except Sundays. The Fettercairn diversion leads on to the start of a scenic hill road, the B974 to Banchory, which reaches its highest point at the **Cairn o Mount**. This hilltop cairn gives excellent views southwards over Angus and is typical of skyline cairns which have been altered by generations of travellers. Originally it dates from the 2nd millennium BC.
    Fasque House►, near Fettercairn, has been the home of the Gladstone family for six generations (none of whom seem to have thrown very much out). The most famous of them was William Gladstone, Victorian Prime Minister. Fasque (1809) is a castellated mansion in Georgian Gothic style, with a pleasingly mellowed, lived-in air (*Open May–Sep, daily 11–5.30, last entry 5. Admission charge*).

► **Fochabers**   *162A3*
Worth visiting for its choice of antique shops, this handsome little planned town was built by the Duke of Gordon in 1776. He thought the old village was too near his castle, so knocked it down. He did not think of building a bypass for the A96 which makes the main street very noisy today. Fochabers is the home of Baxters, whose tinned food factory dominates the western approaches. There is an excellent view of the River Spey from a viewpoint south of the town, signposted **The Earth Pillars**, where eroded columns of red conglomerate rock form the foreground to a striking river panorama, seen through the pinewood.
    Fochabers Folk Museum►► is housed in a converted church and is filled with artefacts of a bygone rural life from horsedrawn carts to a turnip-chopping machine (*Open daily 9.30–1 and 2–5, 2–6 in summer. Admission free*).

▶ Forres   162A3

Like Elgin, further east, Forres also maintains its medieval street plan in part. The main street bulges out at the former market place in the town centre, though the buildings are mainly Victorian. The **Falconer Museum** (*Open* Apr–Oct, Mon–Sat 10–5. *Admission free*) explores local history.

Brodie Castle▶▶ is a National Trust for Scotland property, a little to the east of Forres. Brodie is based on a 16th-century Z-plan with later additions, and houses fine French furniture, porcelain and a painting collection (*Open* Apr–Sep, Mon–Sat 11–5.30, Sun 1.30–5.30; Oct, Sat–Sun only. *Admission charge*). Well worth visiting at any season is the **Califer Braes** viewpoint, with a broad view of the Moray Firth.

▶ Fraserburgh   162C3

Fraserburgh is a fishing port with little merit in its townscape. However, it has a superb beach and also a most interesting visitor attraction. **Scotland's Lighthouse Museum▶▶▶** portrays the story of lighthouse service, now ending with automation. There are fascinating displays as well as a tour of Kinnaird Head lighthouse itself (*Open* Apr–Oct, Mon–Sat 10–6, Sun 12.30–6; Nov–Mar, Mon–Sat 10–4, Sun 12.30–4. *Admission charge*).

▶▶ Fyvie Castle   162B2

Open: Apr–Jun and Sep, daily 1.30–5.30; Jul–Aug, daily 11–5.30; Oct, weekends 1.30–5.30. Last entry 4.45. Admission charge

Five-towered Fyvie Castle epitomises northeast castles: a rambling pile, imposing yet hidden away behind its endless walls and tall trees. The original 13th-century quadrangular fortress evolved over the centuries into a magnificent stately home. Famous families in the northeast, the Prestons, Meldrums, Setons and Gordons, held it in turn, each adding to the building. Then it was bought by Alexander Forbes Leith, a local boy made good in America. He refurbished it in parts, adding Edwardian opulence to the mix. The castle has sumptuous interiors and fine furniture, and displays a magnificent painting collection, including a dozen Raeburns.

Forres's Falconer Museum has a very strong local collection

AN EARLY NAME
Some think that the 'Varris' on the map of Ptolemy, the 1st-century AD geographer, refers to today's Forres.

RANDOLPH'S LEAP
Randolph's Leap, a beauty spot on the River Findhorn, where the river narrows amongst rocks and woodlands, is unfairly named. The Randolph was Thomas Randolph, Earl of Moray. He was in hot pursuit of one Alastair Cumming who had just raided his Darnaway Castle. It was Cumming who escaped by leaping the river at this point. Judge for yourself the relative ease of choosing between a downward leap of around 3m or being skewered on a 14th-century broadsword.

Falconer Museum, Forres

The Northeast

AN UNUSUAL VEHICLE
One of the exhibits in the Grampian Museum of Transport is the Craigievar Express. This is a steam-powered tricycle, and was one of Scotland's pioneering road vehicles. It was built in 1895 by the local post-man to help him on his rounds. The one-cylindered, coal-fired, vertical boiler contraption competed in the 1971 London to Brighton Car Rally – and completed the course.

►► Glen Shee   *162A1*

Climbing to over 620m at the Cairnwell, the A93 between Bridge of Cally and Braemar is the highest main road in the United Kingdom (though not the highest motorable road). Surrounded on both sides by Munros (see panel page 149), it has been prey to ski developers and is very popular when snow conditions are right. The solitude of the high tops in the immediate vicinity has been invaded by vast car parks, snow fencing, chairlifts, tows and cater-ing facilities. With the highest hills only a little over 900m, the downhill runs are not very long, however. The chairlift operates outside the winter season. On the steep south side of the pass is the Devil's Elbow, a once fear-some hairpin bend now bypassed, but still visible.

► Grampian Transport Museum   *162B2*
Open: Apr–Oct, daily 10–5. Admission charge
Alford offers plenty for children, in particular the Grampian Transport Museum with its extensive collec-tion of historic vehicles and the adjoining narrow-gauge railway – built on the original site of the long-vanished 'proper' railway – which runs to Haughton Country Park. Take the road north to **Suie Hill** for a peerless view over rural Aberdeenshire. If it is a summer weekend, continue over to the community hall of the enterprising village of Clatt, where the locals serve a real afternoon tea.

►► Haddo House   *162C2*
Open: Easter, May–Sep, daily 1.30–5.30; Oct, Sat–Sun only, 1.30–5.30; last entry 4.45. Admission charge
There is quite a concentration of National Trust for Scotland properties in the northeast. Haddo House, with its country park, is on the **Castle Trail**, the signposted route which

Pastoral landscape near Inverurie

PITMEDDEN GARDEN
About 6km from Haddo House, Pitmedden Garden, another National Trust for Scotland property, is at its best in high summer, thanks to 40,000 annual plants and 5km of box hedging. This is the re-creation of a formal garden originally laid out in 1675 (*Open* May–Sep, daily 10–5.30, last entry 5. *Admission charge*).

178

takes in the best of them, though this William Adam design of 1731 has an elegance far removed from the bold and battered fortresses typical of the Trail. Haddo's interiors are mostly 'Adam revival' from about 1880 and the overall impression is light and cheerful, inside and out, with curving wings on either side of a harmonious façade. Combine this excursion with a visit to Pitmedden Garden (see panel).

Grampian Transport Museum, Alford

▶ Huntly   162B2

A substantial (for Grampian) town serving a rural hinterland, Huntly was the power base of the influential Gordons who built their castle here on a defensive site between the rivers Bogie and Deveron. Today, **Huntly Castle** stands as an imposing ruin, with heraldic adornments on its walls (*Open* Apr–Sep, daily 9.30–6; Oct–Mar, Mon–Wed and Sat 9.30–4, Thu 9.30–12, Sun 2–4. *Admission charge*). Huntley also has an all-weather cross-country ski track down by the river, with equipment for hire.

TOURIST INFORMATION
Huntly: 9a The Square
(tel: 01466 792255).

▶ Inverurie   162B2

Now bypassed by the busy A96, Inverurie is a locally important administrative centre in the prosperous farming area known as the Garioch (pronounced 'geerie'). It is overlooked by one of the northeast's landmark hills, **Bennachie**, with its hilltop vitrified Pictish fort. There are other prehistoric sites in the vicinity (see page 171), including the atmospheric **Loanhead Stone Circle**, near Daviot, 8km to the northwest. At Oyne, 13km northwest of Inverurie, the displays at **Archeolink**▶▶ will tell you much about the prehistoric peoples who built these monuments (*Open* Mar–Oct, daily 9.30–5; Nov–Feb, Mon–Fri 11–4, Sat–Sun 10–4. *Admission charge*).

GORDON BENNETT
Few places can claim to be the home town of an expletive, but Keith was the birthplace of 'Gordon Bennett'. This mild oath refers to James Gordon Bennett, born in the town in 1795. He was the founder and editor of the *New York Herald*, and is sometimes described as the father of chequebook journalism, because of his innovative sensationalist style.

▶ Keith   162B3

Another planned town on the main Aberdeen-Inverness road, Keith is also the gateway to the **Malt Whisky Trail**. This is a signposted drive – presumably for non-tipplers – around seven malt whisky distilleries, one of which, Strathisla, is in Keith, though the others lie in more picturesque settings in the attractive hinterland of the River Spey and around Ben Rinnes.

Drive

The northeast coast

The section of coast between the mouths of the rivers Don and Spey remains comparatively unexplored. Aberdeen to Sandend is 139km, the return along the main road 80km. Allow a full day.

Starting from Aberdeen, the A92 is set back from the coast until the Ythan estuary at Newburgh on the A975. The northern bank of the estuary is a wild habitat of dune and coastal heath, which is explained at the **Forvie Nature Reserve Visitor Centre** (run by Scottish Natural Heritage).

Continue north, diverting to tiny Whinnyfold, which has a view of the Bay of Cruden and the village of Cruden Bay. Bram Stoker used to holiday here, and the nearby ruin of Slains Castle reputedly inspired his *Dracula*.

At the gloomy **Bullers of Buchan**, the sea has burst through the cliff in a deep, tide-filled, kittiwake-haunted hollow. Beyond, **Peterhead**, the largest white-fish landing port in Europe, and also a North Sea oil servicing centre, has a maritime museum.

Peterhead's harbour – busy with fishing boats

After St Fergus comes the lonely coastline around **Rattray Head**. **The Loch of Strathbeg**, Scotland's largest land-locked coastal lagoon, is an important wintering ground for wildfowl.

Off the B9033 the fishing villages of St Combs and Cairnbulg huddle with gable ends to the sea. **Fraserburgh**, dour in grey granite, has **Scotland's Lighthouse Museum** on Kinnaird Head and a fine beach.

Turning west, the sands are left behind for grey rocks which rear up beyond Rosehearty and reach impressive heights around Pennan. Seabird colonies are spectacular around the fearsomely precipitous **Troup Head** (not suitable for young children). **Gardenstown** has an attractive little harbour, as well as a fine walk to the west, to the ruin of the 11th-century Kirk of St John the Evangelist.

The cliffs stretch unbroken to **Macduff**, another fishing port with a marine aquarium to visit, and twinned with **Banff** across the River Deveron. Some fine Georgian domestic architecture can be admired here, along with the Adam-designed **Duff House**, an outstation of the National Gallery of Scotland and full of fine paintings.

Continue west to **Portsoy**, with a restored 17th- and 18th-century harbourfront. Westwards again is **Sandend**, with the very best beach in the northeast 3km to the west. Return to Banff for a speedy return to Aberdeen on the A947.

Stromness

Kinnairds Head
Sandhaven
Rosehearty
Fraserburgh
Pitsligo Castle
Peathill
Cairnbulg
Troup Head
Crovie
Pennan
Inverallochy
Gardenstown
Protstonhill
New Aberdour
St Combs
irk of St John he Evangelist
Dubford
Memsie
Minnonie
Rathen
B9033
A98
221m
Bracklamore Hill
Loch of Strathbeg
Rattray Head
A98
New Pitsligo
234m
Waughton Hill
A981
A92
Crimond
Blackhill
New Leeds
A952
St Fergus Moss
St Fergus
Mintlaw
Rora
Kirkton
NE of Scotland Agricultural Heritage Centre & Aden Country Park
Longside
Ugie
A950
Peterhead
Clola
Nether Kinmundy
Boddam
Buchan Ness
Moss of Cruden
A92
Hatton
A952
Coldwells
Bullers of Buchan
Slains Castle
Cruden Bay
Bogbrae
Chapel Hill
Bay of Cruden
A975
Whinnyfold
Lerwick

Tarves
Ellon
Kirkton of Logie Buchan
Pitmedden Garden
A920
Pitmedden
Ythan
Sands of Forvie
Collieston
Forvie Nature Reserve
Oldmeldrum
Whiterashes
Foveran
Newburgh
A92
Inverurie
Kinmuck
Drums
A947
Delfrigs
Newmachar
Balmedie Country Park
Balmedie
Hatton of Fintray
Kintore
Don
Potterton
Corby Loch
Blackdog
Blackburn
Dyce
A96
266m
Brimmond Hill
Bucksburn
Bridge of Don
Kirkton of Skene
Westhill
ABERDEEN
Loch of Skene
A944
A92
Girdle Ness
Greg Ness
Leuchar Burn
Cults
Dee
A956
A93
Peterculter
Cove Bay

0   5   10 km
0   1   5 miles

Kildrummy Castle, seat of the Earls of Mar; this is the great triple window of the chapel

A TRAITOR'S REWARD
Kildrummy was besieged by the English in 1306. Sir Nigel Bruce (King Robert's brother) held out but was betrayed by Osbarn the smith, who had been promised gold by the besiegers. After the castle fell he got his reward – poured molten down his throat. Or so the story goes.

AN ECCENTRIC BIRD
Among the Leith Hall soldiers was Colonel Alexander Sebastian Leith Hay, who became laird in 1862. He was in the Thin Red Line at Balaclava and also helped crush the Indian Mutiny. He returned home with a white cockatoo named Cocky, which spoke Hindustani and lived for 50 years at Leith Hall. On its death it was given a burial with full military honours.

TOURIST INFORMATION
Stonehaven: 66 Allardice Street (tel: 01569 762806).
Tomintoul: The Square (tel: 01807 580285).

▶▶ Kildrummy Castle and Gardens   *162B2*

Open: castle Apr–Sep, daily 9.30–6; gardens Apr–Oct, daily 10–5. Admission charge

Kildrummy is one of the best-preserved medieval castles in Scotland – though far from complete, as one glance at the shattered walls will confirm. Built to an unusual shield-shape plan and echoing the fortresses at Caernarvon and Harlech in Wales, Kildrummy controlled the routes through Donside to the north. It withstood many sieges and was finally dismantled after its role as Jacobite headquarters in the 1715 rebellion.

Kildrummy Castle Gardens are a separate concern from the castle, though the two make a good combined visit. They occupy the adjacent quarry from which the castle rock was cut. In this sheltered bowl are many unusual varieties of rock plant and shrubs, as well as a water garden designed by a Japanese engineer. There is often a chance to buy surplus plants.

▶▶ Leith Hall   *162B2*

Open: Easter, May–Sep, daily 1.30–5.30; Oct, weekends only, last entry 4.45; grounds daily 9.30–sunset. Admission charge

The archetypal 'big hoose', Leith Hall was occupied by the Leiths, later the Leith Hays, for 300 years. They were a military family, and the National Trust for Scotland, who have been here since 1945, have made the most of this with an exhibition within the grand mansion. There are fine walks within the grounds and a pleasant garden.

▶▶ North East of Scotland Agricultural Heritage Centre   *162C2*

Open: May–Sep, daily 11–4.30; Apr and Oct, weekends 12–4.30. Admission free

Anyone navigating the bleak hinterland of the old county of Aberdeenshire will realise that the forefathers of today's rural communities must have been a hardworking lot. They were the ones who turned a poorly drained, boulder-strewn, exposed shoulder into a fertile and prosperous landscape. Their story is told in this heritage centre, housed in the old home farm of the former Aden (pronounced 'aa-din') estate. The centre's displays include a fine exhibition '*Weel Vrocht Grun*', defiantly entitled in the northeast's own speech and meaning the 'well-worked ground'. The estate is now a 93-hectare country park.

▶ Stonehaven   *162C1*

While Aberdeen's growth has turned many nearby places into dormitories, the centre of Stonehaven appears to have retained its character. Originally a fishing settlement, it was extended in 1795 by the local laird who built spacious streets round a main square a short distance from the old harbour. Today, there are only a few working boats. The local museum is housed in the old town's 16th-century Tolbooth, close to the harbour edge (*Open* Jun–Sep, Mon, Thu–Sat 10–12 and 2–5, Wed and Sun 2–5. *Admission free*).

Dunnottar Castle▶▶▶ (*Open* Mar–Oct, Mon–Sat 9–6, Sun 2–5; Nov–Feb, Mon–Fri 9–dusk. *Admission charge*). A few minutes down the coast, this 14th-century fortress is worth visiting for its spectacular setting on a rocky headland. Dunnottar was a stronghold of the Earls Marischal of Scotland. In the wars of the Commonwealth, the Scottish crown jewels were hidden here from Cromwell's army.

THE EARLS MARISCHAL
The title of Marischal origi-nally meant the keeper of the king's mares. The Keith family of Dunnottar were the hereditary Earls Marischal until their extinc-tion in the 18th century.

Stonehaven harbour. This former fishing port also used to have a seaside holiday trade, now diminished, like other east coast resorts

183

▶ Tomintoul   *162A2*

Near the southern end of the Malt Whisky Trail, Tomintoul lies among the uplands of Moray, with the Cairngorms on the far horizon. It was founded by the Duke of Gordon in 1779. The village makes a good base for exploring the Glenlivet Estate (part of the Crown Estate), which offers a variety of outdoor activities amongst the high moors and forests. Tomintoul also has a local museum, part of the Tourist Information Centre (closed in winter). It lies on the A939 to Cockbridge, which rises to 600m, giving access to the Lecht skiing area, and has gained a certain notoriety as it is usually the first road in Scotland to be blocked by snow. However, it is an important link for tourers between Speyside and Deeside.

SCOTTISH HEIGHTS
Tomintoul is the highest village in the Highlands at 354m, though the highest village in Scotland is Wanlockhead (421m) in Dumfries and Galloway.

The Great Glen & Western Highlands

*Carrbridge; the arch
across the River Dulnain
dates from 1715*

The Great Glen & Western Highlands

186

THE GREAT GLEN
The wrenching and sliding of the earth's crust formed this coast-to-coast fault line from the searoads of Loch Linnhe to the inner Moray Firth. Granite from Foyers above Loch Ness on its eastern side matches granite around Strontian, over 95km away to the west, in the hills of Ardgour.

WEST HIGHLAND CONTRASTS
One example of the interplay between loch and high ground which typifies the West Highlands is the summit of Ben Nevis. Though it is the highest point anywhere in the UK, it is only 8km from the salt waters of Loch Linnhe.

THE GREAT GLEN The area surrounding this coast-to-coast fault line that splits the Highlands takes in Scotland's highest mountains and greatest lochs. With the exception of the gentler landscape around Nairn on the inner Moray Firth, and the greenness of the far end of Kintyre, reminiscent of pastoral Ayrshire, most of this terrain is rugged. Though the central Cairngorms have been almost tamed in recent years by ski lifts, which spill visitors all year round onto the fragile arctic plateau, the western Cairngorms remain the province only of the hardy hillwalker. West of the Great Glen, the big glens of Cannich and Affric carry hydroelectric dams but emptiness still lies beyond. Loch Morar, deepest of all in the far west, still leads in to the trackless reaches of the Rough Bounds of Knoydart. Even some of the shores of Loch Linnhe are roadless.

As for the Great Glen itself, its hills just fail to reach truly magnificent proportions: it is large without being impressive. Yet it remains firmly on the touring route of those determined to 'do' the Highlands in a day or two and especially of those who hope to find the essence of the Highlands in the busy town of Inverness. Excursions off this main through-route are rewarding, to places such as Glen Roy with its curious Parallel Roads, or to the far reaches of Loch Arkaig and the mysteries of hidden Jacobite treasure.

SPEYSIDE This region, among the old pinewoods, is subtly different. The blue shadows on the Cairngorm backdrop change as the sun goes round, first highlighting then casting shadows deep into the Larig Ghru, the ancient mountain pass that links Speyside with Deeside. Adding to the enticements of birch and Scots pine, lochs with ospreys and other unusual birds, long hill passes and high level excursions, are the commercial developments which range from steam railways to Highland estate safaris.

THE WEST HIGHLANDS The Argyll area, taking in Loch Linnhe, is different again. Here is the picture-postcard interplay of sea loch and wooded hillslope. The mountains diminish in height the further south you travel, yet the landscape still retains a ruggedness, amongst the drowned valleys of Knapdale for example. Only towards the far end of Kintyre is a sense of the Highlands lost almost entirely. Most of the main population centres in the area have been involved with generations of tourists. Inverness is a large commercial centre servicing all of the Northern Highlands. Aviemore was a custom-built 1960s development. Re-development seems always just around the corner: it is looking seedy and is a definite culture shock for those expecting quaint little cottages on the road north. Fort William is an all but unavoidable natural route centre in the West Highlands. It has no pretensions towards the picturesque but is practical in terms of its services. Further

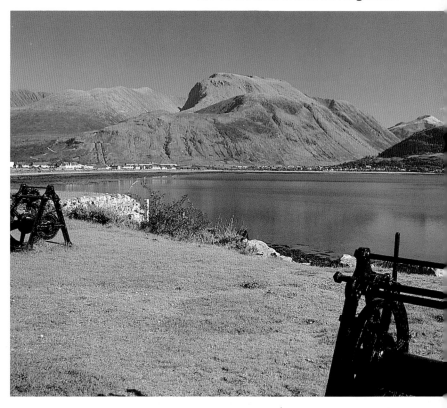

south, Oban is a gateway to the Hebrides and an old-established resort. The often overlooked Campbeltown at the south end of Kintyre is a self-contained working community.

Away from the main towns, there are plenty of smaller places but the essence of this area is definitely rural and rugged, with extensive forestry plantings and a sense of mossy green lushness. When the cloud is down on the hills and the prevailing south-westerlies are dumping their moist contents on campsites and luxury hotels alike, consider it only to be an interlude in the ever-changing pattern of western weather (though it has to be admitted that some of the wettest parts of Scotland lie around the Great Glen). When the sun returns, the colours of hill and loch shine out in breathtaking clarity and the West Highlands can be for-given for everything (except perhaps the midges). This is picture-postcard Scotland, if you time it right.

Ben Nevis from Corpach; this view of Britain's highest mountain hints at the great corries and cliffs hidden when looking up from Fort William

The true Highland cattle of old were wiry black beasts – unlike the modern cuddly version such as this calf

188

CONTROVERSIAL NAME
The area around the River Spey is sometimes known as Speyside and sometimes Strathspey. The local tourist board's introduction of 'Spey Valley' to its name provoked fierce correspondence in Scotland's quality press from numerous partisan Scots decrying the 'anglicising' of Scotland's place names. Even road signs, at one stage, had the new name unofficially blanked out.

►►► (Aviemore) and Strathspey   185D4

The transformation of **Aviemore►** from sleepy Highland railway junction to upmarket St Moritz-type ski resort never quite worked. Concrete shoeboxes amongst birches failed to appeal to the desired clientele who, unaccountably, still preferred the Alps. Skiing is very popular here, however, although a combination of gale-force winds and the icy upper slopes of the Cairngorm might deter those who just want to pose in fashionable ski gear. Aviemore bustles all year round with tourists and skiers, but is fortunately a very small blot on a very large and impressive landscape. **Strathspey►►►** itself is magnificent. Aviemore is a good base with shops and a variety of leisure facilities: ice rink, theatre, cinema, restaurants, discos, amusements, snooker and so on all within the Aviemore Centre, plus a whole range of activities and places to visit within easy reach.

The innovative **Landmark Visitor Centre►►►** at Carrbridge was the first of its kind and portrays many aspects of Scotland, from history to wildlife, by means of audiovisuals and displays. There is also a range of outdoor attractions: mazes, water slides and adventure playgrounds (*Open* Apr–mid-Jul, Sep, Oct, daily 10–6; mid-Jul–Aug, daily 10–7.30; Nov–Mar, daily 10–5. *Admission charge*).

Rothiemurchus Estate►► This working Highland estate, just southeast of Aviemore, offers estate and farm tours by tractor and trailer, Land Rover safari-type excursions, guided walks, a trout farm, fishing lochs and other activities. Its visitor centre opens daily all year.

Highland Wildlife Park Not just today's wildlife, but fauna such as wolves (now extinct in Scotland) can be seen safely fenced off at the Highland Wildlife Park at Kincraig (*Open* daily 10–4, extended hours in summer. *Admission charge*).

Loch an Eilean►►► There is a good walk right round this inspiring loch close to Aviemore amid ancient pinewood, a low level option well within the capabilities of most visitors. Crested tits and crossbills are a speciality. Mind your head on the door lintel of the visitor centre beside the loch, which is open daily.

The Great Wood of Caledon – natural pine forest on Speyside

Inshriach Nursery▶▶ (*Open* Mon–Sat) This wonderful specialist nursery on the B970 west of Loch an Eilean is popular with rock-garden enthusiasts. It has a good range of arctic alpine species – and if it grows at Inshriach, it will probably survive in your garden.

▶▶ Boat of Garten   185D4

Though singling out just one little community from the many in Speyside seems arbitrary, Boat of Garten is typical. It makes a peaceful base for exploring the area, being at a little distance from Aviemore. It has an excellent golf course and a choice of walks through sheltered pinewoods. It is also a steam railway base.

Offering the best view (the Cairngorms) of any preserved steam railway line in Britain, the **Strathspey Railway▶▶▶** is pure nostalgia, especially at the original Boat of Garten Station, near the Boat Hotel. There is a small museum here as well. The line runs to Aviemore. Check the opening hours in advance, but it operates most of the main season.

BIRD LIFE
Speyside is home to a number of rare bird species, not only the osprey, but the increasingly rare capercaillie. This is like a cross between a large grouse and a very aggressive turkey. It is still found in the old Scots pinewoods, but its habit of failing to spot high deer fences when it is in flight does little for the species' wellbeing.

TOURIST INFORMATION
Aviemore: Grampian Road (tel: 01479 810363).

Loch Garten▶▶▶ Another gem lies within easy reach – here you can spy upon the domestic arrangements of Scotland's most famous pair of ospreys. They get on with the serious business of first catching fish and then feeding it to their voracious offspring, all before the relentless gaze of closed-circuit television cameras, large telescopes and terribly earnest wardens. Ospreys are again becoming almost common in quite a few lochs and rivers hereabouts, though they were extinct in Scotland by the early years of this century, persecuted by gamekeepers guarding fish stocks, and returned only in 1959. Look for large hovering broad-winged birds, a little like giant lapwings at first glance. The visitor hide is open daily (ospreys permitting) in the breeding season (May to August); the reserve opens daily all year.

Speyside steam trains link Aviemore and Boat of Garten. There are plans to extend the tracks to Broomhill and eventually on to Grantown-on-Spey. Outstanding Cairngorm views are guaranteed

Cairngorm chairlift

A CAIRNGORM GHOST
Few Scottish ghosts are rugged enough for life on top of the Cairngorms plateau, except for one: the Grey Man of Ben Macdhui. He first terrified the life out of a respectable professor who was walking on the plateau in mist when he became aware of something which followed him, taking one step for every three of his. In 1943, another walker, who happened to be armed, fired his revolver at a 'thing' which loomed at him out of the mist. Other tales are told by climbers and local stalkers around the fireside – especially after a dram or two.

Skiing in the Cairngorms – big business for Aviemore

▶▶ Cairngorms 185D4

The Cairngorms contain four of the five highest mountains in Britain, some of the finest hill passes and arguably the best ice, snow and rock climbing. They represent the country's largest continuous stretch of high ground – an arctic tundra plateau. They are flanked by foothills whose slopes carry Britain's largest surviving fragments of natural pine forest. There are endless opportunities for ski touring, walking, climbing and other activities which respect the fragile environment. The area is under threat from intrusive skiing and tourism developments (see page 188), excessive deer numbers, the proliferation of bulldozed tracks and commercial afforestation, but still remains magnificent.

▶ Caledonian Canal 185C4

The Caledonian Canal, linking east and west coasts, was started in 1803 under the engineer Thomas Telford. It took 19 years to complete and is about 107km long. Approximately 72km is along the natural passage formed by three lochs, Lochy, Oich and Ness, which lie in the Great Glen fault line. The canal has 29 locks, the most famous being the series of eight near Banavie (3km north of Fort William) known as Neptune's Staircase. The project received priority as it was considered to have strategic importance for Britain's navy, but was never wide enough to accommodate large naval craft. Today its chief use is recreational. One good place for watching canal activity is at Fort Augustus with its series of locks through the centre of the village.

▶▶▶ Cawdor Castle 185D5

Open: May–mid-Oct, daily 10–5. Admission charge
Some castles in private hands impress with their opulence, others display stuffy collections while the owner lives elsewhere. Cawdor Castle, the romantic family home of the Earls of Cawdor, does neither of these things, but instead combines the appearance of a fortified stronghold with an air of friendliness.

Though it has a legendary association with Shakespeare's *Macbeth*, it post-dates the historical events around which Shakespeare wrote the well-known tragedy. Most of Cawdor is 16th- or 17th-century, though the central tower dates from around 1370, with 15th-century fortifications. Unoccupied for about 100 years after the last Jacobite uprising in 1745, the castle owes much of its charm to its appearance, which remains unaltered since those days.

Generations of the family have accumulated a variety of artefacts: portraits, Flemish tapestries, Venetian bed hangings and so on, as well as historical material, including the iron gate or yett from Lochindorb Castle (see page 195) which the 6th Thane of Cawdor was ordered to destroy. But Cawdor is much more about the overall effect than individual display items.

Best of all are the room notes. Far from breathlessly tiptoeing past objects, visitors can be heard laughing out loud at the witty captions – a scenario unique in a Scottish castle, which makes it well worth visiting for that reason alone. There are also attractive gardens.

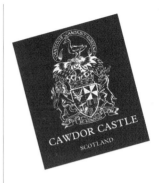

▶ Cowal and the Kyles of Bute   *184B2*

Cowal reaches down towards the island of Bute and is bounded by the long, fjord-like sea lochs of Loch Long and Loch Fyne. It is sometimes overlooked in the headlong dash for the west coast but is a most attractive part of Argyll. It is also easy to reach from the south via the Gourock to Dunoon ferry crossing. The Arrochar Alps guard its northern approaches and it has a number of scenically spectacular roads, of which the Rest and Be Thankful, the A83 west of Arrochar, is the best known.

Much of this area is contained within the **Argyll Forest Park** with its diversity of walking and pony trekking routes. There are more exotic trees to see in the **Younger Botanic Garden** at Benmore. This outstation of Edinburgh's Royal Botanic Garden features some of the largest trees anywhere in Scotland and a world famous rhododendron collection. It is closed in winter.

Cowal's outstretched fingers on either side of Bute form the **Kyles of Bute** (from the Gaelic *caolas*, a strait) These peerless stretches of coastal scenery can be enjoyed from the A886, en route to or from the Bute ferry at Colintraive.

191

BRODIE CASTLE
After Cawdor, castle enthusiasts can travel eastwards, just into Moray, to enjoy Brodie Castle (see page 177). The long and unbroken line of Brodies (they were here by 1160) has allowed a unique continuity in its acquisitions. Cawdor and Brodie could be fitted into a morning and afternoon, with lunch at Brodie Country Fayre en route.

One of the most entertaining of Scotland's castles, Cawdor also has attractive gardens and nature trails

ON TOP OF THE MOUNTAIN

A weather observatory operated from 1883 to 1904 on Ben Nevis, surviving the fierce winds and driving snows which so often beset the dangerous summit plateau. There was also a hotel until 1915.

EMPTY THREAT

Do not be unnerved by the stacked powder barrels in the Grand Magazine at Fort George. They are empty replicas. Besides, the building was designed to withstand a direct hit.

Crarae Garden, of interest throughout the year, but perhaps best in late spring

►►► Crarae Garden   184B2

Open: daily 9–6, or sunset if earlier. Admission charge

If there is time for only one Argyll garden, then Crarae should be chosen. All the natural advantages of topography and climate have been used to create this woodland garden on a hillside with a tumbling burn. Snow does not linger, rainfall is copious, and these soft conditions are appreciated by many tender shrubs, acer and eucryphia, and a range of Himalayan species. Particularly arresting are the large-leaved rhododendrons, including *R. macabeanum*. There is good colour here in spring and autumn too. Be prepared to walk a little way uphill to take it all in – you will see why Crarae has been described as being like a wild corner of some Himalayan gorge.

►► Crinan Canal   184B2

Designed so that ships could avoid the long haul around the Mull of Kintyre, the 14km Crinan Canal was begun in 1794. After many construction problems and the help of

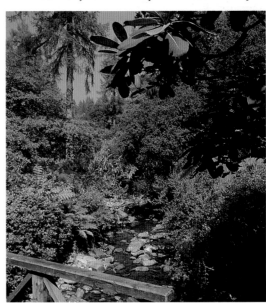

trouble-shooting engineer Thomas Telford, it was pronounced satisfactory in 1817. Once used by the Loch Fyne herring fleet seeking new grounds, the canal is mainly used now by yachts, picturesque concentrations of which can be found at the Crinan end, where there is a good hotel and a coffee shop.

►►► Fort George   185D5

Open: Apr–Sep, daily 9.30–6; Oct –Mar, Mon–Sat 9.30–4; Sun 2–4. Admission charge

Fort George is one of the most vivid experiences of Scotland's history available today. It is also Europe's finest surviving piece of 18th-century military architecture – a huge Georgian fort on a headland jutting out into the Moray Firth like a vast battleship forever anchored to the land.

It was built in response to the Jacobite rebellion of 1745, to ensure that the Highlands never rose again in revolt. It has never fired a shot in anger. Weapon development soon made it redundant. Yet, oddly, it still has a military presence. You can stroll along the great walls with their sentry boxes and embrasures, noting that the whole

Crinan Canal, west end, at Crinan

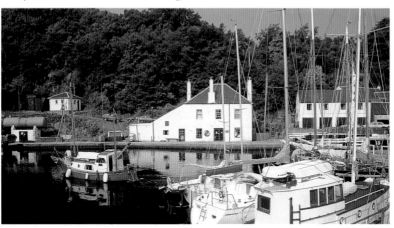

193

design is in the form of a pentagon with a bastion at each angle. This is the place to learn a whole new military language: ravelin, casemate, counterscarp, firing step and so on. There is a visitor centre, period rooms of soldiers' quarters, and the regimental museum of the Queen's Own Highlanders.

Perhaps the toughest of the various hill races throughout Scotland, the Ben Nevis race has a summit checkpoint at 1,343m

▶ Fort William   184B4

Fort William is famed for its proximity to **Ben Nevis**, though Britain's highest mountain, at 1343m, hides its best profile from the town itself.

The fort that was founded here in 1690 was named after William, Prince of Orange. It was finally demolished in the 1880s to make way for the railway. Fort William is a natural route centre in Lochaber, all but unavoidable for touring traffic heading for the Great Glen. Like Inverness at the northern end, Fort William is far from picturesque but has an excellent range of services and shops for books, outdoor wear, tartans, tweeds, woollens and so on.

The West Highland Museum▶▶ has an exhibition on tartan, and touches upon the area's Jacobite connections; there is a fascinating hidden portrait of Prince Charles Edward Stuart (Bonnie Prince Charlie), painted on a cylinder and viewed with a mirror. (*Open* Jul–Aug, Mon–Sat 10–5, Sun 2–5; Jun–Sep, closed Mon; Oct–May, Tue–Sat 10–4, Sun 2–5. *Admission charge*).

A trip into Glen Nevis is also worthwhile for its spectacular hill scenery. (Look for the signpost from the roundabout at the north end of the town.)

Parallel Roads of Glen Roy▶▶ These curious parallel lines etched on the sides of the glen are the shorelines of an Ice Age loch, dammed by a glacier at the mouth of the glen, which melted in stages, hence the parallel shorelines, the highest being the oldest.

TOURIST INFORMATION
Fort William: Cameron
Centre, Cameron Square
(tel: 01397 703781).

THE GLEN COE MASSACRE

There have been several larger massacres in the bloody history of clan warfare. However, none convulsed Scotland as much as the killing of around 38 members of the Maclan MacDonalds of Glen Coe on 13 February 1692 by a force of Campbell militia (that is, government troops). The official line was that the clan chief had been late in taking an oath of allegiance to King William (of Orange) so his clan was taught a lesson. Nevertheless, the troops had been billeted with their MacDonald hosts, observing an old Highland custom of hospitality even to bitter enemies. The breaking of this code and the resulting 'murder under trust' shocked Scotland. The king had blood on his hands – and, besides, the job was botched.

TOURIST INFORMATION
Grantown-on-Spey: 54 High Street (tel: 01479 872773).

A Highlander tops the Glenfinnan Monument rather than Bonnie Prince Charlie

▶▶▶ Glen Affric   185C5

Glen Affric has a reputation as one of the most beautiful glens in Scotland – and this even with a hydroelectric dam. As a way of getting into the excellent hill and (in some places) natural pinewood scenery, there is a choice of Forestry Commission walks. The best known is around the **Dog Falls**, themselves close to the twisty road up the glen. This trip could also take in the **Aigas Dam Fish Lift ▶** on the scenic A831 through Strathglass to the northwest; a facility for viewing migrating salmon (*Open* Jun–Oct, daily 10–3).

▶▶ Glen Coe   185C3

Glen Coe is probably the most famous glen in Scotland, partly because it carries a main road which allows some of the finest hill scenery in the central Highlands to be viewed with no effort whatsoever. This includes the impressive view of Buchaille Etive Mor guarding the eastern approaches to the glen, and the 'Three Sisters', the three long spurs running off Bidean nam Bian, the highest peak in Argyll. Matching these south side features is the long wall of the Aonach Eagach ridge enclosing Glen Coe to the north. This is the most spectacular ridge-walk on the Scottish mainland – but definitely not for the faint-hearted, the unfit or the novice.

The National Trust for Scotland is in charge of much of the glen, hence the obtrusive visitor centre (*Open* Apr–mid-May and Sep–Oct, daily 10–5; mid-May–Aug, daily 9.30–5.30, last entry 30 mins before closing. *Admission charge*). These hills are awesome and high – but certainly not lonely. Also worth exploring is Glen Etive, a road down to the head of a sea loch with a fine, wild flavour.

At Ballachulish, a former slate-quarrying village west of Glencoe, **Highland Mystery World** explores the myths and spirits believed in by the Highlanders of old. (*Open* Apr–Oct, daily 10–5. *Admission charge*).

▶▶ Glenfinnan   184B4

The view down Glenfinnan is a typical Western Highlands landscape, and is an image that is used on everything from picture postcards to place-mats. The rash

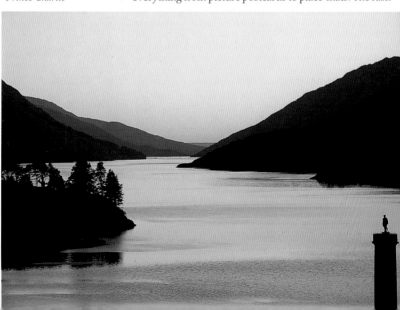

adventurer, Bonnie Prince Charlie, hardly chose this location for scenery alone when he raised the flag of rebellion in August 1745. However, the subsequent Glenfinnan Monument, recalling the escapade, adds interest to the foreground in the view from the main Mallaig road. There is a National Trust for Scotland visitor centre here, which tells the story of the prince's campaign (*Open* Apr–mid-May and Sep–Oct, daily 10–5; mid-May–Aug, daily 9.30–6. *Admission charge*).

Equally photogenic is the **Glenfinnan Viaduct►►►** on the 'Mallaig Extension' of the West Highland Railway of 1901. The engineer Robert MacAlpine ('Concrete Bob') pioneered the use of mass concrete for such large works while building the line. Unlike Bonnie Prince Charlie's excursion here, this brought only benefit to the West Highlands.

Glenfinnan Station and Museum

195

► Grantown-on-Spey   185D5

James Grant of Castle Grant planned his new town in 1766, intending to get some return on the poor moorland site. Handsome buildings of local silver granite soon sprang up, and local trades such as weaving developed. The town became popular with tourists and is still a handsome place, well worth strolling around especially for a complete contrast to Aviemore. It has interesting shops, if quality souvenirs and gifts are on your list, and a good café or two.

The **Speyside Heather Garden Centre►►** (*Open* Mon–Sat 9–6, Sun 10–6). Within easy reach of Grantown, this venue will sell you a huge variety of heather species, but will also inform you at its Heather Heritage Centre of the many different and remarkable uses of heather in the Highland economy of old, from folk remedies to rope-making.

Another excursion north of Grantown-on-Spey leads across endless moors to lonely Lochindorb Castle, a shattered remnant on an island, once the lair of the Wolf of Badenoch (see page 175).

THE RAILWAY VIADUCT
Concrete Bob's railway viaduct at Glenfinnan has 21 spans and is 390m long. It receives much attention from photographers when it is carrying one of the steam locomotives running a regular summer service between Fort William and Mallaig.

THE 'LONE ROWAN'
On the way to Glen Coe from the south, on the left-hand side beyond Loch Tulla, look out for the 'Lone Rowan' on the approaches to the empty stretches of Rannoch Moor. This single tree grows from a crack on a large boulder. It has survived for years and has become a kind of symbol amongst conservationists seeking to restore Scotland's natural tree cover.

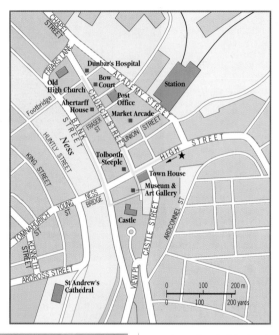

Walk

Around Inverness

Ancient Inverness was regularly burned by marauding clansmen, so little remains. Today, it is a bustling gateway town serving the north of Scotland. Allow one hour for this walk.

West along High Street, the **Tolbooth Steeple's** spire, dating from 1791, was damaged and repaired after an earth tremor in 1816. Opposite is Inverness Town House, where in 1921 the then prime minister Lloyd George held the first-ever Cabinet meeting outside London.

Walk up Castle Wynd to **Inverness Castle**. Though its site is ancient, the present building only dates from 1834–47 and is the Sheriff Court. Note the nearby statue of Flora MacDonald, helpmate of Bonnie Prince Charlie.

Go down steps and follow the River Ness north to Fraser Street. **Abertarff House**, one of the oldest houses in Inverness, is on Church Street. A little further down Church Street is the much-restored **Dunbar's Hospital**. Look for the plaque on the side of the nearby **Bow Court**, which dates from the 17th century.

Turning south, the best shopping is on Church Street and in the fine Market Arcade to the east of Church Street. Return to High Street.

Inverness Castle and the River Ness

Culloden was the last major battle on British soil, fought two and a half centuries ago in order to decide a civil war between the ruling House of Hanover and the Jacobites, who wished to return the exiled House of Stuart – in the guise of Bonnie Prince Charlie – to power. The battle, just to the east of Inverness, accelerated the final demise of a way of life already beginning to disintegrate in the Highlands: the Scottish clan system had become something of an anachronism in an increasingly mercantile age.

Anti-Jacobites Only 5,000–6,000 of the estimated 30,000 fighting men in the Highlands rose in support of the young Stuart prince Charles Edward, known as Bonnie Prince Charlie or the Young Pretender. Anti-Jacobite sentiment prevailed in many parts of Scotland. On his way north from his expedition into England, the prince had no help from Dumfries; and Glasgow was reluctant to supply him with the provisions he demanded. Edinburgh gave the Freedom of the City to the Duke of Cumberland as he took government troops north to confront the Jacobite forces.

The battle On a sleety day in April 1746, about 5,000 Jacobites, exhausted after marching for an aborted surprise attack on the Hanoverians, faced 9,000 regular soldiers, including 15 infantry regiments. Through a tactical blunder by the prince's Irish adviser, the Highlanders were lined up at perfect shooting range for the superior government artillery.

The Jacobites were blown away in less than an hour. The Highland charge, when it finally came, was ragged and ineffective. The government troops then went on to commit, with their commander's blessing, the worst series of atrocities ever carried out by the British Army.

Today, the episode is graphically described in an excellent audiovisual in the **Culloden Visitor Centre**. This does much to counter the myth that this was a simple Scottish-English conflict. (Some say there were more Scots on the government side than with the rebels.) Whatever the truth, Culloden Moor is a strange and poignant place, the scene of much waste and little glory.

BUTCHER CUMBERLAND
Butcher Cumberland acquired his unsavoury nickname due to the conduct of his army after Culloden. Because the rebels were judged to be beyond the law and also because London was a long way off, no mercy was shown, a state of affairs made easier by the fact that the victims were perceived as being racially different in dress and language. This may explain the slaughter which took place on the road to Inverness where bystanders, including women, who had come to watch, were sabred. Wounded rebels were despatched wherever they were found. Military looting was legalised throughout the Highlands, irrespective of the sympathies of the victims.

Drive

A loop to the isles

Castle Tioram

You could use part of this drive to reach Skye via the Mallaig to

Armadale ferry link, or to make an excursion to the Small Isles from Arisaig – but, if the weather is good, the stupendous island views from Moidart alone make the trip enormously worthwhile. Without the Ardnamurchan option (an extra 70km return) the drive is 185km: it can be driven in three hours or so, using the Corran ferry, but it is best to allow a whole day.

If approaching from the south, note the Corran Ferry off the A82, useful on the return leg. Go through Fort William to take the A830 along the shores of Loch Eil. You climb away from the sea-weedy levels of Loch Eil to reach the **Glenfinnan Monument** by Loch Shiel. Though the hills on either side of the loch are not especially high, their steeply tilting slopes receding down the loch into a blue haze make them the very distillation of Scottish scenery. The National Trust for Scotland Centre outlines the story of (Bonnie) Prince Charles Edward Stuart's rebellious escapade here.

Rail buffs will doubtless admire the **Glenfinnan Viaduct**. Its twelve spans are 390m long. Take care, as the train enthusiasts travelling by car are occasionally inclined to chase the locomotive – and it's quite possible that you may be overtaken several times along this stretch.

Continue to Lochailort, then keep right on the A830 for Mallaig. Do not expect to have the dazzling **Sands of Morar** all to yourself in high season. You could also drive down for a close-up view of **Loch Morar**, though its reputed resident, a monster named Morag, has been extremely quiet in recent years. Back on the main road,

of the MacDonalds of Clan Ranald, who burned it in order to prevent the Campbells getting their hands on it after the 1715 Jacobite rebellion. The castle has a grand setting, on a bracken-covered islet barely attached to the mainland by a sandy beach.

Continue through Acharacle and Salen to Loch Sunart to decide on the Ardnamurchan option. If taking the B8007 across the peninsula to the

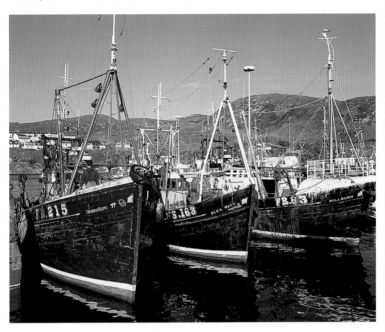

the approach to the town of **Mallaig** is picturesque, with plenty of interest. Actually being there, at the end of the road (and railway) is, however, something of an anticlimax. The **Mallaig Marine World** has fishing displays on the local fleet, a marine aquarium and exhibition (*Open* Jun–Aug, daily 9.30–9; Sep–May, daily 9.30–5.30. *Admission charge*).

Return to take the A861 loop at Lochailort. Here are the classic Scottish views of islands set in ultramarine – over the Sound of Arisaig to Eigg, Muck and Rum – unless it is raining, which is statistically and regrettably very probable. Beyond Kinlochmoidart, **Castle Tioram** is a worthwhile diversion. It was the home of the chief

Mallaig harbour

most westerly point on mainland Scotland at the lighthouse, then allow plenty of time as the road is single track and winding. Otherwise continue east to **Strontian**, the community which gave its name to the element strontium, formerly mined nearby. If you go up the road that led to the mining area, you will see a variety of craft businesses on the way.

Continue on the A861 through **Glen Sanda**, joining the faster double track section and, unless returning to Fort William, exit via the Corran Ferry. Alternatively, note the two roads going south into Morven. Both are attractive ways to reach Mull, via the back-door short ferry crossing at Lochaline.

Inveraray Jail with real-live jailor

BRIDGES
18th-century town planning is seen at its best at Inveraray. The stylishness even extends to its bridges, a notable feature on its northern approaches by the A83. One of at least three good examples is the Garron Bridge of 1747–9, reminiscent of those seen on willow pattern plates.

Kilmartin grave slabs

▶▶▶ Inveraray   184B2

Inveraray is one of the most handsome of Scottish towns and owes its appearance to the mighty chiefs of the Clan Campbell. One of them, Archibald, 3rd Duke of Argyll, planned his grand new town in 1743 at a little distance from his castle. Churches and courthouse, bell tower and Georgian façades all stand together in harmony. Sadly, Inveraray is one of the wettest places in the Highlands. However, it has some indoor attractions. These include **Inveraray Castle**, the stately pile of the present duke. There are fine interiors and valuable portraits to admire (*Open* Jul–Aug, Mon–Sat 10–5.45, Sun 1–5.45; Apr–Jun and Sep–mid-Oct, Mon–Thu and Sat 10–1 and 2–5.45, Sun 1–5.45. *Admission charge*).

Inveraray Jail▶▶ This is a re-creation of a 19th-century county prison, complete with courtroom and cells with live prisoner and jailer. It is more enticing than it sounds (*Open* Apr–Oct, daily 9.30–6; Nov–Mar, daily 10–5, last entry 1 hour before closing. *Admission charge*).

Auchindrain Old Highland Township▶▶▶ This fascinating survivor from an earlier age and authentic glimpse of Highland rural life of the past is the last communal tenancy farm township to have survived on its original site in something like its original form. Many of the buildings have been restored and there is an on-site museum (*Open* Apr–Sep, daily 10–5. *Admission charge*).

▶▶ Kilmartin and Dunadd   184B2

Argyll has plenty of early sites and there is a profusion around Kilmartin, a small village on the main Oban–Lochgilphead road. The youngest are the medieval grave slabs in the churchyard at Kilmartin, the work of craftsmen from the so-called Loch Awe school of carving. The prehistoric monuments of the valley to the south of Kilmartin are also curious: 3,000-year-old cairns at **Nether Largie**, one with axe-head and cup and ring decoration on the slabs of the cist (burial place) within. Among other early sites, the **Templewood Stone Circles** are close by, and the **Ri Cruin Cairn** further south is in a group of five cairns in a straight line.

Dating from around AD 500, on a rocky hillock dominating the mossy flatland all around, **Dunadd Fort▶▶**

was a stronghold or capital of the first kingdom of the Scots after they arrived from Ireland. This kingdom was known as Dalriada. Some early walling survives, but the chief point of interest of this hillfort is the carvings: a boar, an outline of a footprint, and a hollowed-out basin can be

Shopping choice in Inveraray: for a small loch-side town, the range is fairly wide

seen, as well as several lines of inscription in the ancient ogham system of writing (see panel). These features have been linked to the early kingship rituals of the embryonic Scotland. Altogether, it is a mysterious place, with superb views across the levels toward the Crinan Canal. Access at all times.

▶ Kingussie 185D4

Kingussie (pronounced 'kin-*yoo*-see', from the Gaelic for the head of the pinewood) is a typical Speyside tourism community which benefits from the visitor trade, summer and winter. Nearby **Ruthven Barracks▶**, destroyed by retreating Jacobites after Culloden, still dominate the valley floor near Kingussie. They can be visited en route to the Royal Society for the Protection of Birds' **Insh Marshes▶▶▶**, Scotland's largest inland marsh. Goosander and red-breasted merganser breed here, spotted craik and water rail are often heard; and there are wood and common sandpipers in summer, with hen harriers and buzzards all year. In winter 10 per cent of the United Kingdom population of whooper swans is found here, along with greylag geese and goldeneyes.

Highland Folk Museum▶▶▶ Not just a passive show of half-forgotten artefacts, this museum recaptures the past with a programme of events and activities: you can smell bannocks toasting or hear a horse being shod if you choose the right day. Costumes, musical instruments and everyday bits and pieces can be seen, as can authentically reconstructed buildings such as a 'black house' from Lewis (*Open* Apr–Oct, Mon–Sat 10–6, Sun 2–6; Nov–Mar, Mon–Fri 10–3. *Admission charge*).

TOURIST INFORMATION
Inveraray: Front Street (tel: 01499 302063). Kingussie (Apr–Oct): King Street (tel: 01540 661297).

HIGHLAND WILDLIFE PARK
KINCRAIG

►► Kintyre 184B1

This is the longest peninsula in Scotland, with the Mull of Kintyre at its tip. Kintyre's gateway is Tarbert on the isthmus where there is a heritage centre. Some visitors get no further, which is a pity, as Kintyre offers splendid sea views from both its east- and west-facing coasts, as well as an unexpectedly Lowland air in places. (The Campbell Dukes of Argyll once settled the area with Lowland farmers.) The raised beaches backed by ancient sea cliffs, typical west-side landscapes, are bright pasture lands, echoing Ayrshire over on the 'mainland'.

Near Southend on the southern tip of the Mull of Kintyre, an area neither Highland nor Lowland in character, but with an ambience all its own

202

COLUMBA'S FOOTSTEPS
This is the name given to two footprint-shaped impressions on a flat-topped rock near an ancient chapel site. By tradition, this is where Columba first stepped ashore on Scottish soil. As he could still see Ireland, his home, he took to the sea again before ending up on the island of Iona.

With the impressive outlines of Islay, Jura and Gigha parading along the horizon, the main road leads down to Campbeltown, a substantial town, busy with whisky, creameries and fishing. It seems a lot further than 19km down the narrow roads to the Mull of Kintyre itself. Facing west, this spot is very romantic at sunset. The best views are from the moorland before the road drops to the lighthouse, which is built well down the steep slope. This trip can also be combined with the loop which goes past **Columba's Footsteps**, on top of a flat-topped rock at Keil, moments from the road (see panel). Return north from Campbeltown by the B842 (on the east side of the peninsula), which is narrow but scenically rewarding.

►► Knapdale 184B2

Knapdale is an area defined by the Crinan Canal to the north and West Loch Tarbert to the south. Without high mountains or overwhelming scenery, Knapdale nevertheless has a special charm. The woods which drop to the salty tidelines of the sealochs clothe rugged hills. There are primroses in spring and, later, twining honeysuckle. Extensive plantings supplement the natural oakwoods, and there is some farming (the area was once noted for its beef cattle). There are no large towns; instead the small villages have often grown up round natural anchorages.

The stone walls of **Castle Sween►** overlook the loch of the same name. Possibly dating from the mid-12th century, the ancient fortress is one of the oldest in Scotland, and can be viewed at any time. There are also finely carved medieval grave slabs and crosses of the Knapdale School to be viewed at Kilmory and further south, Kilberry, with the further advantage of a good pub near the latter. Knapdale is a spot for slow tourers. Choose a fine day for the sea views.

▶▶ Loch Awe   *184B3*

Loch Awe is Scotland's longest loch. Once it drained southwards, until with the last Ice Age a breach was made in a fault line. The loch now empties by the Pass of Brander westwards to Loch Etive. Loch Awe is most often seen from the A85, the main Perth to Oban road, where its length is not appreciated. However, there are numerous points of interest along this stretch.

At the **Cruachan Dam Visitor Centre▶▶▶** there are displays about the impressive hydroelectric project which generates 400MW of electricity by running water from a dam high on Ben Cruachan down into Loch Awe (and pumping it back at off-peak times). Minibuses take visitors 1km into the mountain to see the turbine hall (*Open* Apr–mid-Nov, daily 9–4.30. *Admission charge*).

The former 15th-century Campbell stronghold of **Kilchurn Castle▶▶▶** is just a short walk across the flats by the loch. Interpretative boards help identify features in the extensive panorama (*Open* Apr–Sep, daily 9.30–6; Oct–Mar, Mon–Sat 9.30–4, Sun 2–4. *Admission charge*).

Duncan Ban McIntyre Monument▶▶▶ Take the road behind Dalmally for one of the very finest vistas in the Western Highlands. Also worth a look are **Ardanaiseig Gardens▶** (*Open* daily in season) and, further west by Loch Etive, the **Bonawe Iron Furnace▶** (*Open* Apr–Sep, daily 9.30–6. *Admission charge*). Here Historic Scotland look after the well-preserved remains of a charcoal furnace for iron-smelting founded in 1753; a reminder that industry even reached these peaceful Highland shores 250 years ago.

203

Kilchurn Castle on the shores of Loch Awe offers outstanding views from its battlements toward Ben Cruachan and its satellite peaks

The Great Glen & Western Highlands

AN UNSUCCESSFUL SPEED ATTEMPT
Between Invermoriston and Drumnadrochit on the A82 a cairn recalls the world water speed record attempt by John Cobb. He was killed here in 1952 when his jet-boat hit a mysterious patch of ripples at high speed. Inevitably, this tragedy is linked to the monster phenomenon, as the loch was otherwise calm.

TOURIST INFORMATION
Fort Augustus (Apr–Oct): Car park (tel: 01320 366367).

Although a ruin, Urquhart Castle, on the side of Loch Ness, remains popular in the summer months – perhaps with those hoping to see the loch's famous resident

▶ Loch Ness   *185C5*

Loch Ness has a larger volume of water than any other Scottish loch. It is around 250m deep in places, and the water in this great glacier-gouged trench is said never to freeze. Because of its mysterious reputation, it is very popular with tourers. Take time to explore the area away from the main loch itself, particularly the big glens to the west around Strathglass and also peaceful Stratherrick eastwards. Though Loch Ness ends up on most people's touring list, like Inverness, Loch Lomond and the Trossachs, the loch itself can be a mild anticlimax – a big sheet of water, certainly, yet lacking in real grandeur.

The west-bank road, the busy main A82, goes through Drumnadrochit with its 'Official Loch Ness Monster Exhibition' and 'Original Loch Ness Monster Visitor Centre' among other enticements. With souvenir shops and cafés as well, it is all-year monster marketing here. Nearby **Urquhart Castle** was once one of the largest castles in Scotland but was blown up in 1692 lest it fall into Jacobite hands. The castle viewpoint is popular with fast-moving coach parties 'doing' Scotland in a day. It is a relief to escape to the gentler and more subtle attractions of the east side road. These include **Loch Tarff**, north of Fort Augustus on the B862, and the superb viewpoint beyond (towards Inverness) with its panorama of the Monadhliath and waves of northern Highland hills. The route here follows the old military road, completed by General Wade's men in 1726. The road runs to Whitebridge, with a handsome preserved Wade bridge, then on to Foyers, where the **Falls of Foyers**▶▶ are worth a visit. (Park beside the post office, but take care with young children on the slippery paths.) Inverfarigaig is lower down. Starting from the Forest Centre, a forest walk leads up to a fine prospect of the loch.

Scottish folklore has plenty of references to water-spirits which lurk in and around lochs and burns, often with evil intent. The water kelpie is blended with Gaelic each-uisge, the water horse, and other beasts in a fantastic menagerie of the Celtic imagination.

The start of the story One quiet week on the *Inverness Courier* in May 1933, there was space for a report which had come from a local correspondent and water bailiff. He had heard of a couple who had seen a strange animal disporting itself in the dark waters of the loch. The couple was thought to be running one of the hotels in Drumnadrochit.

Soon other sightings flooded in. National papers took up the story and 'monster mania' hit the headlines. A pre-war AA patrolman reported that he could create pandemonium amongst the lines of cars parked by the loch merely by pointing over the water. Meanwhile, Inverness Town Council voted to reduce its publicity expenditure substantially for 1934.

The story has refused to go away. It has spawned books, supported a variety of tourism-related businesses both by the loch and in Inverness, and attracted scientists, dedicated amateurs and hoaxers. It has generated dubious cine film and still photographs, echo soundings and sincere testimony from dozens of eye-witnesses who have seen something.

There is undoubtedly a strange phenomenon to be witnessed here, whose manifestation is of great importance to the local economy. Its appearance is in inverse proportion to the number of cameras trained on the loch at any given moment. Loch Ness is a very large body of water, prone to mirages in still, calm conditions – ideal visitor and monster-spotting weather.

In the Scottish legal system there is a verdict 'not proven'. Without enough evidence for a conviction, Nessie has to remain a modern myth – the water kelpie with an excellent publicity machine.

SUNDAY OBSERVANCE
A Free Church minister in Fort Augustus wrote of the 1930s monster craze: 'the word "monster" is really not applicable to the Loch Ness animal, but is truly applicable to those who deliberately sin against the light of law and revelation.' He was objecting to visitors going monster-spotting on a Sunday.

SOME EXPLANATIONS
Swimming red deer, diving otters, floating logs or vegetation, cormorants, boats' wakes, seals and many more everyday things have been suggested as explanations for monster sightings.

Not the real thing at Drumnadrochit

ROAD-BUILDING EXPECTATIONS
One explanation often given for the sudden flurry of sightings in the 1930s was the new road which gave better views of the loch. Some even said the beast or beasts had been disturbed by the blasting. Yet General Wade and his men built a military road down the east side of the loch to supersede the first high-level road of 1726. They also blasted out rock above Inverfarigaig and must therefore have created quite a disturbance. Perhaps Wade's forces were too busy keeping a sharp lookout for Jacobites to notice long-necked creatures.

Busy ferry port and yachting haven, Oban's harbour also has room for more traditional commercial fishing activities

TWO CULTURES
It was once the boast of the Stuart monarchs that they had a town in their realm so large that the inhabitants spoke different languages at either end. This was a reference to Nairn, where the Lowland fishers at the sea end of town used the Scots tongue (still heard eastwards along the Moray Firth today). At the landward end of the town, the farmers spoke Gaelic. Thus Nairn has for long been on the dividing line between Highland and Lowland cultures.

TOURIST INFORMATION
Nairn (Apr–Oct): 62 King Street (tel: 01667 452753).
Oban: Argyll Square (tel: 01631 563122).

THE ATLANTIC BRIDGE
The Clachan Bridge is a single-arched bridge of 1792 linking the island of Seil with the mainland. Seil is one of the so-called 'slate islands', recalling an industry which lasted for 200 years until a violent storm in 1881 flooded the quarry workings and closed down the industry overnight. The Clachan Bridge is often called the Atlantic Bridge, because it spans an arm of that ocean. Other bridges on the western seaboard do likewise, but only the Clachan Bridge is so labelled.

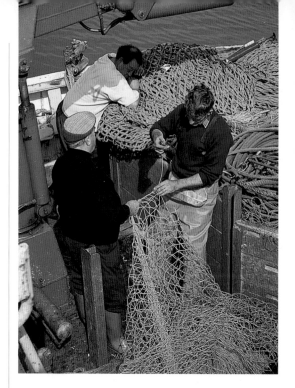

▶▶ Nairn   185D5

More Lowland than Highland, Nairn, with its resort air and famous golf courses, always seems to have had a split personality. The former fisher town by the harbour is separated by the main road from the main shopping streets of a centre once dependent on agricultural activities. Both lie apart from the mansions and hotels of the seaside resort development that benefited from the arrival of the Highland Railway in the mid-19th century. The holiday atmosphere is doubtless helped by the low rainfall – a mere 56cm annually.

Nairn Fishertown Museum▶▶ This pleasingly informal museum, staffed by helpful enthusiasts, tells how the harbour was built by Thomas Telford in the 1820s and how, about a hundred years later, the herring fishery declined. The harbour is now mainly used by pleasure craft (*Open* Jun–Sep, Mon–Sat 2.30–4.30; also Wed and Fri 6.30–8.30. *Admission charge*).

The **Nairn Museum** is a classic, slightly old-fashioned museum which includes relics from Culloden (*Open* mid-May–Sep, Mon–Sat 10–4.30. *Admission charge*). Then there are golf courses and miles of beach backed by dunes, stretching east to Culbin Forest. Fort George, and Cawdor and Brodie castles are also within easy reach.

▶ Newtonmore   185D4

Newtonmore is a Speyside community made more peaceful by the A9 bypass. The old Celtic game of shinty (like a suicidal form of hockey) has quite a hold here and at nearby Kingussie. The village also has the **Clan Macpherson Museum▶** (*Open* Apr–Oct, Mon–Sat 10–5, Sun 2.30–5. *Admission free*) with its display of clan artefacts. Within easy reach of Newtonmore, along the A86, west of Laggan, a track leads to the **Corrieyairack Pass▶**, completed by General Wade's men in 1732. This high-level military route from Speyside to the Great Glen that zig-zags up to about 760m, soon fell into disuse because of the severe Scottish winters. Now it is disintegrating due to the attentions of four-wheel drive enthusiasts.

▶▶ Oban   184B3

When the railway arrived in 1880, Oban was described as the new 'Charing Cross of the Highlands'. The railway company initiated trips to the islands and the sealochs around. Today, the railway is still here, though most of Oban's visitors now come by road rather than rail.

On the way from the east, the A82 passes the **Falls of Lora** at Connel Bridge. This curious turbulence at the mouth of Loch Etive can be seen below the bridge when the tide runs strongly. Even nearer to Oban is the 13th-century **Dunstaffnage Castle**, an old MacDougall stronghold that once controlled the sea-roads of Argyll (*Open* Apr–Sep, daily 9.30–6. *Admission charge*).

Oban is built round a sheltered bay. Unashamedly visitor-centred, many of the well-built, solid houses have 'B & B' signs outside and there is a wide choice of hotels. Oban is both a transit point for the ferry connections and a resort. Within the town is a good choice of commercial attractions with long main-season opening hours, including a distillery, audiovisual shows, and other summer entertainments.

McCaig's Tower▶ is prominent above the harbour. Sometimes called McCaig's Folly, it recalls a local banker who had it built as a family memorial to ease local unemployment. It is open at all times. Both the tower and **Pulpit Hill▶** make excellent viewpoints over this quite handsome town. There are numerous excursions by boat – on spectacular Loch Etive, for example.

Sea Life Centre▶▶▶ This is at Barcaldine, 16km north of Oban, and makes a popular and rewarding excursion. Britain's marine life is revealed to be every bit as flourishing and exotic as anything in the tropics (*Open* Jan–mid-Feb, weekends 10–5; mid-Feb–Jul and Sep–Nov, daily 10–6; Jul–Aug, daily 9–7. 1st 2 wks Dec, Sat–Sun 10–5. *Admission charge*).

207

A World in Miniature – ½-scale exhibition, at Kilninver, south of Oban

Feeding seals at the Sea Life Centre, Barcaldine

The Northern Highlands

THE JOURNEY NORTH From a southern viewpoint, it is easy to assume that Scotland shrinks as you go north. But take care when route planning in this area, as there is still a lot of ground to cover. Inverness to Thurso, for example, is further than Carlisle to Glasgow and the dual carriageway sections of the A9 come to an end not very far over the Kessock Bridge beyond the Highland capital.

However, this is an area which has seen many road improvements in recent years. Ullapool is no longer a single track crawl made hazardous by southbound fish lorries. Instead, it is an easy hour from Inverness. Scourie and Laxford Bridge, far north on the western seaboard, are another two places which can be reached without resorting to single track driving.

All of this means there is more time to look at the scenery, the chief attraction of the north. The eastern side continues to resemble a Lowland farming strip most of the time. Look for the use of lines of Caithness flagstones set on edge as field boundaries, highly characteristic of the sparse wind-honed pastures of the north. Yet the moors with their attendant sense of wildness reach down to the eastern seaboard in places – around Helmsdale, for example. There are also spectacular sea-cliffs.

Destitution Road and the shoulders of An Teallach, near Ullapool

Travelling westward, away from the coastal cultivation,

WEATHERBEATEN HILLS
Some mountains are disappearing fast. The popular Stac Polly in Coigach has lost a few pinnacles in recent years and its red sandstone is powdering and strewing great screes down its flanks. Meanwhile, it is said that on Foinaven, a northern peak just below the magic Munro mark (see page 149), you can hear erosion-the gentle tinkle of chips of Cambrian quartzite intermittently falling from its fast-weathering grey rock summits. So visit soon!

uplands are soon reached – the boggy flows of Caithness, for instance, with their long open vistas ending in blue hills beyond the blocks of alien and controversial conifers. In the far north, the transition westwards into uncultivated landscape is gradual. In the old county of Ross-shire it can be more abrupt. One point which typifies this transition is on the main A832 west of Contin, near the Falls of Rogie (see page 223). Quite suddenly, the last of the Lowland barley, woods and pasture drops back eastward and its vivid greenness is replaced, at a single bend, by enveloping Highland pinewoods, grey hills and a choppy loch.

EMPTY SPACES Beyond, you enter the empty quarter. Settlement in the north is mainly, though not exclusively, coastal. The interior conforms to the pattern of much of Highland Scotland. Generally, it is a network of substantial privately owned estates, with vast areas given over to deer stalking, often bought as an investment by absentee landlords. It is the owners of these exclusive sanctuaries, determined to make their land pay by offering shooting rights, who feel threatened by the increasing numbers of other countryside users, notably hillwalkers intent on 'bagging' not a stag, but another Munro.

Fortunately, some of the very best chunks of landscape, such as the Torridons, Kintail and parts of Coigach, are owned or managed by conservation agencies determined to compromise with all parties.

Beyond the backbone of Scotland in Wester Ross and particularly in Sutherland, the old sandstone peaks sit on their plinth of ancient glacier-scoured rock. It is this spare and empty landscape of a thousand lochans scratched out of the Lewisian gneiss, overlooked by cliffs, rock terraces and shattered hills that is the essence of the far north.

Summer daylight hours lengthen noticeably hereabouts – it is perfectly possible to read outdoors at 11pm around midsummer (if the midges will let you) and it never seems to get dark. However, the climate does not alter in a uniform way. The far north sometimes has periods of a curious flat calm, especially away from the hills and out on the headlands. Golfers can be enjoying a round at Gairloch in good conditions while climbers in the Torridons are taking compass-bearings and extracting waterproofs from rucksacks. Even at low level, for example walking by Loch Clair, admiring the profile of Liathach in Glen Torridon, you may well experience four seasons within an hour.

It is all too easy to be hopelessly beguiled by the north-west landscapes, especially in the Torridon hills or, further north, around Inverpolly. Certainly, the Northern Highlands have attracted lots of permanent newcomers from other parts of the United Kingdom throughout the 1980s, with a noticeable improvement in eating-out options, compared with 20 years ago. Though many tourers want to make their way north and west, do not forget the gentler attractions of Easter Ross and Caithness with their old-established communities such as Cromarty and Dornoch, just two of the handsome little places on the eastern seaboard.

In this northern region, all roads seem to lead to the 'Capital of the Highlands'. Inverness is now bypassed but is still a natural route centre, with roads to the north and west leading out like the spokes of a wheel. And though caution is advised when planning touring routes – it may be further than you think – it is also true that no matter how great the sense of emptiness, of remoteness and spare beauty in these lands of ancient rock, if it all becomes a little too intimidating, then you can always rush back in a few hours to Inverness with its supermarkets, traffic lights and other comforting signs of civilisation…

Durness school children's wallhanging of the Highland Clearances

AN OVERVIEW OF THE NORTH

From the summit of Ben More Assynt, one of Sutherland's Munros (see page 149), on a clear day it is possible to see not only a great swathe of the Northern Highlands but simultaneously Orkney and the Western Isles.

Duncansby Stacks, near John o'Groats, Caithness

Remembering Queen Victoria's Diamond Jubilee, Dingwall

212

HIGH-LEVEL GROUSE
There are few places in Scotland where you can see ptarmigan from the car, but this sometimes absurdly tame high-altitude grouse makes its home amongst the frost-shattered boulders on the exposed plateau at the top of the Bealach-na-Ba (Gaelic, meaning the pass of the cattle). This is the spectacular way to Applecross, reaching 626m, with magnificent views to Skye.

FOSSIL FISH
Cromarty-born Hugh Miller (1802–56) was a pioneering self-taught geologist, who started work as a stonemason. He developed an interest in the fossils he found in the local sandstone quarries, and eventually achieved an international reputation for his discoveries and classification of primitive fishes. His birthplace in Cromarty (National Trust for Scotland) may be visited

The road to Applecross, towards the Bealach-na-Ba

▶ **Achiltibuie and the Summer Isles** *208B3*

A side-road through Coigach beyond Ullapool offers spectacular views of the impossible crenellations of Stac Polly on the skyline. The single track road eventually runs through the 5km straggle of homesteads which is Achiltibuie. The Summer Isles make up part of the peerless sea views. This bleak group off the mainland of Wester Ross holds a strange fascination for some. Cruises go from Ullapool (enquire at the Tourist Information Centre there) and Achiltibuie (ask at the post office).

▶▶ **Applecross** *208A1*

Access to Applecross used to be easiest by sea, especially when the high-level Bealach-na-Ba was closed by snow. Since the 1970s, the settlement has had a low-level road built from Shieldaig. Applecross is associated with St Maelrubha, who established a monastery here in AD 673. Only a few fragments of early crosses survive from its ancient religious past, but the place still has the air of a remote sanctuary.

▶▶▶ **Cromarty** *209C2*

Well worth the Black Isle diversion, this is one of the most satisfying of Scottish towns: full of character, a place which has seen its fortunes rise and fall, with herring and coastal trading, and rise again with oil.

Cromarty Courthouse▶▶▶ is perhaps the best place to start a tour of the town. Now a visitor centre, it portrays the development of Cromarty into a prosperous 18th-century trading burgh. If time permits, take the 'personal tape tour' of the town's fine buildings (*Open* Apr–Oct, daily 10–5; Nov, Dec, Mar daily 12–4; Jan–Feb by appointment. *Admission charge*).

▶ **Dingwall** *209C2*

The former county town of Easter Ross has long been an administrative centre – its name, from the Norse *thing-vollr*, place of assembly, is a reminder that it was an important settlement in 11th-century Viking times. Within easy reach is the little-known **Black Rock Gorge**▶▶ above Evanton. The River Glass runs through a gorge, about 30m deep in parts, yet hemmed in by black and mossy rocks only 4m apart at their narrowest. The spot has a decidedly sinister atmosphere.

Brahan is an estate near Dingwall whose name is now strongly associated with the most famous of Highland prophets, the Brahan Seer. Various stories and legends have become attached to him, and fact and fiction inter-woven. The Brahan Seer is thought to have been a certain Coinneach Odhar (the Gaelic for 'Brown Kenneth', pronounced 'co-in-yach oar') who came to work on the estate in the late 17th century.

His prophecies The Brahan Seer predicted the railways: 'Long lines of carriages without horses will run between Inverness and Dingwall and Skye.' The rise of Strathpeffer as a spa was likewise noted. Of the well he said: 'Uninviting and disagreeable as it now is...the day will come when it shall be under lock and key.' Some prophesies are eerie, especially one curious prediction concerning the terrible disaster that would befall the world when the River Ness in Inverness was spanned by five bridges. A fifth bridge was opened on the river a few days before the outbreak of World War II.

The most unsettling of his prophesies has already partly come to pass. In it he saw the 19th-century coming of the sheep and the emptying of the glens of people. Complete fulfilment of the ending has yet to happen: 'The deer and other wild animals in the huge wilderness will be exterminated and browned by horrid black rains. The people will then return and take undis-turbed possession of the lands of their ancestors.' This meaning is still discussed in the Highlands, with oil pol-lution and nuclear fallout as two unpleasant alternatives.

An unforeseen end Brown Kenneth came to an unfortu-nate end when, at an aristocratic gathering to which he had been invited, perhaps as a novelty act, he reported what the husband of Lady Seaforth was doing at the time (being unfaithful while on a visit to Paris). For such an insult in front of her assembled guests, the furious Lady Seaforth had him burned in a tar barrel – or at least that's how the story goes.

BURNED IN A BRAHAN TUB
On the orders of Lady Seaforth, the Brahan Seer was rolled down a hill in a burning tar barrel at Chanonry Point near Fortrose in the Black Isle. A memorial can be seen there to this day. However, this may not have happened to the 17th-century seer but to another Brown Kenneth accused of witchcraft a century earlier. It seems unlikely that someone with a gift for foretelling the future could not have foreseen the consequences of insulting his hostess.

213

Inverness, where the fifth bridge over the Ness turned out to be 'a bridge too far'

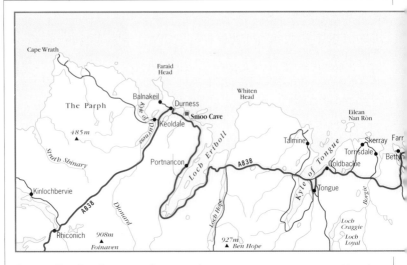

Dunnet Head to Durness along the north coast

By travelling in an east–west direction on this north coast drive, you can see the open, flagstone-bordered fields of the edge of Caithness gradually giving way to the moors and mountains of wild Sutherland. This

Crossing the Kyle of Durness for the Cape Wrath minibus

route (in all 133km long) could be driven in two hours or so, but to get the best from it you might wish to

arrange an overnight stay in either the Durness or Tongue area.

Dunnet Head is the most northerly point in Scotland and makes a worthwhile short excursion from Thurso. Heading west from the town, you will see the unmistakable profile of Dounreay, which became the world's first fast reactor to produce commercial electricity, on a site about as far from the Houses of Parliament as it could possibly be. It is now being decommissioned.

At **Melvich**, the landscapes start to become more rugged. If time permits, divert to lighthouse-tipped **Strathy Point**, with the dunes and coastal grasslands en route harbouring some rare plants, notably the tiny Scots primrose in May and June. (The more conspicuous blue among the grass is spring squill.) Back on the main road, **Bettyhill** is a post-clearance settlement. The name refers to Elizabeth, Countess of Sutherland, whose husband ordered the removal of 1,200 people from their dwellings to the coast during the shameful Highland Clearances (see page 38), as the **Strathnaver Museum** relates. More cheerfully, little coastal loops lead down to empty and beautiful, if windswept, pale sand beaches.

The A836/838 leads on to the **Kyle of Tongue**, with its breathtaking view of spiky Ben Loyal from the causeway which shortens the route round the sea loch. Across the empty moors, with vast and remote seascapes around Whiten Head to the north, lies the next great sea inlet. **Loch Eriboll** was a former wartime convoy assembly point, known to mariners as Loch 'orrible. There is a well-preserved prehistoric wheelhouse, among other barely acknowledged sites in the vicinity, just a walk across the moorlands – but you should take a map.

Smoo Cave by Durness is a popular spot, a series of caverns by the shore, cut into the limestone by water action. The other Durness attraction is the excursion to **Cape Wrath**, the northwesternmost tip of mainland Scotland. Note that you cannot take your car. A small ferry crosses the Kyle of Durness and then a minibus goes to the lighthouse. The tallest mainland cliffs are nearby as well, with the whole area carrying a faintly sinister air, thanks partly to the military range that lies between the Kyle and the Cape. A gentler option is puffin-watching at Faraid Head, a very pleasant walk from Durness: leave the car near the beach at Balnakeil.

Smoo Cave, Durness

THE DESTITUTION ROAD
The roads from Gairloch to Poolewe and northwards were built in a poverty relief programme following the famine after the failure of the 1840s potato crops. Government boards put up half the cash on the understanding that local landowners would match the funds. The lairds benefited from the improved communications, their estates increasing in value. Instead of wages, the half-starved locals were paid in meal, as both government and landowners wished to avoid a 'dependency culture' developing. Part of the A832 is still known as the Destitution Road.

▶▶▶ Dornoch   209C2

Were it not for its northerly location, Dornoch would be better known: a mellow sandstone burgh with a handsome cathedral on its skyline, a picturesque setting by a great sweep of beach and a famous golf course. The opening of the Dornoch road bridge on the A9 has, however, been of benefit. It is one of the most pleasingly attractive of Scottish towns, also known as the 'St Andrews of the North' because of its reputation for great golf. Though much rebuilt and altered, **Dornoch Cathedral▶**, (*Open* daily), dates from the 13th century. The town was the seat of the Bishops of Caithness. As well as just strolling around, admiring how the yellow sandstone sets off the roses in the little gardens, things to do in Dornoch include visiting the town jail, now a craft and exhibition centre (*Open* Easter–Sep, daily 9–5; Oct–Easter, Mon–Fri 10–1 and 2–4. *Admission free*). Another of the peaceful little town's delights are its golden beaches to north and south. Ripple-patterned and unpolluted, long shoals and banks at the mouth of Dornoch Firth are exposed at low tide.

Between Dornoch and Golspie stands **Beinn a Bhragaidh**, a hill west of the A9 whose top is crowned by a massive statue. This colossus by Sir Francis Chantney is in memory of the first Duke of Sutherland (d. 1833), a prime mover in the Highland Clearances which resulted in mass emigration.

▶ Dunrobin Castle   209C2

Open: Apr, May, Sep, Oct, Mon–Sat 10.30–4, Sun 12–4. Jun–Aug, daily 10.30–5. Admission charge
The largest house in the Northern Highlands, Dunrobin

On this sparsely populated and wild coastline, the settlement of Gairloch, with golf course, beaches and choice of accommodation, is the local equivalent of a resort town

started as a 13th-century sandstone keep on a raised beach overlooking the Dornoch Firth. The original keep was progressively enveloped by newer work, the last and most spectacular being 1835–50 extensions. These were by Sir Charles Barry, architect of the Houses of Parliament in London. He gave the pile its present French-style look with spires and elaborate stonework.

For centuries this has been the seat of the Dukes and Earls of Sutherland. The 3rd Duke (d. 1892) was Western

Europe's largest landowner – his holdings included most of the county of Sutherland. However, Dunrobin has also been an auxiliary naval hospital and a boys' school in the present century. Stuffed with the goods acquired by one of the wealthiest families in the land, it has a makeshift air, a series of rooms laid out to impress with displays of uniforms, trophies, medals, endless portraits, tapestries and such eccentricities as the Duke's own steam-powered fire engine.

The old summer house is a museum containing hunting trophies, from which you gain the impression that the Sutherlands must have kept a squad of taxidermists in work over the years. The attractive gardens below the castle were inspired by Versailles.

► Fortrose   209C2

With its neighbours, Avoch and Rosemarkie, on either side, Fortrose is an attractive village by the shores of the Moray Firth. The community originally grew around the cathedral, completed in 1485 but now a red sandstone roofless ruin. Avoch, with its fishing heritage, is like the Lowland towns on the south side of the Firth. North of the three villages is Eathie beach, where pioneering 19th-century geologist Hugh Miller (see panel on page 212) made important discoveries about the origin of the local sandstones.

►► Gairloch   208A2

Gairloch overlooks the safe anchorage of the Gair Loch. Largest of the settlements along this fine stretch of Wester Ross seaboard, Gairloch combines some sea fishing (and processing) activity with tourism, an industry that established itself here in mid-Victorian times. It is a small resort which relies on its own scenic charm. The local sandy beach helps attract families, as does the golf course. Also in the vicinity are **Inverewe Garden** (see page 221) and the beauties of **Loch Maree** (see page 218), as well as **Gairloch Heritage Museum►►** (*Open* Apr–Oct, Mon–Sat 10–4).

Dunrobin Castle, grandest home in the Northern Highlands, is irrevocably associated with the Highland Clearances

GOLFING HISTORY
Many of the priests who came to Dornoch Cathedral had been trained in St Andrews, where the close-cropped coastal turf was already being used for a curious game with a ball and stick. These religious men were soon exploiting the similar terrain around Dornoch. Thus golf took a very early hold here on the magnificent links, perhaps even as early as the 16th century.

In Fortrose

The mountains of Torridon are exactly to the taste of modern travellers eager to escape from urban pressures. Austere and uncompromising, notched and carved into terraces and ridges, they have a beauty which has made an impact for as long as tourists have made their patient way over the long reaches of Strath Bran to Achnasheen, then the high pass over Glen Docherty.

A TRAIL WITH VIEWS
From a clearly marked parking place by the shore of Loch Maree, a hill path ascends the steep slopes leading on to the flanks of Beinn Eighe. This Scottish National Heritage nature trail is for the well-shod walker, but gives excellent views over Slioch and Loch Maree as height is quickly gained and the ancient pinewoods peter out.

218

Far from being a long way off across the backbone of Scotland – now that the roads have been improved across the empty middle – the western seaboard and the Torridons are all too accessible. An easy excursion from Inverness will give a flavour, though the mountains deserve much more time.

The main mountains Glen Torridon runs from the sea towards the southern end of **Loch Maree**. A single-track road runs through the glen, becoming double-track by the shores of **Loch Torridon**. It is from the southern side of Loch Torridon, on the way to or from Shieldaig, that the best views of **Beinn Alligin** can be obtained. This is the most westerly of Torridon's peaks, a half-horseshoe ridge of red sandstone with a spectacular gash on its southern cliffs, casting a sinister shadow by late afternoon. Its equally lofty companion, **Liathach**, lies east of it. Rising precipitously from sea level, its quartzite-topped sandstone terraces and summit pinnacles are best appreciated from the east, by Loch Clair. Next is **Beinn Eighe** – several kilometres of summits on a quartzite ridge with grey-white rocks cascading down its flanks in long scree slopes. These three mountains are the main performers in the Torridon spectacular.

The National Trust for Scotland owns much of the land by the glen and above Loch Torridon – about 6,500 hectares. The visitor centre by the Diabaig road junction is the starting point for ranger-led walks as well as giving an introduction to the unique geology and wildlife of the area. The east end of the glen and much of the west side of Loch Maree was Britain's first National Nature Reserve, now under Scottish Natural Heritage, which operates a visitor centre by the loch (on the A832).

Take your time – but do not hold up the locals!

Walks in the area Though much can be seen from the roadside, the Torridons are best explored on foot. All the rules of Scottish mountain walking obviously apply: and even at lower level, the terrain is rough enough to make proper walking boots a necessity. One popular but demanding low-level walk is the 'circumnavigation' of the Liathach massif. This demands either two cars, extreme fitness or a confident approach to hitchhiking. Start either at the waterfall car park beyond Torridon House on the Diabaig road or at the car park half-way along Glen Torridon. The off-road section of the walk is 11km. The views take in the northern slopes and corries of Liathach and, notably, the less well-known **Beinn Dearg** with its spectacular rock terraces.

Another popular excursion is to view the mighty triple buttresses of **Coire Mhic Fhearchair**. This diverges from the 'round Liathach' path to circle into one of the most magnificent corries in the Scottish hills. Alternatively, take advantage of the nature trails on the Loch Maree side, though the mountain trail goes steeply up through the old pines and demands some particularly careful footwork. There are breathtaking views over the loch to Slioch, the peak on its eastern shore.

Fit hillwalkers have many possible excursions. The pinnacles of Liathach are not for the vertigo-prone, though there is a path round them. The **Horns of Alligin**, on Beinn Alligin's eastern end, demand a little bit of hand-work and need great respect. Meanwhile, the long ridge of Beinn Eighe should not be underestimated. If in doubt, stay at low level, explore the shore path by Diabaig, or the route to the headland near Shieldaig, or stroll by Loch Clair, admiring one of Scotland's finest views, with Liathach filling the skyline like an upturned boat.

NORSE PLACE NAMES
Diabaig is derived from the Norse *deop-vik* (deep bay), while Shieldaig is *sild-vik* (herring bay). Both little villages are in attractive locations and both offer some accommodation, though Kinlochewe at the east end of the glen is a slightly larger centre.

Beinn Eighe from Glen Torridon

Caithness craftsman

SPANIARDS' PEAK
Eilean Donan's destruction by naval gunfire in 1719 came about because of its involvement in the Jacobite rebellion of that year. A force of 300 Spanish soldiers landed nearby to link up with local Jacobites, mainly Mackenzies and Camerons (plus Rob Roy and a few Macgregors). They joined battle in Glen Shiel with government forces, whose superior firepower made retreat or surrender inevitable. The Glen Shiel place name Sgurr na Spainteach (Spaniards' Peak) recalls the incident.

Kintail sunset

▶ John o'Groats   209D4

'From Land's End to John o'Groats' is the age-old expression denoting the length of Britain. Yet the place is not the most northerly point of mainland Scotland – that distinction belongs to **Dunnet Head▶▶** to the west. The seascapes here are, however, spectacular, notably around **Duncansby Head▶▶▶** with its rock stacks. There is a passenger-only summer ferry service from John o' Groats to Orkney.

▶▶▶ Kintail   208A1

Just how much landscape perceptions have changed is indicated by Dr Johnson's remark, when travelling hereabouts. He described the main mountains west of the Great Glen as '...matter incapable of form or usefulness, dismissed by nature from her care and disinherited of her favours'. Kintail today is highly prized for the same elemental qualities that so appalled the urban doctor. The National Trust for Scotland cares for much of the area, which includes the famously picturesque **Five Sisters of Kintail▶▶▶** as its centrepiece. These five peaks are all Munros (see page 149), as indeed are many others further east up Glen Shiel. Also within the National Trust for Scotland sphere are the spectacular **Falls of Glomach▶▶**, tumbling 113m in remote Glen Elchaig, accessible only by an 8km path over rough country – treat it as a hillwalk and dress accordingly.

The best-known low-level landmark is **Eilean Donan Castle▶** on its islet on Loch Duich. This was wrecked in 1719 (see panel) and rebuilt between 1913 and 1932. It includes a memorial to the Clan Macrae, whose seat it was (*Open* Apr–Oct, daily 10–5.30. *Admission charge*).

A dead-end minor road heads off from the end of Glen Shiel to Glenelg. This route is worth exploring, to view not only Skye and Knoydart but also the best preserved brochs (see panel page 229) on the Scottish mainland. **Dun Telve** stands over 9m high. Also nearby are the ruins of the **Bernera Barracks**, originally built around 1722 to control Jacobite activities (see pages 34–5).

Inverewe Garden is on the same latitude as Labrador, but has a cool and temperate climate because it is favoured by the lapping waters of the North Atlantic Drift. The western seas blunt the keen edge of the winter frosts and extensive shelter belts create the micro-climate beloved of rhododendrons, mahonia and other lovers of dappled shade and moisture. Plants from cool temperate zones all over the world can be found here.

History Until 1862, the garden site was a windy, bare headland with only the island of Lewis between it and Northern Canada. But Osgood Mackenzie, whose father and grandfather had been lairds of Gairloch, started his lifetime's work to create a garden in this unpromising landscape. Some of the first trees were planted, not by digging a hole in soil (since often there was none), but by carving out solid rock.

Osgood Mackenzie died in 1922, with the now maturing garden appreciated by temperate eucalyptus trees from Tasmania, species rhododendrons from the Himalayas and pernettyas, olearias, nothofagus and other southern hemisphere plants that found this Highland home compatible with the Patagonian plains or the high forests of the Andes. By 1952 the garden was in the care of the National Trust for Scotland.

The garden today Inverewe is a late garden, which can mean that you might add a month to six weeks on to flowering times quoted in the gardening manuals – particularly in the early months. This cautious start also means that there is a running together of late spring – and early summer – flowering plants into a more continuous display than in many southern gardens. Its most attractive feature is the sense of different 'rooms' within the overall structure – turn a corner to reinvigorated plantings and geographically linked species, a deliberate management policy in which the team of gardeners is given comparatively free rein within their own patches.

EARTH MOVING
Osgood Mackenzie's labours in creating Inverewe did not only involve excavating holes in solid rock for trees. Soil by the basket load had to be moved in as even the thin blanket of peat which had originally overlaid the rock had been stripped off for fuel by previous crofting tenants.

OPENING TIMES
Open daily mid-Mar–Oct 9.30–9; Nov–mid Mar 9.30–5. Head gardener - guided walks: Apr–Sep, Mon–Fri at 1.30. *Admission charge*

Inverewe Gardens; a tribute to its determined founder, Osgood Mackenzie, as well as a reminder of the winter warming effect of the North Atlantic Drift on the western seaboard of Scotland

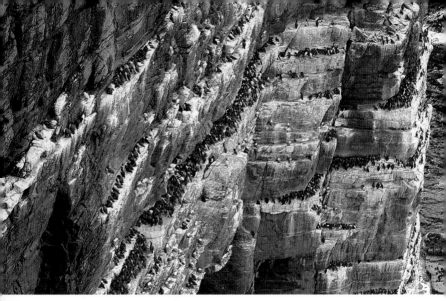

Guillemots, razorbills and kittiwakes on Handa's cliffs

TOURIST INFORMATION
Lochcarron (Apr–Oct): Main Street (tel: 01520 722357).
Lochinver (Apr–Oct): Kirk Lane (tel: 01571 844330).
Strathpeffer (Apr–Oct): The Square (tel: 01997 421415).

▶ Lochcarron   208A1

Glen Carron seems mostly empty: its soaring hills are clothed with forestry. The blueness of Loch Carron, on the western seaboard, is almost a relief after the unpeopled wildness. The village of Lochcarron is a long ribbon of dwellings, shops, guest-houses, hotels and so on, without a real focal point (it even boasts a golf course). Across the loch, beyond the road and the railway with its avalanche shelter, is one of Scotland's larger virtually uninhabited areas. With the Applecross Hills and the Torridons to the north, Lochcarron is ideal for exploring wild country. The A896 northwards passes through Kishorn and then opens up breathtaking views of the series of corries on the Applecross hills. Also nearby is the **Rassal Ash Wood**▶ nature reserve (administered by Scottish Natural Heritage), where fenced grazing 'exclosures' show a rich woodland fauna, contrasting with the over-grazed moors around.

▶▶ Lochinver   208B3

Lochinver is the largest centre in Assynt, and a busy little fishing port. Seen from across the sea loch, the blunt bows of Suilven (731m) rise end on in the rough lands behind the village, as a reminder of the eye-catching Assynt landscapes. Though far north on the map, Lochinver has double-track road all the way, and also offers magnificent touring options on (single-track) loops to both north and south. The B869 goes round via Stoer and Drumbeg, giving fine views of **Quinag**. From this road at Stoer, there are unclassified roads leading out to the Stoer peninsula with its scattered crofts. Park near the lighthouse for a clifftop walk to see the rock stack, the **Old Man of Stoer**▶▶. (It is further than you think.)

For equally spectacular coastal scenery, a longer excursion (by car) goes via the Kylesku Bridge and on beyond Scourie to Tarbet, where a boatman can take you over to **Handa**▶▶▶. This Royal Society for the Protection of Birds reserve has impressive seabird colonies – including puffins – on awesome cliffs as well as skuas in the interior which alarmingly dive-bomb intruders near their nest sites. Southwards, there is more wildlife interest to be found by taking the unclassified road leading towards the **Inverpolly National Nature Reserve**▶▶ (look out for wild cat and golden eagles). There is an information centre at Knockan Cliff, close by the A835.

▶▶ Plockton 208A1
Too impossibly neat to be true, Plockton was a fishing settlement but now has a number of holiday properties. Complete with rambling roses and hardy palm trees, the neatly painted coastal village makes the most of its sheltered east-facing position – unusual in Wester Ross – and turns its back on the prevailing westerly winds. Other points of interest on the Lochalsh peninsula include the **Lochalsh Woodland Garden**▶, a National Trust for Scotland woodland garden with pleasant sheltered walks by the lochside (open throughout the year). Many of the trees are over 100 years old, but the garden is still being developed.

▶▶ Strathpeffer 208B2
The mineral springs in this spa town were described in print by 1772. The first pump room was built in 1819. The local lairds gave the town their blessing and further development took place, assisted by the arrival of the railway which conveyed a regular clientele to the spa to

take the sulphurous waters. The spa attracted royalty and even George Bernard Shaw. The great Victorian heyday lives on in the town's confident and solid architecture. The waters can still be sampled. Though the railway has gone the station is now an attractively converted craft and gift complex with a small **Highland Museum of Childhood**▶ (*Open* mid-Mar–Oct, Mon–Sat 10–5, plus 7–9 Mon–Fri Jul–Aug, Sun 2–5. *Admission charge*).

Nearby are a number of points of interest, including the vitrified walling of the fortified hilltop of **Knock Farril** (as yet unexcavated) which can be reached on foot from Strathpeffer. **Strathconon** is also worth exploring, as this long glen often offers good views of red deer. **The Falls of Rogie** are signposted from the main road west of Contin and also make an enjoyable short stroll.

THE BATTLE OF STROME PIER
Sabbatarianism is still quite strong in certain parts of the Highlands and in May 1883 it resulted in a bizarre incident. East coast fishermen started landing herring at Strome Pier for rail shipment seven days a week. The west coast fishermen opposed the Sunday activity. Along with the locals, they seized the pier, thus preventing the loading of fish on to the trains bound for the London market. The protestors fought off six local constables and the loading crews. Matters escalated. The War Office in London was informed. Only a large police presence and a troop train on standby the following Sunday ensured that religious beliefs did not stand in the way of commerce.

Plockton, arguably Wester Ross's prettiest village

Inspiration by Loch Carron

Though the fishing industry was vital to Wick, no harbour existed here before about 1803. Until then the 200 or so boats that sailed for herring had only the river mouth for shelter

AN UNSAFE SANCTUARY
Tain may have been a shrine and sanctuary of St Duthac, but that did not stop it being violated. In 1306, the wife and daughter of King Robert I (the Bruce) fled the tightening English siege of Kildrummy (see page 182) to find sanctuary at Tain. This proved no obstacle to the local Earl of Ross (who supported Balliol, not Bruce). He snatched them from the sanctuary and made them prisoners. In the next century, a MacNeil warrior pursued his foes to the chapel and set fire to it.

Whaligoe Steps near Ulbster, south of Wick – not for the vertigo-prone

▶ Tain   209C2

Some say Malcolm Canmore granted Tain's first charter in the 11th century. The little town has a fine tolbooth and steeple. The ruins of nearby **St Duthac's Chapel** (built 1065–1256) mark the site of the birthplace of St Duthac, an early missionary to the Picts. Tain was a place of pilgrimage for centuries, the chapel a sanctuary and shrine. **St Duthus Church▶** was built in 1360 and also served the many pilgrims, a story told in the **'Tain through Time' Pilgrimage Visitor Centre▶** and museum (*Open* Apr–Sep, daily 10–6; Oct–Mar, daily 12–4. *Admission charge*).

▶▶ Timespan Heritage Centre   209C3

Open: Apr–Oct, Mon–Sat 9.30–5, Sun 2–5, open until 6pm Jul–Aug. Last entry 1 hour before closing. Admission charge
Timespan, in Helmsdale, is the work of a local group of enthusiasts who wanted to preserve the area's heritage, and knew how to acquire funding. The centre portrays many aspects of life in the Highlands of old, from Neolithic and Pictish times right up to the Clearances, with a mixture of tableaux, artefacts and audiovisuals. It also has a fascinating account of the 'gold rush' in the nearby Strath of Kildonan which took place in 1869. What makes Timespan different is the thought-provoking way the exhibits tell the story. There is only one jarring note: the centre also has a bizarre shrine to the romantic novelist Barbara Cartland, who has property nearby.

Further up the Strath is the site of the gold rush town. At **Baile an Or** 'gold town', 13km to the northwest, it is still possible to pan for gold, using equipment hired from a craft shop in Helmsdale. Do not expect to be able to subsidise your trip this way!

▶▶ Ullapool   208B2

In contrast to many ancient settlements with obscure origins, Ullapool can be dated precisely. The abundant herring in Loch Broom inspired the founding of a fishing station and village there soon after the formation of the

British Fisheries Society in 1786. This society paid for the infrastructure of curing sheds, storehouses, a pier, inn and even a school and some of the dwelling houses. All was laid out on a regular grid plan and mostly completed by 1792. However it soon became clear that the herring were not a reliable harvest. Ullapool's fortunes rose and fell, and many turned to the land for a living. Overall, however, Ullapool has maintained a strong fishing connection, rising into prominence in the 1980s with the arrival of the Eastern Bloc 'klondykers' – vessels buying fish direct for on-board processing.

Two small museums in the town, plus a number of shops and a pottery factory provide diversion for the strolling tourists, as this is one of the largest centres on this stretch of seaboard. Ullapool also has an important ferry link with Stornoway in the Outer Hebrides.

Corrieshalloch Gorge▶▶▶ On the A835 south of Ullapool this is just one of the area's many scenic attractions. Meltwater from a glacier at the end of the last Ice Age cut a 60m deep gorge, into which the **Falls of Measach** now plunge, half hidden by trees and lush greenery. It is viewed from a spindly, vertigo-inducing suspension bridge.

▶ Wick

209D3

The workaday, east-wind flavoured town of Wick made a big contribution to the development of fishing. **Wick Heritage Centre▶▶**, with its wide ranging displays of fishing artefacts, recalls the time when herring brought great prosperity to the town in spite of a dangerous and inadequate harbour (*Open* Jun–Sep, Mon–Sat 10–5, last entry 4.15. *Admission charge*).

North of the town, a pleasant walk along the coastal grazings from the signposted car park soon leads to **Castles Girnigoe** and **Sinclair**, perched on the cliffs above Sinclair's Bay. These adjacent gloomily ruined strongholds were the works of the Sinclair Earls of Caithness and can be visited any time – but take care, as their situation is exposed.

ALONG THE A99
Diversions off the A99 near Wick include: trips to Whaligoe Steps, where a dizzying set of steps leads down the cliff to a former fishing station; and, inland from Whaligoe, to the Grey Cairns of Camster, Neolithic burial cairns of the area's first farmers. Nearby is the Hill o Many Stanes: 200 stones arranged in 22 rows, dating from the early Bronze Age. Their purpose is a mystery.

TOURIST INFORMATION
Helmsdale (Apr–Oct): Coupar Park (tel: 01431 821640)
Ullapool (Apr–Oct): Argyle Street (tel: 01854 612135).
Wick: Whitechapel Road (tel: 01955 602596)

On the Stornoway to Ullapool ferry

The Islands

226

Changeable weather, Cladach Chairinis, North Uist, with Eaval beyond

The CalMac ferry doing the Ardrossan– Brodick (Arran) run

Caledonian MacBrayne

The Islands

THE ISLANDS Scotland's western seaboard is about 416km in a straight line but, counting all the indentations and island shores is around 3,200km long. On such a complicated and rocky coast, even counting islands can be difficult (it all depends on the definition) but it is usually said that Scotland has 790, of which 130 are inhabited.

Apart from the outliers like North Rona or St Kilda, the island clusters fall into natural groupings: the islands of the Clyde which lie within the estuary between the mainland and the Kintyre peninsula; the Inner Hebrides, comprising the main islands of the western seaboard between Kintyre and Skye; the Outer Hebrides, now usually called, somewhat confusingly, the Western Isles, and stretching in a long line from the Butt of Lewis to Barra and beyond; and finally Orkney and Shetland, utterly different in culture and outlook from anything western.

THE CLYDE ISLANDS Access has much to do with character. The Clyde islands were for generations an easy-to-reach holiday playground for the workforce of the Glasgow conurbation and, no matter how much the local authorities try to change this image, just a little of earlier days still hangs around. A 1950s air clings on in the occasional café in Arran or Bute – that is part of their charm. **Arran** is sometimes labelled 'Scotland in miniature' because of its scenic attractions. The granites of the Goatfell ridges (the principal hill complex) have enticed generations of outdoor enthusiasts.

FAIR ISLE
Sometimes the P & O ferry
between Lerwick and
Aberdeen sails close to
Fair Isle to give passengers
a glimpse of this isolated
island midway between
Orkney and Shetland. It is
called the remotest inhabited island in the UK, and
has outstanding coastal
scenery, bird colonies and
a bird observatory, as well
as the George Waterston
Memorial Centre, dis-
playing the island's folklore
and history. A ferry runs
from Grutness, Sumburgh.

**MENDELSSOHN AND THE
HEBRIDES**
The basalt columns
carved by the sea into
caves on the island of
Staffa, west of Mull,
inspired the composer
Mendelssohn to write his
overture *The Hebrides*, or
Fingal's Cave. This little
island has recorded a
series of famous literary
visitors: Scott, Tennyson,
Keats and Wordsworth,
as well as the artist
Turner, all came to
admire the soaring
cathedral-like symmetry.
It can be visited from
Iona or from Mull.

Orkney tractor

Bute, meanwhile, still echoes the old days of traditional holidays, with its seafront mansions built by wealthy industrialists in Victorian times. It is now a very peaceful place, with an attractive rural hinterland to which the spectacular Victorian Gothic Mount Stuart House provides an unusual contrast.

THE INNER HEBRIDES Islay and Jura are often grouped together because of their proximity and ferry connections (the Jura ferry leaves from Islay). Yet they are completely different in character. Because of its farming and whisky, **Islay**, at least in part, still has a sense of a community held together without recourse to too many twee craftware ventures earnestly worked by urban refugees – the characteristic feature of all too many parts of the west.

Jura is simply empty. Not literally devoid of people, perhaps, but there are few other places where depopulation has been quite so spectacular. The island has been divided up into a few sporting estates. Some come to the island because of its connection with George Orwell's *Nineteen Eighty Four*, which was written at Barnhill, a remote house well up the east coast. Neither this spot nor the famous but seldom seen Whirlpool of Corrievreckan, a tidal conflict at the tip of Jura, is accessible by ordinary car.

Mull boasts the only other island Munro apart from Skye: Ben More. There is also some highly attractive coastline. Like Skye, Mull has proved a magnet for a new breed of resident, eager to escape the pressure of life in the south of the UK.

As for smaller Hebridean islands, **Colonsay** is the very distillation of Hebridean charm. With only 22km of roads it is hardly worth bringing a car. Colonsay is popular both as the ultimate in relaxing Scottish hideaways and as a good place for birdwatchers, with its excellent variety of habitats. These include sand, cliff, machair (see page 283), moor and garden, and its own rather stunted woodland. Note that **Oronsay**, its companion to the south, with an interesting ruined priory, is a separate island only at high tide – take your wellington boots for the walk. **Coll** and **Tiree** are also interesting Hebridean destinations, with machair and long beaches. The so-called Small Isles – **Rum**, **Eigg**, **Muck** and **Canna** – also offer a true island experience, very definitely away from it all, with Rum the best for scenery.

SKYE AND THE WESTERN ISLES Skye – strictly part of the Inner Hebrides – is the most scenically spectacular island of the western seaboard, with glorious mountain landscapes. It is therefore very popular. However, the main ridge of the Cuillins (with the possible exception of Bruach na Frithe) is not a place for the inexperienced climber . The ascent of many of the Cuillins peaks demands rock-climbing skills or, at the very least, a good head for heights.

One of the ways in which the **Outer Hebrides (Western Isles)** differs from most of the mainland is in

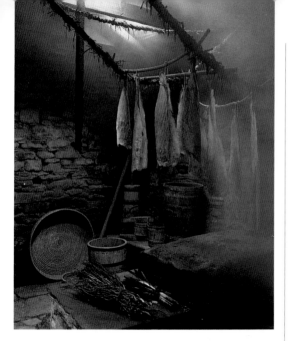

These are circular defensive structures, dry-stone walled and double skinned, of which the Broch of Mousa is the best preserved. There are about 400 of them scattered in Shetland, Orkney, Caithness and Sutherland and further down the western seaboard. Brochs are presumed to have been built for defensive purposes around the 1st century BC to 3rd century AD, probably against sea-borne raiders in the turbulent Celtic world of the time.

Orkney Farm and Folk Museum, Kirbister, Orkney

their deeply felt Sabbatarianism. Once widespread in the west, the setting aside of Sunday for almost exclusively religious pursuits has retreated to a stronghold here. All too easy for outsiders to dismiss as curiously joyless, the staunch faith must be a source of strength for those who choose to live amongst the bleak landscapes of the north end of the island. Visitors should respect it.

The lower end of the island chain is Catholic with a more relaxed community to be found there. Beaches receding to infinity, corncrake-haunted hayfields, and outhouses tied down to escape the wind are just a few of the far Hebridean images – as is the very real sense of a rhythm of life attached to tide and ferry times.

ORKNEY AND SHETLAND Orkney and Shetland look to their Scandinavian heritage. **Orkney** also looks further back, to a time when the climate was warmer and the ancient peoples who farmed here left more prehistoric monuments than anywhere else in Britain. These include Skara Brae, an ancient settlement where, amid the Stone Age furniture, an idea of the life of these shadowy ancestors of ancestors can be gained.

Most northerly of all, from the average Briton's point of view, **Shetland** is almost like having a foreign holiday without leaving Britain. Shetland's specialities include awesome seascapes – Esha Ness on Mainland, for example – and brochs (see panel).

Do not let the sea be any kind of barrier to visiting any of these islands. Access by the main ferry gateways – Oban, Mallaig, Ullapool, Scrabster, Aberdeen and others – is straightforward. All of Scotland's main islands are viable communities, with reliable car-ferry links and, in the case of the Outer Hebrides, Islay, Orkney and Shetland, with good air services as well. And if you want the island experience but do not like ferry travel, then the new bridge to Skye is the answer.

Trimming hoofs on Shetland; on the poor pastures and brown moors of the islands only the hardy sheep survive

HUTTON'S UNCONFORMITY

A rough 10-minute walk over the sheep-cropped raised beach beyond the north shore of Loch Ranza takes you to Hutton's Unconformity. In 1787 the geologist James Hutton noticed a change in the angle of the rocks, where 600-million-year-old grey-green Cambrian schist dips and is overlain by the sprightly young red Devonian sandstone, a good 200 million years its junior. This observation helped Hutton work out his theories about the age of the earth.

230

The Arran tapestry, Brodick, displays aspects of island life

Islands of the Clyde

▶▶ Arran   230A1

Arran has long enjoyed a reputation as an island for outdoor-lovers and walkers. The Highland Boundary Fault runs through the island: Arran's southern end is accordingly less hilly. Its largest township is Brodick, with a frontage spaciously set back from promenade and beach.

Brodick Castle and Country Park▶▶ is Arran's most famous attraction. On the north side of Brodick Bay and in the care of the National Trust for Scotland, the former seat of the Dukes of Hamilton displays furniture, paintings, silver and sporting trophies, but the real attraction is the rhododendrons, particularly in late spring and early summer. There is also a walled garden, and many other shrubs among the great-trunked trees (*Open* Easter–Oct, daily 11.30–5, last admission 4.30. Garden and park, daily 9.30–dusk. *Admission charge*).

Much of the settlement on Arran is clustered round the coast: pottery and crafts at **Corrie**, with its mountain backdrop; even better views at **Mid Sannox** with its bay of ground-down granite. **Lochranza**, where Loch Ranza spills in shallows up the flat-bottomed glacial glen, is yet another focus of craft activity. Here too is **Lochranza Castle** where Robert the Bruce is said to have first landed in 1307 at the start of the independence campaign. Look out for the '**Twelve Apostles**' at Catacol – a row of former fishermen's houses, identical except for differing window shapes, in order to be identified from offshore.

On the west side, around **Machrie Moor**, are atmospheric

standing stones, chambered cairns and hut circles. On the east shore, **Lamlash** has a cheerful air and views to Holy Island (now a religious settlement) and a sobering boulder memorial to the Highland Clearances (see pages 38–9).

▶ Bute

230B3

The old traditional waterfront resort of **Rothesay** contrasts with the pasture, peace and brackeny woodland found on the rest of this little island. The resort was popular in the heyday of the steamer network on the Clyde, a story told at the **Bute Museum** in Rothesay (*Open* Apr–Sep, Mon–Sat 10.30–4.30 also Sun 2.30–4.30 May–Sep; Oct–Mar, Tue–Sat 2.30–4.30. *Admission charge*).

Rothesay Castle▶▶ This fortress in the town centre is built round a circular courtyard. The Norse assailed it in 1230, breaching the wall (*Open* Apr–Sep, daily 9.30–6; Oct–Mar, Mon–Wed and Sat 9.30–4, Thu 9.30–12, Sun 2–4. *Admission charge*).

Just outside Rothesay is **Mount Stuart House▶▶▶**, ancestral home of the Marquesses of Bute. A splendid Victorian Gothic palace, it has plenty to admire inside, from the Marble Hall's galleries, stained glass and astronomical painted vault, to outstanding furniture, paintings and tapestries (*Open* gardens May–mid-Oct, Mon, Wed, Fri–Sun 10–5; house 11–4.30, last entry 4. *Admission charge*).

Bute has beaches and interesting walks up the west coast overlooking the Kyles of Bute. There are also ancient hill forts and faint echoes of Neolithic folk, but the most peaceful place has to be **St Blane's Chapel**, a 6th-century religious foundation with a 12th-century ruined chapel, set amid the hushed trees and sheltering mossy rocks.

Evening calm on Bute

MEDICAL SUPPLIES
The soft and mossy woods of Bute once provided an unusual harvest. During World War I, cotton wool became scarce and sphagnum moss, with its antiseptic and absorbent properties, was used instead for dressing wounds. It was gathered from the Balnakeilly Woods, dried, sorted and packed for hospitals and field units.

THE CUMBRAES
Often overlooked, these are the smallest of the main Clyde islands. Like Arran they are fondly regarded by many visitors, who come for the beaches, sailing, cycling, gentle walks and traditional entertainment. Great Cumbrae and its even smaller neighbour are only a few minutes off Largs on the Ayrshire coast, to which they are linked by ferry.

Cart decoration, Arran & Argyll Transport Museum, Brodick

CHOUGHS
These very rare crows (pronounced 'chuffs') are a Colonsay (and Islay) speciality. From a distance, they look black, in common with most of their cousins. If you observe choughs closely as they poke about for insects in old cowpats, you may glimpse their bright red beaks and feet. In flight they look like square and ragged-winged jet-black jackdaws. Their survival, research shows, seems to be dependent on the overwintering of cattle outside. Hence the cowpats.

232

Spectacular coastal scenery on Colonsay, an island which offers coastline and sandy beaches and dunes

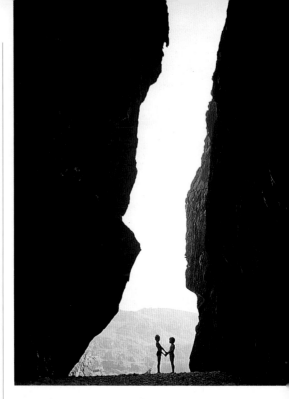

The Inner Hebrides

▶ Coll and Tiree   233A4/A3

Coll and Tiree duck low on the Hebridean horizon to let the Atlantic weather systems pass over, thus boasting good sunshine records. Tiree looks friendlier in cream and green, while Coll is rockier, with more acid moorland. Tiree has long been famed for its fertile, sandy soil, and the crofting way of life is still followed, more so than in Coll with its cattle rearing. Both islands were cleared, at least in part, with Ayrshire dairy farmers the new tenants in Coll in the 1850s. In Tiree the clearances were less severe: even today its population, around 750, is five times that of Coll.

Long beaches with crashing Atlantic surf are popular with surfers. Tiree has reliable conditions almost all year. Visit these islands if wide skies, open seas, wild flowers on windy dunes and a pace of life governed by the tide and the ferry is your idea of Hebridean bliss.

▶▶ Colonsay   233B2

Two hours from Oban lies 13km-long Colonsay, its grey rock rubbing through threadbare moorland. If you only have time for one Hebridean island, this is the one to choose. Colonsay's farms raise sheep and cattle, the rabbit-cropped coastal strip is shadowed by hunting buzzards, while wild goats browse round the edges of protected patches of unusual Hebridean natural woodlands of oak, hazel and willow. Bird habitats include gleaming sandy beaches and extensive tidal sandflats as well as impressive sea-cliffs and a loch. Colonsay's most

JURA
Jura has one road, one distillery, one hotel, six sporting estates and 5,000 red deer – outnumbering the people by at least 20 to one. Jura's human population was cleared to make the island into a deer forest and sheep walk. It is a haunting kind of place, with a few traces of the vanished villages – the faint shapes of the 'lazy-beds' (cultivated strips) still show through the heather. Otherwise, especially near the road end, the bracken and yellow flag-irises, mossy woods and strands of seaweed crisping on the salty grass form idyllic pictures of summer on the Hebrides.

famous (and scarcest) bird is the chough.

Lord Strathcona's family owns Colonsay, residing at Colonsay House. The grounds of this rambling pink mansion, **Kiloran Gardens**, with their tender rhododendrons, thickets of rampant escallonia and many much rarer species, are open to the public all year.

▶▶ Gigha   233C1

Tucked out of the weather off Kintyre, 8km-long Gigha has a mild climate. Its main attraction is **Achamore House Gardens**. These 130-hectare gardens were originally created by Sir James Horlick in 1944, who saw the place as ideal for exotic shrubs. Within the wooded windbreaks he created one of Scotland's finest woodland gardens. There are thickets of camellias, azaleas hoary with lichen, heather banks and damp places as well as a superb viewpoint revealing Jura's spectacular profile. The gardens are open all year and it is possible to visit them by ferry from the mainland in a long morning or afternoon.

ORONSAY
Oronsay is separated from Colonsay at low tide by 2km of sand flats, a splashy cockle-strewn haunt of plover. Bring wellington boots to visit Oronsay Priory, an abandoned 14th-century Augustinian foundation with impressive grave slabs and a magnificent early 16th-century cross. Make sure you keep an eye on the tide to avoid being cut off.

The map of Islay showing places including Rubh a Mhail, Colonsay, Rubha Bholsa, Nave Island, 364m, 785m, Gortantaoid, Bunnahabhainn, Ardnave, Tayovullin, Killinallan, Ardnahoe, Jura, Sanaigmore, Kilnave, Loch Gruinart Nature Reserve, Port Askaig, Feolin Ferry, Braigo, Leckgruinart, Aoradh, Craigens, Finlaggan Centre, Daimh-sgeir, Ballinaby, Saligo Bay, Loch Gorm, B8017, Gruinart Flats, Moin a choire, Ballygrant, A846, Coul Point, Aruadh, A847, Blackrock, Redhouses, Ardfin, Machir, Kilchoman, Bridgend, Kennacraig, Machir Bay, Bruichladdich, Loch Indaal, Barr, McArthur's Head, Kilchiaran, Museum of Islay Life, Bowmore, Kilennan, 491m, Rubha Liath, Tormisdale, 232m, Port Charlotte, Gartbreck, Laggay, Islay, Beinn Bheigeir, Ardtalla, Lossit, Nereabolls, Laggan, Duich, 454m, Claggain Bay, Portnahaven, A847, Easter Ellister, B8016, Trudernish, Ardmore Point, Orsay, Port Wemyss, Rinns Point, Laggan Bay, Glenegedale, Kintour, Kildalton Cross, Machrie, Kintra, Kennacraig, Rubha Mor, 165m, Ardbeg, Glenastle, Carnmore, Lagavulin, Rubha na Gainmhich, Lower Killeyan, Port Ellen, Laphroaig, Texa, Mull of Oa, Inerval, Rubha nan Leacan

0 2 4 6 km
0 2 4 miles

Drive

Around Islay

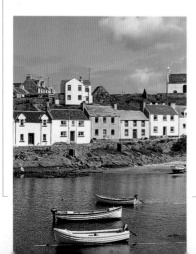

Islay has a quite different feel from the rest of the Hebridean islands. In the western half in particular, it is a place of farms, rather than crofts, and a number of distilleries provide work for the local community. For both the 91km round trip from Bowmore and the southern excursion via Mull of Oa (84km) make sure you allow plenty of time for short walks and sea views.

Bowmore is a tidy little town which gives its name to the whisky made in the distillery (founded 1779) by the shore. The dominating parish church of 1767 was built to an unusual circular design so that the devil could not find a corner to hide in.
   Take the A846 north out of Bowmore to Bridgend, then the A847 to skirt the sand flats at the

Portnahaven, Islay

head of Loch Indaal, following its shores to **Bruichladdich**, a village with a distillery and another malt whisky name. Continuing south for a few minutes you reach Port Charlotte. On the right of the road, in a converted church, is the **Museum of Islay Life** (*Open* Apr–Oct, Mon–Sat 10–5, Sun 2–5. *Admission charge*).

Return north to take the B8018 turning, then take a minor road which ends close to **Machir Bay** with its superb sandy beach. The nearby derelict church of **Kilchoman** has some interesting grave-slabs and two late medieval crosses. Circle **Loch Gorm**, pausing to enjoy the fine seascapes at Saligo Bay beyond the former war-time camp.

Return east, turning right on to the B8018, then left on the B8017. Take a left for **Kilnave**, where the chapel is associated with the massacre of Maclean clansman after a skirmish with the Macdonalds in 1598. In the graveyard is a weathered 8th-century carved cross.

The Royal Society for the Protection of Birds have several farms here, including **Aoradh Farm**, a visitor centre with full information on their nature reserve. The low-lying lands are still farmed, the extensive acreage providing a wintering ground for geese around the splendidly wild dunes and endless beaches of **Loch Gruinart**. Drive up its east shore and park before a gate, where the road deteriorates. Walk as far as the headland –

The Paps of Jura from the northern part of the Mull of Kintyre. Jura, the fourth largest island of the Inner Hebrides (45km long), is very sparsely populated

Killinallan Point – on this peerless and lonely coast before returning to Bowmore.

To the south of the island is the southern peninsula of **The Oa**, a region of caves, cliffs and smuggling tales. At the tip, the **Mull of Oa**, a monument recalls 650 men who lost their lives when the troopships *Tuscania* and *Otranto* went down nearby in 1918. Further east near Ardmore Point is the highly wrought 8th-century **Kildalton Cross**, carved from a single slab of epidiorite rock.

En route for the Jura ferry take in the **Islay Woollen Mill** and, a little further, **Loch Finlaggan**, former power base of the Macdonalds, the Lords of the Isles. Their story is told in a small visitor centre overlooking the loch with its little island on which their headquarters stood.

The magnificent Kildalton Cross

ACCESS TO IONA
This is via the well-used A849 on Mull through Bunessan to a long car park opposite the houses of Fionnphort. The ferry service is frequent in summer and takes only a few minutes.

Torosay Castle, Mull

SUNKEN TREASURE
After England's defeat of the Spanish Armada, several vessels were driven into northern waters. The *San Juan de Sicilia* put into Tobermory for supplies. Rumours spread that it was carrying £300,000 in gold. Donald Maclean of Duart sneaked on board and fired the ship's magazine, though how this would have helped him acquire a fortune is unclear. The ship blew up and sank with the loss of over 300 lives. Since then, every so often, salvage attempts have been made but with little success.

In Torosay Castle Gardens, Mull

►► Mull   *233B3*
Eilean Moula, Isle of Mull, is an island of great beauty and emptiness. It has a history of emigration and eviction. Today it is sometimes called 'The Officers' Mess', because of its popularity with retired military men.

You can take the ferry from Oban to Craignure, though it is more interesting to use the short (summer-only) ferry crossing from Lochaline to Fishnish. Both ferries are within easy reach of Torosay and Duart Castles.

Torosay Castle►►► Scottish baronial-style Torosay (*Open* Easter–mid-Oct, daily 10.30–5.30, last entry 5; gardens summer daily 9–7, winter dawn–dusk. *Admission charge*) is full of interest and humour with its information boards and family albums. The energetic can walk along the shore from Torosay to **Duart Castle►**, otherwise reached off the A849. This ancient Maclean seat was restored by Sir Fitzroy Maclean in 1911 (*Open* May–mid-Oct, daily 10.30–6. *Admission charge*).

Tobermory is the largest settlement, and, like Ullapool was founded as a fishing station. Its gradual decline was hastened by the arrival of the railhead at Oban, which took away fish traffic. However, the brightly painted crescent of mainly 18th-century buildings gives Tobermory a faintly Mediterranean air. A museum and a distillery stand on the waterfront, both opening weekdays all season.

Mull's attractions tend to the ruggedly scenic. Near the tip of the dramatic cliff ramparts of Ardmeanach is **The Burg►**, with its fossil tree reached by a rough walk. There is more coastal spectacle at Carsaig, where a very rough path leads west, below lava cliffs, to the impressive **Carsaig Arches►►**.

Even from the road, there is plenty of dramatic scenery, notably on the west coast loops. North of Loch Scridain, the B8035 breaches stepped cliffs and drops to the shore with fine views of the island of Ulva. This is a remote stretch with unnervingly fresh-looking rock splinters strewn on it.

TOURIST INFORMATION
Mull: Tobermory (tel: 01688 302182).

Isle of Mull Weavers

Although St Ninian, the first named mission-ary to Scotland, is said to have built a church at Whithorn in Galloway around AD 397 (see pages 120–1), it is the tiny island of Iona which is called the cradle of Scottish Christianity, because of its association with St Columba.

Foundation of the monastery The fiery and argumentative Irish monk Columba chose Iona for the setting up of a monastery in AD 563 because it was the first place he reached from which Ireland could not be seen – or so the tale is told. The word of St Columba's church was spread widely amongst the northern Picts, these early missionar-ies being regarded as some kind of superior 'medicine men'. Such was the importance of this religious commu-nity that it eventually became the burial place of the kings of Scotland.

It also suffered dreadful atrocities during repeated Norse sackings which finally caused the evacuation of the community to Kells in Ireland. Even after this it was not abandoned entirely and many monks were martyred here. It became a Benedictine foundation around 1203, finally falling into ruin by the Reformation. Restoration work began at the turn of the present century, the Iona Community was founded in 1938 and today the restored buildings are a spiritual centre under the jurisdiction of the Church of Scotland.

Iona today Today the ambience within the complex is a curious mix of the ancient and the earnest, but beyond the restored cloisters the most mystifying aspect of all is the little island's ability to absorb its visitors and still feel peaceful. Most people only make the short walk from the ferry pier via the nunnery to the abbey. They miss the beautiful white shell beaches and the machair with its undisturbed rich insect and bird life beyond the bare rocks and the thin pasture of the interior. The best place to see the shape of the island is from the top of the low (and oddly-named) hill Dun I (see panel).

A LITERARY LOCATION
From Dun I (a low hill), look for Erraid island, lying close inshore to the south, and difficult to see separately from Mull. Robert Louis Stevenson came from a famous light-house engineering family and knew the area well, as there was a shore base and quarry on Erraid in 1867 for the building of the Dhu Heartach light-house, on an outlying tooth of rock 18km to the southwest. In *Kidnapped* Stevenson set the wreck of the brig *Covenant* on the reefs offshore, the treacherous Torran Rocks.

The 15th-century MacLean's Cross, Iona

237

KITCHENER'S MEMORIAL
The huge bird colonies of
Marwick Head are below
the clifftop memorial to
Lord Kitchener. He was on
his way to Russia in 1916
aboard HMS *Hampshire*
when it hit a mine and
sank, with the loss of the
warlord and most of the
ship's crew.

TICKET BARGAIN
Buy a Historic Scotland
joint ticket to all Orkneys
prehistoric sites, and save
money. It is valid until you
have seen them all.

Stromness garage

Orkney

▶▶ Mainland   *238A2*

Orkney is an ancient archipelago of gently contoured
islands, with place-names identifiable from the rich Norse
heritage of the Viking sagas. It has the greatest concentration of prehistoric sites anywhere in Western Europe.
Mainland is the largest island and quite a lot of visitors
never venture beyond it. **Kirkwall** is the largest town and
island capital, built by a natural harbour. This early
Christian settlement took its name from the Old Norse
kirkjuvagr, 'church bay', and has several attractions.

Earl Patrick's Palace and the **Bishop's Palace▶▶** The
Bishop's Palace dates originally from the mid-12th cen-
tury as accommodation close to the then new cathedral.
Earl Patrick's Palace, Scotland's finest example of French
Renaissance architecture was built in 1600 for Patrick
Stewart, ruler of the islands, executed for treason soon
after (*Open* Apr–Sep, daily 9.30–6. *Admission charge*).

Orkney Wireless Museum▶▶ Crammed together are
numerous examples of wartime communications equipment, including some tiny radio sets, used by spies (*Open*
Apr–Sep. *Admission charge*).

St Magnus Cathedral▶▶▶ This magnificent church's
harmonious proportions belie its smallness. Founded in
1137 by Earl Rognvald Kolsson and dedicated to his uncle
St Magnus, the red sandstone structure took three centuries to complete. Visit any day, to admire its
Romanesque, Transitional and Gothic styles.

Tankerness House▶▶ This 16th-century merchant-
laird's mansion is now a museum of Orkney life from prehistoric times to the present (*Open* Mon–Sat 10.30–12.30,
1.30–5, also Sun 2–5 May–Sep. *Admission charge*).

Maes Howe▶▶▶ Off the A965 14km from Kirkwall,
this huge burial chamber dates from around 2500 BC and

has workmanship unsurpassed in Western Europe. It was almost 3,500 years old when Vikings scratched graffiti on the walls (*Open* Apr–Sep, daily 9.30–6; Oct–Mar, Mon–Wed and Sat 9.30–4, Thu 9.30–12, Sun 2–4. *Admission charge*).

Marwick Head Nature Reserve▶▶ Orkney has a wealth of wildlife, notably seabird colonies. These easily reached great red cliffs are stacked with 35,000 guillemots, among other species.

The Ring of Brogar▶▶▶ Orkney's best-known stone circle has 36 stones surviving from around 60. Other mounds and standing stones all add to the mystery of these monoliths. The **Stenness Standing Stones** are also in the vicinity. Open at all times.

Skara Brae▶▶▶ At this unforgettable prehistoric site, 5,000-year-old stone dressers, beds and cupboards have survived as fitments to the snug circular dwellings built before the Pyramids; (*Open* Apr–Sep, daily 9.30–6; Oct–Mar, Mon–Sat 9.30–4; Sun 2–4. *Admission charge*).

Stromness is the main ferry port for mainland Scotland connections. The little town became important in the 18th century as a watering place for shipping. Whalers, Hudson Bay traders and round-the-world explorers all stopped off here. Today, with its own fishing fleet and boatyards, its narrow lanes and old traders' houses, it has a decidedly pleasant period feel. Visit the **Pier Arts Centre** (*Open* Tue–Sat 10.30–12.30, 1.30–5; Jul–Aug 10.30–5) for exhibitions and a permanent 20th-century collection.

VIKING INSCRIPTIONS
The party of Vikings who came into the Maes Howe tomb in the winter of 1153 not only contributed to one of the largest surviving collections of runic inscriptions, but also executed some fine animal drawings on a buttress. These include the Maes Howe Dragon (though some say it looks like a lion) which has inspired artists and jewellery designers ever since its rediscovery in 1861.

239

A FAMOUS MARINER
Captain Bligh (of later *Mutiny on the Bounty* fame) was one of many well-known mariners who called at Stromness. This was in 1780 when he was with the *Discovery* and *Resolution*, returning home from the South Seas after Captain Cook's death. He dined at the Whitehouse of 1680, which can still be seen today.

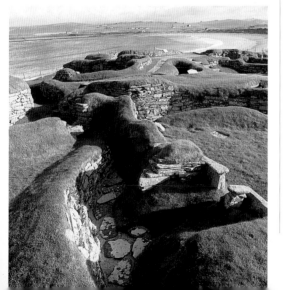

Skara Brae on Mainland Orkney is perhaps the most spectacular of the island's prehistoric sites. This extraordinary slice of Stone Age life lay buried beneath the sands until a storm revealed it in 1850

A SCUTTLED FLEET
It was off the islands of Cava and Flotta that the interned German High Seas Fleet scuttled itself on Midsummer Day in 1919. In doing so, they not only created a massive amount of scrap metal that was salvaged for years after, but they also became what is now rated as Britain's best amateur diving site, as not all of the German ships were cut up.

240

Many of Orkney's landscape features come together at St Margaret's Hope, South Ronaldsay: the prevailing greenness of the pasture, the sturdy, grey-slated dwellings and the ever-present sea

A WALK ON HOY
Naturalists who want to explore the rugged Hoy hinterland can reach Rackwick on foot by a well-marked track that goes round the north side of Ward Hill, the highest point on Orkney at 479m. Look out for great skuas bathing at the Sandy Loch on the way.

▶▶ **Hoy** 238A1

Hoy, the second largest island in the group, is the exception to Orkney's prevailing low-lying greenness, its north and west being high and craggy. Here the red sandstone has weathered into almost Highland scenery, with a west coast of spectacular natural beauty, glimpsed from the ferry en route to Stromness. With the most northerly natural woodland in Britain, glacial features such as small corries at comparatively low levels and U-shaped valleys, plus an arctic-alpine flora (and mountain hares), Hoy has a very distinct character.

The eerily deserted **Lyness Naval Base** on the east coast was the shore base which serviced the key anchorage for the Royal Navy in two world wars. The former Pump House is an interpretation centre. Here, too, is the cemetery as an inevitable epilogue to warfare, with sailors' graves from many famous ships, including HMS *Hampshire*, mined and sunk in 1916, HMS *Vanguard*, accidentally blown up off Flotta in 1916, and HMS *Royal Oak*, torpedoed at anchor here in 1939. Also nearby are the Martello Towers, on either side of Longhope Bay, first built in 1813–15 as protection for Baltic-bound British convoys against American privateers.

A road leads west to **Rackwick**, a crofting township gradually coming back to life after a period of decline. This is one of the most attractive parts of all of Orkney, amid the heathery hills with steep shoreward cliffs nearby. From here a footpath leads to the **Old Man of Hoy**, a spectacular sea stack.

North Hoy Nature Reserve▶▶▶ This area takes in the Old Man of Hoy and is noted not only for its seabird colonies, but also species such as the piratical great skua, of which 1,500 pairs breed on the island. It is administered by the Royal Society for the Protection of Birds.

Dwarfie Stane▶ Yet another curiosity, reached on foot from the Rackwick Road, is the so-called Dwarfie Stane, the only rock-cut tomb in Britain. Quite why its 3rd millennium BC excavators should have bothered to chip away at this natural block of red sandstone in its windy valley is a mystery. The tomb has been empty since recorded time.

▶ South Ronaldsay

Though strictly speaking a separate island, this can be easily visited from Mainland by the road link over the Churchill Causeway, formed by lines of tipped concrete blocks. Sir Winston Churchill ordered its construction during World War II in order to close off the eastern arm of the Scapa Flow anchorage after a German U-boat slipped in and torpedoed HMS *Royal Oak* with great loss of life. Rusty shipwrecks, previously scuttled as part of the navy defences, still line part of the route, adding a surreal quality to the scene.

Italian Chapel▶▶ Starting with a Nissen hut, Italian POWs in 1943 built this extraordinary *trompe l'oeil* building (even the windows are painted on), creating an intricate embellishment with only scrap metal, cement and other scrounged bits and pieces. Years after World War II had ended, the Italian labour of love began to fall into decay. By this time the local Orcadians had become so fond of it that they used the Italian media to find the original builders, who then returned to Orkney to restore it. It stands on Lamb Holm, half-way along the Churchill Causeway, and is open at all times.

The road continues to **St Margaret's Hope,** grey houses tucked next to a seaweedy harbour and on to Burwick on the southern tip.

OTHER ORKNEY ISLANDS Among the further-flung Orkney islands are **Papa Westray**, where two 5,000-year-old dwellings (believed to be the oldest houses in Europe) can be seen at Knap of Howar; **Sanday**, where a tomb of the Maes Howe type – and many other remains – suggests that this was a burial place of great importance in the 2nd millennium BC; and **Westray**, with its ancient church and **Noltland Castle**, a very impressive 16th-century Z-plan edifice, guarding the natural harbour at Pierowall. These and almost all of the other northern outliers of Orkney are well served by the inter-island aeroplane and ferry network from Kirkwall.

VICTORIAN TOURISTS
The Dwarfie Stane is mentioned in Sir Walter Scott's *The Pirate* as the favourite dwelling of Trolld, a dwarf of Norse legend. By Victorian times, the spot was visited regularly, as can be gauged by the surviving graffiti. This includes an inscription in Persian, carved in 1850 by a certain Major William Mouncey. He was an ex-Afghanistan and Persian spy of eccentric habits, including adopting Persian costume and spending several nights inside the tomb.

241

The Old Man of Hoy, a spectacular sandstone sea stack

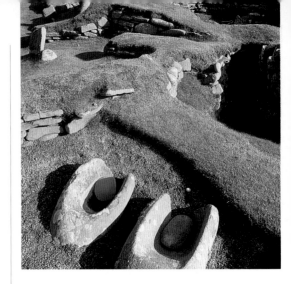

Many-layered Jarlshof, near Sumburgh Head on the southern tip of Shetland

SUMBURGH HEAD
With its cluster of attractions, South Mainland alone needs a couple of trips from Lerwick, particularly if you are interested in the birdlife. Though there are plenty of other places to see puffins, the Sumburgh Head colony is particularly convenient. Park before the wall that marks the lighthouse area, go through the gap in the wall and walk up the road to the first hairpin bend. Look over the cliff to the right for the puffins.

A fairly quiet day at Esha Ness

Shetland

With its ever-changing seascapes, its Norse heritage and the sheer challenge of its ocean-girt northerly setting, Shetland confounds any stereotypes of tartans and glinting lochs. Nowhere is more than 8km from the sea, thanks to the voes and (smaller) geos, the long fingers of sea that find their way far inland. The ocean is a glittering or grim backdrop to every view, and has historically made Shetland into a surprisingly cosmopolitan place.

The islands themselves are subtly different, with a prevailing inland landscape of crofts and small fields or eroded peatland vegetation, and virtually no trees. The biggest island, Mainland, has the island 'capital' Lerwick, the only town of any size, and also some excellent seascapes and nature interest as well as historic sites.

▶▶▶ Mainland   243A2
Esha Ness▶▶▶ Here the sea has hammered away at the cliffs and quarried out awesome rock features: the Holes of Scraada, the Heads of Grocken and the Grind of the Navir. South of the B9078, **The Drongs**, sea stacks in the bay, resemble a Norse galley under sail. North of Ronas Voe, the scoured hump of Ronas Hill can be seen. Though only 450m high, its exposed northerly situation has created a low altitude arctic environment, with a variety of interesting arctic and alpine plants on its boulder fields.

Explanatory panels at the Jarlshof site help unravel the complex pattern of settlement

Minutes from Sumburgh Airport, the important archaeological site of **Jarlshof▶▶** (in the care of Historic Scotland) represents waves of settlement from the Bronze Age right through to medieval times. Among the earliest huts was a bronze smiddy (blacksmith's). The buildings were then covered by an Iron Age broch (see panel page 229) whose walls still stand about 2m high. This in turn became a wheelhouse, and there are examples of others on site. Then there are traces of possible Pictish occupation, probably between the 6th and 8th centuries AD, before the Viking farm was built over them. A series of medieval homesteads and finally a late 16th-century house of the Earls Patrick and Robert Stewart were built. The latter's ruins dominate the site today (*Open* Apr–Sep, daily 9.30–6. *Admission charge*).

Nearby look for puffins and otters on **Sumburgh Head** and bonxies (great skuas) loafing around the Loch of Spiggie before their next spot of air piracy. Also within easy reach is **St Ninian's Isle**, where a treasure was discovered in 1951 near an ancient chapel site. **St Ninian's Isle** is a tombolo – an island joined to Mainland by a spit of dazzling cream sand.

The Shetland Croft House Museum▶▶▶ is a 19th-century thatched building once typical of the style of croft house found throughout the islands (*Open* May–Sep, daily 10–1 and 2–5. *Admission charge*). The museum gives an excellent insight into rural life in Shetland, and the helpful attendant answers any questions. Walk down to the fascinating 'click mill' – a miniaturised horizontal water-mill powered by a tiny burn.

MAVIS GRIND
Mavis Grind is the appealing name given to a point on the A970, west of Brae, where Mainland all but splits in two, except for a narrow rocky waist that carries the road. It is said to be the only place in Scotland where it is possible to throw a stone from the North Sea to the Atlantic, though it still needs a strong arm.

The Islands

A NORSE LEGEND
The Orkneyinga Saga tells how Mousa Broch, or Moseyjarborg, already a thousand years old, was used as a refuge in 1153 by a wayward Orkney earl who had abducted the woman of his dreams (a rival earl's mother, hence the complications).

▶ Lerwick

243B1

This is by far the largest town in Shetland. No settlement existed here before the 17th century, as the area was not considered very fertile. The Norsemen named the area *leir vik* – mud bay – but muddy or not, the sheltered stretch of water between modern Lerwick and the island of Bressay was a safe anchorage for enterprising Dutch fishermen. Lerwick started as a fishing season trading post, then in the Anglo-Dutch wars of the mid-17th century, it became a permanent town, built around Fort Charlotte, whose walls still survive. Now it has around 8,000 people, one third of the total Shetland population.

Today, the centre of Lerwick is full of character, especially the waterfront, with the older buildings hard against the sea still retaining their 'lodberries' built out over the water. These were shops-cum-houses-cum-storage-areas with their own private loading and unloading areas. The main commercial street is flagged and at least partly for pedestrians only, with as good a range of shops as anywhere else in Scotland. There are also fine and sturdy Victorian buildings as well as the housing boom on the edge of town

Lerwick and its harbour are inseparable, always busy with ferries, fishing boats and oil-supply vessels

Exclusive knitwear labels, Lerwick Museum

prompted by the oil developments. The **Shetland Museum** (*Open* Mon, Wed, Fri 10–7, Tue, Thu, Sat 10–5. *Admission free*) covers the main Shetland themes of folk life, shipping, art and archaeology.

Once solitary on the edge of a boggy loch, now with lots of new housing nearby, **Clickhimin Broch▶▶** has the complication of being a broch built within an Iron Age fort. Open any time, it makes a good preamble to an excursion to Mousa Broch.

Mousa Broch▶▶▶ is the most complete example of a broch anywhere in Scotland, with 12m walls. As it is on the island of Mousa, the visit involves taking a boat, which runs daily in summer – check with the Tourist Information Centre in Lerwick. Mousa Broch is impressive because it is eerily complete. Boats can be hired on summer afternoons, also weekend mornings and some evenings.

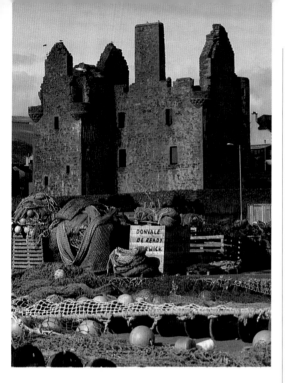

THE SHETLAND BUS
This was the name given to the small craft that maintained the highly dangerous sea connection from Shetland to Norway during World War II. It was used by the Norwegian Resistance for taking in saboteurs and taking out refugees.

245

Scalloway Castle adds a sense of drama to the skyline of the little town

Another very worthwhile Lerwick excursion is across the neighbouring island of Bressay to visit the nature reserve of **Noss▶▶▶**, a much smaller island looked after by Scottish Natural Heritage. Though its vertiginous seabird colonies are not for the faint-hearted, the massed puffins and rapier-beaked gannets offer spectacle on a grand scale. Take the regular Lerwick–Bressay ferry, then walk, cycle, drive or take a taxi 5km across Bressay for a small boat crossing to Noss, and walk all round the island.

Scalloway▶▶ The second biggest settlement on Mainland (and in all of Shetland) is older than Lerwick. It lies in a more fertile area on the west coast and was the original main town. Dominating the roofs of the town are the ruins of **Scalloway Castle**. After the demise of Norse power, Shetland gradually came under the sway of a particularly predatory breed of Scottish baron, of which Earl Patrick Stewart was a typical specimen. As the displays within the castle tell, he used forced labour from the surrounding area to build his fortress in 1600. He was executed in Edinburgh in 1615, the castle thereafter gradually falling into ruin. The key-keeper lives nearby and access is at any reasonable time.

By the Town House, Lerwick

Also nearby is the locally run **Scalloway Museum** which, among other maritime matters, tells the story of the Shetland Bus (see panel) which used Scalloway as a base (*Open* May–Sep, Tue–Thu 2–5, Sat 10–1, 2–5. The museum can be visited at other times by telephoning one of the numbers displayed outside). Access to the lesser islands of Trondra and East and West Burra is by the B9074, also near Scalloway. All are linked to Mainland by bridges and the road eventually ends at Papil. At the road end, walk through a little gate to find another fine beach, with views to distant Foula framed by rocky headlands.

CURIOUS ENCLOSURES
First-time visitors to 'the bonnie isle' of Whalsay are often puzzled by the small circular stone-built enclosures that dot the landscape. The locals will inform you that they are 'planticruives' (variously spelt). They were used to grow winter fodder of the brassica variety. The round wall kept the sheep out and provided shelter. The structure was usually covered with net to keep out birds.

246

FOULA
Foula (from a Norse word for bird island) offers spectacular coastal scenery even by Shetland standards. The Kame on the west coast is a sheer 365m cliff, the second highest in Britain. (Only the cliff by Conachair on St Kilda is higher at 430m.) Foula is 43km west of Scalloway.

A variation on the theme of a boathouse at Gutcher, Yell

▶▶ **Unst**   *243B3*

Thanks to cheap prebookable inter-island ferries, getting up to Unst is not a problem. It is worth going, if only to see the United Kingdom's most northerly just about everything, from post office to lighthouse.

Muness Castle▶ Scotland's most northerly stone castle was built on low ground by the sea for yet another tyrannous Shetland laird, Lawrence Bruce, half-brother to Scalloway Castle's Earl Patrick Stewart. Muness shares approximately the same building date as Scalloway (1598) and the same architect, Adam Crawford. He created a handsome yet functional oblong fortress flanked by two towers on the diagonal, though the second floor and roof are now missing. His client's invocation in verse carved above the main entrance – 'To help and not to hurt his work always' – did not impress the French privateers who burned the building within 30 years of its completion. Access is at all reasonable times, via a key-keeper, and the building can also be seen from the road.

Hermaness National Nature Reserve▶▶▶ At the other end of Unst from Muness, this is the very end of the United Kingdom. However, the RAF community at Baltasound and the conspicuous radar station on top of Saxa Ford, one of the twin headlands on top of Unst, give the area a slightly sinister ambience. To make the most of the headland, climb the 200m high Hermaness Hill. Strong shoes are advised on the rough moorland path. There is a good hilltop view of Muckle Flugga with its lighthouse. Take care if investigating the puffin-hollowed cliffs and gannet-plastered stacks on the west side as the grassy edges slope away treacherously. Look out too for dive-bombing great and arctic skuas breeding on the moor and keep on the path.

Other features of Unst to note are the most northerly post office at **Haroldswick,** as well as a number of broch sites and other prehistoric places; also, for the botanist, the **Keen of Hamar,** a low, domed hill near Baltasound with plant species from the arctic tundra (Scottish National Heritage permit access only – though the general terrain can be seen from the road).

▶ Whalsay   243B2

The Hanseatic League, the trading confederation of European cities that flourished until the 17th century, was important for Shetland. The most vivid reminder of those sea-trading days can be seen at Symbister on the island of Whalsay. The **Bremen Böd** (booth) is a curious little building by the harbourside, a restored Hanseatic storage and trading booth, possibly dating from the 17th century. The key-keeper is nearby, so visiting is possible at reasonable times. Otherwise, Whalsay is an island for bird lovers, with several rarities recorded on migration here. It is also a wealthy island, as it is the home of many of the successful local skippers.

▶ Yell   243B2

Yell is a dark brown stepping stone between Mainland and Unst. It has more peat than any other part of Shetland, and this is widely cut for fuel. The **Old Haa of Burravoe** is a 17th-century house (or hall) built by the local laird on the best spot to keep an eye on shipping entering Burra Voe. It has been restored as a local museum with extras such as genealogy, crafts and a good cup of tea (*Open* late Apr–Sep, Tue, Wed, Thu, Sat 10–4, Sun 2–5). Up at the north end of Yell, it's worth tracking down the **Gloup Fishermen's Memorial** in a field behind one of the crofts. Gloup Voe is long and narrow and once had a large fishing community, which was devastated in July 1881 by the loss of 58 men from ten 'sixerenes', the native six-oared craft.

Clickhimin Broch, Lerwick

VIKING QUARRIES
Among the variety of rock types in Shetland is steatite or soapstone, a soft, easily worked rock extensively used by the Vikings for making a variety of vessels including lamps. One source was near Clibberswick, east of Haroldswick on Unst, where traces of quarrying can still be seen. Sometimes the vessels were formed while still attached to the living rock. They were chiselled into shape, upside down, then removed and hollowed out.

THE WHITE WIFE
On the way up Yell by the B9081, look towards the sea edge for the White Wife near Otterswick and Queyon. She was the figurehead of the German sail training ship *Bohus* and now looks over the waters in which her ship was wrecked. The Old Haa at Burravoe has a copy of her, as well as details of the drama.

Skye and the Western Isles

▶ Barra   251A1

The sea-going Macneil clan owned Barra for centuries, and often practised piracy. One chief sold the island to pay debts in 1838, and part of it was bought back in 1937 by the 45th chief, an American architect, who restored **Kisimul Castle** (also known as Kiessimul)▶ in Castlebay (*Open* Apr–Sep, Mon, Wed, Sat 2–6). Castlebay itself was once a thriving fishing port.

As well as the open shell-sand beaches, one of which achieved fame as the island's landing strip, and the rough inland walking, other points of interest on Barra include **Kilbarr Church**, a ruinous medieval church dedicated to the saint who gave his name to the island. The last thatched croft house on the island is at **Craigston**, northwest of Castlebay. It is now a little museum (*Open* Jun–Sep, Mon–Fri 11–5; other times, contact Tourist Information Centre at Castlebay).

▶ Benbecula   251A2

Benbecula, joined to the Uists by causeways, is patterned and interlaced with inland waters. It presents great sweeps of sand to the Atlantic, with flowery machair beyond and attendant crofts. To the west, a missile range points into the ocean. To the east there is much rough bogland. The highest point, Rueval, is barely 120m above sea level and overlooks endless peaty lochans, beloved of fishermen.

▶▶ Harris   251B3

Harris has austere rocky landscapes, except for some western machair and the highest hill in the Outer Hebrides, **Clisham**, at almost 800m. The 'border' between Lewis and Harris runs east from Kinlochresort. Traditionally, the Macleods of Lewis held the island of their name, while Harris was under the sway of the

LEVERBURGH
One odd chapter in Harris's story is encountered at Leverburgh, near Rodel, which recalls the efforts of one of Britain's most successful industrialists, the soap magnate Lord Leverhume, to spend some of his riches turning a tiny fishing village into a major fish processing port. He owned most of Lewis and Harris at the time.

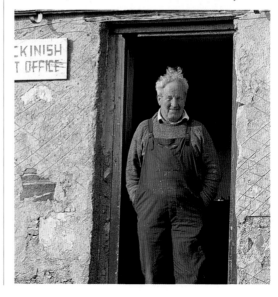

Stockinish post office and postmaster, on Harris

Macleods of Dunvegan in Skye.

Walking, fishing, birdwatching and visiting beaches are the main activities. **St Clement's Church**▶▶ at Rodel, on the southern tip, is a cruciform church built around 1500 by the eighth chief of the Macleods, sometimes known as Alasdair Crotach, who died 20 years after the construction of his magnificent tomb within the church. Visit it at any reasonable time.

Kisimul (Kiessimul) Castle and Castlebay, Barra

249

Above East Loch Tarbert, Harris

ERISKAY
This island between Barra and South Uist was the place where Bonnie Prince Charlie first landed on Scottish soil. Its other claim to fame is that the SS *Politician* was wrecked there in 1941 while carrying 20,000 cases of whisky. The subsequent events inspired Compton Mackenzie's *Whisky Galore*.

If visiting Rodel from Tarbert, take in the endless empty sands of **Traigh Luskentyre**▶▶▶ and loop back towards Tarbert from Rodel by the east coast road, enjoying the wild and remote bouldery country before a whole mountain is removed and a new sea loch is created. This gigantic feat of engineering will make way for a new superquarry which is planned here for the future. Another very twisty drive along the B887, northwest of Tarbert towards uninhabited Scarp, passes the former whaling station at **Bunavoneadar** (which was abandoned in 1930 – look for the sentinel chimney stack beside the road), and **Amhuinnsuidhe Castle** with its 'no stopping' notices. This grand structure was built by the then owners of Harris, the earls of Dunmore, in the 1860s.

The Islands

Callanish Standing Stones

TOURIST INFORMATION
Lewis: 26 Cromwell Street
(tel: 01851 703088)

SCOTLAND'S OLDEST UNIVERSITY
Some historians maintain that the Teampuill na Trionaid (Trinity Temple) on North Uist is Scotland's oldest university. This monastery and college founded in the early 13th century lies in ruins, ransacked in the Reformation, its valuable books said to have been cast into the sea. A number of other historical sites are near this ancient seat of learning.

250

LORD LEVERHUME
Perhaps Lewis's owner, Lord Leverhume, with his English public school background and wealth, failed to understand the Gaelic mind. He became deeply involved in post-World War I politics on the island, in a complex confrontation with land raiders – ex-servicemen returning from war and eager to acquire crofts. Yet many on Lewis supported his vision of an industrialised island society. He eventually turned his attentions to Harris, his grand dream for Lewis unfulfilled.

An abandoned croft at Barvas, Lewis

▶ **Lewis**   *251B4*

Most of Lewis's townships are close to the coast, forming a narrow green strip between the ocean and the inland brown sea of endless lochan-dotted peatlands. This initially unpromising landscape has a long history of settlement dating from neolithic and Norse times.

Callanish Standing Stones▶▶▶ This is the most famous of the prehistoric sites, possibly dating from 3000 BC, sometimes described as Scotland's Stonehenge. It is a cruciform setting of stones: 19 monoliths form an avenue running north-south from a circle of 13 other stones, with outliers adding to the inexplicable design. View any time.

Dun Carloway Broch▶ A fairly well-preserved structure visible from the main A858. The walling stands in part over 9m high. View any time.

Black House at Arnol▶▶▶ This once typical local dwelling is in the care of Historic Scotland. The byre is under the same roof (*Open* Apr–Sep, Mon–Sat 9.30–6; Oct–Mar, Mon–Thu, Sat 9.30–4. *Admission charge*).

Callanish, Carloway and Arnol are all on the west coast. It is worth continuing northeast on the main road, the A857, all the way to Port of Ness to see the **Butt of Lewis** and its lighthouse. Though the cliffs are not spectacularly high, the ambience is wild and windswept. There are streams of gannets, other seabirds, skuas, and sometimes dolphins or whales can be seen.

Lewis also offers good seascapes on the way to Great Bernera, an island joined to the 'mainland' by a causeway: there are plenty of diving gannets and terns off the little beach at the road end at **Bosta**. Arguably the finest beach on Lewis is on the east coast: **Tràigh Mhór** (literally in Gaelic 'big beach') can be seen near at the Tolsta road-end.

Stornoway is the main administrative centre for the Western Isles. It is not overtly picturesque and is very hushed on Sundays but has a fine asset in the **An Lanntair Gallery** with its changing exhibition programme (*Open* Mon–Sat, 10–5.30. *Admission free*).

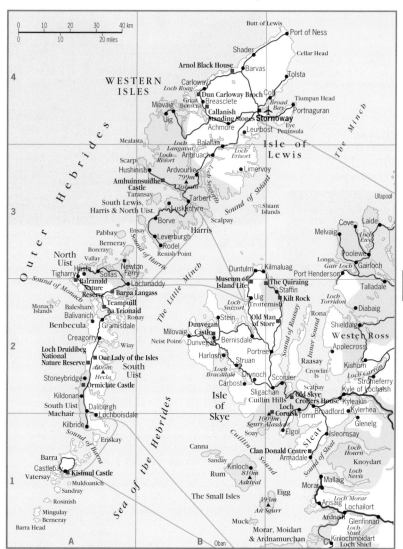

▶ **North and South Uist**   *251A2*

These are classic Hebridean islands of shell-sand and peaty lochans, golden beaches with crashing Atlantic surf and a rocky, wild and forbidding easterly coast. All of this provides a varied habitat for wildlife, hence the importance of the RSPB's **Balranald Reserve** on North Uist. There is a reception cottage for information on what to see on the reserve, which is open daily.

On South Uist **Loch Druidibeg** is another wildlife area under the care of Scottish Natural Heritage and noted for its breeding greylag geese, among many other species. Check with the warden's office for visiting details. There is access to machair land at several points on the Uists, where the full glory of wild flowers and bird life can be seen in late spring and early summer.

THE TALLEST MONOLITH
The Callanish stones may be tall, but tallest of all on the islands is the Clach an Trushal, a solitary monolith standing by the township of Ballantrushal (between Barvas and Shader) on the A857 (north of the junction with the A858). This grey, grizzled, lichen-covered tooth reaches a height of around 6m.

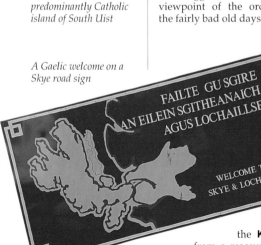

Pony trekking at Sligachan, Skye

Roadside shrine on the predominantly Catholic island of South Uist

A Gaelic welcome on a Skye road sign

FAILTE GU SGIRE
AN EILEIN SGITHEANAICH
AGUS LOCHAILLSE

WELCOME TO
SKYE & LOCHALSH

▶▶▶ Skye 251B2

Superlatives and Skye scenery go together. The big hill masses catch southwesterly weather systems, so it does rain a lot here, but when it is clear, the hills make the heart ache. Skye is unforgettable.

Though there is a Mallaig-Armadale ferry link, most people arrive via the new Skye Bridge near Kyle of Lochalsh, which replaced the ferry to Kyleakin. Among attractions on the way to Portree is the **Luib Folk Museum▶**, north of Broadford (*Open* Apr–Oct, daily 10–6. *Admission charge*). This thatched, traditional period-piece shows the kind of dwelling that the crofters of Skye once lived in.

En route for Portree, the **Cuillins** first show themselves around Sligachan and are still distantly in view from the 'capital' of Skye itself. Fairly picturesque (depending on the angle of view) **Portree** has quite a good range of shops and services.

The **Skye Heritage Centre▶▶▶** is a good starting point for understanding the island, particularly the struggles of the crofters. It tells Skye's story from the viewpoint of the ordinary folk who lived there in the fairly bad old days, rather than dwelling upon heroic tales of clans and chieftains. The centre uses headphones which pick up and relay information, depending on which part of the exhibition you are in (*Open* Apr–May, Mon–Sat 9–6; Jun–Oct 9–9; Nov–Mar 10–5. *Admission charge*).

The most interesting of Skye's scenic road loops is the **Trotternish** peninsula. Beyond the curious rock form of the **Old Man of Storr▶▶**, one popular stop is the **Kilt Rock▶▶** at Elishader. Seen from a reassuringly safe viewing platform, the cliff edge has alternate bandings of sedimentary rock with dolerite, giving the strong impression of kilt pleats. Much of the coastline around here is scenically spectacular, including the 90m seaward vertical drop of the **Mealt Falls**.

Beyond the impressive **Quiraing**▶▶ with its rock towers and pinnacles, and round the top of the peninsula, the Skye **Museum of Island Life**▶▶ by the main road at Kilmuir portrays crofting life as it was lived in a self-contained township. The staff are helpful and eager to tell you more. Flora Macdonald's grave is nearby (*Open* Easter–Oct, Mon–Sat 9.30–5.30. *Admission charge*).

Though there are other places to track down on your way round Trotternish, **Dunvegan Castle**▶ is the big attraction in the northern half of Skye. For 700 years the chiefs of the Clan Macleod have inhabited this rock above the sea loch, and between the 19th-century front entrance and the 14th-century keep there is plenty of historic lumber to enjoy. Amongst the relics is the Fairy Flag. All true Macleods believe this ancient cloth has the power to save the clan one more time if waved in battle (*Open* mid-Mar–Oct, daily 10–5.30, last entry 5. *Admission charge*).

Clan Donald Centre▶ The Sleat peninsula is sometimes overlooked by visitors heading for Trotternish and the Cuillins, unless they are travelling from the ferry port at Armadale. The area's principal attraction is this centre in a restored portion of Armadale Castle. It tells the story of the MacDonalds when they held sway over the western seaboard and beyond as the Lords of the Isles. Around the castle are gardens and nature trails (*Open* Apr–Oct, daily 9.30–6, last entry 5. *Admission charge*).

The Small Isles▶▶ This is the collective name for Muck, Eigg, Rum and Canna. Accommodation is very limited (though not impossible) on all of them, so they are usually visited on a day-trip from either Arisaig or Mallaig. Rum is the most spectacular and entirely in the care of Scottish Natural Heritage. Red deer are studied here and there are large numbers of breeding burrow-nesting shearwaters.

A VIEW OF THE CUILLINS
The B8083 runs to Elgol and offers a close view of the Cuillins. Hardy walkers can get into the interior via a rough track which leads to Camasunary. This starts some 6km from Elgol itself. There is also a coastal path from Elgol.

TOURIST INFORMATION
Skye: Bayfield House, Bayfield Road (tel: 01478 012137).

253

...AND ANOTHER CUILLINS VIEWPOINT
Follow the minor road, off the B8009 near Drynoch, into Glen Brittle. An obvious track, starting from the large car park right at the end of the road by Loch Brittle, rises on to rough moorland for a closer view of the Cuillin ridges. Strong footwear is advised, otherwise enjoy the roadside views, especially from where the road descends into Glen Brittle.

Dunvegan Castle is on the itinerary of most visitors to Skye. It offers a wide range of historic artefacts with Clan Macleod connections

Skye's 80km length is the distilled essence of Scottish scenery. In geological terms it has a greater area of basaltic plateau than anywhere else in the United Kingdom. It also has what some writers claim to be the finest view: the view of the Cuillin Hills from Elgol. Sir Walter Scott was inspired by it, so was the painter Turner who was one of many artists who journeyed here.

SKYE MARBLE

Among the many geological complexities of Skye, the island even has its own marble. This grey-, green- and white-striped rock is not only found in lamp bases and paperweights in souvenir shops, but is also exported for decorative, building and agricultural purposes from the Torrin Quarry on Loch Slapin (visible from the Elgol road). The marble has come about by 'thermal metamorphism' millions of years ago – limestone in contact with neighbouring igneous rocks in their molten state has been converted and hardened into the attractive stone found here today.

254

Sgurr nan Gillean from the Old Bridge at Sligachan

South of the island Skye starts off gently enough, from a tourer's point of view, with the **Sleat** peninsula. Even the bulky granite flanks of the **Red Hills** (sometimes known as the Red Cuillin) give no hint of the spectacle just around the corner. Then the pinkish granite gives way to dark toothed gabbro, and the **Cuillins** reveal themselves at Sligachan with the spire of Sgurr nan Gillean, well over the 914m (3,000ft) contour. More than 20 of its high companions also reach this magic Munro mark (see page 149), the highest being Sgurr Alasdair at 1,009m, on a spiky arête which eventually tumbles into **Loch Scavaig** in the west. Complicated volcanic geology has been further notched and splintered by more recent glaciation.

The Trotternish peninsula Yet even with the Cuillins, Skye has not finished with scenic spectacle. Most of the north of the island is basalt plateau, the ancient lavas suddenly ending in a long line of slipping cliffs, again the most spectacular of their kind in Britain. The **Old Man of Storr** on the horizon is a 49m pinnacle adrift from its parent cliff. It stands insecurely on a jumbled complication of clays and limestones unable to support the weight of the lava-plateau above. The infinitesimally slow rotational slippage of great slabs of lava cliff has also created the extraordinary rockforms of the **Quiraing**, into whose confines only sure-footed walkers should venture. Skye is unbeatable – when the sun shines.

MORVERN

5
4

Communications map

In all, Scotland has about 790 offshore islands, most of which are uninhabited. Ferry routes between larger islands, and between them and the mainland, are shown on this map, as are other communication routes

Arriving

By air

You can fly direct from London to Edinburgh, Glasgow, Aberdeen and Inverness. There are also Scottish connections from other English airports. Main operators within Scotland are British Airways, British Midland [New York office call (203) 661 8980, fax (203) 661 9221] and KLM UK. British Airways operates many internal routes within Scotland as well as cross-border routes. Some carriers offer fly-drive deals; check with your travel agent.

There are direct services by major carriers from a number of European cities into Scotland's larger airports, principally **Edinburgh**, **Glasgow** and **Aberdeen**. All transatlantic scheduled services to Scotland fly into Glasgow, though this option is under increasing pressure, particularly from London Heathrow, and there has been a reduction in the number of North American carriers serving Glasgow. Transatlantic visitors can also fly to Frankfurt or Amsterdam, and connect with a wide choice of flights to Scotland. A departure tax of £10 for flights within the European Union, and £20 for flights elsewhere, is payable.

By sea

From Europe There are frequent ferry services from the Continent to the north of England within easy reach of the Scottish Border. There are a variety of Scandinavian connections to **Newcastle**, within 90 minutes of the border, and **Hull**, 3–4 hours away, has ferries to Rotterdam and Zeebrugge.
From Northern Ireland There are frequent regular sailings from **Larne** to **Stranraer** and to **Cairnryan**. Full details are available from Sealink or from P & O appointed travel agents. There is also a SeaCat service from **Belfast** to **Stranraer**.

By train

Rail services connect the main cities of Scotland with the south, though with privatisation of the rail network, matters are in a state of flux. Fast electrified routes run from **London Kings Cross** to **Edinburgh Waverley** and between **London Euston** and **Glasgow Central**. Some Kings Cross services also run to Glasgow Central. In addition there are some (non-electrified) through services from London to Aberdeen and Inverness. The journey time between Edinburgh and London is just under four hours (the fastest timing) with many services taking around four hours 30 minutes including stops. The fastest direct service between London Euston and Glasgow Central takes around 5–5½ hours, with services linking Glasgow and Kings Cross taking about the same time. Rail services also connect main English cities and towns with Scottish destinations: for example, Birmingham, Carlisle, Crewe, Manchester, Newcastle, Penzance, Peterborough, Preston, Plymouth, York and many others. Overnight travel by sleeper services is available.

By bus

There are a number of companies in the UK operating express services to Scotland. They offer direct services, many of which run daily throughout the year, to a variety of destinations. Overnight travel is available on most major routes.

Many services offer facilities such as steward or hostess service with hot and cold drinks and light refreshments, toilet and washroom facilities, air-conditioning and seating in smoking or non-smoking areas. Further details on all services and ticket prices can be obtained from appointed travel agents or main city bus stations.

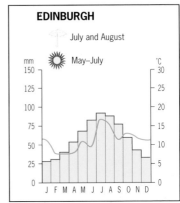

EDINBURGH

July and August

mm   May–July   °C

By car

Many travellers from the south use the M6 motorway, which becomes the M74 and A74 north of the Border. Using this route to Glasgow, and then taking the M80 and M/A90 north, it is possible to reach as far north as Aberdeen by motorway or dual carriageway all the way from London or even Exeter.

Alternatively, the M1, A1(M) and A1 is the main route on the eastern half of the country, though it is not possible as yet to reach Edinburgh, the capital, without encountering some single carriageway stretches of the A1 north of the Border. Allow seven or eight hours to reach Edinburgh comfortably from London, including stops and keeping reasonable average speeds.

WICK

October–January
April–June

DUMFRIES

July–January
May–July

Customs

There are no border checkpoints between England and Scotland. Transatlantic visitors flying direct to Glasgow will find the standard UK regulations apply with regard to quantities of duty-free cigarettes, alcohol and perfume. There are higher allowances for duty-paid goods bought in the EU.

When to go

Most Scots would say that May and June are the best months. Peak holiday season is July and August, when there is less accommodation choice in some of the smaller places in the west. Festival time in Edinburgh

(late August to early September) is very busy. Scotland's indigenous biting insect, the midge, is active from late May–mid-September on the west coast and the islands. Though an irritation, it poses no serious threat.

In terms of visitor attractions open, most properties belonging to the National Trust for Scotland (see address page 269) are closed by the beginning of November and open again at Easter. However, the grounds of many of these properties stay open throughout the year. Many Historic Scotland properties are open throughout the year, though some opening times are quirky, with Thursday afternoon and all-day Friday closing between October and March. Many privately owned castles also close between November and March.

Most municipal museums and art galleries stay open in the winter, as do some nature reserve visitor centres, plus a number of other attractions. Cromarty Court House and Scotland's Lighthouse Museum are just two places of interest in the north open year-round (but remember winter daylight hours are very short).

Rainfall, Edinburgh
Average rainfall in mm (1961–90)

	Jan	Feb	Mar	Apr	May	Jun	Jul	Aug	Sep	Oct	Nov	Dec
mm	57	42	51	41	51	51	57	65	67	65	63	58

Essentials

Climate
The Scots say that Scotland does not have a climate: it only has weather. Scotland's position on the edge of Europe, surrounded by sea on three sides, means that the weather is varied – though plenty of east coast places have less rain than Rome.

The east coast of Scotland tends to be cool and dry, the west coast milder and wetter. Remember also that only a short distance can make a great deal of difference to the weather. The occasional outbreak of haar (summer sea mist) along the east coast is usually a sign of brilliant sunshine only a little way inland. Most important, if you do meet rain, with Scotland's ever-changing weather patterns, the chances are that it will not last for long. See also **When to go** on page 259.

Hours of daylight
There are longer summer daylight hours in the north of Scotland – up to an hour's difference on Mid-summer Day (24 June) depending on how far north from Edinburgh you go.

Public holidays
In Scotland, 'bank holidays' apply only to banks and some other financial and commercial offices, although in England and Wales they are general public holidays. **Christmas Day**, **Boxing Day** (26 December) and **New Year's Day** (and **2 January**) are usually taken by everyone.

In place of the general holidays in England, Scottish towns and cities normally have a spring and autumn holiday. The actual dates when these local holidays take place varies from place to place but they are

There are five major banks in Scotland: Bank of Scotland, Royal Bank of Scotland, Clydesdale Bank, TSB Scotland and Girobank, three of which issue their own bank notes.

Bank of England and Northern Ireland bank notes are legal tender in Scotland. Note also that, unlike England, there are £1 notes (issued by the Royal Bank of Scotland) as well as £1 coins.

The opening hours of Scottish banks are approximately 9.15–4.45, with some closing later on Thursdays. A very few banks open on Saturday mornings.

In Scotland generally, banks give the best exchange rates for foreign currency. All banks offer this facility. It is also possible to change money in airports, larger rail stations, travel agents, and some of the larger hotels (if you are a resident). Travellers cheques can be used in some shops, and can be cashed in banks.

Several major English banks have branches in Edinburgh, Glasgow and Aberdeen. There are also several foreign banks in Edinburgh and Glasgow. For details of these see the Yellow Pages, the *Phone Book* or ask at the local Tourist Information Centre.

almost invariably on a Monday. In general, all visitor-orientated places including restaurants, remain open but a local holiday in a small town means that local businesses and many shops will be shut for the whole day.

Time differences
Scotland observes the same time as the rest of the UK. Between the end of October and the end of March, Greenwich Mean Time operates: thus at 12 noon in Edinburgh it is 8–10pm in Australia, 4–8.30am in Canada, 12 noon in Eire, midnight in New Zealand and 4–7am in the USA. From the end of March to the end of October, British Summer Time operates (one hour ahead).

Visas and vaccinations
Scotland's visa requirements are identical to those of the rest of the UK. US citizens need a valid passport, though visas are not required for a stay of less than six months. No special vaccinations are required.

Money and banking
English currency is accepted in Scotland and a sign to this effect can be seen decorating the till of many a Highland shop.

Credit cards Most larger shops, stores, hotels and restaurants in Scotland will accept the majority of British and international credit cards, such as Access, MasterCard, Visa, American Express, and Diners Club. Debit cards and cheques are also widely accepted, but it is advisable to carry some cash in case of difficulty. Many smaller accommodation establishments, such as bed and breakfasts, are unlikely to accept any form of credit card. American Express has offices in Glasgow, Edinburgh and Aberdeen.

Above: near Aberfeldy in Tayside…
Left: the weather closes in

Driving

Car rental

Scotland has a selection of car rental firms. Both national and local companies offer competitive rates. Major operators can often arrange in advance for a car to be available at your destination. Some hotels also offer this service. It is advisable to contact several companies in order to compare the rates. Away from the main cities and in northern Scotland, the choice decreases and may be restricted. There are car rental companies at the major airports in Scotland.

A familiar sight – a Caledonian

Aberdeen Airport
Avis
tel: 01224 722282
Europcar
tel: 01224 770770
Hertz
tel: 01224 722373

Edinburgh Airport
Alamo
tel: 0131 344 3250
Avis
tel: 0131 333 1866
Europcar
tel: 0131 344 3114
Hertz
tel: 0131 333 1019
National Car Rental
tel: 0131 333 1922

Glasgow Airport
Alamo
tel: 0141 848 1166
Avis
tel: 0141 887 2261
National Car Rental
tel: 0141 887 7915
Europcar
tel: 0141 887 0414
Hertz
tel: 0141 887 2451

Inverness Airport
Avis
tel: 01667 462787
Hertz
tel: 01667 462652
At the smaller airports in Scotland, many local car rental companies can deliver and collect cars from the airport by prior arrangement.

Car rental at a railway station You can arrange to collect a Hertz car at any station on the rail network. Hertz have car rental offices at many principal stations. When travelling to such stations during normal office hours, make your reservation just before starting your rail journey and your car will be waiting on your arrival.
Hertz reservation centres:
Aberdeen
tel: 01224 210748
Edinburgh
tel: 0131 557 5272
Glasgow
tel: 0141 248 7736

Car rental companies can, in many instances, arrange for your rental car to be available at a ferry terminal.

Driving in Scotland
Driving in Scotland, like the rest of the UK, is on the left side of the road.

Scotland's roads include an efficient motorway network in central Scotland, with good roads to key places further north such as Aberdeen – a dual carriageway, now the A90(M) – and Inverness (partly dual carriageway via the A9). In some parts of the north and west there are still some single track roads with passing places.

Radio Scotland (FM 92.4–94.7MHz/ MW 810kHz) broadcasts details of road conditions throughout the day, as do all Scotland's local radio stations.

Rush hour in the Highlands

Insurance Visitors bringing their own cars from overseas will require 'green card insurance' and should also have in their possession the registration documents of their car.

Driving licence Any holder of an overseas driving licence may for a period of up to one year drive a motor vehicle in Britain, but only for a class of vehicle which the original licence authorises.

Speed limits On motorways and dual carriageways 70mph/112kmh; on single carriageways 60mph/96kmh; in built-up areas 30mph/48kmh unless otherwise signposted.

Drinking and driving The police in Scotland strongly advise against drinking alcohol and driving afterwards. This advice applies to citizens of Britain and overseas visitors alike. Anyone caught driving with more than the legal limit of alcohol in their bloodstream by the police is subject to prosecution.

Motorway breakdowns If you break down on the motorway there is a 'hard shoulder' where you can stop your car. Free emergency telephones are positioned at regular intervals (approximately every kilometre) on the hard shoulder. The hard shoulder is for emergency use only. You must never use it simply to stop for a rest.

Single Track Roads In some of the more remote areas of Scotland there are still some single track roads. When two cars approach from opposite directions, the car which first reaches a passing place should pull in or stop opposite to allow safe passage. It is an offence to hold up a following vehicle and not give way. It should also be noted that passing places are not to be used as parking places.

Parking Parking is difficult in Scotland's cities and you are advised not to take chances. Traffic wardens are vigilant, fines for parking offences are high and you could have your car impounded.
There are usually coin-operated meters for individual parking spaces or else ticket-issuing machines. There are also car parks run by the local authority or National Car Parks (NCP). These can be the best option, saving you the time and frustration of looking for a space on the street.

An unusual – and comprehensive – cast-iron milepost in Fife

263

Public transport

By train

Scotland has a reasonable internal network, with fast connections to the four main Scottish cities and points between. In addition, there are 260km of track north of Inverness and also west coast railheads such as Mallaig and Kyle of Lochalsh, with superb scenery on the way. Privatisation of the service means changes to the current structure of tickets. Check with your travel agent, main rail station or the nearest Tourist Information Centre in Scotland.

Glasgow Underground

By bus

A network of operators covers the smaller towns and rural areas of Scotland. Local Tourist Information Centres carry full details and timetables. Alternatively, for further information on getting around by bus contact the following:

Aberdeen & Grampian Tourist Board
27 Albyn Place
Aberdeen AB10 1YL
tel: 01224 288800
fax: 01224 581367

Angus & City of Dundee Tourist
  Board
Market Place
Arbroath
Angus DD11 1HR
tel: 01241 872609
fax: 01241 878550

The Borders Council
Public Transport Unit
Newtown St Boswells
Melrose TD6 0SA
tel: 01835 824000, ext. 5123

Dumfries & Galloway Council
Public Transport Unit
Council Offices, English Street
Dumfries DG1 2DD
tel: 0345 090510
fax: 01387 260111

Edinburgh & Scotland Information
Centre
3 Princes Street
Edinburgh EH2 2QP
tel: 0131 557 1700
fax: 0131 473 3881

Fife Council
Public Transport Unit
Fife House, North Street,
Glenrothes, Fife KY7 5LT
tel: 01592 416060
fax: 01592 413061

Highland Council
Public Transport Unit
Glenurquhart Road
Inverness IV3 5NX
tel: 01463 234121
fax: 01463 702606

Orkney Tourist Board
6 Broad Street, Kirkwall
Orkney KW15 1DH
tel: 01856 872856
fax: 01856 875056

Shetland Islands Tourism
Market Cross, Lerwick
Shetland ZE1 0LU
tel: 01595 693434
fax: 01595 695807

Stirling Council
Public Transport Unit
Viewforth
Stirling FK8 2ET
tel: 01786 442707
fax: 01786 442631

Strathclyde Passenger Transport
Authority
Travel Centre, St Enoch Square
Glasgow
tel: 0141 226 4826

Tourist Information Centre
Granada A1 Service Area
Oldcraighall, Musselburgh
East Lothian EH21 8RE
tel: 0131 653 6172
fax: 0131 653 2805

Western Isles Council Public
Transport Unit
Sandwick Road, Stornoway,
Lewis, Western Isles, HS1 2BW
tel: 01851 703773, ext 319
fax: 01851 706426

Postbus Many remote areas are
served by Postbuses, small minibuses
delivering mail which also have seats
for fare-paying passengers. Space on
these buses, however, is limited, so
do not plan an entire or a tight
itinerary round the Postbus network,
especially if you have a lot of
luggage. There are over 130 rural
routes throughout Scotland; timetables are available from:

Royal Mail
7 Strothers Lane
Inverness 1VI 1AA
tel: 01463 256200
fax: 01463 256220

By ferry

Ferries are a major means of
transport on the western seaboard
and also around Orkney and
Shetland.

Caledonian MacBrayne Ltd, The Ferry
Terminal, Gourock PA19 1QP,
Renfrewshire, tel: 01475 650100,
fax: 01475 637607. Reservations:
tel: 0990 650000, fax: 01475 635235.

P & O Scottish Ferries sail regularly
to Orkney and Shetland from
Aberdeen and Scrabster (near
Thurso). The main Orkney crossing is
from Scrabster to Stromness. There
are also some sailings between
Orkney and Shetland, although these
are not as frequent as the ferries to
and from the Scottish mainland. Make
sure that you book in advance for cars
on all sailings and also for passengers
from Aberdeen to Lerwick. Information is available from: P & O Scottish
Ferries, P O Box 5, Jamieson's Quay,
Aberdeen AB9 8DL, tel: 01224 572615,
fax: 01224 574411.

Western Ferries operate ferries
between the mainland towns of
Gourock and Dunoon and between
the islands of Islay and Jura. Information on these services is available
from:
Western Ferries (Clyde) Ltd, 16
Woodside Crescent, Glasgow G3 7UT,
tel: 0141 332 9766, fax: 0141 332 0267.

265

Kirkwall Harbour

Caledonian MacBrayne Ltd (CalMac)
operate the majority of ferry services
on the River Clyde and west coast of
Scotland, sailing to 23 islands. Most
ferries carry vehicles, although some
(to the Small Isles, for instance) only
convey passengers. On many
services, it is advisable to make
advance vehicle reservations,
especially during the summer and at
other peak times. Caledonian
MacBrayne offer flexible tickets
which make island touring easier.

Orkney Islands Shipping Co Ltd
operate services between the various
Orkney islands. Information is
available from:
Orkney Ferries Shipping Co Ltd,
Head Office, Shore Street, Kirkwall
KW15 1LG, tel: 01856 872044,
fax: 01856 872921.

The **Shetland Isles Council** operate
ferry services within the Shetland
Isles. Information on these is
available from:
Shetland Isles Tourism,
Market Cross, Lerwick, ZE1 0LU,
tel: 01595 693434, fax: 01595 695807.

Media and communications

The media Scotland has its own indigenous media, at both the quality and tabloid ends of the market. *The Scotsman*, based in Edinburgh, aspires to the crown as Scotland's national newspaper, though challenged by its Glasgow-based competitor, *The Herald*. Both are exceeded in circulation by the unashamedly regional, if not parochial, Aberdeen-based *Press and Journal*. (It is said that the P & J headlined the *Titanic's* sinking with 'North-East Man Drowns at Sea'). All of these have their evening equivalents. Scotland's other popular daily is the tabloid *Daily Record*.

   The Sunday Post is a top selling Scottish institution peddling its own unique brand of homespun, Conservative, family-orientated journalism, while *Scotland on Sunday*,

weather forecasts. The commercial television networks north of the Border include Border Television, the influential STV (Scottish Television), based in Glasgow, and Grampian Television from Aberdeen. One curious anomaly of the 1990s is the availability of funding for the making of Gaelic programmes which both the BBC and independents beam out not just

The Scotsman, *voice of Edinburgh*

from the same stable as *The Scotsman*, is a heavyweight which sees off *The Sunday Times* north of the Border. Scotland also has many local weekly newspapers worth dipping into to see what entertainment is on offer in your chosen holiday locality. *The List* is excellent for both Glasgow and Edinburgh listings. There is also a reasonably widespread circulation and availability of quality and tabloid newspapers printed in England, partly servicing the many English people in Scotland.

   Scotland's television choice is essentially what is broadcast from south of the Border, with home-based material slotted in as appropriate. Both BBC1 and BBC2 have Scottish opt-ins, including, on BBC1, substantial Scottish news coverage and the all-important

to the Gaels but to chunks of Scotland where the language has not been spoken since the 13th century, such as the northeast and even Orkney and Shetland, where it has never been spoken.

   BBC Radio Scotland has a loyal following. Though also on FM, its medium-wave transmissions can easily be found by locating Radio 4 on long-wave (sometimes referred to as 'Radio England' north of the Border) and pressing the medium-wave button (not guaranteed to work on all radios!). Radio Scotland is very useful for *Scottish* weather forecasts. Otherwise, the station broadcasts a broadly based mix of news, discussion, travel, magazine format and music programmes. There are also various commercial radio stations, some of which are good, some of which are startlingly amateurish.

Post offices

Post offices in reasonably sized Scottish towns were formerly instantly recognisable and housed in distinguished, often handsome, buildings. However, recently they have become heavily disguised as chemists or grocers, for example,

Some old style red phone kiosks survive in Scotland

and are much harder to identify. Look for the sign 'Post Office', in yellow lettering on red. Beware of the tendency for small post offices to shut on half days and local holidays, which means a journey to the nearest large town if postal services are required urgently. Otherwise, all post offices open for 'conventional' shop hours, approximately 9am to 5pm and also on Saturday mornings. Most smaller post offices close for an hour at lunch.

Telephones

Telephones are standard throughout the UK. Modern payphone equipment usually means that the amount of money inserted is shown on a display which 'counts down' throughout the conversation. Fax machines are often available at hotels, as well as at printing and photocopying bureaux in larger towns.

Language guide

English-speakers will be able to understand just about anyone north of the Border unless people are using a particularly dense form of Scots. Scots speakers frequently 'modulate' almost unconsciously into some form of 'standard English' when dealing with non-Scots. As for the Gaels, all speak English anyway, so there should be absolutely no problem. See also page 283 for a select glossary of commonly used Scots terms and phrases.

267

Scottish post offices come in all shapes and sizes

Emergencies

In general, Scotland is an extremely safe destination, though the police would certainly advise using common sense.

Thefts from cars (and of cars) do occur, especially in the main cities and in crowded car parks, for example, at the Cairngorm chairlift, and also at popular beauty spots. It is not a good idea to keep valuable material of any sort in an unattended vehicle. If this is unavoidable then cover your belongings or lock them in the boot.

As for personal safety, again, use common sense. You are probably perfectly safe late at night in any Scottish city centre, but from time to time, incidents – muggings and worse – do occur, often alcohol-related.

One Scottish activity which all too often requires emergency action by the authorities is hillwalking. It must be strongly emphasised that Scotland's hills are rugged and should be treated with respect. Snow can occur above 900m in any month, and hill conditions can change very rapidly. Proper water-and windproof clothing and equipment and – most importantly – properly soled hillwalking boots (definitely not with a cut-away heel) should be worn. **Always** take a map and compass, and know how to use them. The police also advise leaving word, for example, with your hotel, about your proposed route and estimated time of return. Though there are some obvious security implications, it is also advisable to leave a similar note displayed on or in your car.

Embassies and consulates

As Scotland is part of the UK, the chief foreign embassies are located in London. However, a number of representatives for other nations have consular offices within Scotland and these can be found in the *Yellow Pages*.
These include:

The American Consulate General
3 Regent Terrace
Edinburgh
tel: 0131 556 8315.

The Australian Consulate
25 Bernard Street
Leith
Edinburgh EH6 6SH
tel: 0131 555 4500

Emergency telephone numbers
As in the rest of the UK, dial **999** to summon police, fire and ambulance services, as well as coastguard and mountain rescue. These calls are free from all phones, including public payphones.

Lost property
The police operate an efficient lost property service, as do both the railways and major bus operators. Broadly speaking, the Scots are fairly honest and if an item is left behind in a restaurant or other establishment it is always worth going back or making enquiries by phone.

Health
Medical insurance If you fall ill in Scotland, unless you are a UK or EU (European Union) citizen, you are eligible only for free emergency treatment at National Health Service Accident and Emergency departments of hospitals. If you are hospitalised even from an Accident and Emergency department or referred to an out-patient clinic, you will be asked to pay. Therefore you are strongly advised to take out adequate insurance cover before travelling to Scotland. Your travel agent will advise.

Pharmacies Except in remote rural areas, where some doctors do their own dispensing, you must take a doctor's prescription to a pharmacy. These part-prescribing, part-retail businesses have normal shop hours plus a rota system whereby one pharmacy in a given area stays open to cover half-day closings and other holidays. In cities, there is usually a pharmacy staying open at other times to deal with urgent prescriptions. In all cases, a notice usually prominently displayed on the shop door will tell you where you can get the prescribed medication. In addition – in an emergency – police can contact a pharmacist and request him or her to attend.

Other information

Camping and caravanning

There are over 400 licensed and recognised camping and caravan parks in Scotland. All area tourist boards carry listings of parks within their own area while the Scottish Tourist Board produces a comprehensive annual guide called *Scotland: Where to Stay Caravan and Camping Parks*. This is available both direct from the STB (address on page 272) and from bookshops.

Caravanning is popular in Scotland. Any roads which are unsuitable for towed caravans are clearly marked. Towing a caravan on single track roads demands extra vigilance and care should be taken to ensure that following traffic is not held up. Please note that most local authorities do not permit overnight parking of caravans in laybys and other car parks, and in several places barriers of a suitable height prevent their entry.

So-called 'wild camping' is still fairly popular in Scotland. In fact, Scotland is recognised as one of the last areas of the UK where camping away from recognised parks is still possible. It is always polite and in your own interests to seek out permission from the landowner first if intending to camp in the countryside.

Self-catering

The main single source of listings of self-catering properties is the Scottish Tourist Board's *Scotland: Where to Stay Self-Catering* guide, published annually and available direct from the STB (address on page 272) or from bookshops. There are also a number of agencies specialising in self-catering property rental.

Visitors with disabilities

Disability Scotland has a comprehensive bank of disability information. The holiday database include information on hotels, camping and caravanning, sports and leisure facilities, guest-houses and so on. A holiday directory is also published, covering the whole of Scotland. Information is avalible from: Disability Scotland, Princes House, 5 Shandwick Place, Edinburgh EH2 4RG. Tel: 0131 229 8632, fax: 0131 229 5168.

A wide range of information for disabled visitors can also be found in the Scottish Tourist Board's *Practical Information for Visitors with Disabilities*, available directly from the board or from Tourist Information Centres.

Opening times

Opening times are given within the text for all main attractions and tourist sights. Information on opening times has been provided for guidance only. We have tried to ensure accuracy, but things frequently do change and we would advise readers to check locally before planning a trip to avoid any possible disappointment.

Scotland's supermarkets and DIY stores often open on Sundays even in quite small towns, and in the main cities shopping malls may also be open. In popular tourist areas most shops will open daily. Beware the local half-day, usually a Wednesday or Thursday, on which many little shops in small towns close.

Evening opening for shopping is usually confined to Thursdays in the cities, though, certainly in Edinburgh, bookshops in particular are tending to open late in the evening. In addition, many superstores stay open most nights till around 8pm.

Conservation bodies
Historic Scotland

Longmore House, Salisbury Place, Edinburgh EH9 1SH (tel: 0131 668 8800).
The government agency which is responsible for the preservation of a huge range of monuments from standing stones to castles and industrial buildings.
Many of its properties have standard opening hours: April–September, daily 9.30–6. October–March, Monday–Saturday 9:30–4, Sunday 2–4.

National Trust for Scotland,

5 Charlotte Square, Edinburgh EH2 4DU (tel: 0131 226 5922).
The leading charitable organisation which cares for castles and other grand properties, as well as a smaller range of humbler places, and also wild land of high landscape value.

Other information

Scottish Natural Heritage, 12 Hope Terrace, Edinburgh EH9 2AS (tel: 0131 447 4784, fax: 0131 446 2277). The main government agency with responsibility for environmental matters and nature conservation, it operates nature reserves in some of Scotland's finest unspoilt places.

Royal Society for the Protection of Birds, 17 Regent Terrace, Edinburgh EH7 5BN (tel: 0131 557 3136, fax: 0131 557 6275). The leading charitable body in the preservation of habitat suitable for birdlife, this operates a number of nature reserves of high ornithological interest.

Scottish Wildlife Trust, Cramond House, 16 Cramond Glebe Road, Edinburgh EH4 6NS (tel: 0131 312 7765, fax: 0131 312 8705). Scotland's own charitable conservation agency, concerned with the preservation of habitat for all kinds of wildlife, operates a number of nature reserves.

Places of worship
Scotland recognises many religions. The most widespread is the (Presbyterian) Church of Scotland. Roman Catholics, Episcopalians, Baptists and Free Presbyterians are also represented as well as a variety

Dunblane Cathedral, a historic setting for Sunday worship

of non-denominational 'chapels' and other sects. Because of liberal Sunday drinking laws and shopping hours, Sabbath observance is fairly low-key, with the notable exception of Lewis and Harris and also Skye. The local press usually carries church notices with times of worship, though the local Tourist Information Centres will also help.

Toilets
Public toilet provision in Scotland is fairly good but does seem to vary in standard between local authorities. Some are free, some attended toilets require a small fee.

Photography
With its spectacular scenery, Scotland is a great place for photography. Because it is also a popular hobby north of the Border, even quite small towns often have photography businesses where a wide range of film can be obtained. Pharmacists and other shops, particularly in tourist areas, also carry stocks of film. Films of larger format than 35mm can sometimes be trickier to find.

Electricity
Voltage is 240V 50Hz AC, as in all the UK. Almost all accommodation in Scotland has square pin sockets for 3, 5 and 13amp fused plugs.

Etiquette: dealing with the Scots
Preconceived images can make it easy to see the Scots as being more 'different' than they actually are. Certainly, the Scots can be defined as an ethnic minority within the United Kingdom, but they differ from the other groups in quite subtle ways. However, the Scots have an intense dislike of being labelled English.

Also to be noted is the curious double meaning of the word 'national' which within the Scottish media can mean either Scottish or UK-wide British, depending on the context. Radio Scotland, for instance, announces itself as 'The National Network'. Many of the subtle distinctions which mark out the Scots are actually linguistic, and in everyday speech, there are opportunities for misunderstanding.

A number of minor points of etiquette apply to food and drink. Do not be surprised to be given biscuits and home-bakes if invited into someone's house for coffee or tea, no matter what the hour of the day. When ordering beer in Scottish pubs listen out for the local words 'export', 'heavy', and 'special', rather than the English word 'bitter' which is virtually absent north of the Border. And finally, if your host offers you a dram (a glass of whisky) and suggests malt whisky rather than an everyday blend, make sure that you only add water, if anything, to it. Ginger or other soft drinks will be at least an irritation, if not an insult.

However, no one is going to mind if you put sugar instead of salt in your porridge; nobody is going to arrest you for wearing the 'wrong' tartan (there is no such thing); and hardly anyone will even notice if you get the words of 'Auld Lang Syne' wrong at the end of the ceilidh. (Most Scots do as well.)

Please note. For reasons quite unknown, the Scots do not like to be 'Scotch' and much prefer 'Scottish'. See also below.

Scotch a word for whisky never used by Scots people.

Scotch broth broth made with a meat stock, plenty of vegetables and lots of barley to give it a glutinous texture.

Scotch egg a boiled egg in sausage meat and breadcrumbs.

Scotch mist a characteristic western weather condition of relentlessly damp misery, created to test cheap summer anoraks.

Scotch bluebell *Campanula rotundifolia*, called the harebell south of the border, and common on Scottish heaths.

Scotch thistle the national emblem of Scotland, sometimes called the cotton thistle, though not a native plant.

Scotch verdict 'not proven', a peculiarity of Scotland's legal system.

CONVERSION CHARTS

FROM	TO	MULTIPLY BY
Inches	Centimetres	2.54
Centimetres	Inches	0.3937
Feet	Metres	0.3048
Metres	Feet	3.2810
Yards	Metres	0.9144
Metres	Yards	1.0940
Miles	Kilometres	1.6090
Kilometres	Miles	0.6214
Acres	Hectares	0.4047
Hectares	Acres	2.4710
Gallons	Litres	4.5460
Litres	Gallons	0.2200
Ounces	Grams	28.35
Grams	Ounces	0.0353
Pounds	Grams	453.6
Grams	Pounds	0.0022
Pounds	Kilograms	0.4536
Kilograms	Pounds	2.205
Tons	Tonnes	1.0160
Tonnes	Tons	0.9842

MEN'S SUITS

UK	36	38	40	42	44	46	48
Rest of Europe	46	48	50	52	54	56	58
US	36	38	40	42	44	46	48

DRESS SIZES

UK	8	10	12	14	16	18
France	36	38	40	42	44	46
Italy	38	40	42	44	46	48
Rest of Europe	34	36	38	40	42	44
US	6	8	10	12	14	16

MEN'S SHIRTS

UK	14	14.5	15	15.5	16	16.5	17
Rest of Europe	36	37	38	39/40	41	42	43
US	14	14.5	15	15.5	16	16.5	17

MEN'S SHOES

UK	7	7.5	8.5	9.5	10.5	11
Rest of Europe	41	42	43	44	45	46
US	8	8.5	9.5	10.5	11.5	12

WOMEN'S SHOES

UK	4.5	5	5.5	6	6.5	7
Rest of Europe	38	38	39	39	40	41
US	6	6.5	7	7.5	8	8.5

271

Tourist Information Centres

Tourism in Scotland is in the overall control of the Scottish Tourist Board (STB), 23 Ravelston Terrace, Edinburgh EH4 3EU, tel: 0131 332 2433, fax: 0131 343 1513. Personal callers are asked to use the Edinburgh and Scotland Information Centre (see below). There are two other STB offices for visitors en route to Scotland:
- Scottish Tourist Board, 19 Cockspur Street, London SW1Y 5BL tel: 0171 930 8661/2/3, fax: 0171 930 1817
- Southwaite Tourist Information Centre, (Southwaite Service Area M6, south of Carlisle) tel: 01697 473445/6

In Scotland there is an integrated network of Tourist Information Centres. As well as comprehensive information services, they offer on-the-spot accommodation bookings both locally and into other areas. The main year-round 'TICs' are given below.

- Edinburgh and Scotland Information Centre, Waverley Market, 3 Princes Street, Edinburgh EH2 2QP, tel: 0131 557 1700 fax: 0131 473 3881
- Greater Glasgow and Clyde Valley Tourist Board, 11 George Square, Glasgow G2 1DY, tel: 0141 204 4400 fax: 0141 221 3524

The South
- Burns House, Burns Statue Square, Ayr KA7 1UP, tel: 01292 262555, fax: 01292 269555
- Murray's Green, Jedburgh TD8 6BE, tel: 01835 863435, fax: 01835 864099
- Horsemarket, Ladyacre Road, Lanark ML11 7LQ, tel: 01555 661661, fax: 01555 666143
- Burgh Halls, The Cross, Linlithgow EH49 7AH, tel: 01506 844600, fax: 01506 671373
- Granada Service Area, Oldcraighall, Musselburgh, East Lothian EH21 8RE, tel: 0131 653 6172, fax: 0131 653 2805
- High Street, Peebles EH45 8AG tel: 01721 720138, fax: 01721 724401

Central Scotland
- 4 City Square, Dundee DD1 3BA, tel 01382 434664, fax: 01382 434665
- 45 High Street, Perth PH1 5TJ, tel: 01738 638353

- 70 Market Street, St Andrews KY16 9NU, tel: 01334 472021
- 41 Dumbarton Road, Stirling FK8 2QQ, tel: 01786 475019

The Northeast
- St Nicholas House, Broad Street, Aberdeen AB9 1DE, tel: 01224 632727, fax: 01224 620415
- 17 High Street, Elgin, Moray IV30 1EG, tel: 01343 542666, fax: 01343 552982

The Great Glen and Western Highlands
- Grampian Road, Aviemore, Inverness-shire PH22 1PP, tel: 01479 810363, fax: 01479 811063
- 7 Alexandra Parade, Dunoon, Argyll PA23 9AB, tel: 01369 703785, fax: 01369 706085
- Cameron Square, Fort William, Inverness-shire, PH33 6AJ, tel: 01397 70378, fax: 01397 705184
- Castle Wynd, Inverness IV2 3BJ tel: 01463 234353, fax: 01463 710609
- Boswell House, Argyll Square, Oban, Argyll PA34 4NN, tel: 01631 563122, fax: 01631 564273

The Northern Highlands
- The Square, Dornoch, Sutherland IV25 3SD, tel: 01862 810400, fax: 01862 810644
- Auchtercairn, Gairloch, Wester Ross IV21 2DN, tel: 01445 712130, fax: 01445 712071
- Whitechapel Road, Wick, Caithness KW1 4EA, tel: 01955 602596, fax: 01955 604940

The Islands
- 6 Broad Street, Kirkwall, Orkney KW15 INX, tel: 01856 872856, fax: 01856 875056
- Market Cross, Lerwick, Shetland ZE1 0LU, tel: 01595 693434, fax: 01595 695807
- Bayfield House, Bayfield Road, Portree, Skye IV51 9EL, tel: 01478 612137, fax: 01478 612141
- 26 Cromwell Street, Stornoway, Lewis HS1 2DD, tel: 01851 703088, fax: 01851 705244
- Ferry Terminal Building, Stromness, Orkney KW16 3AA,tel: 01856 850716

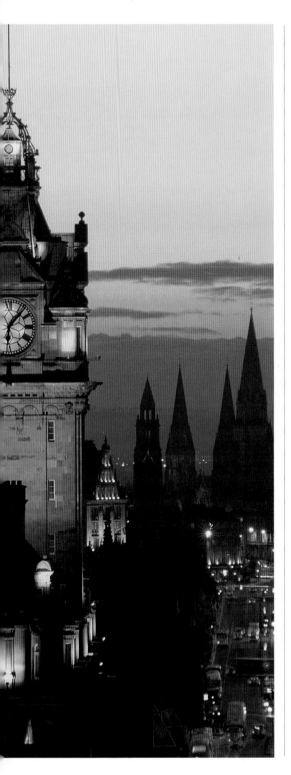

Hotels & Restaurants

Accommodation

Finding good accommodation is not a problem. (Use the Scottish Tourist Board's grading and classifications if in doubt.) Off season rates vary, and may be negotiable.

As a rough guide in this listing £££ is over £60 per person for dinner, bed and breakfast; ££ is between £20 and £60; and £ is under £20 for bed and breakfast only.

The AA Hotel Booking Service is a new service exclusively for AA personal members. It is a free, fast and easy way to find a place for a short break, holiday or business trip; tel: 0990 050505. Full listings of the British and Irish hotels and B&Bs available through the service can be found and booked at the AA's Internet site: http://www.theAA.co.UK/hotels.

EDINBURGH

Balmoral Hotel (£££) Princes Street, Edinburgh EH2 2EQ (tel: 0131 556 2414). £23 million bought a total refurbishment of Edinburgh's landmark hotel in the early 1990s. High standards in 189 rooms.

274

Caledonian Hotel (£££) Princes Street, Edinburgh EH1 2AB (tel: 0131 459 9988). Another old-established hotel, 236 rooms. Like the Balmoral, a former railway hotel.

Carlton Highland (£££) North Bridge, Edinburgh EH1 1SD (tel: 0131 556 7277). Close to the Royal Mile, 197 rooms and extensive leisure facilities. A popular business and tourist hotel.

Channings (££) 12–16 South Learmonth Gardens, Edinburgh EH4 1EZ (tel: 0131 315 2226). A superbly stylish conversion of five Edwardian terraced town houses. A place for comfort and indulgence. 48 rooms.

Edinburgh Grand Sheraton (£££) 1 Festival Square, Edinburgh EH3 9SR (tel: 0131 229 9131). This opulent and stylish hotel adds a subtly Scottish stamp to Sheraton quality without resorting to clichés.

George Hotel Inter-continental (£££) George Street, Edinburgh EH2 2PB (tel: 0131 225 1251). Supremely convenient, luxury standard in elegant surroundings, 195 rooms.

Hilton National Edinburgh (£££) 69 Belford Road, Edinburgh EH4 3DG (tel: 0131 332 2545). A modern hotel in a quiet West End location, yet convenient for Princes Street. 144 rooms.

Howard Hotel (£££) Great King Street, Edinburgh EH3 6QH (tel: 0131 557 3500). Ideal central location amid New Town refinement. Very comfortable. 15 rooms.

King James Thistle Hotel (££) 107 Leith Street, Edinburgh EH1 3SW (tel: 0131 556 0111). Conveniently situated modern hotel, slightly anonymous in feel, with helpful staff. 143 rooms.

Malmaison (£££) 1 Tower Place, Leith, Edinburgh EH6 7DB (tel: 0131 555 6868). Elegantly converted from a former seamen's mission, close to the waterfront. 10 minutes from the city centre. 60 rooms.

Norton House (£££) Ingliston Edinburgh EH28 8LX (tel: 0131 333 1275). In parkland setting on the western outskirts of the city, a country house hotel close to airport and motorway system. 47 rooms.

Roslin Glen (££) 2 Penicuik Road, Roslin, Midlothian EH25 9LH (tel: 0131 440 2029). Small hotel in centre of quiet conservation village south of the city. Close to bypass and 20 minutes to city centre.

Roxburghe (£££) 38 Charlotte Square, Edinburgh EH2 4HG (tel: 0131 225 3921). Right in the heart of the New Town, with 75 well-equipped bedrooms and a choice of restaurants.

Swallow Royal Scot (£££) 111 Glasgow Road, Edinburgh EH12 8NF (tel: 0131 334 9191). Modern hotel on western outskirts, 259 bedrooms, recently refurbished. Leisure centre with swimming pool.

Thrums Private Hotel (££) 14 Minto Street, Edinburgh EH9 1RQ. (tel: 0131 667 5545). 14 rooms in two adjoining Victorian town houses on the city's south side, with frequent bus service (5 minutes to city centre).

GLASGOW

Cameron House Hotel (£££) Balloch G83 8QZ (tel: 01389 755565). Top-quality hotel on banks of Loch Lomond, a 30-minute drive from city centre. 96 luxurious bedrooms. Sports facilities.

The Devonshire (£££) 5 Devonshire Gardens, Glasgow G12 0UX (tel: 0141 339 7878). Note the correct address of this simply sumptuous town house. 14 rooms, superb throughout.

Glasgow Hilton (£££) 1 William Street, Glasgow G3 8HT (tel: 0141 204 5555). Hilton style hit Glasgow in 1992 with themed eating and drinking, wide-ranging leisure facilities and 319 rooms.

Glasgow Marriott (£££) 500 Argyle Street, Glasgow G3 8RR (tel: 0141 226 5577). Close to the Kingston Bridge and SEC, modern 300-bed hotel with sports facilities.

Glasgow Thistle (£££) 36 Cambridge Street, Glasgow G2 3HN (tel: 0141 332 3311). Very central, with own car park. 302 recently refurbished bedrooms.

Holiday Inn Garden Court (££) 161 West Nile Street, Glasgow G1 2RL (tel: 0141 332 0110). New central city hotel with 80 modern bedrooms. Parking nearby.

Kelvin Park Lorne Hotel (££) 923 Sauchiehall Street, Glasgow G3 7TE (tel: 0141 314 9955). A 99-room hotel, with friendly staff. It makes an excellent base for Kelvingrove and Hunterian or Transport museums.

Malmaison (£££) 278 West George Street, Glasgow G2 4LL (tel: 0141 221 6400). Style-conscious hotel with 73 rooms (CD players, minibars) and good French cuisine in brasserie restaurant.

Glasgow Moat House (£££) Congress Road, Glasgow G3 8QT (tel: 0141 306 9988). Located in what seems rather like an endless car park by the river, a stylish modern hotel with 282 rooms.

One Devonshire Gardens (£££) 1 Devonshire Gardens, Glasgow G12 0UX (tel: 0141 339 2001). Adjoining elegantly furnished town houses. Very high reputation in all departments, 27 rooms.

THE SOUTH
Abbotsford
Woodlands House Hotel (££) Windyknowe Road, Galashiels TD1 1RG (tel: 01896 754722). Gothic Revival-style hotel with stunning views over Tweeddale.

Ayr
Grange Hotel (££) 37 Carrick Road, Ayr KA7 2RD (tel: 01292 265679). Small hotel in residential area, with 8 rooms. In walking distance of seafront.
Piersland House Hotel (£££) Craigend Road, Troon, Ayrshire KA10 6HD (tel: 01292 314747). Fine Edwardian mansion with 15 rooms, originally built for whisky firm owner.

Castle Kennedy Gardens
North West Castle Hotel (££–£££) Stranraer, Wigtownshire DG9 8EH (tel: 01776 704413). Excellent range of leisure facilities at this former home of Arctic explorer. 70 rooms.

Chatelherault
Strathaven Hotel (££–£££) Hamilton Road, Strathaven, Lanarkshire ML10 6SZ (tel: 01357 521778). Adam fireplace and stairway feature in this refurbished house, 22 rooms, making ideal base for Glasgow.

Culzean Castle
Turnberry Hotel (£££) Turnberry KA26 9LT (tel: 01655 331000). Famous golfing hotel with spa, leisure suite and every comfort.

Dalbeattie
Balcary Bay Hotel (££) Auchencairn DG7 1QZ (tel: 01556 640217). Waterside hotel dating from 1625. 17 well-equipped rooms with 3 acres of gardens.

Dirleton (Castle)
Open Arms Hotel (££–£££) Dirleton, East Lothian EH39 5EG (tel: 01620 850241). Old-established, much-loved, comfortable hotel in attractive village, easy access to Edinburgh. 10 rooms.

Galloway Forest Park
Kirroughtree House (£££) Minnigaff, Newton Stewart DG8 6AN (tel: 01671 402141). A 17th-century mansion house set high above Wigtown Bay. Elegant interior decoration, including antiques, and stunning views. 17 rooms.

Gatehouse-of-Fleet
Cally Palace Hotel (££) Gatehouse-of-Fleet, Kirkcudbrightshire DG7 2DL (tel: 01557 814341). Georgian mansion set in a large forested estate. Extensive leisure facilities. 56 rooms.

Jedburgh
Sunlaws House Hotel (£££) Heiton, Kelso, Roxburghshire TD5 8JZ (tel: 01573 450331). Luxurious country house of the highest standards, owned by the Duke of Roxburghe. 22 rooms.

Kelso
Cross Keys (££) 36–37 The Square, Kelso TD5 7HL (tel: 01573 223303). Former coaching inn in town centre. 24 rooms, café bar.
Dryburgh Abbey Hotel (£££) St Boswells TD6 0RQ (tel: 01835 822261). Stone-built mansion set beside Dryburgh Abbey ruins. Spacious, with 25 rooms and pool.
Ednam House Hotel (££) Bridge Street, Kelso TD5 7HT (tel: 01573 224168). Georgian mansion beside the River Tweed, with 32 rooms and choice of public areas. Run in traditional style.

Logan Botanic Garden
Fernhill Hotel (££) Heugh Road, Portpatrick DG9 8TD (tel: 01776 810220). Family-run, elevated position on coastal site, excellent service. 19 rooms.

275

The Machars
Corsemalzie House Hotel (££) Port William, by Newton Stewart, Wigtownshire DG8 9RL (tel: 01988 860254). Welcoming country house in total seclusion.

Melrose
Bon Accord Hotel (££) Market Square, Melrose TD6 9PN (tel: 01896 822645). Town centre hotel with cheerfully furnished bedrooms. Restaurant, and bar meals.
Burts Hotel (££) Market Square, Melrose, Roxburghshire TD6 9PN (tel: 01896 822285). Friendly, family-run hotel of the kind that generates a loyal local clientele. Ideally placed for Border touring.

Moffat
Moffat House Hotel (££) High Street, Moffat, Dumfriesshire DG10 9HL (tel: 01683 220039). An elegant, 20-room Adam house, near town centre, well placed for north-bound travellers and Border explorers.

North Berwick
Greywalls (£££) Muirfield, Gullane, East Lothian EH31 2EG (tel: 01620 842144). Architecturally exciting house by Edward Lutyens adjacent to some of Scotland's best golf. A hotel of much finesse.

Peebles
Cringletie House (£££) Eddleston, Peebles-shire EH45 8PL (tel: 01721 730233). Plenty of personal and professional attention in rural, family-run, 13-room baronial mansion.
Park Hotel (£££) Innerleithen Road, Peebles EH45 8BA (tel: 01721 720451). 24-room hotel with valley views; guests can use leisure facilities of sister hotel, the Hydro.

Hotels & Restaurants

CENTRAL SCOTLAND

Aberfeldy
Guinach House (££) Urlar Road, Aberfeldy, Perthshire PH15 2ET (tel: 01887 820251). A small country house hotel emphasising great cuisine in peaceful, rural surroundings.
Weem Hotel (££) Weem, by Aberfeldy, Perthshire PH15 2LD (tel: 01887 820381). Refurbished 17th-century inn with plenty of country pursuits close at hand in Perthshire countryside.

Arbroath
Letham Grange Resort Hotel (£££) Colliston, Arbroath DD11 4RL (tel: 01241 890373). Country house hotel with two golf courses and curling rink. Many original Victorian features and choice of traditional or modern style in the 41 bedrooms.

Balloch
Cameron House Hotel (£££) Loch Lomond, by Alexandria, Dunbartonshire G83 8QZ (tel: 01389 755565). Luxury resort hotel by loch shore, 96 rooms. Very wide range of leisure facilities.

Blairgowrie
Kinloch House Hotel (£££) by Blairgowrie, Perthshire PH10 6SG (tel: 01250 884237). Mid-19th-century oak-panelled country house with 21 rooms, fine antiques (and 130+ malt whiskies).
Moorfield House (££) Myreriggs Road, Coupar Angus PH13 9HS (tel: 01828 627303). In a country setting, with 12 spacious, handsomely furnished bedrooms, a library, lounge, restaurant and bar.

Callander
Lubnaig Hotel (££) Leny Feus, Callander FK17 8AS (tel: 01877 330376). Spotless hotel in pretty gardens, with 10 rooms, three lounges and dining room.
Roman Camp Hotel (£££) Callander, Perthshire FK17 8BG (tel: 01877 330003). Beautiful riverside site for this charming 17th-century house, like a small château. 14 rooms.

Dundee
Old Mansion House Hotel (£££) Auchterhouse, by Dundee, Angus DD3 0QN (tel: 01382 320366). 16th-century baronial house with original plasterwork and other features, in grounds. Six rooms.

East Neuk Villages
Old Manor Hotel (£££) Leven Road, Lundin Links KY86 AJ (tel: 01333 320368). On village outskirts with sea views. 24 rooms with modern furnishings.

Forfar
Idvies House (££) Letham, Forfar DD8 2QJ (tel: 01307 818787). In woodland setting, a Victorian country house with 11 rooms.

Perth
Auchterarder House (£££) Auchterarder, Perthshire PH3 1DZ (tel: 01764 663646). A sumptuously furnished country house with notable conservatory. The 'house guest in private home' approach makes for an interesting alternative to neighbouring Gleneagles. 15 rooms.
Gleneagles Hotel (£££) Auchterarder, Perthshire PH3 1NF (tel: 01764 662231). Arguably Scotland's best-known hotel, with the ambience of an ocean-going liner. 236 rooms and every need catered for – you will never need to step outside the hotel grounds.
Green Hotel (££) 2 The Muirs, Kinross, Perthshire KY13 7AS (tel: 01577 863467). A 47-room independent hotel, with an excellent range of leisure facilities.

Pitlochry
Knockendarroch House (££) Higher Oakfield, Pitlochry, Perthshire PH16 5HT (tel: 01796 473473). Victorian mansion, 12 rooms, of considerable charm and style.
Pine Trees Hotel (££) Strathview Terrace, Pitlochry PH16 5QR (tel: 01796 472121). With marble staircase and ornate plasterwork, this 20-room mansion offers high standards in all areas.

St Andrews
Rufflets Country House (£££) Strathkinness Low Road, St Andrews, Fife KY16 9TX (tel: 01334 472594). Country house in its own grounds; garden provides fresh produce for restaurant. 25 rooms.
The Old Course Hotel (£££) Old Station Road KY16 9SP (tel: 01334 474371) Superb setting beside the 17th hole of the famous championship course. There is a choice of lounges and the bright conservatory provides an informal dining option. 125 rooms.
Russell Hotel (££) 26 The Scores, St Andrews KY16 9AS (tel: 01334 473447). Family-run hotel with 10 rooms, close to Old Course on seafront.
St Andrews Golf Hotel (£££) 40 The Scores, St Andrews KY16 9AS (tel: 01334 472611). Close to the Old Course, large Victorian terraced building with high standards throughout. 22 rooms.

Stirling
Stirling Highland Hotel (£££) Spittal Street, Stirling FK8 1DU (tel: 01786 475444) Fascinating conversion of former high school, full of character and very comfortable. 78 rooms.
Terraces Hotel (££) 4 Melville Terrace, Stirling FK8 2ND (tel: 01786 472268). Town centre business hotel, with 18 modern bedrooms and good restaurant.

THE NORTHEAST

Aberdeen
Atholl Hotel (££) 54 King's Gate, Aberdeen AB15 4YN (tel: 01224 323505).

Handsome building in residential area, close to city centre. Personally-run establishment, friendly staff.

Craighaar Hotel (££) Waterton Road, Bucksburn, Aberdeen AB21 9HS (tel: 01224 712275). Behind a plain exterior there is plenty of design flair and a high standard of comfort.

Marcliffe at Pitfodels (£££) North Deeside Road, Pitfodels, Aberdeen AB15 9YA (tel: 01224 861000). Luxury hotel run by proprietors with plenty of experience of local hotel scene. 42 rooms.

Palm Court Hotel (££) 81 Seafield Road, Aberdeen AB15 7YU (tel: 01224 310351). Close to ring road, a comfortable business hotel with 24 rooms and memorably decorated split-level restaurant.

Simpsons (££) 59 Queens Road, Aberdeen AB15 4YP (tel: 01224 327777). The granite facade of two converted town houses hides a most exciting hotel development. One building contains the modern bedrooms, whilst the other contains a large split-level bar and Mediterranean brasserie. 38 rooms.

Thainstone House Hotel and Country Club (£££) Thainstone Estate, Inverurie Road (N), Inverurie, Aberdeenshire AB51 5NT (tel: 01467 621643). Up-market Georgian mansion in large grounds, 48 rooms.

Ballater
Balgonie Country House (£££) Braemar Place, Ballater AB35 5NQ (tel: 01339 755482). Creeper-clad Edwardian house with sweeping lawns, 9 bedrooms and excellent modern Scottish cuisine.

Darroch Learg (££) Braemar Road, Ballater AB35 5UX (tel: 013397 55443). Country house in-town hotel, with Deeside views.

Banff
Banff Springs Hotel (££) Golden Knowes Road, Banff AB45 2JE (tel: 01261 812881). A modern business and leisure hotel with 31 rooms. Sea views and gymnasium.

Craigellachie
Craigellachie Hotel (££) Craigellachie, Banffshire AB38 9SR (tel: 01340 881204). Imposing fishing and shooting hotel with excellent food and 29 well-appointed rooms.

Elgin
Mansion House Hotel (£££) The Haugh, Elgin, Moray IV30 1AW (tel: 01343 548811). Peacefully situated baronial mansion with excellent leisure facilities.

Fyvie Castle
Lodge Hotel (££) Old Rayne AB52 6RY (tel: 01464 851205). In a country setting beside A96, with 7 rooms (4 in annexe). Family run.

Meldrum Arms Hotel (££) The Square, Oldmeldrum AB51 0DS (tel: 01651 872238). Family-run traditional town centre hotel with 11 rooms, restaurant and bar.

Huntly
Kildrummy Castle Hotel (£££) Kildrummy, by Alford, Aberdeenshire AB33 8RA (tel: 019755 71288). Imposing mansion house close to ancient castle in rural setting. Very high standard of accommodation and cuisine. 16 rooms.

Old Manse of Marnoch (££) Bridge of Marnoch, by Huntly, Banffshire AB54 7RS (tel: 01466 780873). 19th-century country house in secluded gardens. Fine food and high standards throughout. Five rooms.

THE GREAT GLEN & HIGHLANDS
Aviemore
Boat Hotel (££) Boat of Garten PH24 3BH (tel: 01479 831258). A holiday hotel right beside the Strathspey Steam Railway, with Cairngorm views. 32 rooms with modern furnishings.

Fairwinds (££) Carrbridge PH23 3AA (tel: 01479 841240). A Victorian former manse with 5 rooms and extensive gardens. Conservatory lounge/dining room.

Muckrach Lodge (£££) Dulnain Bridge PH26 3LY (tel: 01479 851257). A former shooting lodge with mountain views, conservatory dining room and 10 bedrooms.

Cowal
Enmore Hotel (££) Marine Parade, Kirn, Dunoon PA23 8HH (tel: 01369 702230). Sea views, squash courts, 10 traditionally furnished bedrooms and a genuinely friendly welcome.

Crinan
The Stag (££) Argyll Sreet, Lochgilphead PA31 8NE (tel: 01546 602496). Town centre hotel with live music in downstairs bar at weekends. 17 (small) bedrooms.

Fort William
Allt-nan-Ros (£££) Onich, by Fort William PH33 6RY (tel: 01855 821210). Fine family-run hotel with superb Loch Linnhe views. 21 modern bedrooms.

Inverlochy Castle Hotel (£££) Torlundy, by Fort William, Inverness-shire PH33 6SN (tel: 01397 702177). The by-word for luxury country house-style accommodation in Scotland. 17 rooms.

Kilcamb Lodge Hotel (£££) Strontian, Argyll PH36 4HY (tel: 01967 402257). Sturdy Georgian house with private shoreline on Loch Sunart. 11 rooms.

Letterfinlay Lodge (££) Letterfinlay PH34 4DZ (tel: 01397 712622). Family-run hotel with 13 rooms, 12 miles north of Fort William on A82. Views over Loch Lochy.

Moorings Hotel (££) Banavie, Fort William, Inverness-shire PH33 7LY (tel: 01397 772797). Canal-side location with panoramic mountain views. Ideal touring base. 24 rooms.

Nevis Bank (££) Belford Road, Fort William PH33 6BY (tel: 01397 705721). On town outskirts at entrance to Glen Nevis. Gymnasium, 31 rooms plus 8 annexe rooms.

Hotels & Restaurants

Glen Coe
Ballachulish Hotel (££) Ballachulish, Argyll PA39 4JY (tel: 01855 811606). Imposing old baronial hotel with 54 rooms, overlooking main road and Loch Linnhe.
Holly Tree (££) Kentallen, by Appin, Argyll PA38 4BY (tel: 01631 740292). A comfortably converted Edwardian station, on superb loch-side location.

Grantown-on-Spey
Garth Hotel (££) Castle Road, Grantown-on-Spey PH26 3HN (tel: 01479 872836). Relaxed and friendly town centre hotel with log fires. 17 modern bedrooms.

Inverness
Bunchrew House (£££) Bunchrew, Inverness IV3 6TA (tel: 01463 234917). A 17th-century mansion set on shores of Beauly Firth that is popular with sporting, business and leisure guests. 11 luxurious bedrooms.
Dunain Park Hotel (££) Inverness IV3 6JN (tel: 01463 230512). Georgian country house in secluded grounds, six bedrooms, eight suites, pool and sauna.
Kingsmills Hotel (£££) Calcabock Road, Inverness IV2 3LP (tel: 01463 237166). An 84-room hotel with good leisure facilities, catering for tourist and business clientele.
Travel Inn (££) Millburn Road, Inverness IV2 3QX (tel: 01463 712010). Modern hotel with 40 spacious rooms. Good for families.
Windsor Hotel (££) 22 Ness Bank, Inverness IV2 4SF (tel: 01463 715535). Riverside town house hotel with 18 pine-furnished bedrooms, lounge and dining room.

Loch Ness
Knockie Lodge Hotel (£££) Whitebridge, Inverness-shire IV1 2UP (tel: 01456 486276). A 10-room hotel with simple high quality.

Oban
Ardanaiseig Hotel (£££) Kilchrennan, by Taynuilt, Argyll PA35 1HE (tel: 01866 833333). Superb country house in romantic setting with outstanding garden.
Falls of Lora Hotel (££) Connel, by Oban PA37 1PB (tel: 01631 710483). Popular vacation hotel with restaurant and bistro bar. 30 rooms, ranging from luxury to basic.
Isle of Eriska (£££) Ledaig, by Oban, Argyll PA37 1SD (tel: 01631 720371). Family-owned baronial mansion offering the highest standards of comfort.
Manor House Hotel (£££) Gallanach Road, Oban PA34 4LS (tel: 01631 562087). Top-quality hotel in Georgian mansion close to centre. Sea views. Excellent restaurant.

THE NORTHERN HIGHLANDS
Dornoch
Burghfield House (££) Dornoch, Sutherland IV25 3HN (tel: 01862 810212). Victorian mansion in extensive gardens, with antiques and open fires. 14 rooms.

Dornoch Castle Hotel (££) Castle Street, Dornoch, Sutherland IV25 3SD (tel: 01862 810216). Originally the local bishop's palace, a hotel with plenty of ambience in the centre of this pleasant town.
Royal Golf Hotel (£££) Dornoch, Sutherland IV25 3LG (tel: 01862 810283). Established hotel with views over the famous golf course. Popular with golfers, non-golfers and business people. 25 rooms, plus 8 annexe rooms.

Gairloch
Aultbea Hotel (££) Aultbea IV22 2HX (tel: 01445 731201). A small family-run hotel on the shores of Loch Ewe. Relaxed atmosphere. 11 rooms, lounge and restaurant.
Creag Mor (££) Charleston, Gairloch IV21 2AH (tel: 01445 712068). Comfortable holiday hotel with 17 rooms and harbour views.

Lochinver
Eddrachilles Hotel (££) Badcall Bay, Scourie IV27 4TH (tel: 01971 502080). Spectacular island-studded views. 11 recently upgraded bedrooms.
Inver Lodge (£££) Lochinver, Sutherland IV27 4LU (tel: 01571 844496). Modern hotel with wide coastal views, 20 rooms with good facilities.
Kinlochbervie Hotel (£££) Kinlochbervie, Sutherland IV27 4RP (tel: 01971 521275). Family-run hotel overlooking sea loch and fishing harbour. 14 rooms.

Thurso
Park Hotel (££) Thurso KW14 8RE (tel: 01847 893251). Modern hotel with lounge bar and restaurant. 11 rooms.

Torridons
Loch Torridon Hotel (£££) Torridon, by Achnasheen, Wester Ross IV22 2EY (tel: 01445 791242). Extensively refurbished hotel, now of very high standard and earning excellent reputation. 21 bedrooms.
Tigh an Eilean Hotel (£££) Shieldaig, by Strathcarron, Wester Ross IV54 8XN (tel: 01520 755251). Refurbished hotel, personally run, 11 rooms. Good seafood.

Ullapool
Ceilidh Place (££) West Argyle Street, Ullapool IV26 2TY (tel: 01854 612103). A unique hotel with very relaxed style, live music, restaurant, coffee-shop and bars, welcoming lounge and 13 rooms (bunkhouse also available).
Dundonnell Hotel (££) Dundonnell, by Garve, Wester Ross IV23 2QR (tel: 01854 633204). Family-run for over 30 years, popular haven in wild country. Quality accommodation, 30 rooms.

THE ISLANDS
Arran
Auchrannie Country House Hotel (£££) Brodick, Arran KA27 8BZ (tel: 01770 302234). Previously home to a dowager

duchess, 28-bedroom hotel with luxurious add-on leisure facilities.

Kilmichael Country House Hotel (£££) Glen Cloy, Brodick KA27 8BY (tel: 01770 302219). Delightful small mansion close to Brodick, with flowers, books and excellent food. 9 rooms.

Colonsay

Isle of Colonsay Hotel (££–£££) Colonsay, Argyll PA61 7YP (tel: 01951 200316). A superb location and a very well equipped hideaway. (Try the fresh oysters.) 10 rooms.

Harris

Ardvourlie Castle (££) Aird a Mhulaidh, Harris HS3 3AB (tel: 01859 502307). An impressive-looking castle in a loch shore setting amid wild scenery. Offering excellent home cooking and personal attention. Four rooms.

Harris Hotel (££) Tarbert, Isle of Harris HS3 3DL (tel: 01859 502154). Down-to-earth family-run hotel located close to ferry. 25 rooms.

Scarista House (£££) Scarista, Isle of Harris HS3 3HX (tel: 01859 550238). Elegance and comfort are provided in this Georgian house overlooking an endless shell sand beach. The hotel has a high reputation for its cuisine. Five rooms.

Two Waters Guest House (££) Lickisto, Harris, Western Isles PA85 3EL (tel: 01859 530246). Small, four-room establishment in a wild hill and loch setting. Home cooking.

Lewis

Caberfeidh Hotel (££–£££) Manor Park, Stornoway Lewis HS1 2EU (tel: 01851 702604). 46-room modern hotel thought to be the finest on the island. Good local seafood.

Galston Farm Guest House (££) South Galston, Lewis, Western Isles HS2 0SH (tel: 01851 850492). 18th-century restored working croft by the shore with Butt of Lewis views. Three rooms.

Mull

Western Isles Hotel (££) Tobermory PA75 6PR (tel: 01688 302012). Traditional hoilday hotel with extensive views. 26 rooms and 2 restaurants.

Shetland (Mainland)

Busta House (£££) Busta, Brae, Shetland ZE2 9QN (tel: 01806 522506). Scotland's most northerly top-flight country house-style establishment, 20 rooms, considerable charm and elegance.

Lerwick Hotel (£££) 15 South Road, Lerwick ZE1 0PW (tel: 01595 692166). Recently refurbished hotel, near town centre with 35 rooms.

Shetland Hotel (££) Holmsgarth Road, Lerwick ZE1 0RB (tel: 01595 695515). Modern 64-roomed hotel conveniently located for ferry.

Unst (Shetland)

Baltasound Hotel (££) Unst ZE2 9DS (tel: 01957 711334). Informal hotel with open-plan lounge/restaurant/bar, 10 rooms and 17 log cabins.

Restaurants

It is possible to eat very well in Scotland, though locals sometimes argue that the best produce is sent south to market. This is not entirely true. Scotland's cities are notably cosmopolitan in their offerings.

As a rough guide in this listing, £££ is over £25 per person for a three-course meal excluding drinks, ££ is between £25 and £15, and £ is under £15.

EDINBURGH

Atrium (£££) 10 Cambridge Street, Edinburgh EH1 2ED (tel: 0131 228 8882). Fresh Scottish produce, with a strongly theatrical element. Popular with locals.

L'Auberge (££) 56 St. Mary's Street, Edinburgh EH1 1SX (tel: 0131 556 5888). French staff, excellent French food close to the Royal Mile.

Ducks at Le Marche Noir (££) 2/4 Eyre Place, Edinburgh EH3 5EP (tel: 0131 558 1608). French country cuisine in a little New Town restaurant popular with locals.

The Grill Room (££) Sheraton Grand Hotel, 1 Festival Square, Edinburgh EH3 9SR (tel: 0131 229 9131). Classic French cuisine served in elegant, tartan-clad surroundings.

Jackson's Restaurant (£–££) 2 Jackson Close, 209–213 High Street, Edinburgh EH1 1PL (tel: 0131 225 1793). On a main tourist thoroughfare and achieving authentic Scottish tastes without resorting to 'whisky sauce with everything'.

Kalpna (£) 2/3 St Patricks Square, Edinburgh EH8 9EZ (tel: 0131 667 9890). Inexpensive, full-flavoured vegtarian cuisine. One of the most distinctive Indian places in town.

Malmaison Brasserie (££) 1 Tower Place, Leith, Edinburgh EH6 7DB (tel: 0131 555 6868). Simple, Mediterranean-style food in docklands setting.

Martin's (£££) 70 Rose Street North Lane, Edinburgh EH2 3DX (tel: 0131 225 3106). Tucked well away in a city-centre service lane but in the top-flight. Simply one of the very best anywhere in Scotland.

No. 1 The Restaurant (£££) Balmoral Hotel, 1 Princes Street, Edinburgh EH2 2EQ (tel: 0131 556 2414). Deep red decor, deep-cushioned seats, and top quality modern Scottish cuisine, served in supreme style.

Pompadour (£££) Caledonian Hotel, Princes Street, Edinburgh EH1 2AB (tel: 0131 459 9988). Gracious establishment – supremely high standards with a Scottish flavour.

Vintner's Room (£££) The Vaults, 87 Giles Street, Leith EH6 6BZ (tel: 0131 554 6767). An eating place of high repute, housed in a 17th-century building in Edinburgh's port.

Hotels & Restaurants

The Witchery by the Castle (££) Castle Hill, Edinburgh EH2 1NE (tel: 0131 225 5613). Two atmospheric candlelit rooms in which to savour the latest cooking trends and a huge choice of wines.

GLASGOW

The Buttery (£££) 652 Argyle Street, Glasgow G3 8UF (tel: 0141 221 8188). An old-established restaurant with famously polite, unobtrusive service – great food.

Camerons Restaurant (£££) Glasgow Hilton, 1 William Street, Glasgow G3 8HT (tel: 0141 204 5555). Hunting lodge theme, but plenty of style and panache.

Drum and Monkey (£) 93–5 St Vincent Street, Glasgow (tel: 0141 221 6636). Atmospheric pub with appetizing snacks, moving up a gear in back-room bistro.

Malmaison Café Bar and Brasserie (£) 278 West George Street, Glasgow (tel: 0141 221 6401). British favourites mix with classic French dishes in this booth-lined basement restaurant.

October Café (£–££) Princes Square, 46 Buchanan Street, Glasgow (tel: 0141 221 0303). Persevere – go to the roof of the modern shopping mall to find this 1930s-style café, serving exciting but simple food.

One Devonshire Gardens (£££) 1 Devonshire Gardens, Glasgow G12 0UX (tel: 0141 339 2001). Stylish cuisine in the most luxurious surroundings.

Papingo Restaurant (££) 104 Bath Street, Glasgow G2 2EN (tel: 0141 332 6678). City-centre café bar/restaurant serving modern Scottish dishes.

La Parmigiana (£) 447 Great Western Road, Glasgow G12 8HH (tel: 0141 334 0686). Deservedly popular local trattoria featuring regional Italian cooking.

Rogano Restaurant and Café Rogano (£££) 11 Exchange Place, Glasgow G1 3AN (tel: 0141 248 4055). Remodelled in art-deco style in 1935, the long-established Rogano is a top class restaurant.

Stravaigin (££) 30 Gibson Street, Glasgow G12 (tel: 0141 334 2665). Cheerful basement restaurant serving excellently prepared dishes from around the world – Hanoi, Chile, Mexico – using Scottish ingredients.

Ubiquitous Chip (££–£££) 12 Ashton Lane, Glasgow G12 8SJ (tel: 0141 334 5007). A sophisticated interpretation of Scotland's larder is guaranteed at 'the Chip' – the discriminating Glaswegian's restaurant choice.

Victoria and Albert (£) 159 Buchanan Street, Glasgow G1 2JX (tel: 0141 248 6329). Yet another bar-restaurant straddling the categories, depending on chosen menu.

Yes (£££) 22 West Nile Street, Glasgow G1 2PW (tel: 0141 221 8044). A sophisticated city-centre crowd enjoys the eclectic menu featuring Scottish seafood, lamb, and game cooked in modern style. Paintings by Glasgow artists hang all around.

THE SOUTH

Ayr

Fouters Bistro Restaurant (££) 2A Academy Street, Ayr KA7 1HS (tel: 01292 261391). A highly regarded establishment taking full advantage of Ayrshire's own produce. Exciting food, interesting ambience – old bank vaults.

Biggar

Shieldhill Hotel (£££) Quothquan, by Biggar ML12 6NA (tel: 01899 220035). In a fortified mansion built in 1199, enjoy superb innovative modern Scottish cuisine.

East Neuk Villages

Cellar Restaurant (£££) 24 East Green, Anstruther, Fife KY10 3AA (tel: 01333 310378). Probably one of the best seafood restaurants in Scotland. Don't miss it if visiting Fife.

Gifford

Bonars Restaurant (££) Main Street, Gifford EH41 4QH (tel: 01620 810264). This former country tearoom now offers an admirable menu of modern Scottish delights. Leave plenty of room for the delicious desserts on offer.

Girvan

Wildings (£) Montgomerie Street, Girvan KA26 9HE (tel: 01465 713481). Enjoy the cheerful enthusiasm of this busy restaurant. It majors in seafood, though meat-eaters will also be happy with the menu.

Logan Botanic Garden

Knockinaam Lodge (£££) Portpatrick DG9 9AD, Galloway (tel: 01776 810471). A place of pilgrimage for foodies in the far west, basically modern French and highly inventive.

North Berwick

La Potinière (£££) Main Street, Gullane EH31 2AA (tel: 01620 843214). Near-legendary restaurant in golfing resort, transcending fashion to go its own sophisticated way.

Open Arms Hotel (££) Dirleton, East Lothian EH39 5EG (tel: 01620 850241). Food with panache from very experienced hoteliers.

Swinton

Wheatsheaf Hotel (££) Main Street, Swinton TD11 3JJ (tel: 01890 860257). The menu at this country inn – situated by Swinton's village green – features carefully cooked seasonal produce.

Troon

Highgrove House (££) Old Loans Road, Troon KA10 7HL (tel: 01292 312511). Popular venue overlooking the Firth of Clyde, serving well-pre-pared traditional food – country paté, roasts and traditional desserts.

CENTRAL SCOTLAND

Arbroath

Gordon's Restaurant (££) Homewood House, Main Street, Inverkeilor, by Arbroath, Angus

DD11 5RN (tel: 01241 830364). Cosy village restaurant, decorated in cottage style.
Balloch
Grill Room (£££) Cameron House Hotel, by Alexandria, Dunbartonshire G83 8QZ (tel: 01389 755565). Very sophisticated cuisine of the highest standards at this country club hotel overlooking Loch Lomond.

Blairgowrie
Kinloch House Hotel (£££) Blairgowrie PH10 6SG (tel: 01250 884237). Fruit and vegetables from the 19th-century walled garden of this country house are married to the best Scottish meats and seafood, cooked with a light, precise touch.

Callander
Roman Camp Hotel (£££) Callander, Perthshire FK17 8BG (tel: 01877 330003). Cooking with Scottish flair at the restaurant of this old country house by the river.

Carnoustie
11 Park Avenue (££) 11 Park Avenue, Carnoustie DD7 7JA (tel: 01241 853336). Unpretentious town-centre restaurant offering good, simply cooked food such as mussels in white wine and grilled fillet of salmon.

Dundee
Stakis Dundee (££) Earl Grey Place, Dundee DD1 4DE (tel: 01382 229271). Quayside setting for a modern hotel with open-plan restaurant. The menu includes Highland game terrine, Finnan haddock and other Scottish classics.

Killiecrankie
Killiecrankie Hotel (£££) Killiecrankie, Pitlochry PH16 5LG (tel: 01796 473220). Enthusiastically run, with a great atmosphere and cuisine proving beyond doubt that modern trends do penetrate far beyond the big cities.

Perth
Auchterarder House (£££) Auchterarder, Perthshire PH3 1DZ (tel: 01764 663646). The style and flair of this opulent Victorian country house are reflected in the imaginative menus. A dining experience.
Let's Eat (££) 77/79 Kinnoull Street, Perth (tel: 01738 643377). Housed in former theatre premises and popular with locals, this restaurant offers an ideas-packed ranging from fashionable salsas to char-grilled ribeye steak with fries.
Number Thirty Three Seafood Restaurant (£££) 33 George Street, Perth PH1 5LA (tel: 01738 633771). A café bar/restaurant that majors in fish dishes. With adjoining oyster bar.

St Andrews
Ostlers Close (££) Bonnygate, Cupar, Fife KY15 4BU (tel: 01334 655574). Hidden up a 'close' or alleyway is outstanding cuisine, consistent over the years.

Trossachs
Braeval (£££) Braeval, Aberfoyle FK8 3UY (tel: 01877 382711). TV chef Nick Nairn's home base. Sample his unique style of cooking in this converted mill.

THE NORTHEAST
Aberdeen
Ardoe House Hotel (£££) South Deeside Road, Blairs, Aberdeen AB1 5YP (tel: 01224 867355). Country-house style paneled dining room in a baronial mansion, featuring a menu of game, roasts and seafood.
The Marcliffe at Pitfodels (£££) North Deeside Road, Pitfodels, Aberdeen AB15 9YA (tel: 01224 861000). A team of chefs emphasise local produce here: lobster, halibut, Aberdeen Angus beef, venison.
Patio Hotel (££) Beach Boulevard, Aberdeen AB24 1EF (tel: 01224 633339). Specialising in seafood and appropriately sited on the seafront.
Q Brasserie (££) 9 Alfred Place, Aberdeen AB1 1YD (tel: 01224 595001). A former church-owned building is the slightly unexpected setting for innovative modern Scottish cuisine.

281

Ballater
Darroch Learg Hotel (£££) Braemar Road, Ballater AB35 5UX (tel: 01339 755443). A Victorian mansion on Royal Deeside with a choice of two set-price menus offering Scottish produce cooked with great flair.
The Green Inn, (££) 9 Victoria Road, Ballater, Aberdeenshire AB35 5QQ (tel: 01339 755701). Fresh, health-conscious local dishes. Speciality Scottish cheeses.

Craigellachie
Archiestown Hotel (££) Archiestown, Aberlour AB38 7QX (tel: 01340 810218). A popular angling hotel with informal bistro; the blackboard menu features casseroles, fish, steaks, and treacle pudding to follow.
Rib Room Craigellachie Hotel (£££) Craigellachie, Banffshire AB38 9SR (tel: 01340 881204). Thoroughly Scottish in ambience, professional hotel cooking of the highest standard.
A Taste of Speyside (£–££) 10 Balvenie Street, Dufftown, Banffshire AB55 4AB (tel: 01340 820860). Good home cooking with extra touches (plus a huge malt whisky selection).

Elgin
Old Monastery (££–£££) Drybridge, by Buckie, Banffshire AB56 2JB (tel: 01542 832660). Sophisticated, honest cooking without pretension. The best for miles around.

Kildrummy Castle
Kildrummy Castle Hotel (£££) Kildrummy AB33 8RA (tel: 019755 71288). Victorian country house hotel beside medieval castle ruins, featuring the excellent local game, Aberdeen Angus beef and salmon.

THE GREAT GLEN & WESTERN HIGHLANDS

Arduaine

Loch Melfort Hotel (££) Arduaine, by Oban PA34 4XG (tel: 01852 200233). Set beside Arduaine Gardens and with sea views, a hotel restaurant emphasizing seafood.

Cowal

Beverley's Restaurant (££) Ardfillayne Hotel, Bullwood Road, Dunoon, Argyll PA23 7QJ (tel: 01369 702267). Classical French cooking meets Scottish traditional amid high Victoriana.

Fort William

Arisaig House (£££) Beasdale, by Arisaig, Inverness-shire PH39 4NR (tel: 01687 450622). Special country house in impressive location with food to match.
Crannog Seafood Restaurant (££) Fort William, Inverness-shire PH33 7NG (tel: 01397 705589). Here the catch is off-loaded directly into the kitchen. Good value.

Grantown-on-Spey

Garth Hotel (££) Castle Road, Grantown-on-Spey PH26 3HN (tel: 01479 872836). A friendly sporting and holiday hotel offering straightforward, French-influenced cooking using prime Scottish produce.

Inverness

Dunain Park Hotel (£££) Inverness IV3 6JN (tel: 01463 230512). Top-quality Scottish game and seafood, with home-grown vegetables and home-baking, are merged in Scottish-French cuisine.

Kingussie

The Cross (£££) Tweed Mill Brae, Ardbroilach Road, Kingussie, Inverness-shire PH21 1TC (tel: 01540 661166). A mill conversion full of character, but do not be distracted from the high quality food.

Oban

Airds Hotel (£££) Port Appin, Argyll PA38 4DF (tel: 01631 730236). This elegant hotel, housed in a former ferry inn, offers creative food with great finesse.
Isle of Eriska Hotel (£££) Isle of Eriska, Ledaig, by Oban, Argyll PA37 1SD (tel: 01631 720371). An island setting for a hotel dining room starring a daily roast, ably supported by Scottish game, fish and seafood.
Taychreggan Hotel (££) Kilchrenan, Taynuilt PA35 1HQ (tel: 01866 833211). A 300-year-old drovers' inn on the tree-clad shores of Loch Awe offering an eclectic menu, stressing local produce.

THE NORTHERN HIGHLANDS

Cromarty

The Dower House (£££) Highfield, Muir of Ord IV6 7XN (tel: 01463 870090). The daily menu here might include spinach tagliatelle with scallops or fillet of beef with rosti. The dining room is enhanced by elegant antiques, Persian rugs and paintings.

Dundonnell

Dundonnell Hotel (££) Dundonnell IV23 2QS (tel: 01854 633204). Highland hospitality beside Little Loch Broom, where the chef excels at fish and seafood.

Kylesku

Kylesku Hotel (££) Kylesku, Lairg, Sutherland IV27 4HW (tel: 01971 502231). Small waterside hotel offering seafood landed minutes earlier on the pier nearby.

Lochinver

Lochinver Larder's Riverside Bistro (££) Main Street, Lochinver, Sutherland IV27 4JY (tel: 01571 844356). Panoramic bay views, with steaks and seafood prominent on the menu.

Timespan (Helmsdale)

Royal Marine Hotel (££) Golf Road, Brora KW9 6QS (tel: 01408 621252). The dining room offers a wide-ranging menu making good use of local produce.

Tongue

Ben Loyal Hotel (££) Tongue IV27 4XE (tel: 01847 611216). A family-run hotel offering traditional Scottish cooking, including leek and potato soup, cod in cheese sauce, with Atholl brose for dessert.

Ullapool

Altnaharrie Inn (£££) Ullapool IV26 2SS (tel: 01854 633230). Guests talk in reverent tones about food here. It can only be reached by boat – so you will want to stay.

THE ISLANDS

Mull

Druimard Hotel (££) Dervaig, Isle of Mull PA75 6QW (tel: 01688 400345). Enjoy potted wild salmon with oatcakes, game terrine, or saddle of venison for a pre-theatre dinner (Mull Little Theatre is next door).

Orkney

Creel Restaurant (££) Front Road, St Margaret's Hope, South Ronaldsay, Orkney KW17 2SL (tel: 01856 831311). A very popular restaurant working wonders with seafoods, as well as Orkney beef and lamb.

Skye

Ardvasar Hotel (££) Ardvasar, Skye IV45 8RS (tel: 01471 844223). Straightforward cuisine using island produce: potted crab, roast chicken glazed with honey and mustard, and game pie are dishes typically found on the menu.
Three Chimneys Restaurant (£££) Colbost, nr Dunvegan, Skye IV55 8ZT (tel: 01470 511258). Cuisine of the highest order at the most westerly point of Skye in a converted crofter's cottage.

Entries with asterisks indicate words of Gaelic origin

bastel	a characteristically Scottish fortified house (*cf* French *bastille*)
ben*	a mountain, hill (usually used as a prefix)
bonnie	bonny, pretty, fine, handsome
brae*	slope, road with steep gradient, hillside
broch	a late-prehistoric round tower
burgess	a citizen of a burgh (see below)
burgh	Scottish town with special privileges granted by (royal) charter
burn	a stream
byre	a cowshed
cairn*	a pile of stones, often now marking hilltops or landmarks, or a memorial
ceilidh*	originally an informal gathering or visit to neighbours at which stories and songs were performed, now a concert or entertainment in a hall or hotell
clachan*	a small Highland village
clan*	a Highland family group or tribe, owing allegiance to a chief
claymore*	a large double-edged sword, often a basket-hilted, single-edged sword
Clearances	the economic reorganisation of Highland estates, mainly taking place 1800–50, which resulted in the suppression or discouragement of arable farming and the clearing and resettlement of tenants, either on less productive coastal ground or by forced emigration
corrie*	a deep hollow on the face of a mountain, scooped out by glacial action
Covenanter	a supporter of the National Covenant (1638), a manifesto drawn up in protest against King Charles I's religious reforms
craig*	a crag, cliff
croft	a small-holding
dram	a single drink (or 'nip') of whisky; to drink whisky
factor	a Scottish estate manager

firth	a wide sea inlet or major river estuary
Gael*	a Gaelic-speaking Highlander
Gaeltacht*	the Gaelic-speaking community
geo	in Orkney, Shetland and Caithness, a narrow gully-like sea inlet
glen*	a Highland valley, often U-shape in profile
haar	coastal mist, often occurring in summer on the east coast
howe	a hollow or low-lying piece of ground
Jacobite	a (Catholic) supporter of the exiled King James VII (of Scotland), his son and grandson (Bonnie Prince Charlie)
kirk	church
kirk elder	an ordained member of the Presbyterian Church, elected to hold office
kyle*	either an inlet or strait between the mainland and an offshore island
laird	the owner (or the landlord) of an estate
linn*	a cataract or the pool below a cataract or waterfall
loch*	a lake
lochan*	a small lake
machair*	grassland lying immediately behind a sandy beach
manse	the house of the kirk minister
mercat cross	a market cross, symbol of the trading rights of a Scottish burgh
Munro	a Scottish peak over 3,000ft (914m) in height (named after Sir Hugh Munro, the first compiler of such mountains)
neuk	corner, as in East Neuk, the eastern corner of Fife
ogham, ogam	an ancient Celtic alphabet with 20 characters
policies	the enclosed grounds or parkland of a large house
quaich*	a shallow, two-handled drinking bowl, now usually ornamental
sassenach*	a non-Gaelic speaking Lowlander – Scots or English – often now used simply to indicate a non-Scot
strath*	a broad open valley
tolbooth	the former administrative centre of a Scottish burgh
tombolo	a narrow sand strip joining an island to the mainland
voe	a bay or creek in Orkney and Shetland

Index

285

Index

286

Picture Credits

The Automobile Association would like to thank the following photographers, libraries and associations for their assistance in the preparation of this book.

ABERDEEN UNIVERSITY LIBRARY 42–3 Embarking at Broomielaw, Glasgow   MARY EVANS PICTURE LIBRARY 25 19th-century shipbuilding, 28 Bannockburn, 30–1 execution warrant, 30b Mary Queen of Scots, 34–5 Battle of Prestonpans, 104–5 Robert Burns, 197a Culloden   D HARDLEY 110 Culzean Castle, 120 Logan Gardens, 202 Mull of Kintyre, 231a Rothesay Harbour, 232 Colonsay, 234 Islay, 235a Ferry to Jura, 235b Kildaton Cross   HULTON DEUTSCH COLLECTION LTD 205a Loch Ness Monster   IMAGE BANK Front cover b, sailor   NATIONAL GALLERY OF SCOTLAND 33 Earl of Seafield   ROYAL GEOGRAPHICAL SOCIETY 37a map   SCONE PALACE 150 Scone Palace   SPECTRUM COLOUR LIBRARY 39 Dunrobin Castle   THE MANSELL COLLECTION LTD 26a seal and coins of Alexander III, 28–9 Bannockburn Battle, 30a Mary Queen of Scots, 36b Adam Smith, 41 Andrew Carnegie, 42 building of Queen Mary, 123a Lanark, 123c Robert Owen   TONY STONE Front cover a, castle and cow.
The remaining photographs are held in the Automobile Association's own library (AA PHOTO LIBRARY) and were taken by the following photographers: M ADLEMAN 38, M ALEXANDER, 18–9, 23b, 40b, 76, 77, 78a, 81a, 81b, 82a, 82b, 83b, 83c, 86a, 86b, 87a, 90, 91, 94, 97, 98, 99, 100a, 100b, 101, 102, 106a, 106b, 107, 112a, 112b, 113a, 114a, 115, 118a, 124, 125a, 125b, 127a, 127b, A BAKER 17a, 131, 147a, 154, 155a, 155c, 172–3, 190a, 190b, J BEAZLEY 5c, 9, 35a, 108b, 109a, 109b, 114b, 116a, 117, 118b, 121a, 121b, 122a, 122b, 128b, 192, 193a, 196, 200b, 213b, 216, 221a, 221b, P & G BOWATER 169b, J CARNIE 2, 10a, 10b, 14, 15, 20b, 31, 34, 130, 138b, 151c, 184, 189, 191, 199, 200a, 204, 205b, 212a, 213a, 226, 230, 231b, D CORRANCE 20a, 23a, 48a, 50, 51a, 51b, 55, 59a, 64, 67, 111, 119, 129a, 129b, S L DAY back cover, spine, 11a, 13b, 18, 19, 21b, 22a, 22b, 24a, 29a, 29b, 35b, 128a, 132, 133a, 133b, 135a, 135b, 135c, 136, 137, 138a, 139, 140, 141a, 141b, 142b, 143a, 143b, 144a, 144b, 145a, 145b, 147b, 148, 149, 151a, 151b, 152, 153a, 153b, 156, 157, 158, 159a, 159b, 160–1, 160, 161, 167b, 186, 187a, 187b, 188a, 193b, 194, 195a, 195b, 198, 203, 206, 207a, 207b, 260, 261b, 263a, 263b, 266a, 270, E ELLINGTON 5a, 7, 16–7, 26b, 163, 164, 165a, 166, 167a, 168, 170b, 174, 175a, 176a, 176b, 177a, 177b, 179, 182a, 210, 211a, 212b, 214, 215, 217a, 217b, 218–9, 218, 220a, 223a, 223b, 224b, 228, 229a, 229b, 238, 239a, 239b, 240a, 240b, 242a, 242b, 243, 244a, 244b, 245, 245b, 246, 247a, 247b, 262, 265, 267a, R G ELLIOTT back flap, 6–7, 49, 64–5, 68, 69, 70b, 95b, 96, 220b, 225, 226–7, 236a, 236b, 237a, 237b, 248, 249a, 249b, 250a, 252b, 252c, 254a, 254b, 255, 267b, 273, S GIBSON PHOTOGRAPHY 43, 79b, 80, 83a, 85a, 88a, 88b, 89a, 92, 93a, 93b, 95a, 108a, 264, D HARDLEY 27, 146, 219, A J HOPKINS 188b, 222, R JOHNSON 241, S KING 148–9, S & O MATHEWS 126, K PATERSON 3, 8, 11b, 12a, 12b, 13a, 16, 17b, 21a, 32a, 32b, 36a, 37b, 44, 46, 47, 48b, 52a, 52b, 53, 54a, 54b, 56a, 56b, 57, 58, 59b, 60a, 61a, 61b, 62, 63a, 63b, 65, 66, 70a, 71, 72a, 72b, 73, 74a, 74b, 75a, 261a, 266b, D ROBERTSON 5b, P SHARPE 84, 103a, 103b, 105, 170a, 201, M TAYLOR 171a, 171b, 171c, 178, 180, 211b, 224a, R WEIR 4, 24x, 134, 165b, 169a, 172, 173, 175b, 182b, 197b, 252a, 253.

Contributors

Original copy editor: Barbara Fuller   Original designer: Design fx;   Revision copy editor: Jillian Stewart
Revision verifier: Gilbert Summers   Indexer: Marie Lorimer